CW01237409

Creating and Consuming the American South

UNIVERSITY PRESS OF FLORIDA

Florida A&M University, Tallahassee
Florida Atlantic University, Boca Raton
Florida Gulf Coast University, Ft. Myers
Florida International University, Miami
Florida State University, Tallahassee
New College of Florida, Sarasota
University of Central Florida, Orlando
University of Florida, Gainesville
University of North Florida, Jacksonville
University of South Florida, Tampa
University of West Florida, Pensacola

CREATING AND CONSUMING THE AMERICAN SOUTH

Edited by Martyn Bone, Brian Ward,
and William A. Link

University Press of Florida
Gainesville · Tallahassee · Tampa · Boca Raton
Pensacola · Orlando · Miami · Jacksonville · Ft. Myers · Sarasota

Copyright 2015 by Martyn Bone, Brian Ward, and William A. Link
All rights reserved
Printed in the United States of America on acid-free paper

This book may be available in an electronic edition.

20 19 18 17 16 15   6 5 4 3 2 1

Library of Congress Cataloging-in-Publication Data
Creating and consuming the American South / edited by Martyn Bone, Brian Ward, and William A. Link.
pages cm
Includes bibliographical references and index.
ISBN 978-0-8130-6069-9
1. Southern States—History. 2. Southern States—Social conditions. 3. Regionalism—Southern States. I. Bone, Martyn, 1974– editor. II. Ward, Brian, 1961– editor. III. Link, William A., editor.
F209.C69 2015
975—dc23
2014048358

The University Press of Florida is the scholarly publishing agency for the State University System of Florida, comprising Florida A&M University, Florida Atlantic University, Florida Gulf Coast University, Florida International University, Florida State University, New College of Florida, University of Central Florida, University of Florida, University of North Florida, University of South Florida, and University of West Florida.

University Press of Florida
15 Northwest 15th Street
Gainesville, FL 32611-2079
http://www.upf.com

CONTENTS

List of Figures vii
Preface: Understanding the South ix

Introduction. Old/New/Post/Real/Global/No South: Paradigms and Scales 1
Martyn Bone

PART I. CREATING AND CONSUMING THE "REAL" SOUTH

1. From Appalachian Folk to Southern Foodways: Why Americans Look to the South for Authentic Culture 27
W. Fitzhugh Brundage

2. God and the MoonPie: Consumption, Disenchantment, and the Reliably Lost Cause 49
Scott Romine

3. Toward a Post-postpolitical Southern Studies: On the Limits of the "Creating and Consuming" Paradigm 72
Jon Smith

PART II. CREATING AND CONSUMING THE SOUTH: CASE STUDIES

4. Southern (Dis)Comfort: Creating and Consuming Homosex in the Black South 97
E. Patrick Johnson

5. Serpents in the Garden: Historic Preservation, Climate Change, and the Postsouthern Plantation 117
Michael P. Bibler

6. Creating and Consuming "Hill Country Harmonica": Promoting the Blues and Forging Beloved Community in the Contemporary South 139
Adam Gussow

7. Pride at Preservation Hall: Tourism, Spectacle, and Musicking in New Orleans Jazz   158
Anne Dvinge

8. Recovering through a Cultural Economy: New Orleans from Katrina to Deepwater Horizon   178
Helen Taylor

PART III. CREATING AND CONSUMING THE SOUTH IN TRANSNATIONAL CONTEXTS

9. Creating a Multiethnic Gulf South: Vietnamese American Cultural and Economic Visibility before and after Katrina   203
Frank Cha

10. A "Southern, Brown, Burnt Sensibility": *Four Saints in Three Acts*, Black Spain, and the (Global) Southern Pastoral   226
Paige A. McGinley

11. Southern Regionalism and U.S. Nationalism in William Faulkner's State Department Travels   248
Deborah Cohn

12. The Feeling of a Heartless World: Blues Rhythm, Oppositionality, and British Rock Music   268
Andrew Warnes

13. Me and Mrs. Jones: Screening Working-Class Trans-Formations of Southern Family Values   289
John Howard

Afterword: After Authenticity   309
Tara McPherson

List of Contributors   325
Index   329

FIGURES

5.1. The Arbor Day Foundation 2006 map   133

10.1. A shop window plays on the title of *Four Saints in Three Acts*   227

10.2. Procession scene, *Four Saints in Three Acts*   243

12.1. "Negroes jitterbugging in a juke joint on a Saturday afternoon, Clarksdale, Mississippi"   274

PREFACE

....

Understanding the South

In 2008 the Arts and Humanities Research Council in the United Kingdom agreed to fund an international research network dedicated to the theme "Understanding the South, Understanding America: The American South in Regional, National and Global Perspectives." The network was based at the University of Manchester, with the universities of Copenhagen, Cambridge, and Florida as partners. Between May 2008 and August 2010, each of these institutions hosted a network conference. These meetings brought together scholars from a range of disciplines and allowed them to explore together the current state and future prospects for the study of that section of the North American continent that eventually became known as, with all due disclaimers about the definitional slipperiness of the term, the American South.

This series of books from the University Press of Florida extends the work of the network, initially in three volumes grouped around the themes of creating citizenship in the nineteenth-century South, the South and the Atlantic world, and creating and consuming the South. While each volume stands alone as a valuable contribution to a particular aspect of southern studies, collectively they allow us to take stock of a rich and diverse field, to ponder the substantive disagreement and methodological tensions—as well as the common ground—among scholars of the South, and to think about new areas and techniques for future research. Each volume and many of the individual essays are marked by an interest in interdisciplinary and multidisciplinary approaches to the region. Indeed, one aim of the series is to juxtapose the work of historians with that of scholars associated with the New Southern Studies in the belief that historians and those working out of literary and cultural studies traditions have much to learn from each other in their quest to understand the American South in a variety of overlapping temporal, geographic, symbolic, cultural, and material contexts.

The coeditors of the series wish to thank all those colleagues who participated in the four conferences. Special thanks are due to Tony Badger at the University of Cambridge for his generous financial support and for hosting the Cambridge conference; to James Broomall, Heather Bryson, Angela Diaz, and Angie Zombek at the University of Florida for their logistical help; at the University of Manchester, to David Brown for co-editing the *Citizenship* volume; at Louisiana State University, to Michael Bibler (formerly of the University of Manchester) for his consistently constructive engagement with all aspects of the network; and to Tom Strange and Jennie Chapman for their invaluable administrative assistance. We would like to thank Lisa Williams for her careful copyediting of this third and final volume and Martina Koegeler for compiling the first draft of its index. We would also like to express our gratitude to the Arts and Humanities Research Council for its sponsorship of the network; to the British Academy and the United States Embassy's Cultural Affairs Office in London for important additional funding; and to Meredith Morris-Babb at the University Press of Florida for her enthusiastic support of the Understanding the South series of books.

Brian Ward, Northumbria University
Martyn Bone, University of Copenhagen
William A. Link, University of Florida

INTRODUCTION

Old/New/Post/Real/Global/No South

Paradigms and Scales

MARTYN BONE

This book explores how an eclectic range of narratives and images of the American South have been created and consumed—indeed, often created *for* consumption. However, the contributors also seek to move beyond both traditional southernist and more recent postmodernist understandings of how, when, where, and why the American South has been created and consumed. The thirteen essays in this volume reorient our attention to the ways in which ideas and stories about "the South" and "southernness" have social and material effects that register on various local, regional, national, and transnational scales.

As an academic field in which even constituent disciplines like history and literary studies have often remained separate, U.S. southern studies traditionally has cohered around and returned to certain well-worn themes like "southern distinctiveness." This has involved recurring debates over whether said distinctiveness (usually assumed to have existed, even if its sources are contested) has survived or has succumbed to social and economic forces (usually perceived to be external and pernicious). This seemingly endless and often anxious discourse around distinctiveness—a prime example of what Scott Romine sees as southern studies' "overdeveloped eschatological sense"—has also permeated popular media: in 2013 journalist Tracy Thompson lamented that the South "has been urbanized, suburbanized, strip-malled, and land-formed to a point that at times I hardly recognize it anymore." Conversely, southern partisans continue to insist on the endurance of regional difference: when Apple's iPhone voice recognition software struggles with the dialect and accent of "we Southerners," such corporate malfeasance serves to validate the subcultural (or neonational) persistence of "a distinct people with our own culture."[1]

Such contemporary responses to the suburbanization, modernization, or homogenization of Dixie are fairly consistent with those narratives of decline and endurance, invasion and resistance, that have shaped discussions of southern identity for decades. Commentators on the right and left alike have long complained that "industrialism," "Americanism," and the postmodern "cultural logic of late capitalism" have rendered the region less and less real, more and more indistinct and simulated.[2] For decades, both conservative and liberal elegies for the loss—as well as paeans to the survival—of a putatively authentic "southern way of life" have carried the whiff of warmed-over outtakes from the Nashville Agrarians' manifesto *I'll Take My Stand* (1930). If this testifies to the legacy of the conservative neo-Agrarian ideology that so thoroughly informed the institutionalization of southern literary studies in the 1950s, it is also now fully four decades since the appearance of the most prominent liberal version of the end-of-southern-distinctiveness jeremiad: John Egerton's *The Americanization of Dixie* (1972), which worried out loud and at length that "the South is just about over as a separate and distinct place," due to "an obsession with growth and acquisition and consumption" combined with "a steady erosion of the sense of place, of community."[3]

Since the 1970s, however, and especially in the early twenty-first century, scholars have emphasized that "the South" is a discursive, ideological, or commercial construct rather than a material, geographical site (Egerton's "separate and distinct place"). In their introduction to *South to a New Place* (2002), Suzanne Jones and Sharon Monteith remark that the South's "mythic properties have traditionally exceeded its realities." Tara McPherson's *Reconstructing Dixie: Race, Gender, and Nostalgia in the Imagined South* (2003) opens by asserting, "The South today is as much a fiction, a story we tell and are told, as it is a fixed geographic space below the Mason-Dixon line." Jennifer Greeson states on the first page of *Our South: Geographic Fantasy and the Rise of National Literature* (2010), "This South that we hold collectively in our minds is not—could not possibly be—a fixed or real place . . . it is a term of the imagination, a site of national fantasy." Anthony Stanonis, in his introduction to *Dixie Emporium: Tourism, Foodways, and Consumer Culture in the American South* (2008), remarks, "As mass-produced goods and travelers unfamiliar with local customs increasingly penetrated the region beginning in the antebellum period, the South became as much an evolving set of images as an actual place."[4]

Though this more recent emphasis on the imagined South has offered a way around decline-and-death narratives about the tragic erasure or heroic endurance of southern distinctiveness, it has itself become rather rote, congealing into a kind of postmodern-constructionist consensus. One aim of the present volume, then, is to explore more nuanced ways of understanding the region as both a circulating discourse *and* a social, material locus—in Romine's terms, as both "the real South" and "the South-under-no-description"—at conceptual and geographical scales ranging from the local to global.[5]

Around half of the chapters in *Creating and Consuming the American South* focus partly or wholly on the twenty-first century, and not without reason. If *The Americanization of Dixie* is now over forty years old, it is also more than a decade since Jon Smith interrogated and inverted Egerton's Americanization thesis by suggesting that "as the South becomes more 'Americanized'—as identity becomes more and more structured as a lack to be filled by consumption—the paradoxical result may be the increasing commodity-fetishization of southernness itself." Both Smith in 2002 and historian James Cobb in 2005 saw this trend expressed in the promotion by southernness.com of a perfume that supposedly bottled "the celebrated Southern 'sense of place.'"[6] Almost a decade later, it is one more irony of southern cultural history that Romine's chapter in the present volume identifies a similar process and result in the fetishization of "southern foodways" by the Southern Foodways Alliance, a semi-academic organization cofounded by Egerton. Yet in the contemporary era of economic globalization, and especially after the global financial crisis that began in 2007, scholarly musings on a brand of perfume or form of foodway can themselves seem kitschy or quaint (especially when, as Smith remarks in his chapter for this volume, that perfume is no longer produced). While for some southern(ist) partisans globalization simply supersedes Americanization as the latest external leviathan threatening Dixie, the perceived danger may also intensify emotional *and* economic investment in "southernness" through what Smith identifies as a combined narrative- *and* commodity-fetishism.[7] Cobb observes further contradictions and ironies arising from the Globalization of Dixie: "Paradoxically enough, by threatening to take our national, regional, or ethnic identities away from us, the global economy first stimulates our desire to preserve them, and then through a combination of commodification and clever marketing, it proceeds to sell them back to us."[8] But there is another twist, for as Smith stresses in *Finding Purple America* (2013), southernness is not simply being commodified and sold by "them" to "us." In the twenty-first-century arena of "Southern civic brand identities," where "the civic brand Dixie and its logo the Confederate battle flag" compete with Birmingham's attempt to "alter its brand image" on the back of a native son's *American Idol* victory, the creation and consumption of "the South" is a process in which "we Southerners"—including academic southernists—are active participants.[9]

But as Stanonis reminds us, the creation, commodification, and consumption of the South as "an evolving set of images" is nothing new either: like ideas of southern distinctiveness, such images date back to at least the antebellum period. For this and other reasons, *Creating and Consuming the American South* can hardly confine itself to the twenty-first century. Even when focused on the recent past, many of the chapters also range back through the history of the region in the nineteenth and twentieth centuries and attend to the uncanny recurrence of images and narratives of older Souths—from the plantation and the Lost Cause to "folk" cultures and the civil rights movement.

It is worth adumbrating some of the ways in which "the idea of the American South" has *always* been subject to invention and reinvention by, among other things, political ideologies and market forces.[10] Greeson insists that narratives of "our South" as the United States' "internal other" began with the birth of the nation during the War of Independence, and that these northern and national narratives of the "Plantation South" and the "Slave South" intensified during the early nineteenth century.[11] James Peacock suggests that below the Mason-Dixon line (white) southern self-fashioning took on fuller form after 1830: following two centuries in which "the South was a node in a network stretching from Europe through the Caribbean ... around 1830 the South as a region was invented, as people migrated inland and formed a regional identity that turned inward, in opposition to the nation."[12] Both politicians like James Henry Hammond and novelists like William Gilmore Simms contributed to this process of inventing "the South," culminating in what Drew Gilpin Faust calls "the creation of Confederate nationalism."[13]

Daniel Aaron has observed that once the Union army defeated the Confederate army, "[t]he ideal of the Old South—order, beauty, freedom—remained."[14] As I have noted elsewhere, this detachment of an idealized South from the defeated nation-state proved rather convenient to authors like Thomas Nelson Page, who produced romantic neo-Confederate narratives that elided the CSA's true lost cause: the maintenance of racial slavery.[15] Such narratives were wildly popular, and not only in the South: by 1888 they were so prevalent nationwide that war veteran and novelist Albion Tourgée observed in exasperation, "Our literature has become not only Southern in type, but distinctly Confederate in sympathy."[16] As Ted Ownby notes, such "Southern" literature was successful because "white northerners literally bought into the romance of reunion [with white southerners] at the expense of any concern for the injustices African Americans faced."[17] David Blight emphasizes that the creation and consumption of this romantic Old South often had an economic as well as ideological base: "Sectional reconciliation was . . . staged in part as a means of cementing commercial ties between Northern money and Southern economic development." As part of the "southern mythmaking" process that Paul Gaston termed the "New South Creed," boosters like Henry Grady and plantation fiction authors like Page and Joel Chandler Harris advocated southern economic progress empowered by northern capital even while extolling a deeply nostalgic vision of the Old South that appealed to, and extracted profit from, a receptive national audience anxious about the dislocating dimensions of modern, urban, industrial capitalism.[18]

In the late nineteenth century, the burgeoning southern tourist industry began to capitalize on northerners' attraction to the increasingly accessible (by railroad) southern states: Civil War battlegrounds were marketed as historic sites; east Florida towns such as Saint Augustine and Palm Beach promoted themselves to northerners as winter retreats; and numerous southern cities organized expositions.[19] Images of the South as simultaneously nostalgic, exotic, and authentic permeated other nascent forms of popular culture: as Karen Cox notes in her analysis of early-twentieth-century sheet music (the MP3 file of its time), "'Dixie' was not simply a reference to a region: it was a brand purposefully linked to the nation's nostalgia for the antebellum South."[20] Cox's study reminds us that Smith's "civic brand called Dixie" is what marketers would call a "mature brand." The maturation process continued between the two world wars, the period that W. Fitzhugh Brundage terms "a watershed in the self-conscious commercialization of the southern past."[21] During the 1920s and 1930s, Savannah and Charleston, "America's Most Historic City," embarked on programs of "historic preservation" that became inextricable from the emergence of heritage tourism valorizing plantation culture and colonial gentility—the "Old and Historic Charleston District" was established in 1931—while downplaying slavery and Denmark Vesey. As J. Mark Souther has observed, New Orleans followed suit as its political and business elite "gradually recognized the value of cultivating the image of their Old South legacy, albeit one that erased slavery and cleaned up the messiness of the auction block." Cotton, sugar, shipping, and the slave trade had made New Orleans the nation's third-largest city by 1840; however, by 1940 New Orleans was being superseded by "more economically dynamic southern cities," like Atlanta, Houston, and Miami. Hence, New Orleans "constructed a tourist image that showcased the heritage embodied in its architecture," and began marketing its supposedly exceptional status as "America's Most Interesting City."[22]

One can also trace today's ongoing debates and anxieties about the commodification of "authentic" southern culture to the 1920s and 1930s. Not unlike Marxists (and later southern liberals like Egerton), the Nashville Agrarians critiqued the creation of consumer culture by capitalism for generating a kind of false consciousness. In the introduction to *I'll Take My Stand*, John Crowe Ransom claimed that because industrial "production greatly outruns the rate of natural consumption," "modern advertising" sought "to persuade the consumers to want exactly what the applied sciences are able to furnish them." By contrast, Ransom claimed, the traditional "agrarian life of the Old South" was "deeply founded" on a material culture and social forms that were part of "the way of life" itself, rather than commodities that their owners had been duped into buying as consumers.[23] But even as Ransom's Agrarian fellow traveler Donald Davidson articulated an "autochthonous ideal" in which (white) southerners supposedly existed in unselfconscious harmony with the land, Charleston's "memory theaters . . . provided settings in which southerners performed their 'southernness' before eager audiences."[24] While it is doubtful that Davidson's ideal was ever a social and cultural reality, capitalist modernity—not least the rise of a tourist economy—contributed to a growing sense that southernness was performative and self-conscious, rather than inherently authentic and autochthonous.

Yet for population groups almost entirely ignored by the Agrarians and rather less invested in their image of "the South and the Agrarian Tradition," the rise of consumer culture provided opportunities to re-create and even repudiate "southern" identities. In *American Dreams in Mississippi* (1999), Ownby explores how blacks "could reject old Mississippi identities as subservient workers by embracing and reshaping American identities as consumption."[25] Poor whites too gave the lie to the Agrarians' fantasy of southern agricultural antipathy for consumer culture: author Harry Crews recalled how during his pre–World War II youth in Bacon County, Georgia, white tenant farmers "loved *things* the way only the very poor can. They would have thrown away their kerosene lamps for light bulbs in a second. . . . For a refrigerator they would have broken their safes and burned them in the fireplace."[26]

The interwar years also saw the rise of what Jack Temple Kirby termed "media-made Dixie" through the new conduits of mass communication: radio, film, and television.[27] Yet despite their formal modernity, radio and film reiterated and disseminated nationwide decidedly familiar nostalgic narratives about the South.[28] Furthermore, if literary fiction sometimes seemed to be ceding cultural clout to these new aural and visual media— even as critics hailed a "Renascence" in southern writing—the success of cinematic adaptations of novels like Stark Young's *So Red the Rose* and Margaret Mitchell's *Gone With the Wind* strengthened the persistence of Old South romance in the national imaginary. As with plantation fiction in the late nineteenth century, the success of such fiction and films also brought tourists southward in search of the "real" Old South. Even today, scholars in the vanguard of the New Southern Studies keep turning to Tara: McPherson identifies Mitchell's 1936 novel with "the instrumental role that the plantation home and the southern lady play in the selling of the South," especially heritage tourism, while Romine's *The Real South* (2008) deems Tara the "ground zero of southern cultural reproduction."[29]

By the early 1960s tourism had become the second- or third-largest employer and wealth generator throughout the southern states.[30] This growth was not significantly hindered by the recurring images of white southern racism playing out in the national and global media at the zenith of the civil rights movement. Founded in 1966, *Southern Living* magazine pitched a highly stylized "positive image of the South," which, according to Amy Elias, "turns all of history into romance: in this South, there is no Civil War anguish, only Civil War memorials . . . no slavery or racial strife, only quaint bed-and-breakfast plantations with golf courses and four-star accommodations."[31] Historians have argued that the movement itself became fodder for the "commercialization of the southern past" as public-private partnerships from Montgomery to Memphis created a "civil rights industry" no less "manufactured" and "ahistorical" than *Southern Living*.[32] These historians' insistence that remembrance and representation of the movement matters, and cannot be left to heritage tourism, resonates with McPherson's argument that "[t]ourist zones are political combat zones, terrains of struggles over the contemporary meanings of history"—especially when "[t]he South receives more than one-third of all American tourists, more than any other region."[33] Though marketers have become savvy about promoting black southern heritage tourism to an affluent African American middle class, the region's tourist sites remain racially inflected in ways that are consistent with a larger history of segregation and spatial inequality. Moreover, the kind of revisionist history that the movement seemed to compel was trumped during the 1970s by the expansion of antebellum heritage tourism in smaller cities like Richmond ("Down Where the South Begins"), Baton Rouge ("Plantation Country"), and Natchez ("Where the Old South Still Lives").[34] Heated disputes over the redevelopment of New Orleans following the devastation caused by Hurricane Katrina in 2005 offered a salient recent reminder of how and why "tourist zones" continue to be "political combat zones" for the future, as well as history, of southern places. Witness, for example, the controversy in 2012 when mayor Moon Landrieu sought state approval to direct substantial tax revenues into the establishment of a "formal hospitality zone" centered on the French Quarter. The costly proposal contrasted with the notorious absence of financial and infrastructural support for those many black New Orleanians "pushed into apartments beyond the city's fringes" or relocated (initially as Katrina refugees, then as more permanent settlers) to other southern cities from Baton Rouge to Houston.[35]

Though necessarily selective, this brief overview reminds us that there is a considerable history of creating and consuming the South, and of inventing and performing southern distinctiveness, that predates Romine's "artificial Taratoriality" or McPherson's "neo-Confederates in cyberspace."[36] Contra Davidson's autochthonous ideal, Faust writes that "the 'creation' of culture has almost always been a necessary and self-conscious process," and that "[t]he study of Confederate nationalism must abandon the notions of 'genuine' or 'spurious,' of 'myth' or 'reality.'"[37] Faust's thinking about the short-lived Confederacy resonates with Romine's insistence that scholars should abandon their stubborn tendency today to seek out and valorize "real" or "authentic" Souths; indeed, Romine opens *The Real South* by proposing that perhaps "a mechanically reproduced South is preferable to an authentic one" and concludes "Better a cyber-Confederacy than a real one."[38]

Still, narratives, images, and fantasies of the South also have real social, political, and economic origins and effects, whether they emanate from Chambers of Commerce, neo-Confederate websites, or forces outside the region. McPherson insists, "The emergence of a new 'Old South' coincides both with the political agendas of the Reagan–Bush years and with the economic pressures of late capitalism, re-inscribing the region as a site of authenticity and the local at the very moment that globalization blurs the boundaries of the nation." The transnational turn in the South—the intensification of economic globalization and influx of immigrant labor—requires us to think more about how the region is created and consumed at global as well as national scales. Several chapters in this book are devoted to such thinking, from considerations of how Vietnamese immigrants and their descendants complicate the South's established black–white racial binary, to the circulation of "southern" expressive forms (theater, film, music, and literature) in various "foreign markets." Of course, such global processes have historical antecedents too, from the transatlantic slave trade, via the agricultural-industrial nexus between southern plantations and Manchester cotton mills, to the avid consumption and re-creation of black southern blues by British rock and roll bands. In *Circling Dixie* (2001), Helen Taylor considered how various "southern cultural industries" have circulated in Europe (especially Britain) and concluded: "Rather than seek an authentic 'southernness,' we should recognize that southern culture is itself hybrid, the product of black and white Atlantic or transatlantic intercultural influences and movements—a living process of 'call and response.'"[39]

However, beneath such hopeful visions of hybridity and mobility, transatlantic "circling" has often had an exploitative economic base. New Southern Studies scholarship has been increasingly attentive to how, as Leigh Anne Duck puts it, "previous phases of globalization—including imperialism and the transatlantic slave trade—influence present-day forms of immiseration."[40] In recent years, even the poorest Deep South states, Mississippi and Alabama, have attracted Japanese car manufacturers as well as African, Asian, and Latin American workers. Yet even as those manufacturers receive massive tax breaks, their employees eke out nonunionized salaries. Meanwhile, illegal immigrants encounter draconian legislation—Alabama's HB-56 law, passed in 2011, is so stringent it outstrips even Arizona's notorious SB 1070—and agricultural working conditions so coercive that Justice Department officials have categorized rural Florida as "ground zero for modern slavery."[41] Furthermore, "recent decades have seen the widespread migration of manufacturing jobs from the U.S. South to the global 'South' of Latin America and southern Asia."[42] As McPherson and Bethany Moreton demonstrate, southern companies like Wal-Mart play a significant role in this process by outsourcing manufacturing across the global South and exporting "the South's long-standing, business-friendly, antilabor policies."[43]

For these and other reasons, "prevailing images of the American South [that] have been framed in relationship to the nation" are being superseded by an "understanding of the U.S. South [that] must be broader . . . to take in the perspective of the world."[44] Recent fiction like Cynthia Shearer's novel *The Celestial Jukebox* (2005), with its global-southern emphasis on the role of African and Latin American immigrant labor in rural Mississippi, helps drive home McPherson's point that the notion of "a self-contained and authentic South is simply an isolationist fantasy, albeit one with powerful material effects." Precisely because "[t]here is no pure South now—indeed, there never was—specific understandings of how the South is represented, commodified, and packaged become key."[45] The "worldly" perspectives provided in this volume, especially its third and final section, seek to extend such understandings.

* * *

Like the two previously published volumes in this series, *Creating Citizenship in the Nineteenth-Century South* and *The American South and the Atlantic World* (both 2013), *Creating and Consuming the American South* brings southern historians into dialogue with literary and cultural studies colleagues associated with the New Southern Studies. However, this collection also pointedly includes scholars who do not identify as "southerners," and who approach the subject from a variety of other disciplinary perspectives, including American studies, performance studies, jazz studies, and queer studies.

The book is organized into three parts. Part I features three wide-ranging chapters by leading scholars in southern history and the New Southern Studies. W. Fitzhugh Brundage's opening chapter assesses more than a century of national interest in southern culture as a site and source of "authenticity." Brundage demonstrates how, in the first half of the twentieth century, fascination with Appalachian folk music and Mississippi Delta blues was bound up with ideas of racial purity and premodern life. White and black music alike was conceived of and consumed as sourced from a South that was simultaneously the nation's primitive internal other and the last, best hope of authentic American values. By contrast, more recent southern musicians such as the Allman Brothers have been celebrated as authentic for their syncretic fusion of musical forms across racial and social divides. Brundage identifies the rise of "southern foodways" as another striking example of how the authentic has become associated with the syncretic, especially in images of the southern kitchen as a site of multicultural fusion and harmony. Scott Romine's chapter explores how this most literal act of consumption, eating "southern food," has become freighted with semiotic significance, from bestselling cookbooks to the semischolarly publications of the Southern Foodways Alliance (SFA). Romine is more skeptical than Brundage about the SFA's "irrepressibly upbeat" cross-racial vision of southern culture. However, Romine remains equally suspicious of the decline narratives that, as we have seen in this introduction, so often determine discussions of southern identity. Boldly stating that "the idea of the South has mostly been a bad idea," he argues that the thin gruel of southernness served up by "foodways" discourse is at least relatively benign, and as such preferable to the thick identitarian politics that coagulated around the Lost Cause.

The chapter closing Part I challenges both Romine and the very premise of this volume. Jon Smith begins by suggesting that the "creating and consuming paradigm" mires the field of southern studies in an outmoded postmodern emphasis on constructions of the region. For Smith, the very concept of "the South" no longer has any political or academic use-value; he has little patience either for the "postsouthern," which he sees as enmeshed with the traditional southern studies it claims to disavow. Smith insists on the need to look beyond symbolic or discursive ideas of southern identity to a kind of "real": the ways in which "real bodies" in the region continue to be subjected to the inequities of global capitalism, the rollback of the civil rights movement, and environmental degradation. Smith repudiates prominent criticism of the New Southern Studies—most notably by Michael O'Brien, in a keynote lecture later reworked for *Creating Citizenship in the Nineteenth-Century South*—as too invested in postmodernism and too dazzled by globalization to discern its discontents. But Smith also critiques Romine's "postmodern relativism," which he sees as insufficiently suspicious of neoliberal capitalism. Smith's chapter concludes with a clarion call for a "post-postpolitical" southern studies: scholarship that moves beyond postmodernism's politically neutered focus on signification, marketing, and branding to reengage with the real world shaped by economic neoliberalism.

Part II of the book is made up of five chapters that offer innovative case studies of how aspects of the South have been created and consumed, in an array of expressive forms and economic contexts. All five contributors focus on the recent past, while situating their case studies in longer southern histories. In the opening chapter, E. Patrick Johnson, author of *Sweet Tea: Black Gay Men in the South—An Oral History* (2008), returns to that book's source material to consider how his interviewees re-created a variety of southern loci—New Orleans, black colleges, golf courses, and country clubs—in ways that facilitated homosexual identity formation while challenging established binaries between gay and straight, black and white, and work and play.

Michael Bibler's chapter offers a sobering check on postmodern deconstructions of "the South" by looking at the looming threat of climate change. Echoing Smith, Bibler notes the limitations of postsouthern literary criticism which figures the South as only and always a textual or ideological construct; he argues that both postsouthern and environmental criticism must confront the ways in which "the physical, economic, and material actualities of the southern landscape" are threatened by devastation. Bibler then offers a postsouthern-environmentalist reading of Scott Elliott's novel *Coiled in the Heart* (2003), which depicts the economic and ecological transformation of rural landscapes in dystopian, even apocalyptic terms. The chapter proceeds to stress the political urgency of confronting the prospect of ecological catastrophe; Bibler warns that a grimly deterministic form of southern distinctiveness may yet emerge if climate change makes all too real the burden of living in a landscape already wracked by hurricanes, floods, and droughts.

The next two chapters can be read together as related case studies in the creation and consumption of (black) southern music. Anne Dvinge's chapter examines the dialectic between tradition and commercialization so common to New Orleans, but especially the city's celebrated jazz culture. Dvinge begins by exploring the low-class, creolized origins of jazz—origins that excluded it from the early branding of New Orleans as a European city—before tracing the music's incorporation into discourses of cultural authenticity, where it has served as a signifier of local, regional, and even national identity ("America's Classical Music"). The chapter then homes in on Preservation Hall in the French Quarter. Rather than dismissing Preservation Hall as either a musical museum that preserves traditional New Orleans jazz in amber, or a tourist trap that sells out the true spirit of jazz, Dvinge argues that the ongoing process of "musicking" at the Hall—a process that involves both the Hall's musicians and its sometimes maligned tourist audiences—sustains a dynamic art form.

Adam Gussow's chapter reflects on his own involvement in Hill Country Harmonica (HCH), an annual blues event established in 2010. Gussow considers the complex nexus of subject positions he occupied during the planning of HCH: academic; amateur entrepreneur; blues harmonica player; and the white northern husband of a black southern woman with whom he has a son. He also explores the mixed motives behind HCH: a wish to showcase local black blues performers excluded from similar events; a commitment to racial justice and reconciliation; a desire for profit; and the opportunity to employ and even exploit his expert understanding of Mississippi blues mythology, which extended to inventing a blues tradition of his own. At first glance, both Dvinge's analysis of Preservation Hall and Gussow's account of creating HCH may seem to prove Romine's point that "the South is increasingly sustained as a virtual, commodified, built, themed, invented or otherwise artificial territoriality." Yet Dvinge's emphasis on a quotidian process of performance that involves inexpert audiences as well as skilled musicians, and Gussow's complicated but rewarding collaboration with his black southern business partners, proves Romine's corollary point: that the South and its cultural forms, however commercialized, are not "removed . . . from the domain of everyday use."[46]

Dvinge's microscale analysis of Preservation Hall also serves as a prelude to the final chapter in Part II: Helen Taylor's broader assessment of New Orleans' attempt to re-create itself as a cultural economy before and after the devastation wrought by Hurricane Katrina in August 2005. Like Dvinge, Taylor attends to the role of music as part of the commodity culture of New Orleans tourism; however, she situates it in the context of a wider attempt to brand the city's cultural forms as part of a postindustrial economy. Referencing Richard Florida's influential argument that cities should strive to attract the "creative class," Taylor shows how New Orleans has followed other global cities by rebranding itself as a city of culture. One might note here too the similarity with other *regional* cities, and that Taylor's timely take on the Crescent City's "creative" turn should be read not as another narrative of or about "New Orleans exceptionalism," but rather as a case study of contemporary southern urbanism. Indeed, her analysis invites comparison with sociologist Wanda Rushing's account of the creative class's courting by another southern city in *Memphis and the Paradox of Place: Globalization in the American South* (2009).[47] Taylor proceeds to discuss how, after the deluge, Louisiana boosters redoubled their attempts to exploit an—in the words of an official report—"economic asset that other states can only dream of: a deeply rooted, authentic culture." However, she also considers creative responses that offered a more critical, oppositional take on post-Katrina New Orleans. These responses ranged from the local (brass band marches through the French Quarter, theater productions in the devastated Ninth Ward) to the transatlantic (graffiti art by Bristol-born Bansky, a play about Katrina staged in London).

The five chapters that make up Part III share Taylor's interest in the transnational routes through which the South has been circulated, (re)created, and consumed. Frank Cha's chapter also focuses on New Orleans but diverges from Dvinge's and Taylor's contributions by exploring the simultaneously local- and global-scale experience of a particular ethnic populace: the Vietnamese Americans of New Orleans East (and, along the Gulf Coast, in East Biloxi). Cha addresses the larger history of Vietnamese immigrants to the Gulf South and their attempts since the 1970s to fashion a southern identity beyond the "partly colored" status of "racial interstitiality" that Leslie Bow has identified with the wider Asian American immigrant experience of the segregated South.[48] Cha then analyzes the community's political and cultural imperilment in the wake of Katrina. He reveals how Vietnamese immigrants and their descendants not only forged a newly visible and cross-racial activism but also re-created New Orleans East as a (multi)cultural destination for tourists and locals alike.

In a presentation at the August 2010 "Creating and Consuming the U.S. South" conference in Copenhagen, Brian Ward discussed three "southern operas": *Koanga* (1904), by the British classical composer Frederick Delius; *Singin' Billy* (1953), a folk-opera collaboration between Donald Davidson and Charles Bryan; and the double-LP *Southern Rock Opera* (2001) by Alabama rock band Drive-By Truckers. Ward demonstrated how these "very different artists, working in different idioms at quite different historical moments, all tried to evoke aspects of the South in musical form."[49] Paige McGinley's chapter here unpacks what may be an even more unlikely southern opera: *Four Saints in Three Acts* (1934) by Gertrude Stein. Like *Koanga*, *Four Saints* conflates southernness with blackness. McGinley shows how Stein's ostensibly highbrow modernist opera responded to the massively successful musical *Green Pastures* (1930), which shaped New York audiences' conception and consumption of black southern culture. But *Four Saints* also superimposed a racialized American South onto a southern European country, Spain, which Stein and other modernists figured in primitivist terms as black. Stein's opera thus imagines a "transitive blackness" that, while problematic, moves through a transnational matrix of regional and global southern relations. In doing so, McGinley suggests, *Four Saints* reminds us that we need to revise the periodization of current scholarship on the regional South vis-à-vis the global South, which tends to privilege the recent past, so that it can also account for modernism.

Deborah Cohn, whose previous work on "the two Souths" (the U.S. South and Spanish-speaking Latin America) heralded the hemispheric turn of New Southern Studies, maintains McGinley's emphasis on literary modernism in regional, national, and global matrices. Cohn is concerned with the ways in which William Faulkner's post–Nobel Prize status as a major U.S. writer became enmeshed with the global politics of the Cold War. Discussing Faulkner's world tours as a cultural ambassador for the State Department, Cohn explores Faulkner's creation of his public persona as southerner and farmer, as well as the circulation and consumption during Faulkner's official travels of competing images of the U.S. South—most notably, the racist murder of Emmett Till in Faulkner's home state of Mississippi. Focusing on Faulkner's 1955 tour of Asia and Europe, Cohn shows how the author drew specific historical analogies between the South and Japan as sites of military defeat and subsumed regional and national identities into a universalizing vision of freedom that accorded with anti-communist U.S. policy.

The penultimate chapter brings us back to music: in this case, the transatlantic relationship between black southern blues and white British rock. Rather than rehashing hackneyed debates about the adoption or appropriation of the blues by earlier British rock groups like the Rolling Stones and Led Zeppelin, Andrew Warnes turns to the post-punk period of the late 1970s and early 1980s. Against the hardening critical consensus that British post-punk bands deliberately rejected blues modes and motifs, Warnes argues that songs by Gang of Four and Wire subtly exhibit, on the lower frequencies, a "blues epistemology" and "oppositionality." Warnes links this subterranean post-punk blues back to black southern expressive culture more broadly, from Frederick Douglass's 1845 slave narrative to jitterbugging at a juke joint in 1930s Clarksdale.

Finally, John Howard analyzes British director Moby Longinotto's documentary short *The Joneses* (2009), which depicts the everyday life in rural Mississippi of a sixty-nine-year-old transsexual mother and her two adult sons. Like E. Patrick Johnson's contribution to Part II, Howard's chapter reveals how the rural South emerges as a site in which non-normative sexual identities can be created against the odds. Like both Johnson and Gussow, Howard foregrounds his own subject position vis-à-vis his subject matter: he was an executive producer of *The Joneses*, and the film's central figure, J. Jones, is an old acquaintance who featured in Howard's acclaimed book *Men Like That: A Southern Queer History* (1999). However, this does not preclude Howard critiquing *The Joneses*' failure to depict non-normative sexual activity, even as he powerfully evokes the transnational routes through which J's ostensibly rooted rural-southern life has circulated, beginning with J's sex-reassignment surgery in Brussels and including the documentary's screening at numerous international film festivals.

Taken together, then, these thirteen chapters move beyond not only shopworn debates over the death or survival of southern distinctiveness, but also the consensus that has solidified since 2000 or so that "the South" is first and foremost a discursive or ideological construction. But what if Jon Smith is correct that the "creating and consuming paradigm" mires us in the southern (studies) past, rather than advancing the New Southern Studies or another paradigm shift toward Duck's "Southern studies without 'the South'"? Ultimately that is something for each reader of this book to decide, but Smith's provocative analysis raises some questions of its own. Would or should post-postpolitical southern studies become the "mainstream" mode of New Southern Studies? If work done a decade or so ago is in Smith's view now a kind of *old* New Southern Studies,[50] hoist with its own postmodern petard, at what point might New Southern Studies per se become obsolete, as out-of-touch to emerging scholars as most boomers seem to Smith? How long can a movement that marks itself with tenth-anniversary conference panels remain "new" and cutting-edge? And finally, if we can do "without 'the South,'" should we then renounce the idea and institutional apparatus of *any* kind of "southern studies"?

It is always a perilous business to hazard predictions, but I suspect that the New Southern Studies will be with us for a while yet, not least because it has itself become a brand with considerable academic-cultural capital. Smith himself has been its foremost promoter, most notably as the founding coeditor of the important New Southern Studies book series—complete with its own brand logo. Whatever the current state of southern studies, it and related disciplines surely do need to engage in vigorous debates (what Smith frankly calls arguments) about the interpretative use-value of terms like "the South," "southernness," and "southern studies." One of Smith's most compelling claims is that "'the South' increasingly appears to be an unhelpful scalar unit: far better to work at a larger scale (the nation, conservatism, plantation America) or a smaller one (consumer culture in Mississippi, desegregation in Atlanta or Milwaukee)." Not only do Smith's examples here reflect much of what "we southernists" actually *do*, but his larger point dovetails with current discussions about "scale" across a range of disciplines, from human geography to comparative literature. For southern studies too, globalization poses what Nirvana Tanoukhi terms "the challenge of describing 'world-scale' phenomena" in ways that move beyond familiar "metaphorical deployments of 'space'" (to cite some examples from traditional southern studies, "Dixie," "the former Confederacy," "the Bible Belt") and "toward concrete discussions about the materiality of literary *landscapes*" (or, one might add, any other Souths-under-description). Yet it does not necessarily follow that "the world-system" or "the global South" is a more "scale-sensitive" unit of analysis than "the American South"; as Smith's examples suggest, the appropriate scalar units might be more local and/or more (trans)national.[51] In this book's companion volume *The American South and the Atlantic*

World, Brian Ward employs a different metaphor—poet William Blake's claim to "see a world in a grain of sand"—to suggest that "those studying the American South can benefit from a granular approach" in which global scales like the Atlantic World "are revealed by close attention to a particular southern locale."[52]

In an afterword to this volume, McPherson posits that the next paradigm shift for scholars working on the South may be away from the analyses of "authenticity" that resound throughout this volume to a more thoroughgoing engagement with the impact of globalization, especially neoliberal capitalism. Smith's chapter makes similar noises. If this does represent the next move beyond "the creating and consuming paradigm," some of those historians and social scientists seemingly marginalized by the New Southern Studies may prove to have been more "progressive" all along.[53] Still, Smith and McPherson are surely right that we need to pay more heed to how discursive and imagined Souths interact with and impact social and material realities, and at a variety of scales. My own modest proposal is that *Creating and Consuming the American South* marks a start in that direction.

Notes

1. Romine, "Where Is Southern Literature?," 26; Thompson quoted in Garner, "Crisscrossing"; "Michael," "iPhone Points to Southern Distinctiveness."
2. Two contributors to this book have seen traces of this tendency in my own work: see Romine, *Real South*, 7, and Smith, review of *Postsouthern*, 373.
3. Egerton, *Americanization of Dixie*, xxi, xx.
4. Jones and Monteith, "Introduction," 2; McPherson, *Reconstructing Dixie*, 1; Greeson, *Our South*, 1; Stanonis, "Introduction," 5.
5. See Romine, *Real South*, and "God and the MoonPie" in this volume.
6. Smith, "Southern Culture on the Skids," 83; Cobb, "Beyond the 'Y'all Wall,'" 13.
7. See Smith, "Southern Culture on the Skids," 83.
8. Cobb, "Beyond the 'Y'all Wall,'" 13.
9. Smith, *Finding Purple America*, 107, 109. Sharon Monteith observes that "there is a disconcerting return to the autochthonous" whenever scholars who were born and/or work in the U.S. South continue to express puzzlement that "the mapping of Southern studies is already—and has always been to some extent—a global process" ("Southern like US?" 67–68). Smith notes that such residual southern(ist) nativism includes identifying as "we Southerners" taking a stand against "tourists and carpetbaggers . . . historians and theorists" (*Finding Purple America*, 143n8, quoting the call for papers from the 2010 Society for the Study of Southern Literature conference). See also my own critique of southern studies' "Quentissential fallacy" ("Transnational Turn," 192).

10. See O'Brien, *Idea of the American South*.
11. Greeson, *Our South*, 1.
12. Peacock, "South and Grounded Globalism," 265.
13. See Faust, *Creation of Confederate Nationalism*.
14. Aaron, *Unwritten War*, 293.
15. See Bone, "Neo-Confederate Narrative," especially 87–89.
16. Tourgée quoted in Blight, *Race and Reunion*, 220.
17. Ownby, "Introduction," 21.
18. Blight, *Race and Reunion*, 200; see also Gaston, *New South Creed*.
19. See Brundage, *Southern Past*, 187, and Stanonis, "Introduction," 3; see also Knight, *Tropic of Hopes*.
20. Cox, *Dreaming of Dixie*, 36.
21. Brundage, *Southern Past*, 184.
22. On Charleston and Savannah, see Cox, *Dreaming of Dixie*, 156, and Brundage, *Southern Past*, especially 199–203; on New Orleans in comparison to Charleston and Savannah, see Souther, *New Orleans on Parade*, 2–3.
23. [Ransom], "Introduction," *I'll Take My Stand*, xlix–l, xlviii.
24. Davidson, "The Artist as Southerner," 782; Brundage, *Southern Past*, 184.
25. Ownby, *American Dreams in Mississippi*, 5; see also chapter 6.
26. Crews, *Childhood*, 132.
27. See Kirby, *Media-Made Dixie*.
28. Cox, *Dreaming of Dixie*, 83.
29. Romine, *Real South*, 27; McPherson, *Reconstructing Dixie*, 40.
30. Brundage, *Southern Past*, 221.
31. Elias, "Postmodern Southern Vacation," 259, 261.
32. Eskew, "Selling the Civil Rights Movement," 196; see also Brundage, *Southern Past*, 301–7.
33. McPherson, *Reconstructing Dixie*, 99.
34. Brundage, *Southern Past*, 310.
35. Souther, *New Orleans on Parade*, xi, xvi.
36. Romine, *Real South*, 29; McPherson, *Reconstructing Dixie*, 101–15.
37. Faust, *Creation of Confederate Nationalism*, 5–6.
38. Romine, *Real South*, 2, 236.
39. Taylor, *Circling Dixie*, 11, 23.
40. Duck, "Plantation/Empire," 77.
41. Bowe, "Nobodies."
42. Peacock, Watson, and Matthews, "Introduction," 2.
43. McPherson, "On Wal-Mart and Southern Studies," 696; see also Moreton, *To Serve God and Wal-Mart*.
44. Peacock, Watson, and Matthews, "Introduction," 3.
45. McPherson, *Reconstructing Dixie*, 254, 18.
46. Romine, *Real South*, 9.
47. See Rushing, *Memphis and the Paradox of Place*, especially 78–79, 85, 113. What I term the "timely" nature of Taylor's chapter also meant that its author faced "the perils

of trying to write about the contemporary and the fast-moving!" (personal communication, May 28, 2014). Taylor presented an initial version of this chapter as a keynote lecture at the third "Understanding the South" conference, at the University of Cambridge, in May 2010—less than five years after Hurricane Katrina. The final version of the chapter appears another five years on; in the meantime, much has changed on the ground in New Orleans. For timely recent accounts of "New Orleans exceptionalism," see Campanella, "New Fuel for an Old Disaster," which argues that "the BP oil disaster, like Katrina, breathed new life into the area's oldest historical impression: that *something different happens here*. Call it the exceptionalism narrative"; and Lightweiss-Goff, "Peculiar and Characteristic," which offers a literary-critical history of New Orleans exceptionalism from Frederick Law Olmsted to Katrina.

48. Bow, *Partly Colored*, 8–9.

49. Ward, "Delius, Davidson, and the Drive-By Truckers."

50. Perhaps including Smith's own earlier work: in his 2002 essay for *South to a New Place*, Smith concluded that "punk may—for those young white southerners alert to the implications—have freed white southern identity from its long, narcissistic gaze at its own ancestral navel" ("Southern Culture on the Skids," 95). In 2013 Smith chided his younger self for exhibiting "too much faith . . . in the redemptive functions of subcultures" defined by "the heroic school of subcultural studies" (*Finding Purple America*, 15, 73).

51. Palumbo-Liu, Robbins, and Tanoukhi, "Acknowledgments," vii; Tanoukhi, "Scale of World Literature," 79, 84. Here I am indebted to my participation in Tanoukhi's weeklong seminar "The Scale of World Literature" at the Institute for World Literature, Harvard University, in summer 2013.

52. Ward, "Caryl Phillips," 30. For an example of New Southern Studies scholarship that considers "a variety of geographic scales," see Stecopoulos, *Reconstructing the World*, especially 3, 35, 114, 170 n10.

53. See especially the two collections, published in 2005, *The American South in a Global World* and *Globalization and the American South*—though I would qualify that both conspicuously fail to engage with relevant scholarship in literary and cultural studies.

Works Cited

Aaron, Daniel. *The Unwritten War: American Writers and the Civil War*. New York: Knopf, 1973.

Blight, David W. *Race and Reunion: The Civil War in American Memory*. Cambridge: Belknap Press of Harvard University Press, 2001.

Bone, Martyn. "Neo-Confederate Narrative and Postsouthern Parody: Hannah and Faulkner." In *Perspectives on Barry Hannah*, edited by Martyn Bone, 85–101. Jackson: University Press of Mississippi, 2007.

———. "The Transnational Turn, Houston Baker's New Southern Studies, and Patrick Neate's *Twelve Bar Blues*." *Comparative American Studies* 3, no. 2 (June 2005): 189–211.

Bow, Leslie. *Partly Colored: Asian Americans and Racial Anomaly in the Segregated South.* New York: New York University Press, 2010.

Bowe, John. "Nobodies: Does Slavery Exist in America?" *New Yorker*, April 21, 2003. http://www.newyorker.com/archive/2003/04/21/030421fa_fact_bowe. Accessed May 28, 2014.

Brundage, W. Fitzhugh. *The Southern Past: A Clash of Race and Memory.* Cambridge: Belknap Press of Harvard University Press, 2005.

Campanella, Richard. "New Fuel for an Old Narrative: Notes on the BP Oil Disaster." *Design Observer*, September 7, 2010. http://places.designobserver.com/feature/new-fuel-for-an-old-narrative-notes-on-the-bp-oil-disaster/14828/. Accessed May 28, 2014.

Cobb, James C. "Beyond the 'Y'all Wall.'" In *Globalization in the American South*, edited by James C. Cobb and William Stueck, 1–18. Athens: University of Georgia Press, 2005.

Cox, Karen L. *Dreaming of Dixie: How the South Was Created in American Popular Culture.* Chapel Hill: University of North Carolina Press, 2011.

Crews, Harry. *A Childhood: The Biography of a Place.* In *Classic Crews: A Harry Crews Reader.* New York: Touchstone, 1993.

Davidson, Donald. "The Artist as Southerner." *Saturday Review of Literature*, May 15, 1926, 782.

Duck, Leigh Anne. "Plantation/Empire." *CR: New Centennial Review* 10, no. 1 (2010): 77–88.

Egerton, John. *The Americanization of Dixie: The Southernization of America.* New York: Harper's Press, 1974.

Elias, Amy J. "Postmodern Southern Vacation: Vacation Advertising, Globalization, and Southern Regionalism." In *South to a New Place: Region, Literature, Culture*, edited by Suzanne W. Jones and Sharon Monteith, 253–82. Baton Rouge: Louisiana State University Press, 2002.

Eskew, Glenn T. "Selling the Civil Rights Movement: Montgomery, Alabama, since the 1960s." In *Dixie Emporium: Tourism, Foodways, and Consumer Culture in the American South*, edited by Anthony Stanonis, 175–202. Athens: University of Georgia Press, 2008.

Faust, Drew Gilpin. *The Creation of Confederate Nationalism: Ideology and Identity in the Civil War South.* Baton Rouge: Louisiana State University Press, 1988.

Garner, Dwight. "Crisscrossing a Region of Strip Malls and Ghosts." *New York Times*, April 23, 2013. http://www.nytimes.com/2013/04/24/books/the-new-mind-of-the-south-by-tracy-thompson.html?_r=0. Accessed May 28, 2014.

Gaston, Paul M. *New South Creed: A Study in Southern Mythmaking.* New York: Knopf, 1970.

Greeson, Jennifer Rae. *Our South: Geographic Fantasy and the Rise of National Literature.* Cambridge: Harvard University Press, 2010.

Jones, Suzanne, and Sharon Monteith. "Introduction: South to New Places." In *South to a New Place: Region, Literature, Culture*, edited by Suzanne W. Jones and Sharon Monteith, 1–19. Baton Rouge: Louisiana State University Press, 2002.

Kirby, Jack Temple. *Media-Made Dixie: The South in the American Imagination.* Baton Rouge: Louisiana State University Press, 1978.

Knight, Henry. *Tropic of Hopes: California, Florida, and the Selling of American Paradise, 1869–1929.* Gainesville: University Press of Florida, 2013.

Lightweis-Goff, Jennie. "'Peculiar and Characteristic': New Orleans Exceptionalism from Olmsted to the Deluge." *American Literature* 86, no. 2 (June 2014): 147–69.

McPherson, Tara. "On Wal-Mart and Southern Studies." *American Literature* 78, no. 4 (December 2006): 695–98.

———. *Reconstructing Dixie: Race, Gender, and Nostalgia in the Imagined South.* Durham: Duke University Press, 2003.

"Michael" [no surname given]. "iPhone points to Southern distinctiveness." *Southern Nationalist Network*, December 20, 2011. http://southernnationalist.com/blog/2011/12/20/iphone-points-to-southern-distinctiveness/. Accessed August 29, 2013.

Monteith, Sharon. "Southern like US?" *Global South* 1, nos. 1–2 (2007): 66–74.

Moreton, Bethany. *To Serve God and Wal-Mart: The Making of Christian Free Enterprise.* Cambridge: Harvard University Press, 2009.

O'Brien, Michael. *The Idea of the American South, 1920–1941.* Baltimore: Johns Hopkins University Press, 1990.

Ownby, Ted. *American Dreams in Mississippi: Consumers, Poverty, and Culture, 1830–1998.* Chapel Hill: University of North Carolina Press, 1999.

———. "Introduction: Thoughtful Souvenirs." In *Dixie Emporium: Tourism, Foodways, and Consumer Culture in the American South*, edited by Anthony J. Stanonis, 19–23. Athens: University of Georgia Press, 2008.

Palumbo-Liu, David, Bruce Robbins, and Nirvana Tanoukhi. "Acknowledgments." In *Immanuel Wallerstein and the Problem of the World: System, Scale, Culture*, edited by David Palumbo-Liu, Bruce Robbins, and Nirvana Tanoukhi, vi–vii. Durham: Duke University Press, 2011.

Peacock, James. "The South and Grounded Globalism." In *The American South in a Global World*, edited by James Peacock, Harry L. Watson, and Carrie R. Matthews, 265–76. Chapel Hill: University of North Carolina Press, 2005.

Peacock, James, Harry L. Watson, and Carrie R. Matthews. "Introduction: Globalization with a Southern Face." In *The American South in a Global World*, edited by James Peacock, Harry L. Watson, and Carrie R. Matthews, 1–5. Chapel Hill: University of North Carolina Press, 2005.

[Ransom, John Crowe.] "Introduction: A Statement of Principles." In *I'll Take My Stand: The South and the Agrarian Tradition*, by Twelve Southerners, xxxvii–xlviii. 1930. Baton Rouge: Louisiana State University Press, 2006.

Romine, Scott. *The Real South: Southern Narrative in the Age of Cultural Reproduction.* Baton Rouge: Louisiana State University Press, 2008.

———. "Where Is Southern Literature? The Practice of Place in a Postsouthern Age." In *South to a New Place: Region, Literature, Culture*, edited by Suzanne W. Jones and Sharon Monteith, 23–43. Baton Rouge: Louisiana State University Press, 2002.

Rushing, Wanda. *Memphis and the Paradox of Place: Globalization in the American South.* Chapel Hill: University of North Carolina Press, 2009.

Smith, Jon. *Finding Purple America: The South and the Future of American Cultural Studies*. Athens: University of Georgia Press, 2013.

———. Review of *The Postsouthern Sense of Place in Contemporary Fiction*, by Martyn Bone. *Mississippi Quarterly* 59, no. 2 (2006): 369–73.

———. "Southern Culture on the Skids: Punk, Retro, Narcissism, and the Burden of Southern History." In *South to a New Place: Region, Literature, Culture*, edited by Suzanne W. Jones and Sharon Monteith, 76–95. Baton Rouge: Louisiana State University Press, 2002.

Souther, J. Mark. *New Orleans on Parade: Tourism and the Transformation of the Crescent City*. With a new preface by the author. Baton Rouge: Louisiana State University Press, 2013.

Stanonis, Anthony J. "Introduction: Selling Dixies." In *Dixie Emporium: Tourism, Foodways, and Consumer Culture in the American South*, 1–16. Athens: University of Georgia Press, 2008.

Stecopoulos, Harilaos. *Reconstructing the World: Southern Fictions and U.S. Imperialisms*. Ithaca: Cornell University Press, 2008.

Tanoukhi, Nirvana. "The Scale of World Literature." In *Immanuel Wallerstein and the Problem of the World: System, Scale, Culture*, edited by David Palumbo-Liu, Bruce Robbins, and Nirvana Tanoukhi, 78–99. Durham: Duke University Press, 2011.

Taylor, Helen. *Circling Dixie: Contemporary Southern Culture through a Transatlantic Lens*. New Brunswick: Rutgers University Press, 2001.

Ward, Brian. "Caryl Phillips, David Armitage, and the Place of the American South in the Atlantic and Other Worlds." In *The American South and the Atlantic World*, edited by Brian Ward, Martyn Bone, and William A. Link, 8–44. Gainesville: University Press of Florida, 2013.

———. "Delius, Davidson and the Drive-By Truckers: Three Operas and the Southernness of Southern Music." Paper presented at the "Creating and Consuming the U.S. South" conference, University of Copenhagen, August 2010.

1

Creating and Consuming the "Real" South

1

From Appalachian Folk to Southern Foodways

Why Americans Look to the South for Authentic Culture

W. FITZHUGH BRUNDAGE

If we associate anything with the year 1893 in the United States, it probably is the onset of one of the nation's worst economic depressions, the spectacle of the Chicago Columbian Exposition, or perhaps the tawdry events culminating in the annexation of Hawaii. It is probably not Lila Edmands' publication of three transcribed songs that she had collected in the Roan Mountains of North Carolina. Yet this obscure article, which appeared in the newly established *Journal of American Folklore*, signaled a growing interest in, even fascination with, Appalachian folk songs. During the 1880s, local color writers had begun to win readers by drawing attention to Appalachia, but only in the 1890s did enthusiasts begin to systematically catalogue its "rustic" folkways. Newly established mountain settlement schools became centers of cultural recovery, and there Olive Dame Campbell and other would-be folklorists found the inspiration and materials for their seminal collections of mountain lore. Collecting southern folklore acquired sufficient prestige that scholars at the region's universities took it up; moreover, within two decades of Edmands' article, folklore societies had been launched in North Carolina and other states along the spine of Appalachia. By the 1910s, the annual Georgia Old-Time Fiddlers' Convention was drawing scores of mountain fiddlers, as well as large and enthusiastic audiences, to Atlanta. The romance with southern mountain folkways was so advanced that by 1921 one observer urged those who wanted to "espy pure America in its native haunts" to hasten to the Appalachian South.[1]

Nearly one hundred years after the publication of Edmands' transcriptions, writer John Egerton published *Southern Food: At Home, On the Road, in History* (1987). Egerton's work is a modern paean to the foodways of the South. Recalling the pleasures of a barbecue feast, he attests that the aromas and flavors of southern food penetrate to "the core of thought and remembrance." "No other form of cultural expression, not even music," he concludes, "is as distinctively characteristic of the region. For as long as there has been a South and people who think of themselves as Southerners, food has been central to the region's image, its personality, and its character." Egerton's consuming passion for distinctively southern cooking is hardly idiosyncratic. In the past two decades, shelves of cookbooks have methodically explored all manner of southern foods. The titles of some of these cookbooks suggest the breadth of traditions that are now catalogued and venerated: *Old Carolina Tobacco Country Cook Book*; *Smokehouse Ham, Spoon Bread, and Scuppernong Wine*; *Heritage Corn Meal Cookery*; *Legends of Texas Barbecue*; *Down on the Bayou Cookbook*; *Biscuits, Spoonbread, and Sweet Potato Pie*; *Gullah Home Cooking the Daufuskie Way*; and *Hoppin' John's Lowcountry Cooking*. No mere compilations of recipes, these cookbooks are veritable works of ethnography. Elsewhere in this book, Scott Romine catalogues the traits that define such cookbooks as part of the highly self-conscious creation of "southern foodways": featuring "a folksy voice," they evoke "nostalgic memories of consuming the food item" in question while making "exaggerated claims of its tried-and-true southernness." Like many southern chef-authors, Paul Prudhomme, in his *Louisiana Tastes* (2000), devotes as much space to explorations of the culture surrounding the foods he describes as to the recipes themselves.[2]

Prudhomme and Egerton, like Edmands and Campbell, participated in a defining project of twentieth-century culture—the pursuit and celebration of the authentic. They catalogued what they believed to be the "authentic" culture of the South, and they tried to lead lives steeped in that culture. With their efforts in mind, in this essay I offer a reconsideration of the persistent interest in southern culture during the twentieth century. This topic warrants careful consideration for several reasons. First, southern culture exerted a profound influence on the United States and the world during the twentieth century. It inspired countless practitioners and enthusiasts in almost every genre of cultural expression. Second, now that the Jim Crow "solid" South has given way to the desegregated "Sunbelt" South, now that immigrants from Latin America and Asia have flocked to the region, now that evangelical churches associated with the South have spread their influence across the nation, and now that suburbanization has transformed large swaths of the region into landscapes indistinguishable from those elsewhere, southern culture is, for most Americans and many international observers too, the distinguishing feature of the region. To understand how southern culture has been created (by practitioners and observers like Edmands and Egerton, who in the process of interpreting "southern culture" have also defined it) and consumed is to trace an important theme in the region's shifting identity. My main contention is that southern culture at the dawn of the twentieth century was explained—not to mention exploited—so as to affirm purportedly primordial, innate, and enduring divisions among the region's and the nation's peoples. Now, in contrast, "authentic" southern culture is held up as evidence of the enrichment of American life that results from pervasive cultural exchange across economic, racial, and social divides.

At the outset, a word on the challenge of defining culture is in order. Are we speaking of "high" or "low" culture? Are we talking about culture as the totality of a people's socially transmitted behavior, or as a self-conscious, cultivated mode of artistry? It is worth recalling the evolution of the word *culture* during the twentieth century. According to the definition that prevailed at the dawn of the century, the South was a "Sahara of the Bozart," as Baltimore newspaperman and habitual crank H. L. Mencken cruelly put it in 1917. The South lacked most of the essential institutions of culture, as they were then commonly understood. There were few distinguished universities, museums, libraries, or galleries between the Potomac and the Rio Grande. Conditions clearly have improved in the past three-quarters of a century. But even more striking is the adoption of a broader and more inclusive conception of culture to replace the older notion of "culture" as a synonym for advanced civilization. The South figured prominently in this conceptual evolution, and as a result the "folkways" that Mencken mocked have now become esteemed cultural forms. Indeed, rather than being seen as a Sahara of culture, the South is now commonly viewed as a region where culture is as plentiful as kudzu.[3]

Central to this shifting conception of culture was the pursuit of authenticity. Here again we confront the challenge of definition. An intellectually compelling definition of "authentic" culture may not be possible. Any definition is likely to provoke the response, "Authentic compared to what?" Those Americans who have been keenest to find authentic culture in the South are unlikely to provide much guidance or clarity about the proper measure of "authenticity." Neither do I intend to offer a definition; instead, I propose that we ponder why various groups, with widely divergent cultural aspirations, have found it useful to locate and tap what they insisted was the "authentic" culture of the South.[4]

Let us begin by returning to the burgeoning interest in mountain folkways at the dawn of the twentieth century. Evident in this growing fascination with the Appalachian folk was the influence of nineteenth-century romanticism, especially of German philosopher Johann Gottfried von Herder. For Herder and his disciples in Europe and the United States, folk cultures were an antidote to the Enlightenment's suffocating idolatry of reason and progress. They recoiled from the artificial and abstract universalism that characterized national ideologies in the age of the French Revolution, and which supposedly threatened folkways that revealed the true and distinctive soul of a people. Americans encountered these ideas in the writings of England's romantic poets and novelists even before Harvard professor Frances James Child introduced the techniques of systematic collection and study of folklore to the United States during the 1850s. Before the end of the nineteenth century, then, there was a widely held belief that the purest expression of a nation's collective character was its folkways.

When folklorists in the South tapped this tradition at the beginning of the twentieth century, they were also motivated by decidedly contemporary concerns. New South boosters enthused over mountain folkways in an effort to rehabilitate the image of poor whites and to ease simmering class tensions that had flared during the 1890s. Some devotees were eager to find a cultural patrimony in American songs and lore that compared favorably with those of the European powers. Many more came to understand the ballads and folkways of Appalachia as the cultural seed corn of the Anglo-Saxon race. Englishman Cecil Sharp underscored this point when, after extended research trips in western North Carolina and elsewhere, he published *English Folk Songs from the Southern Appalachians* (1917). What Sharp had discovered, he claimed, was a vast repository of largely uncorrupted English folk songs. His findings strengthened notions that the mountaineers still spoke a version of Old English, worshiped in a centuries-old form of Calvinism, and lived according to timeless traditions that resembled those of English peasants in Shakespeare's day. For Sharp and his ilk, mountain culture was more than quaint traditions; it was the collective expression of the innate racial traits of a pure English stock. As Sharp explained, "the reason why these mountain people, albeit unlettered, have acquired the essentials of culture" was "their racial heritage." Because most folklorists assumed that American culture was, at core, Anglo-Saxon culture, they needed little persuasion to conclude that the mountain South preserved the true American culture that elsewhere had been debased by modernity and immigration.[5]

A striking aspect of this interest in mountain culture was that it distanced white Americans from African American culture. At the same time that folklorists were busy tracking down American renditions of ancient British ballads, they paid scant attention to emerging forms that would define American popular culture during the twentieth century—the blues and jazz. Whites had displayed considerable interest in black spirituals ever since the Fisk Jubilee Singers began touring to raise money for their alma mater in 1871. But conventional wisdom held that the spirituals were a corruption of white hymns and were principally of interest as remnants of a passing culture that was exotic and picturesque but hardly representative of America. Likewise, the popular recordings of Bessie Smith and other black artists during the 1920s were too modern, urban, and risqué to merit inclusion in the catalogue of "authentic" American expression. Such ideas about the purity of white mountain culture led record executives to pointedly refuse to allow white "hillbillies," as they were called in the industry, to record any songs that betrayed African American influences.[6]

While these presumptions about white southern culture would persist (and continue to shape the genre of country music to the present day), the assumptions about black culture came under revision as early as the 1930s. Folklore gadfly John Lomax and his sons John Jr. and Alan were hardly the first folklorists to trace pure Americana to the South, but the Lomaxes, especially Alan, expanded the boundaries of "true" American culture to include the plaintive sounds of black bluesmen. When the Lomaxes began to wander the back roads of the South in 1932, lugging their cumbersome and primitive portable recorder, they specifically sought out "traditional" black music in the "eddies of human society." In the prisons of Mississippi and Louisiana, as well as other isolated locales, they found what they were looking for—blacks who knew and "heard only the idiom of their race." At Angola, the Louisiana state penitentiary, the Lomaxes made their most famous "discovery": Huddie Ledbetter, better known as "Lead Belly." To hear the Lomaxes, Lead Belly's eleven-year confinement had been a blessing that sheltered him from contemporary music. They heard in Lead Belly's music a faithful expression of black America; John Lomax explained, "To me his music is real music." When Lomax began to organize performances for the former convict, he cast Lead Belly as "a 'natural' who had no idea of money, law, or ethics and who was possessed of virtually no restraint." Lomax had Lead Belly dress in his prison stripes, overalls, or other rustic clothes that accentuated his wild aura. White listeners soon parroted the language of the Lomaxes, romanticizing the "deep primitive quality" and "perfect simplicity" of Lead Belly's music and performances.[7]

During the Depression, the bracing voices of Lead Belly and others conjured up America's mythic past. They sounded earthy, sensual, uncontaminated by middle-class propriety or commercialized popular culture, and quintessentially exotic. These musicians were seen to represent, and their records were consumed as, something timeless in the midst of the transparently ephemeral mass culture and squandered prosperity of Swing-era America. Admittedly, Lead Belly's popularity was confined to a comparatively small audience until after his death, but he subsequently became an icon during the folk music boom of the 1950s. By then the corpus of southern music that the Lomaxes and others had collected during the 1930s, and that Lead Belly had vividly embodied, had become a mother lode of American tradition—one that would be tapped by generations of musicians from Johnny Cash and Bob Dylan to Nirvana. In this manner, music that purportedly emerged organically outside the mass marketplace acquired heightened value in postwar consumer society. Pop culture during the late twentieth century, Jon Smith suggests, "seemed saturated with reclamations of the old, weird" South as a source of authenticity within—even subversion of—mainstream commercialism.[8]

While the Lomaxes were tracking down "authentic" voices in the prison pens of the Deep South, others looked to the South Carolina low country for an alternative to machine-age uniformity. During the 1920s and 1930s, the low country was the epicenter of a cultural effervescence that became known as the Charleston "Renaissance." Charleston was an improbable host for a revival of any kind; since the Civil War it had lapsed into economic decline. Nevertheless, in the twenties, when Mencken was still dismissing most of the South as a cultural wasteland, he touted Charleston as a pocket of culture and refinement. The basis for Charleston's cultural standing was the claim put forth by Mencken and others that the city and its environs retained the "authentic" culture of the Old South. As Herbert Sass, one of the most commercially successful writers associated with the Charleston Renaissance, put it: "Charleston has become for thousands the visible affirmation of the most glamorous of all folk legends of America— the legend of the plantation civilization of the Old South. A single morning spent wandering through its older streets, a single afternoon at one of the great plantations which were an essential part of it, prove that there was at least one region—actually there were several—where the Old South really was in many ways the handsome Old South of the legend."[9]

For writers like Sass and artists like Alfred Hutty and Alice Ravanel Huger Smith, as well as tourists who streamed into Charleston each spring, the city perpetuated an otherwise vanished "way of life." At a time when many "old stock" Americans were anxious about the waning of the nation's Anglo-Saxon character, Charleston preserved a reassuringly traditional and stable social order. "Her exclusive families," a tourist brochure announced, "are keeping alive in America some of the best heritages of our ancestors." A travel writer boasted that "Charleston is the last stand of the traditional and original in place and people against the leveling, common-place aspect which is the most marked characteristic of the twentieth century." Protected by a cocoon of tradition, white Charlestonians apparently had almost no business to pursue and instead enforced social protocols that elsewhere had been corrupted by "the vulgarity of materialism" and the hurly-burly of modernity.[10]

While Charleston was a sanctuary for an authentic aristocratic culture, it also purportedly harbored the remnants of an equally distinctive and archaic black culture. Low-country African Americans and their folkways figured prominently in the fascination with the region. Artist Elizabeth O'Neill Verner was not alone in insisting that blacks were "an integral part of the beauty of Charleston." They were certainly essential to the most famous product of the renaissance, DuBose Heyward's *Porgy* (1925). They also enthralled folklorists and anthropologists who roamed the sea islands in search of residual African folkways that had survived the Middle Passage. Whether intentionally or not, the portrait of low-country blacks that prevailed during the Charleston renaissance was of an exotic, childlike race that survived under the indulgent protection of a white aristocracy. Common wisdom held that the region's harmonious racial order fixed whites and blacks in their appropriate and separate roles. In this regard, Charleston stood in marked contrast to northern cities, where black southern migrants were seen to have acquired the troubling affectations of the "New Negro" associated with the era's other renaissance, the Harlem Renaissance.[11]

Because modernity threatened to overwhelm the low country's black folkways, local whites launched the Society for the Preservation of Spirituals (SPS), one of the century's most eccentric cultural preservation movements. Founded in 1922 by white descendants of antebellum planters, the society pledged to preserve black spirituals and to educate "the rising generation in their character and rendition." As the children of slave owners, society members boasted that they understood "the negro character probably as well as any white man ever does." They confined their campaign to the preservation and performance of slave spirituals because they alone possessed the "pure African wildness and beauty of tone, only touched by the religion of the Anglo-Saxon." Society members viewed these spirituals as something that African Americans uncorrupted by mass culture or inappropriate ambition produced naturally. But because too few "authentic" blacks existed, concerned whites claimed that they had to appropriate this traditional black southern culture in order to preserve it.[12]

Had society members recorded black performers or published transcriptions of spirituals, they would have been inconspicuous partners of the Lomaxes, Zora Neale Hurston, and other contemporary folklorists who displayed unprecedented interest in black music and culture. Indeed, Hurston, like society members, lamented that traditional spirituals had been corrupted by mass culture. (Hurston, though, critiqued the very practice that the society promoted: the performance of spirituals—or what Hurston witheringly called "neo-spirituals"—in concert hall settings.) However, society members went further and actually performed black spirituals themselves. Dressed in hoop skirts and in tuxedos with antebellum era bowties, they sang spirituals in the low-country black dialect of Gullah. In addition to singing and "shouting," their performances included commentary about the meaning of the spirituals and the splendors of the antebellum society that supposedly produced them. The SPS's version of black spirituals demonstrated that the institution of slavery had nurtured beauty and faith, but it elided slavery's brutality. The irony of descendants of white slaveholders appropriating and performing black spirituals to glorify slavery and the social order it made possible drew no comment from either SPS members or their audiences. Many audience members apparently agreed with a 1927 concert-goer who vouched that "the negroes themselves could not do so well."[13]

Uniting the pursuit of authentic American culture in the southern low country, the prison camps of Louisiana, and the hollows of Appalachia during the first third of the twentieth century was the allure of uncorrupted essences. The ur-cultures of the Gullah, aristocratic low-country whites, Mississippi Delta bluesmen, and mountain bards provided seekers of "authenticity" with evidence that American folkways were resistant to the solvent of modernity. Always implicit and sometimes explicit in the recovery of the South's folkways was the presumption that assimilation into modern cosmopolitan life could be prevented only by retaining one's authentic, and profoundly racialized, culture. Although the early folklorists held dismissive ideas about black culture that the Lomaxes and some of the participants in the Charleston Renaissance rejected, they all were in fundamental agreement that the nation's richest cultural traditions emerged from cultural isolation. This conviction drove the Lomaxes to seek out cultural "eddies" for decades and inspired white Charlestonians to brag that not only they but also the blacks in their midst were outside of the American mainstream. Despite the decades that separated Lila Edmands' work in the mountains of North Carolina and the Lomaxes' recording expeditions in Louisiana, key assumptions about cultural authenticity persisted. Although Alan Lomax was a left-leaning liberal, and Herbert Sass was a reactionary conservative, both idealized southern communities that seemingly had escaped the undertow of commercialism and modernity. For Lomax, Sass, Edmands, and many others during the early twentieth century, the most profoundly American places in the South paradoxically were those places that were least like the rest of America.

Hunger for authenticity did not end with Pearl Harbor, although it was sometimes difficult to discern amid the subsequent postwar enthusiasm for Tupperware, prepared food mixes, television, and mass consumption. Simultaneously, the image of the South as a picturesque storehouse of U.S. culture waned at a time when many Americans viewed the strife-torn region as deviating in alarming, rather than endearing, ways from the rest of the nation. With opponents of desegregation tracing their defiance to time-honored "southern" traditions, many Americans understandably looked elsewhere for a usable, appealing cultural heritage. New York City and southern California, not the southern backwoods or the low country, seemed to better represent the promise of postwar America. Not coincidentally, during the two decades after World War II, many performers who drew upon southern musical traditions self-consciously set out to modernize their sound. Jazz musicians gravitated toward African, Caribbean, and European musical forms, abandoning the older New Orleans jazz tradition; as Anne Dvinge shows in her contribution to this volume, it would take clean-cut revivalists and "hot" collectors in the North and outside the United States to burnish the image of New Orleans as the hallowed birthplace of jazz. While Mississippi bluesmen like Muddy Waters shed the rambling acoustic country blues of their youth and pioneered hard-driving, electric and urban blues in Chicago, purveyors of country music cleansed their product of its "old timey," rustic traits and created the so-called "Nashville" or "countrypolitan" sound.[14]

Yet in the mid-1960s the South reemerged as a fount of traditional culture. Indeed, it is a challenge to decide where to begin when cataloguing the late-twentieth-century fetish for "authentic" southern culture. It is evident in the earnest but unsuccessful effort, at the taxpayers' expense, to revive French in southern Louisiana. It turned the *Foxfire* books, which compiled mountain wisdom about every conceivable pastoral chore, into a publishing phenomenon. It was codified (and commodified) in the celebrated *Encyclopedia of Southern Culture* (1989). The fetish also fueled some of the nation's most ambitious historic preservation programs, which have transformed Charleston, Savannah, and numerous southern towns and cities into alluring "memoryscapes" that cater to inherited notions of southern charm, gentility, and tradition. The marketing and consumption of "authentic" southern culture also has become a staple of the region's "heritage" tourism industry. It too is the catalyst, as Romine explains in his contribution to this book, for the recent enthusiasm for southern cooking.[15]

The "roots music" phenomenon of the late twentieth century is yet another significant expression of the reclamation of "authentic" southern culture. This phenomenon had many sources of inspiration. The nascent discipline of ethnomusicology performed a function comparable to the folklore movement of the early twentieth century: it elevated the study of American musical cultures into something more than mere antiquarianism. Although ethnomusicology retained some romantic ideas about the "folk," its strongest influence was the cultural relativism associated with anthropologist Franz Boas and his students during the first half of the twentieth century. No longer was the measure of a culture's beliefs and aesthetics an arbitrary, universal standard. Instead of presuming, for example, that European traditions of harmony and counterpoint were the criteria of advanced musicianship, students of southern music now acknowledged the previously denigrated rhythmic and tonal complexities of the blues and bluegrass.[16]

Beyond the ivory towers of academe, both the emerging New Left and "counterculture" made access to "authentic" experience a prerequisite for a just society. The Port Huron Statement of the Students for a Democratic Society voiced a growing sentiment that "finding a meaning in life that is personally authentic" required "full, spontaneous access to present and past experiences." Music's capacity to articulate grievances with piercing clarity and sincerity mesmerized student radicals. White folk troubadours like Bob Dylan, Joan Baez, and Pete Seeger, as well as African American musicians including Odetta and the Selma Freedom Choir, yoked traditional black music to the cause of social justice with unimpeachable integrity. For members of both the New Left and the counterculture who were deeply suspicious of the mass culture and "military-industrial complex" that dominated postwar America, the music of America's disadvantaged and marginalized—not least black southerners—acquired new relevance; the music of the southern "folk" offered the promise of sampling a democratic culture that the "organization men" and their corporate ethos had apparently eviscerated elsewhere. In this context, genres that had previously attracted few listeners outside of isolated regional pockets, ranging from zydeco and Cajun to Tejano and bluegrass, now garnered national and international audiences.[17]

The roots music revival that began in the 1960s was not simply a reprise of the early-twentieth-century discovery of southern folk cultures. The revivalists certainly were intent on rejecting saccharin Nashville country, Brill Building pop, and other mainstream musical genres. However, unlike their turn-of-the-century predecessors, roots music revivalists were not searching for latter-day primitives whose culture was fixed in amber. Instead, they sought to tap American traditions as a means of fashioning an eclectic, cosmopolitan, and explicitly multiracial aesthetic. Barbara Dane, a prominent white folk performer, typified this impulse. The child of parents who had moved to Detroit from Arkansas, Dane earned the nickname of "Bessie Smith in Stereo" for a voice that *Ebony* magazine described as her "powerful dusky alto." In 1966 Dane responded to the call of Bernice Johnson Reagon, a prominent black civil rights activist and performer, to join an interracial group that toured the South raising funds for civil rights groups. For Dane and her fellow performers, the tour provided an opportunity "to tell about the people we come from, and to show how the music has always been intertwined—to show that *no* kind of wall could have separated 'black' music from 'white' music."[18]

This aspiration to erase artificial racial barriers in musical traditions led music buffs, performers, and critics to look for precedents of cultural sharing among the region's polyglot population. This search uncovered previously overlooked southern artists such as black string band leader Howard Armstrong (aka Louie Bluie), a flamboyant and garrulous Tennessee-born fiddler, mandolinist, painter, writer, and storyteller. In 1930 Armstrong and his band, the Chocolate Drops, made their radio debut and cut their first records. Eventually, Armstrong and his band moved to Chicago where they regularly played for tips in the Maxwell Street flea market. However, changing tastes and hard times during the Depression ended Armstrong's professional career until the 1970s, when music buffs rediscovered his recordings. So great was the interest in them that Armstrong reunited his band of four decades earlier and performed steadily until his death, at age ninety-four, in 2003.

At first glance, Armstrong's appeal to audiences may appear to have been much the same as that of Lead Belly during the 1930s. Certainly, Armstrong and his reunited band performed string band music that seemed exotic and uncorrupted by the dictates of the marketplace. Yet it was Armstrong's promiscuous and incorrigible eclecticism that won him acclaim late in his life. He drew upon material not only from the segregated "race music catalogues" but also old-time jigs, reels, waltzes, rags, minstrel show favorites, jazz, Tin Pan Alley hits, and traditional ethnic tunes. In an especially telling anecdote captured in Terry Zwigoff's 1985 documentary *Louie Bluie*, Armstrong recounts using the Italian and Polish that he had learned as a youth in multiethnic La Follette, Tennessee, to perform traditional European songs for white immigrants in neighborhood taverns in Chicago.[19]

Beneficiaries of the new interest in hybrid southern musics included the Tejano greats Little Joe and accordionist Flaco Jimenez, zydeco king Clifton Chenier, the gospel a cappella quintet Sweet Honey in the Rock, Texas bluesman Clarence "Gatemouth" Brown, and bluegrass star Alison

Krauss. Arguably, the archetype of modern southern musical fusion has been the Allman Brothers Band, who demonstrate an exceptional talent for reconfiguring southern musical traditions. Their rousing renditions of Blind Willie McTell's "Statesboro Blues" and Dickie Betts' lyrical country-music-inspired "Blue Sky" demonstrate the breadth of their musical vocabulary. Reflecting the band's multiracial membership and expansive musical tastes, the Allmans dissolve inherited musical boundaries as both an act of artistic creativity and a testament to the permeability of regional and national cultural divisions.

Greg and Duane Allman, the band's founders, grew up in a household of avid country-music listeners who tuned in to WSM out of Nashville and favored the music of Bill Monroe and Roy Acuff. After moving to Daytona Beach, Florida, the Allman boys became enthralled by the black rhythm and blues music they heard on WLAC, and they attended shows by black musicians at Ocean Pier. However, unlike many white aficionados of black music during the 1960s, the Allmans were neither blues revivalists nor purists. They were as conversant in contemporary black R&B as they were in obscure blues from the early twentieth century. Duane, for example, initially made a name for himself as a session guitarist at the FAME Studios in Muscle Shoals, Alabama, where he accompanied the elite of 1960s soul music, including Aretha Franklin, Wilson Pickett, and King Curtis.[20]

From early in their careers, Greg and Duane were fearless in their appropriation and fusion of virtually all of the music traditions of the South and resented efforts to categorize their music. Shirking the title of founders of "southern rock," band members have stressed that they are, as Greg put it, "a contemporary blues and jazz band." The membership of the group has reflected the band's eclectic influences. Guitarist Dickey Betts, who boasted American Indian ancestry, displayed a keen understanding of country music as well as an adventurous jazz sensibility; black Alabamian Johnny Lee "Jaimoe" Johnson brought to the group years of experience as a jazz and soul drummer, most recently for Otis Redding; Butch Trucks was a classical percussion prodigy; and bassist Berry Oakley was steeped in midwestern blues that he grew up listening to in Chicago. In subsequent iterations of the band, new members, especially Derek Trucks, have only broadened the group's influences to include sacred steel and Pakistani and East Indian qawwali music.[21]

The band's early double-LP masterpiece, *Live at the Fillmore East* (1971), underscored the band's commitment to mastering a seamless fusion of blues, rock, jazz, and country that avoided romanticizing or fetishizing any of their sources of inspiration. The band's penchant for shuffling and recasting blues classics was on display in their renditions of songs drawn from virtually all eras and regional traditions of the genre. The two longest performances of their Fillmore date—"Whipping Post" and "Mountain Jam"—are arguably the pinnacle of the band's musical syncretism. "Whipping Post," written by Greg, yokes the classic subject of the blues—the torment and psychic violence of disappointed desire—to lyrical and musical imagery derived from slavery. The song climaxes with Duane and Dickey Betts playing unison guitar lines that mimic the snap of a whip and the cries of the whipping victim. At first glance Greg Allman, a white southerner without any inherited memory of the trauma of slavery, may appear to be engaging in modern-day rock minstrelsy by exploiting the terror of slavery to convey lovelorn pain. Had the Allmans not been a multiracial band (always a rarity in rock, and especially in "southern rock"), and had the band not contractually demanded integrated seating at all of its performances during the late 1960s (which was still uncommon at many venues in the South), the imagery of "Whipping Post" might be dismissed as yet another example of white cultural appropriation and voyeurism. "Whipping Post" avoids trivializing and instead fosters empathy for the plight of the whipping victim. Most striking is that Greg Allman would forthrightly dredge the fraught historical memory of slavery for the song's title and central metaphor; that he did so almost certainly was a reflection of his immersion in black musical idioms and the new possibilities, opened up by the civil rights movement and desegregation, to confront the region's past. Meanwhile, the concluding song on *Live at Fillmore East*, "Mountain Jam," is a marathon instrumental improvisation during which the band displays another facet of its musical hybridity by interpolating musical quotes from avant-garde jazzman Ornette Coleman, 1930s Parisian jazz guitarist Django Reinhardt, British hard rock group Led Zeppelin, rock virtuoso Jimi Hendrix, traditional Protestant hymns, English folk-pop, and the full blues canon.[22]

For a generation of white southerners who came of age after the climax of the civil rights struggle in the early 1960s and during the maturation of the "sunbelt" South, the appeal of the Allmans' musical gumbo was considerable. Although the Allmans never enjoyed record sales or radio play comparable to British blues rockers like the Rolling Stones or Led

Zeppelin, they garnered an enthusiastic fan base both within and outside the South through their relentless touring. In the music of the Allmans, southern-born rock journalist Mike Kemp and his peers discerned a cultural alternative to earlier ideals of southern whiteness, one that was neither reactionary nor racist. Kemp recalled the angst that he felt during the late 1960s: "I loved the land that surrounded me but hated the history that haunted that land." When he listened to the Allmans he heard familiar regional musical references, but they were now recast in new and appealing ways: "This multiracial outfit of hippies and rednecks created a soundtrack that relieved young southerners of the weightiness of their guilt, fear, and economic insecurities: the family legacies of racism, the drudgeries of a rural, working class existence." He was not alone in his perception that the Allmans' mix of music styles was "sonic integration at its purest."[23]

Coinciding with the roots music phenomenon has been an explosion of interest in southern cuisine. That southern foods would become celebrated would have surprised many Americans a century ago, or even a half century ago. New Orleans, of course, was famed for its cuisine as early as the 1880s. Elsewhere, though, only southerners displayed enthusiasm for their cuisine, and this state of affairs lasted throughout most of the late nineteenth century, and the first half of the twentieth century. However vaunted in legend, southern cooking had lamentable shortcomings according to one traveler in the region during the 1880s. He warned tourists that "such villainous, disgusting cooking" as was found in Florida was "surely unequaled." Nearly four decades later an early automobile enthusiast regretted that in Statesboro, Georgia, he had sampled "such food, so badly prepared and so disgustingly presented, it has never been our misfortune to meet." Almost certainly these encounters with southern cooking reflected the poverty that gripped the region and the consequent lack of any significant restaurant industry outside of major cities.[24]

The dramatic rise of incomes and urbanization during the second half of the twentieth century transformed southern kitchens and restaurants. With Americans displaying an unprecedented appetite for foods with robust flavors, a succession of cuisines associated with the South, ranging from Cajun to Tex-Mex, have come into favor. A striking feature of this interest in "southern foodways" has been the reinterpretation of regional traditions. Whereas cookbook authors during the late nineteenth and early twentieth centuries contributed to the romanticization of the Old

South by including nostalgic testimonials to black household cooks, contemporary champions of southern cooking display little sentimentality for the cultural assumptions that pervaded earlier regional cookbooks. Instead contemporary cookbooks and chefs dwell on the multicultural elements of the region's foods. They stress their indebtedness to Native Americans for everything from corn to sassafras leaves and maple syrup; to Africans for okra, black-eyed peas, collard greens, yams, and watermelons; to South Americans and Caribbean islanders for peppers, peanuts, tomatoes, lima beans, chocolate, and potatoes; and Europeans for cream sauces, gravies, and white-flour breads. These diverse sources of inspiration give southern cuisine an appeal that, in the words of John Egerton, "transcends the barriers of race, class, sex, religion, and politics." Leah Chase, a prominent New Orleans chef, agrees: "Food belongs to everybody." Many southerners probably agree with Egerton that "[f]ood has been perhaps the most positive element of our collective character, an inspiring symbol of reconciliation, reverence, and union." He adds that "southern food now unlocks the rusty gates of class and race, age and sex."[25]

This conviction about the unifying influence of traditional southern food suggests just how far the South has traveled, or, more accurately, how far some southerners hope it has traveled, in the twentieth century. In the wake of the black freedom struggle, southerners and Americans in general have searched for a usable past of multicultural adaptation and exchange. Whereas southern culture at the dawn of the twentieth century was exploited to affirm purportedly primordial and innate divisions among the region's and the nation's peoples, it is now celebrated for its traditions of pervasive cultural exchange—traditions that are figured as distinctly "American." This revision of our understanding of southern culture testifies to widespread hope that aesthetic expression and lived culture can break down inherited barriers and inhibitions. These new understandings of southern culture allow for more sophisticated understandings of cultural evolution and innovation.

Of course, champions of southern cultural syncretism are prone to overreach and exaggeration. Kemp's autobiographical rumination about the emancipatory import of southern rock for his generation of white southerners exhibits an understandable but at times facile notion of the redemptive power of popular culture. In this volume Romine brilliantly critiques the contemporary fetishization of southern foodways, pointing out how much the romance of grits and shrimp, barbeque, and collard greens is focused on the pleasures of consumption, and how little attention is devoted to the drudgery of production (growing, harvesting, and distribution); even more glaringly, "foodways" discourse "tends to suppress the racial taboos and prohibitions that for generations dictated the protocols of food consumption in the South." What is more, contemporary reconsiderations of southern culture as multicultural and syncretic are unlikely to address all of the anxieties and needs that have fueled the search for authenticity in the modern United States. Long before German philosopher Walter Benjamin's writings were translated into English, generations of Americans recognized the challenge that mass production posed to aesthetics rooted in artisanal traditions. Unlike Benjamin, who was optimistic about the aesthetic potential of mass production and culture, many Americans recoiled from it and instead craved the verifiably authentic.[26] Their pursuit of the authentic became bound up with a contemporary preoccupation to escape the banality of modernity, to make "contact with reality," and to escape to "a realm of intense experience."[27] Whether by touring "quaint and picturesque" old towns, collecting rustic handicrafts, or listening to folk ballads, Americans have looked to the South for an accessible alternative to the standardization of modern American life. As long as southern culture performed this function, escape from the perceived artificiality of modernity did not require any larger struggle against broader social, economic, and political forces.

Even today, substantial numbers of Americans who are not fully reconciled to modern life and mass culture perpetuate some of the cultural tropes inherited from the nineteenth century and early twentieth century. Many blues aficionados still romanticize the blues as an innately primitive form. For evidence of this we need look no further than the colorful legends that surround Robert Johnson and other early blues musicians. Contrary to conventional wisdom, the Mississippi Delta familiar to Son House, Robert Johnson, and other bluesmen was not cut off from the wider, modern American culture. Many of the early blues musicians boasted broad repertoires that would have been familiar to Blind Willie McTell in Georgia or Howard Armstrong and his string band in eastern Tennessee. We can only imagine how different our conception of Mississippi blues would be if the record producers of the early twentieth century had sampled the full repertoire of the region's bluesmen. We might wonder too whether many Robert Johnson fanatics would be so enamored if he had been recorded performing Tin Pan Alley ditties.[28]

Similar assumptions continue to shape country music. Periodically during the past half century, country musicians have advocated a return to the pure "roots" of country music, whether defined as mountain ballads or honky-tonk shuffles. However, the Carter Family, Fiddlin' John Carson, and other icons of early "hillbilly" music were less backwoods rubes than ambitious artists who listened with open ears to the music of their age, including jazz, blues, and Tin Pan Alley tunes. They were cultural innovators, not preservers of a static culture. Nevertheless, country music retains an unshakable association with rock-solid heartland traditions. It is not happenstance that politicians from the 1920s to the present, from Huey Long to George W. Bush, have exploited country music to vouch for their authenticity and to lend their campaigns an aura of populism. Simply put, in a world beset by unsettling and headlong change, imagined cultures that are figured as distinctive and timeless possess tremendous appeal.[29]

Finally, the idea of southern culture as a product of cultural syncretism is unlikely to resolve the questions of identity and power that have long vexed the South. Even as we acknowledge the extent of cultural exchange in the South, we still lack a satisfactory vocabulary to delineate its complexities. How do we describe with precision the cultural stealing, sharing, borrowing, and creating that gave birth to the South's cultural forms? Because we are eager to celebrate cross-racial, cross-ethnic, and cross-class exchanges as a solvent of inherited prejudices, we tend to overlook the threat that this emphasis poses to the cultural identity of some southerners. Some African Americans, for instance, conclude that whites are yet again claiming the culture of the region's minorities as their own. Southern chefs and food historians continue to tussle over the invention of such iconic southern foods as barbecue. Whereas many whites dwell on the extent of cultural fusion in southern cuisine, food historian and cookbook author Jessica B. Harris and others stress the decisive, even predominant contributions of African Americans. At stake in these arguments is much more than just the finer points of barbecue. Having struggled so long to overcome white condescension, blacks now bridle at the possibility that recognition of their ancestors' creativity will be subsumed in a broader celebration of the multicultural origins of southern folkways.

So where does this survey of evolving ideas about southern culture during the twentieth century leave us? A half century ago William Taylor, in his masterful *Cavalier and Yankee* (1961), argued that the myth of the planter cavalier in the Old South provided antebellum Americans with an antidote to the restless mobility and strident materialism of their age. Fear and envy sustained the allure of a culture that was supposedly immune to acquisitiveness and indiscriminate progress, yet was rooted in place and tradition.[30] Here I have suggested that the South and its "authentic" cultures continued to perform a similar role during the twentieth century. Across the century, southerners and non-southerners reinterpreted the region's culture to bolster shifting ideas about both regional and national identity. As often as southern culture was used to criticize the institutions and values of the United States, it was also used to accommodate Americans to them. In the age of Jim Crow, students of southern culture affirmed the cultural separateness of the region's people. Now, in a more pluralist age, southern culture has been reinterpreted to provide comforting evidence of the possibility and value of cultural exchange. We can find satisfaction that contemporary Americans find fellowship through southern culture. However, we would be naive to assume that the meanings we assign to "authentic" southern culture today will not be subject to revision and re-invention in the future.

Notes

1. Edmands, "Songs from the Mountains of North Carolina," 131–34; Campbell and Sharp, *English Folk Songs from the Southern Appalachians*. On the "discovery" of mountain music, see Campbell, *Music and the Making of the New South*, 100–42; Filene, *Romancing the Folk*, 9–46; Whisnant, *All That Is Native and Fine*, 103–80.

2. Egerton, Bleidt Egerton, and Clayton, *Southern Food*, 2; Prudhomme, *Chef Paul Prudhomme's Louisiana Tastes*. See also Romine, "God and the MoonPie," in this volume.

3. Mencken's essay is reprinted in Cairns, ed., *American Scene*, 157–68.

4. The starting point for any discussion of the pursuit of "authenticity" is Orvell, *Real Thing*. See also Cheever, *Real Phonies*.

5. Campbell and Sharp, *English Folk Songs from the Southern Appalachians*, vii.

6. Huber, *Linthead Stomp*.

7. Filene, *Romancing the Folk*, 47–75; Hamilton, *In Search of the Blues*, 99–115ff; Porterfield, *Last Cavalier*, 330–70.

8. Smith, "Weird Americas," 104.

9. Sass, "Charleston," 72.

10. Law, "Charleston—Queen of Colonial America," 46.

11. Verner, *Mellowed by Time*, 33.

12. On the SPS, see Brundage, *Southern Past*, 216–18; Campbell, *Music and the Making of a New South*, 75, 80; and especially Yuhl, *Golden Haze of Memory*, 124–55.

13. Matthew Page Andrews, quoted in *Charleston News and Courier*, November 26, 1927. For Hurston's lament on spirituals, see her "Spirituals and Neo-Spirituals," 344–47.

14. See Dvinge, "Pride at Preservation Hall," in this volume.

15. Brundage, "Le Reveil de la Louisiane"; Wilson and Ferris, eds., *Encyclopedia of Southern Culture*; Puckett, "Foxfire Reconsidered"; Wigginton, *Sometimes a Shining Moment*; Romine, "God and the MoonPie."

16. For discussions of the emergence of the discipline of ethnomusicology, see Myers, ed., *Ethnomusicology*; and Blum, Bohlman, and Neuman, eds., *Ethnomusicology and Modern Music History*.

17. The Port Huron Statement of the Students for a Democratic Society, 1962, is available at http://www.h-net.org/~hst306/documents/huron.html, accessed July 13, 2011.

18. Quoted in Cohen, *Rainbow Quest*, 232.

19. See also Zwigoff, "Life and Music of William Howard Armstrong."

20. The gestation of the Allmans' music is traced in Freeman, *Midnight Riders*, 3–43; and Poe, *Skydog*, 1–100. On WLAC and its importance in introducing white audiences to black R&B, see Barlow, *Voice Over*, 160–66.

21. Insights into the bands' musical influences can be gleaned from interviews with Duane Allman collected on "Duane Allman Interviews & Radio Shows," http://www.duaneallman.info/duaneinterviews.htm, accessed December 28, 2010.

22. On Fillmore, see Freeman, *Midnight Riders*, 86–96; Poe, *Skydog*, 171–90; and especially Grandt, *Shaping Words to Fit the Soul*, 84–103.

23. Kemp, *Dixie Lullaby*, 29. On the reception of southern rock, see also Cullen, *Civil War in Popular Culture*, 108–38; Butler, "Luther King Was a Good Ole Boy," 41–62.

24. Jarvie, "From Richmond over Proposed Highway to Florida," 182.

25. Egerton et al., *Southern Food at Home*, 4; Chase, quoted in St. John, "Greens in Black and White," accessed December 28, 2010. For a sampling of highbrow southern food writing, see the five volumes of *Cornbread Nation* published under the auspices of the Southern Foodways Alliance between 2002 and 2010. For critical interpretations of the southern foodways "renaissance," see Romine, *Real South*, especially 108–15; and Warnes, *Savage Barbecue*.

26. Benjamin, "Work of Art in the Age of Mechanical Reproduction," accessed July 13, 2011.

27. Lears, "From Salvation to Self-Realization," 11.

28. See Hamilton, *In Search of the Blues*; Schroeder, *Robert Johnson, Mythmaking, and Contemporary American Culture*; Wald, *Escaping the Delta*.

29. See Huber, *Linthead Stomp*; Willman, *Rednecks and Bluenecks*.

30. Taylor, *Cavalier and Yankee*.

Works Cited

Barlow, William. *Voice Over: The Making of Black Radio*. Philadelphia: Temple University Press, 1999.

Benjamin, Walter. "The Work of Art in the Age of Mechanical Reproduction." http://www.marxists.org/reference/subject/philosophy/works/ge/benjamin.htm. Accessed July 13, 2011.

Blum, Stephen, Philip Vilas Bohlman, and Daniel M. Neuman, eds. *Ethnomusicology and Modern Music History*. Urbana: University of Illinois Press, 1991.

Brundage, W. Fitzhugh. *The Southern Past: A Clash of Race and Memory*. Cambridge: Belknap Press of Harvard University Press, 2005.

———. "Le Reveil de la Louisiane: Memory and Acadian Identity, 1920–1960." In *Where These Memories Grow: History, Memory, and Southern Identity*, edited by W. Fitzhugh Brundage, 271–98. Chapel Hill: University of North Carolina Press, 2000.

Butler, Mike. "'Luther King Was a Good Ole Boy': The Southern Rock Movement and White Male Identity in the Post–Civil Rights South." *Popular Music and Society* 23 (summer 1999): 41–62.

Campbell, Gavin James. *Music and the Making of the New South*. Chapel Hill: University of North Carolina Press, 2004.

Campbell, Olive D., and Cecil James Sharp. *English Folk Songs from the Southern Appalachians*. New York: G. P. Putnam's Sons, 1917.

Cheever, Abigail. *Real Phonies: Cultures of Authenticity in Post–World War II America*. Athens: University of Georgia Press, 2010.

Cohen, Ronald D. *Rainbow Quest: The Folk Music Revival and American Society, 1940–1970*. Amherst: University of Massachusetts Press, 2002.

Cullen, Jim. *The Civil War in Popular Culture: A Reusable Past*. Washington, DC: Smithsonian Press, 1995.

Edmands, Lila W. "Songs from the Mountains of North Carolina." *Journal of American Folklore* 6 (April–June 1893): 131–34.

Egerton, John, Ann Bleidt Egerton, and Al Clayton. *Southern Food: At Home, on the Road, in History*. New York: Knopf, 1987.

Filene, Benjamin. *Romancing the Folk: Public Memory & American Roots Music*. Chapel Hill: University of North Carolina Press, 2000.

Freeman, Scott. *Midnight Riders: The Story of the Allman Brothers Band*. New York: Little, Brown, 1995.

Grandt, Jurgen E. *Shaping Words to Fit the Soul: The Southern Ritual Grounds of Afro-Modernism*. Columbus: Ohio State University Press, 2009.

Hamilton, Marybeth. *In Search of the Blues*. New York: Basic Books, 2008.

Huber, Patrick. *Linthead Stomp: The Creation of Country Music in the Piedmont South*. Chapel Hill: University of North Carolina Press, 2008.

Hurston, Zora Neale. "Spirituals and Neo-Spirituals." In *Voices from the Harlem Renaissance*, edited by Nathan Irvin Huggins, 344–47. 2nd ed. New York: Oxford University Press, 1995.

Jarvie, William. "From Richmond over Proposed Highway to Florida." *Club Journal* 2 (May 28, 1910): 182.

Kemp, Mark. *Dixie Lullaby: A Story of Music, Race, and New Beginnings in a New South*. New York: Free Press, 2004.

Law, Margaret Lathrop. "Charleston—Queen of Colonial America." *Travel* 44 (November 1929): 46.

Lears, T. Jackson. "From Salvation to Self-Realization." In *The Culture of Consumption: Critical Essays in American History, 1880–1980*, edited by Richard Wightman Fox and T. Jackson Lears, 1–38. New York: Pantheon, 1983.

Mencken, H. L. "The Sahara of the Bozart." In *The American Scene: A Reader*, edited by Huntington Cairns, 157–68. New York: Knopf, 1977.
Myers, Helen, ed. *Ethnomusicology: Historical and Regional Studies*. New York: W. W. Norton, 1993.
Orvell, Miles. *The Real Thing: Imitation and Authenticity in American Culture, 1880–1940*. Chapel Hill: University of North Carolina Press, 1989.
Poe, Randy. *Skydog: The Duane Allman Story*. San Francisco: Backbeat Books, 2006.
Porterfield, Nolan. *Last Cavalier: The Life and Times of John A. Lomax, 1867–1948*. Urbana: University of Illinois Press, 1996.
Prudhomme, Paul. *Chef Paul Prudhomme's Louisiana Tastes: Exciting Flavors from the State That Cooks*. New York: William Morrow, 2000.
Puckett, John L. "Foxfire Reconsidered: A Critical Ethnohistory of a Twenty-Year Experiment in Progressive Education." PhD diss., University of North Carolina at Chapel Hill, 1986.
Romine, Scott. *The Real South: Southern Narrative in the Age of Cultural Reproduction*. Baton Rouge: Louisiana State University Press, 2008.
Sass, Herbert Ravenel. "Charleston." *Saturday Evening Post*, February 8, 1947, 72.
Schroeder, Patricia. *Robert Johnson, Mythmaking, and Contemporary American Culture*. Urbana: University of Illinois Press, 2004.
Smith, Jon. "Weird Americas, Old, New, and Ongoing." *CR: The New Centennial Review* 10, no. 1 (spring 2010): 101–12.
St. John, Warren. "Greens in Black and White." *Uptown Flavor*. http://uptownflavor.blogsome.com/2006/02/14/mg-diner/. Accessed December 28, 2010.
Taylor, William Robert. *Cavalier and Yankee: The Old South and American National Character*. New York: Harper and Row, 1961.
Verner, Elizabeth O'Neill. *Mellowed by Time: A Charleston Notebook*. 3rd ed. Charleston: Tradd Street Press, 1978.
Wald, Elijah. *Escaping the Delta: Robert Johnson and the Invention of the Blues*. New York: Amistad, 2004.
Warnes, Andrew. *Savage Barbecue: Race, Culture, and the Invention of America's First Food*. Athens: University of Georgia Press, 2008.
Whisnant, David E. *All That Is Native and Fine: The Politics of Culture in an American Region*. Chapel Hill: University of North Carolina Press, 1983.
Wigginton, Eliot. *Sometimes a Shining Moment: The Foxfire Experience*. Garden City, NY: Anchor Press/Doubleday, 1985.
Willman, Chris. *Rednecks and Bluenecks: The Politics of Country Music*. New York: New Press, 2005.
Wilson, Charles Reagan, and William R. Ferris, eds. *Encyclopedia of Southern Culture*. Chapel Hill: University of North Carolina Press, 1989.
Yuhl, Stephanie E. *A Golden Haze of Memory: The Making of Historic Charleston*. Chapel Hill: University of North Carolina Press, 2005.
Zwigoff, Terry. "The Life and Music of William Howard Armstrong, as Told to Terry Zwigoff," *78 Quarterly* 1, no. 5 (1990): 41–55.

2

God and the MoonPie

Consumption, Disenchantment, and the Reliably Lost Cause

SCOTT ROMINE

> Like a good Beaujolais and steak frites, RC Cola and the Moon Pie should be consumed together to achieve the full impact of regional memory exploding on the tongue.
>
> Moon Pie and RC Cola are intimately linked with the country store. Together, they are among the most powerful icons in Southern culture . . . they are mythic symbols of the region.
>
> The Moon Pie anchors the memories of Southerners in their history and culture.
>
> William Ferris, "The Moon Pie: A Southern Journey"

I begin with these passages from William Ferris not because they are unusual, but because they are not.[1] Originally presented at the 2005 Southern Foodways Symposium, Ferris's "The Moon Pie: A Southern Journey" appeared in 2008 in *Cornbread Nation 4*, the penultimate collection to date in what the Southern Foodways Alliance website advertises as "Four Irresistible Collections of Southern Food Writing at its Finest—*Cornbread Nation 1, 2, 3, 4, and 5*."[2] The essay repeats many features of southern food writing, including a folksy voice, an expository background on the food item in question, nostalgic memories of consuming the food item, and exaggerated claims of its tried-and-true southernness. I pause here according to the old rule that in texts, once is happenstance, twice is coincidence, and the third time is a genre. The editors of *Cornbread Nation 4* are attuned to generic convention, observing in a preface to Audrey Petty's

"Late-Night Chitlins with Momma" that "[i]n food writing there is an established genre of articles with titles like 'My Mama's _____' or 'Cooking _____ with Mamaw.'"[3] I take this conventional quality of southern food writing to be significant. If the MoonPie and RC Cola allow regional memory to explode on the tongue, I want to consider how the *discourse* of the foodway makes it possible to eat the South—and not just this or that combination of marshmallow and chocolate, or pork and sauce.

The conventions attending the foodway and its enabling discourses position the cultural practice in an odd limbo. Although various metrics describe foodways as increasingly central to southern culture—they constitute $1/24$ of that culture, by the calculus of the twenty-four-volume *New Encyclopedia of Southern Culture*; $10/12$ of it, by the calculus of the Southern Zodiac; $9/25$ of it, by the calculus of a recent *Southern Living* spread on "25 Tips for Celebrating the Soul of the South"—such calculations are often at least partially ironized.[4] When they are not engaged in lip smacking, tongues—Ferris's, for example, which is clearly *performing* a kind of southernness—often seem at least partially in cheeks. Yet at the same time, foodways are presented straightforwardly as a continuous tradition. The term itself, in alluding to William Graham Sumner's "folkways," signals a deep cultural practice, thereby suppressing that the cultural practices so named are, in contemporary times, mostly a matter of consumerist choice and are often positioned at the high end of market. If you shop in the right places, you can exchange money for heirloom tomatoes; no one actually inherits them.

Such paradoxes abound in a field of cultural production that despite entanglements in food tourism, cookbooks, the restaurant industry, television programs, and academic conferences, understands consumption to mean eating plain and simple, minus any connotations of consumerism. The contemporary, commodity character of foodways inevitably gives way to their "traditional" status, even if the tradition in question is obviously invented or of recent vintage. Miller Union restaurant in Atlanta offers "a modern farmhouse feel" and "heritage breed Poulet Rouge." If, as the *New Encyclopedia of Southern Culture* claims of fried green tomatoes, the "dish has become synonymous with southern culture," it has done so through what Agehananda Bharati calls the "pizza-effect," wherein a culture's self-understanding is refracted through outside sources—in this case, a Hollywood film.[5] The localist valences of many foodways often appear as reactions to the pressures of a globalized world of media and mobility. As *Southern Living* editor M. Lindsay Bierman explains, cooking and gardening are "ways to stay grounded, literally and spiritually, in an age of electronic distractions. In this and future issues, look for more ways than ever to savor a meal and put down roots."[6] In screening practices of producing and consuming southern food, such discourse invents pasts as often as it records them. According to the *New Encyclopedia*, "[m]any southerners have fond memories of going to the tobacco patch to harvest tobacco and to eat tomatoes growing in rows adjacent to the tobacco rows."[7] While I am incredulous of this claim as history—how many southerners, after all, *have* this recollection?—I am interested in it as a kind of imagined memory that circulates throughout the discourse.

In its broad contours, then, and in its particular sublation of commodity form, the contemporary southern foodway appears as yet another iteration of what Pierre Bourdieu identifies as one of the key "inventions" of romanticism—specifically, "the representation of culture as a kind of superior reality, irreducible to the vulgar demands of economics"—that are, in fact, "just so many reactions against the pressures of an anonymous market."[8] But if the cultural position of the foodway appears as a trivial variation on an old theme, there is something significant in this insignificance. This essay traces a somewhat improbable line of descent from God to the MoonPie as guarantors of something called "southern culture," and as they are differently embedded in fields of representation and causality. In developing a contrast between what I will call culture in its fundamentalist and its consumerist modes—that is, between culture as a set of default imperatives regulating desire, and as an object in itself desirable (if never fully attainable)—I argue that what Michael O'Brien calls "the idea of the South" is weakened as it is submitted to a regime of (cultural) consumption and, consequently, exerts less social and historical force.[9] From God to the MoonPie describes an arc between culture as *context*, to use Clifford Geertz's classic formulation, to culture as *content*, positioned in increasingly standardized delivery systems. In describing this arc, I hope to complicate the narratives that typically accrue around it wherein the emergence of commodification signals an undesirable *loss* of culture as it submits to pressures of standardization and bureaucratization. Without approaching the heroic conclusion that the MoonPie represents a domain of freedom wrested from the realm of necessity, I want nevertheless to argue that narratives of cultural *loss*, as articulated by both the right and the left, are equally legible as narratives of cultural *detoxification*.

But how does a mass-produced marshmallow sandwich invented in 1918 serve as a culture-bearing medium in the first place? If we are inquiring of possibilities, the answer seems straightforward: it is no more nonsensical to say that marshmallow can bear culture than it is to say that a communion wafer can bear God or that epidermal pigmentation can bear identity. Such relationships are always arbitrary and conventional, secured through collective practice, and, considered skeptically, irrational. If we are inquiring of actualities—asking, that is, whether the MoonPie *does* these things—the answers are more complex, still more if we inquire as to the conditions and means of such work. Even allowing that the MoonPie is, as a $15.99 T-shirt available at moonpie.com claims it to be, a "Southern Thing" that "You wouldn't understand," what kind of southern thing is it?

That the MoonPie might be a southern thing at all is perhaps most readily legible within an old story of cultural decline: specifically, the South's deterioration from a way of life to a lifestyle. In *Placing the South* (2007), Michael O'Brien claims that the "South begins to become a voluntary lifestyle. And this may be how Southern identity will begin to perish, not with a bang but a whimper." The observation is common enough; versions of it have existed for at least a half century, and for O'Brien it has something of a throwaway feel. What is notable, however, is that O'Brien notes explicitly what most commentators have, in making similar judgments, been at pains to suppress: "The South has always been an effort of will." "The idea of the South," O'Brien writes, "has always been only one of the synthesizing ideas available to those people who have lived in the southeastern United States since about 1820, to accept and use if they wished, to refuse if they wished."[10] In positing a variable relationship between an ideational, willful South—a South to be accepted or refused—and a set of realities existing in the southeastern United States—a South-under-no-description—O'Brien opens a crucial gap whose conceptual implications have not always been sufficiently appreciated. Despite ours being an age of suspicious hermeneutics, a predisposition toward the South as a synthesizing idea explanatory of various social and historical phenomena has existed and continues to exist as a matter of analytical bias and institutional pressure.

In attending to how the idea of the South operates in foodways discourse, I want to scrutinize three of O'Brien's apparent premises, all of which require modification relative to that discourse: first, that the idea of the South is singular; second, that it is synthesizing; and third, that it is consistently optional throughout history. In arguing that the opposing propositions—that the ideas of the South are multiple, discontinuous, and more optional than they were—seem better to explain contemporary practices of consumption, I want to turn to the year 1880, which O'Brien identifies as the apogee of southerners' propensity to accept "'southern' as the social identity most explanatory of their lives and individualities."[11] In a novel published that same year, Albion Tourgée's *Bricks without Straw*, the narrator observes that below "old 'Mason and Dixon's line,'" the people identify "first of all [as] 'Southerners.'" The evidence is everywhere:

> There are "Southern" hotels and "Southern" railroads, "Southern" steamboats, "Southern" stage-coaches, "Southern" express companies, "Southern" books, "Southern" newspapers, "Southern" patent-medicines, "Southern" churches, "Southern" manners, "Southern" gentlemen, "Southern" ladies, "Southern" restaurants, "Southern" bar-rooms, "Southern" whisky, "Southern" gambling-hells, "Southern" principles, "Southern" *everything*! Big or little, good or bad, everything that courts popularity, patronage or applause, makes haste to brand itself as distinctively and especially "Southern."[12]

Although Tourgée does not organize it so, his list breaks down structurally into items such as patent-medicines, restaurants, and whisky, on the one hand, and principles, ladies, and manners, on the other—between consumables and nonconsumables, commodities and things irreducible to market praxis. The collation of disparate items under the aegis of "Southern" indicates the idea's power in generating structures of feeling and performing synthesizing work. Here, the idea of the South is capacious, integrating practices as disparate as religious observance and restaurant patronage, and powerfully binding consumption to the performance of social identities.

Consumption of the MoonPie works differently. There are any number of observations to be made here regarding the nature of the South purportedly realized by MoonPie consumption, the most significant of which is that it lacks coercive force. If "the MoonPie anchors the memories of Southerners in their history and culture," the history and culture so anchored are unintelligible as imperatives—as constituting a determinative field of prohibition and regulation. By way of contrast, consider the items in the following list, said to have "deeply founded in" them a "culture, the whole way in which we live, act, think, and feel": "tables, chairs, portraits, festivals, laws, marriage customs." In *I'll Take My Stand* (1930), John Crowe Ransom could imagine a table as continuous with laws, and as culturally foundational, primarily because it had not gone to market and thus remained integrated within a distinctive mode of production. It was part of a "definite social tradition . . . rooted in the agrarian life of the older South." Although Ferris's claims for the MoonPie are superficially similar, his "history and culture" have nothing to do with laws or modes of production.

Not surprisingly, Ransom omitted the MoonPie from his list: even by 1930, the MoonPie was firmly installed in a regime of mass production and advertising, which Ransom loathed, and hence opposed to God, whom he venerated. For Ransom, religion, which is "our submission to the general intention of a nature that is fairly inscrutable," weakened as nature is "manufactured into commodities," while advertising, "the most significant development of our industrialism," becomes necessary to "coerce and wheedle the public into being loyal and steady consumers."[13]

Ransom's diagnosis had been prefigured by Max Weber a half century earlier. In his analysis of the "disenchantment of the world," Weber argued the sanctity of custom and authority "based on 'knowledge' known 'since time immemorial'" had deteriorated under the rationalizing and bureaucratizing pressures of modernity. Exploring the "conscious tension of religion in relation to the realm of intellectual knowledge," Weber concluded that "where rational empirical knowledge has consistently carried through the disenchantment (*Entzauberung*) of the world and its transformation into a causal mechanism," religion is thereby forced "with each acceptance of the rationalism of empirical science . . . out of the realm of the rational and into the irrational, so that now it is simply *the* irrational or anti-rational transcendent force."[14] In *God without Thunder* (1930), Ransom came to similar conclusions, suggesting that Protestantism had "figured to itself as a determination to rationalize the antiquated religious doctrines," thereby domesticating the old god of thunder into the figure of a New Testament Jesus whose tidy moralism rendered God tractable. "*The peril to which a religion is constantly exposed is that of being regarded as a magic*," Ransom writes, and hence as subject to exposure by anthropology, which he viewed as the "handmaiden of a belligerent scientific party attacking its enemy the party of religionists." Paralleling Weber's account of religion's positioning as "irrational," Ransom conceded that anthropology was "quite correct in charging that the savage who beats his idol in order to compel it . . . is acting with precisely the same intelligence as the modern man who thinks he secures a physical blessing by prayer, baptism, offering, or ceremony, under the forms supposed to be sanctioned by his God." However, in offering his "unorthodox defense of orthodoxy," Ransom defended fundamentalisms as the only possible "first-class" religions, since fundamentalists made no concessions to either science or the market, and thus "regard their God as an actuality, and treat their supernatural objects as natural objects." The crucial act for the fundamentalist was "*to pick out of all the myths a particular one to profess and to keep.*"[15]

By the time of the Agrarian symposium, Ransom had come to profess and keep a different myth. As Mark Malvasi shrewdly observes, if for Ransom "modern Christianity could not on its own resist the dictates of science, perhaps the aesthetic sensibility could endure if nurtured in the premodern, antiscientific soil of the traditional South."[16] Ransom's rough substitution of the South for God as a source of authority and an object of piety was neither idiosyncratic nor capricious. Indeed, that social authority was experienced as supernatural dictate was something of a commonplace for southerners of Ransom's generation. Andrew Lytle enjoined southerners, "Seek a priesthood that may manifest the will and intelligence to renounce science and search out the Word in the authorities."[17] Critics on the left were scarcely less cognizant of the supernatural dimension of social authority. In *Killers of the Dream* (1949), Lillian Smith recounts contemplating as a child the moral lessons of segregation and masturbation authorized by a "God whom we feared and tried desperately to love, [and who] had made the rules concerning . . . our bodies and Negroes."[18] When science did go South, in the person of sociologists such as John Dollard and Arthur Raper, it chose advisedly the metaphor of caste to describe racial solidarity and taboo, and to account for how individuals in the South are (as Dollard put it) "made tractable by culture (i.e., by internalizing social prohibitions)."[19] For Donald Davidson, Raper's scientific method represented a perverse exercise in disenchantment; the locale of Raper's *Preface to Peasantry* (1936) had become, Davidson complained in a 1937 review, "a type and stopped being a beloved place to which men cling with more than rational attachment."[20] The most celebrated formulation of southern solidarity, W. J. Cash's "savage ideal"—"whereunder dissent and variety are completely suppressed, and men become, in all their attitudes, professions and actions, virtual replicas of one another"—reiterates key features of Emile Durkheim's account of how "it is in spiritual ways that social pressure exercises itself."[21] In *The Elementary Forms of the Religious Life* (1912), Durkheim had posited that social regulation depends upon representations of collective opinion that, because their psychical properties seem irreducible to material coercion, "give men the idea that outside themselves there exist one or several powers, both moral and, at the same time, efficacious, upon which they depend." Because "men know well that they are acted upon, but they do not know by what," and because scientific analysis has not yet offered competing explanations, premodern societies "must think of these powers, at least in part, as outside themselves" and thus originating not from profane but sacred sources.[22]

In a January 2009 keynote address at the University of Florida (published in revised form in this book's companion volume *Creating Citizenship in the Nineteenth-Century South*), O'Brien traced the deterioration of God as a referent of southern intellectual history. Commenting on the New Southern Studies, O'Brien identifies in its belief in the "constitutive power of the imagination" what he characterizes as "the deepest heterodoxy of this school, when judged by the standards of older traditions of Southern thought, which stretch back to the Agrarians, but also to the beginnings of the nineteenth century." For O'Brien, those traditions, both liberal and conservative, "shared a powerful sense that, in the balance between freedom and constraint, there was more weight on the side of constraint. . . . There was assumed to be small manouevering room, because the pressure of society and history was so great—great as a nightmare from which one wished to awake or great as a tradition in which one wished to revel—but always great." In its postmodern "indifference to God," the New Southern Studies deviates, according to O'Brien, and probably too much, from the "older traditions of Romanticism and modernism," which "saw God as an indispensable referent. If we were trapped by society and history, it was because this was God's purpose for us, God's trial for us, or God's gift to us."[23]

As concerns an indifference to God as property of scholarly analysis, O'Brien is doubtlessly correct about the New Southern Studies. Still, I do not share his assumption that the constitutive power of the imagination should be understood as a reaction against historicity rather than itself being historically constituted or determined. Here I follow Arjun Appadurai's argument that media and mobility have caused imagination to break out of the protected domains of myth and ritual to become "a part of the quotidian mental work of ordinary people in many societies."[24] God does not fare well, as Ransom correctly foresaw, in an age of consumerism, except when He or She is subjected to consumerist logic and practice. More particularly, however, I would argue that the idea of the South has itself been progressively dehistoricized—that is, has lost social *force*—to the extent that it has been subjected to the historical pressures of market logic and commodification, themselves "southern" in no meaningful sense. The history to which the MoonPie anchors southerners is not very historical if we imagine history as a set of constraints; in Ferris's discourse, God is not an indispensable, but an impossible, referent.

I am inclined to prefer the South as commodity to the South as God, the disenchanted South to the enchanted one. Furthermore, like Weber and Ransom, I am inclined to position these terms oppositionally and in a form legible in the arc from folkway to foodway. Folkways, as Sumner defined them, are those habits and customs that "men unconsciously set in motion" and that "are handed down by tradition and admit of no exception and variation." "[W]ithout rational reflection or purpose," they go without saying because they come without saying.[25] By contrast, foodways not only do not go without saying, they are said at great length. One can arrive at a fairly precise determination of whether a food is a foodway through a simple text-per-calorie metric. In the South, the test is even clearer: does the food have an entry in the *New Encyclopedia of Southern Culture*? We might say, then, that the foodway is overdetermined by virtue of being overrepresented—that the material dimension in which it is eaten is subordinate to its discursive one in which its cultural meaning is assigned.

Considered skeptically, the foodway can be approached as an instance of one of modernity's recurring master plots: the deteriorating relationship between the sign and the thing, often experienced or represented as the loss of the sacred. In 1975 Erich Heller argued that the Protestant revision of the Eucharist began to sunder the natural and the supernatural, thereby initiating a process whereby "the word 'merely' has been attaching itself ever more firmly to the word 'symbol,' soon gathering sufficient strength to bring about a complete alienation between the two spheres" and the consequent loss of humanity's sacramental vision. Heller's alienation depends on precisely what Ransom's fundamentalists, who "regard their God as an actuality," reject: an understanding of representation as existing in a state of play or as "mere" symbolism. Durkheim, too, located the gods' coercive power in representations that, when confronted with "attempted dissidence" within the social order, "repel the representations which contradict [them] and keep them at a distance."[26] Science, in turn, hammers the "merely" to the symbol and pries the symbol from the thing.

Accounts of representation's detachment from the world of things trend toward the dystopian. Moreover, such accounts have tended to associate this process with the rise of consumerism and multinational capitalism. Linking his analysis to "those societies in which modern condition of production prevail," Guy Debord writes, "All that was once directly lived has become mere representation," and in this detachment of images from life, "the former unity of life is lost forever." Apprehended in a partial way, Debord continues, "reality unfolds in a new generality as a pseudoworld apart, solely as an object of contemplation," culminating in "the spectacle"—not a "collection of images," but rather "a social relationship between people that is mediated by images."[27] Again, but this time from the left, we see the loss of a "former unity of life"; again, the identified cause (recuperated as symptom) is the deterioration of representation.

In foodways discourse, images are regularly said to perform the work of social mediation. For Ferris, the MoonPie and RC Cola anchor southerners in culture because, as "mythic symbols of the region," they are "among the most powerful icons in Southern culture." The mythic iconography depends on its being pointed out; the MoonPie is "A Southern Thing" because the T-shirt says so, or because Ferris says so. Occasionally, the syntactical relation is reversed, as in Edna Lewis's "What Is Southern?," which discursively constitutes southernness in a series of fourteen food-centered paragraphs.

> Southern is a mint julep. A goblet of crushed ice with a sprig of mint tucked in the side of the glass, a plain sugar syrup the consistency of kerosene poured over the ice, then a jigger of bourbon. Stir and bruise the mint with a silver spoon. Sip and enjoy. Southern is a hot summer day that brings on a violent thunderstorm, cooling the air and bringing up smells of the earth that tempt us to eat the soil. Southern is Tennessee Williams and *Streetcar*. Southern is a springhouse filled with perishables kept cool by a stream running through. And a spring keeper—a salamander—is there, watching over.[28]

The overwrought prose conceals a complex rhetoric: imagery collides with imperative as the word picture of a mint julep gives way to an injunction to "sip and enjoy." The deictically conjured salamander—that one just *there*—locates us in a place where few have been, in an effort to teach us what "southern is" (springhouses, not refrigerators). This is why, Lewis suggests, food writing is important: "The world has changed. We are now faced with picking up the pieces and trying to put them into shape, document them so the present-day young generation can see what Southern food was like." Having lost access to yet another "former unity of life," the younger generations lacks knowledge of what southern *is*; the discourse of what southern food *was* will (somehow) fill the lack. In his introduction to the "Foodways" volume of *The New Encyclopedia of Southern Culture* (2007), John Edge employs a similarly fraught chronology, writing, "In the two decades since the original *Encyclopedia of Southern Culture* was published . . . the South in particular, has awakened to the cultural import of regional foodways."[29] The recent awakening to the implicitly longstanding import of foodways is due, in no small part, to the efforts of Edge's Southern Foodways Alliance and its production of films, symposiums, essay collections, and iPhone apps. The discourse of foodways—and to belabor the point, there are no prediscursive foodways—is irrepressibly iconographic and, in Debord's terms, spectacular.

As a rule, the iconography is irrepressibly upbeat. Everyone recalls eating their collards, but no one recalls being *made* to eat their collards. Food is positioned, as Egerton suggests in his introduction to *Cornbread Nation 1*, as "central to the South we all like—the Good South of conviviality and generosity and sweet communion."[30] Although they would seem to inhabit different cognitive maps, the two privileged locations of food writing, the local and the global, are often simultaneously valorized: southern food is both the most local and the most global of cuisines. The desire for authentic tradition in no way compromises the desire for innovation, especially where fusion with other cultures is concerned. Down-home foodways are continually put in contact with the cosmopolitan world in dishes like butterbean crostini or the "Big Bad Bacon Rillettes" available at City Grocery in Oxford, Mississippi. Ferris pictures the country store of MoonPie consumption as "a sanctuary where white and black customers could share stories and shop in a common space."[31] Sharing and commonality are the keywords here; there is some editing of racial histories at work. Writing in 1999 to the incipient founders of the Southern Foodways Alliance, Egerton enforces the theme, assuring his audience, "The time has come for all of us—traditional and nouvelle cooks and diners, up-scale and down-home devotees, meat-eaters and vegetarians, drinkers and abstainers, growers and processors, scholars and foodlorists, gourmands and the health-conscious, women and men, blacks and whites and other identity groups, one and all—to sit down and break bread together around one great Southern table."[32]

As an icon widely diffused in the discourse of southern foodways, the "great Southern table" displays a particular kind of attention at the same time it enacts an interested lack of attention. In "Taste of Tradition: Iced Tea," Fred Thompson writes that the beverage is "the sign of hospitality. It transcends race, religion, and politics because it truly welcomes all to the table."[33] Iced tea can "transcend" such historically significant social forces as it "welcomes all to the table" because those forces are already elided from the discourse that controls the signs. Aspirational rather than historical, this discourse of the southern table suppresses the racial taboos and prohibitions that for generations dictated the protocols of food consumption. The pleasures of consumption predominate, while accounts of hunger and lack—Frederick Douglass's or Richard Wright's, say—are lost to history. Similarly edited are accounts of production, which trend strongly toward artisanal forms of labor and local production. Low-wage line cooks and "flexible" immigrant agricultural labor are virtually invisible; the shrimp in shrimp grits is unimaginable as an import, although over 80 percent of the shrimp consumed in the U.S. is imported. The program for a 2007 Southern Foodways Alliance field-trip to Charleston shows the editing at work.

> For over three hundred years, Charleston's fortunes have been intertwined with her natural bounty. Rice fueled the economic engine and appeared on the tables of rich, poor and enslaved. Fortunes made off the land and the sea built this port city. Prosperity has waxed and waned but the wealth of local ingredients—grains, fruits, vegetables, livestock, game and seafood—endured. Planters have given way to artisanal farmers whose passion for excellence enrich [sic] rather than enslave. The abundance from the land and sea continue to delight and inspire professional chefs, home cooks, locals and visitors alike.[34]

Gesturing lightly toward slavery, if only to note its displacement by "artisanal farmers," this account links Charleston's fortunes to "her natural

[sic] bounty." "Rice," not rice plantations, fueled its economic engine and "appeared" on all tables, even the ones the (historical) slaves probably lacked. The constant in Charleston's history is the "wealth of local ingredients." Little wonder, then, that locals and visitors alike are delighted and inspired.

The one great Southern table never existed and, by and large, still does not. But in imagining that it does, or that it might, Egerton generates an idea of the South—a representation or image of it—that potentially, and hopefully, mediates what Debord calls "a social relationship between people." Debord's language suggests the essentially fetishistic nature (in Marx's specific sense of commodity fetishism) of the material objects consumed at that table—that is, as pseudo-intrinsic embodiments of social relations arising only in exchange, and not in production itself. The screening of labor noted above strives to reproduce what Marx identified as the logic of pre-commodity production, wherein "the social relations between individuals in the performance of their labor, appear at all events as their own mutual personal relations, and are not disguised under the shape of social relationships between the products of labor."[35] As G. A. Cohen explains in an analysis of Marx fully consonant with Agrarian labor theory—recall here Ransom's table, or Lytle's agrarian table in "The Hind Tit" that contains no industrial "dairy butter," but rather food that is "particularly relished" because "each dish has particular meaning for the consumer, for everybody has had something to do with the long and intricate procession from the ground to the table"—the pre-commodity product is "socially impregnated before it circulates, in virtue of a nexus of duties or agreements between people."[36] Under commodity production, however, the product "shows a social character only in so far as it circulates, in commodity form." In diagnosing commodity fetishism as the symptom of an atomized market society whose members are in "serial disconnection," Cohen follows Marx in arguing that the fetish allows individuals to be *"joined indirectly on an alienated plane, in illusory forms"*—more particularly, in a "second world [that] arises to confer a surrogate coherence on the fragmented elements."[37]

As a countertactic to such Marxist and Agrarian analyses of the degrading shift from socially meaningful product that can be "relished" to commodity fetish that is merely consumed, foodways discourse romanticizes the product's social impregnation anterior to the market while suppressing the status of food as a commodity. It matters little that, as Edge puts it, "chefs have interpreted traditional recipes for white-tabletop consumers and, in the process, become celebrities": the "tradition" endures, even if celebrities produce it for high-end consumers. Diverse southern foodways thus survive what, for Lytle, would be fatal: the space between home and restaurant. Even when Corby Kummer acknowledges that "the best food, especially ethnic food, is made at home," he assures us that a Mexican restaurant in Houston will suffice if "the home-style Mexican food" is "cooked by four or five Mexican mothers and grandmothers, using the skill bred into their hands and the kinds of modest tools and pots and pans you'd find in a Mexican home kitchen."[38]

Even so, I do not consider the survival—or rather, the invention—of southern tradition under the regime of the commodity to be categorically pernicious. Social coherence is inevitably a "surrogate" matter of "second worlds" enabled by "illusory forms": all communities are imagined communities enabled by representations and the material practices through which those representations are realized. This is not to say that representations and practices function similarly in all cases. When Lillian Smith sat down to eat with African American women at an actual table, she became physically ill and explained the symptom as "how this eating taboo in childhood is woven into the mesh of things that are 'wrong,' how it becomes tangled with God and sex, pulling anxieties from stronger prohibitions and attaching them to itself."[39] Food discourse represents differently; it strives to do the kind of work Tara McPherson identifies in claiming that "it is precisely from within the domain of representation that the difficulties and possibilities of a politics of alliance [might] begin to emerge."[40]

Such hopes are not necessarily facile, even with the most strained efforts to reenchant culture. To the extent that the MoonPie or butterbean crostini or the local barbeque "anchor Southerners in their history and culture," I am rather glad that they do, given the unsavory character of many past (and weightier) anchors. Because the idea of the South has, on balance, exerted a deleterious effect on the South-under-no-description and contiguous spaces, one might argue that we should welcome with open arms its reconfiguration as a set of commodities for sale in the market of what Stanley Fish calls "boutique multiculturalism," the "multiculturalism of ethnic restaurants [and] weekend festivals . . . characterized by its superficial or cosmetic relationship to the object of its affection."

Multiculturalism is impossible, Fish argues, because in its normative instance, the "boutique multiculturalist resists the force of culture he appreciates at precisely the point at which it matters most to its strongly committed members."[41] The market logic of the multicultural boutique exerts as well a pressure on culture as practiced from the inside, weakening the very points at which strong commitments would entail the loss of sales. Jennifer Justus describes Phila Hach, a "humble country cook" from Tennessee, serving her grandmother's recipe for custard pie to a group of "international pastry experts." Hach knows from experience, Justus says, that "sharing a meal connects all walks of life to their common humanity, encouraging appreciation for cultural differences without losing a special place for one's own."[42] Although her custard pie recipe meets the international standard, the grandmother's "cultural differences" on matters of race or religion might not have fared as well. When cultural differences are reduced to pie form, imagining a common humanity becomes easier.

To clarify, I do not claim that going to market or assuming commodity form is necessarily a good thing for culture to do. Rather, I claim that it is a good thing for southern culture to have done, since it has revised and weakened the very points at which the idea of the South has, historically, mattered most to its strongly committed members. In *Southern Food* (1987), Egerton writes, "The South, for better or worse, has all but lost its identity as a separate place, and its checkered past belongs to myth and memory, but its food survives."[43] Although foodways discourse (including Egerton's) would soon revise this logic to claim that the South's identity survives *in* its food, the more interesting question is why equivocation and elegy are necessary in the first place. Since I believe that the idea of the South has been mostly a bad idea, I find it perfectly logical that traditionalists would lament its passing or weakening; for liberals such as Egerton, the elegiac note seems more perplexing, although common enough to warrant examination, especially insofar as they are keyed to the ascendance of consumption.

In *Confederates in the Attic* (1998), Tony Horwitz visits a laser light show at Stone Mountain, home of the massive bas-relief sculpture of Lee, Jackson, and Davis. Following an overture of pop hits, Coca-Cola ads, and Elvis singing "Dixie," lasers outline the sculpted Confederate pantheon, "Dixie" segues into the "Battle Hymn of the Republic," and Lee breaks his sword. "Finally," Horwitz writes, "to expunge any last hint of the Cause, the sound track played 'God Bless the U.S.A.' amidst images of the Lincoln

Memorial, JFK's grave, Martin Luther King, Jr., and a ballot box.... Like so much in Atlanta, Stone Mountain has become a bland and inoffensive consumable: the Confederacy as hood ornament." "Better," he concludes, "to remember Dixie and debate its philosophy than to have its largest shrine hijacked for Coca-Cola ads and MTV songs." Consonant with the premise that commodification means degradation, Horwitz's complaint is likewise symptomatic in its presentation of that diminishment as a loss of meaning: hijacked by Coca-Cola and reduced to a bland consumable, the Confederate shrine no longer facilitates memory and debate but rather sends the message "that there was no message—no real content" to the divisive historical figures whose graven images have given way to laser spectacle.[44] For Horwitz, expunging the (Lost) Cause correlates with a broader loss of causality: without a coherent narrative of how history generates division and solidarity, images "spew" incoherently. But in contrast to the coherence of the graven image it replaces, there is something to be said for the incoherence. Before being overwritten by lasers, the stone image of the Confederate pantheon constituted a monumental effort to, in Fitzhugh Brundage's words, "insinuate memory into public space ... [to] exert... cultural authority, express the collective solidarity, and to achieve a measure of ... permanence ... [designed] to ... underscore the connectedness of past and present."[45] An idea of a solid South underwrites that effort—a South written in stone.

What Horwitz encounters is not the erasure of causality but its transformation—not the loss of the social, but its evolution into new forms. Given the causal density of any human society, causes are always lost. Durkheim says, "Men know well that they are acted upon, but they do not know by what." But they do not remain long in that state, and their use of representation to reduce or eliminate uncertainty may assume radically different forms. Monuments to the Lost Cause exerted a powerful cultural authority because they mobilized a powerful causality: we are who we are, things are as they are, because of history and the primordial loss it involved. Appealing to custom and authority "known since time immemorial," such efforts memorialized and consolidated culture in the imperative mode, thereby acquiring some of what a 1945 essay in Ransom's *Kenyon Review* described as "positive religion['s] character of objective, all-comprising validity, its supra-individual binding force." However, for the author of that essay, Theodor W. Adorno, modernity had rendered that function of religion defunct. "It is no longer an unproblematic, *a priori* medium," Adorno writes, "within which each person exists without questioning. Hence the desire for a reconstruction of that much praised unity amounts to wishful thinking, even if it be deeply rooted in the sincere desire for something which gives 'sense' to a culture threatened by emptiness and alienation."[46] For Adorno, there was no reconstruction of unity available through religion; nor did the market logic of the culture industry offer either solace or "sense" to a culture threatened by emptiness and alienation.

Here Ransom would have agreed, having published two issues previously Adorno's "A Social Critique of Radio Music," an essay that epitomizes the peculiar alignment between right and left against the market logic of commodification. In that essay Adorno argues that music, having been forced "to go to the market" during the late eighteenth century, had come to exist as a commodity—"a means instead of an end, a fetish"—and thus had "ceased to be a human force and [was] consumed like other consumers' goods."[47] For Ransom, this doubtlessly recalled Davidson's claim that industrialism, "[s]eeing the world altogether in terms of commodities, . . . simply proposes to add one more commodity to the list. . . . It will buy art, if any fool wants art."[48] I find Adorno's and Davidson's diagnoses equally unconvincing. Emptiness and alienation exist too easily as postulates; or rather their absence (some "former unity of life") is too easily conjured in the culture prior to this one. Although such sequences are better understood as efforts to mobilize loss *as cause* and as intervention, I am especially wary of them as they have operated in the South. Rather, I am inclined to follow Dominick LaCapra in situating what he calls "absence" at a transhistorical level and asking what happens when it is narrativized, inserted into history, and thereby converted into loss. "Absence," LaCapra writes, "appears in all societies and cultures, yet it is confronted differently and differently articulated with loss." Posing the question of "whether the conversion of absence into loss is essential to all fundamentalisms or foundational philosophies," LaCapra affirms that "the critique of ultimate or absolute foundations is best understood as related to an affirmation or recognition of absence, not a postulation of loss."[49]

Let me offer, then, a distinction between relatively organized (or fundamentalist) and relatively disorganized representations of absence and loss. In the former, such as the mythology of the Lost Cause, the translation of absence into loss acquires great coherence, thereby accumulating explanatory power and generating coercive, inertial force. As O'Brien observes, the experience of being "trapped by society and history" correlates with the belief that "this was God's purpose for us, God's trial for us." In this configuration, agency, even moral agency, is displaced from the social order; Ransom gets to the deterministic heart of the matter in declaring that "the moral order is a wished-for order, which does not coincide with the actual order or the world order . . . the mind must accept the world order."[50] Such a radical conservatism never accumulated in any strict sense around any idea of the South, which has always played unevenly and at different volumes in the South-under-no-description. But at times its volume, its interpellative force, has seemed to be amplified all the way up to eleven.

The interpellative volume of the Stone Mountain laser show is much lower. Its audience is hailed, sequentially, as fans of the Beatles, Georgia peaches, Scarlett O'Hara, the Braves, the Falcons, Elvis, the South, America, Lee, Lincoln, MLK, and Coca-Cola. It weds a narcissism of minor differences to a message that there are no major ones: we are taught to sing in perfect harmony. The medium—flickering lasers, not granite—is the message: there is no anchoring, only momentary tethering. If you are not a Braves fan, the Falcons will be by momentarily; if you dislike Scarlett, wait for Elvis; if you dislike Coke—but everyone likes Coke. This is culture not in the imperative mode, but in the consumptive mode: select what you wish from the cultural boutique. Southern history is no longer much of a Cause, even a lost one; it is something you *like*, in the Facebook sense of the word, not an object of veneration. In the South of the Stone Mountain laser show, there are many gods, none of them very jealous. It is, in Ransom's sense, a South without thunder.

In this South, which is also the South of the foodway, there lies a significant insignificance. Although the bland consumable is often viewed, as Horwitz views it, as merely banal, it constitutes a complex social phenomenon in reconfiguring absence as lack, not loss. Since culture cannot confront absence as such, the translation of absence into lack tends to translate cultural practice from the domain of piety and submission to the domain of consumption and acquisition—acquisition of the thing that will fill the lack. Memory begins to float free from history in a state, as Pierre Nora puts it, of "permanent evolution, open to the dialectic of remembering and forgetting, unconscious of its successive deformations, vulnerable to manipulation and appropriation."[51] Configured in this way, memory attaches itself toward highly edited pasts—the past of the "one great southern table," or of Lee chumming it up with Lincoln—even as its objects of consumption emerge inevitably as cultural fetishes. However, edited pasts are arguably the only ones with much cultural significance, and the fetishism involved is of a weak, half-enchanted form involving the kind of commodity whose value, as Henry Krips puts it, consumers treat "as if it were a real, intrinsic property even when they know that it is an artifice created through the process of exchange."[52] If Ransom's fundamentalist picks out of all the myths a particular one to keep, the postfundamentalist cultural consumer picks out four or five to keep, sort of.

Reviewing the original *Encyclopedia of Southern Culture*, John Shelton Reed calls attention to what he labels a "charming sequence of entries":

Gardner, Dave
Gays
Goo Goo Clusters
Grits
Hammond, James Henry[53]

The subject of the last entry in this list would not have appreciated the sequence. For Hammond, what made the South the South was that it had submitted to the "ordinances of the Scriptures," which revealed "*domestic slavery—precisely such as is maintained at this day in these States—[to be] ordained by God.*"[54] On the same page as the entry for Hammond, Egerton claims that "throughout its history, and in pre-Columbian times as well, the South has relished grits and made them a symbol of its diet, its customs, its humor, and its good-spirited hospitality."[55] As history, this hardly passes muster: no one a century ago, much less in pre-Columbian times, was making grits a symbol of the South's anything. Hammond never mentioned them at all. Moreover, as memory, Egerton's claim is profoundly unconscious of successive deformations. Yet for that reason, Egerton's claim offers itself—as does the discourse of foodways in which it is positioned—as an interesting moment in the story of southern culture; or, more precisely, the story of what counts as "southern culture" as a particular discourse constitutes an idea of "the South." The full story of that discourse would involve many topics that this chapter has neglected entirely. Still, to the degree that telling about the South—what it's like there, what they do there—means telling about grits and MoonPies and good-spirited hospitality, I don't dislike it very much, I don't dislike it very much. There are worse things than banality: southern history is full of them.

Notes

1. Ferris, "The Moon Pie," 154, 55.
2. *Southern Foodways Alliance*, http://www.southernfoodways.com/cookbook/corn bread_nation.html, accessed August 4, 2010.
3. Reed and Reed, "Preface," 218.
4. Bruce and Cole, "25 Tips for Celebrating the Soul of the South," 85–108.
5. Best and Abbott, "Tomatoes," 277; Bharati, "Hindu Renaissance," 273.
6. Bierman, "Welcome Home," 8.
7. Best and Abbott, "Tomatoes," 274.
8. Bourdieu, *Field of Cultural Production*, 114.
9. O'Brien, *Placing the South*, 19.
10. Ibid.
11. Ibid.
12. Tourgée, *Bricks without Straw*, 382–83.
13. [Ransom], "Introduction: Statement of Principles," xliv, xlii, xlvi.
14. Weber, *Essential Weber*, 135, 238–39.
15. Ransom, *God without Thunder*, 27, 92, 93, 94, 95.
16. Malvasi, *Unregenerate South*, 45.
17. Lytle, "Hind Tit," 244.
18. Smith, *Killers of the Dream*, 84.
19. Dollard, *Caste and Class in a Southern Town*, 39.
20. Davidson, "Sociologist in Eden," 184.
21. Cash, *Mind of the South*, 90; Durkheim, *Elementary Forms*, 232.
22. Durkheim, *Elementary Forms*, 238–39.
23. O'Brien, "Place as Everywhere."
24. Appadurai, *Modernity at Large*, 7.
25. Sumner, *Folkways*, 4
26. Heller, *Disinherited Mind*, 266–67; Durkheim, *Elementary Forms*, 238.
27. Debord, *Society of the Spectacle*, 12.
28. Lewis, "What Is Southern?" 9.
29. Edge, "Introduction," xix–xx.
30. Egerton, "Introduction," 1.
31. Ferris, "MoonPie," 154.
32. Egerton, "Founders Letter."
33. Thompson, "Taste of Tradition," 296.
34. "Charleston: Citadel of the Lowcountry."
35. Marx, *Capital*, 89.
36. Lytle, "Hind Tit," 223, 27. Cohen, *Karl Marx's Theory of History*, 120.
37. Edge, "Introduction," xx; Cohen, *Karl Marx's Theory of History*, 120, 122.

38. Kummer, "Cooking for a Sunday Day," 253.
39. Smith, *Killers of the Dream*, 148.
40. McPherson, *Reconstructing Dixie*, 30.
41. Fish, "Boutique Multiculturalism," 378.
42. Justus, "Grace before Dinner," 12, 13.
43. Egerton, *Southern Food*, 3.
44. Horwitz, *Confederates in the Attic*, 288.
45. Brundage, *Southern Past*, 6.
46. Adorno, "Theses upon Art and Religion Today," 677.
47. Adorno, "Social Critique of Radio Music," 211.
48. Davidson, "Mirror for Artists," 30–31.
49. LaCapra, "Trauma, Absence, Loss," 701, 702.
50. Ransom, *God without Thunder*, 47.
51. Nora, "Between Memory and History," 8.
52. Krips, *Fetish*, 15.
53. Reed, *Minding the South*, 98.
54. [Hammond], *Pro-Slavery Argument*, 156.
55. Egerton, "Grits," 495.

Works Cited

Adorno, Theodor W. "A Social Critique of Radio Music." *Kenyon Review* 7, no. 2 (spring 1945): 208–17.

———. "Theses upon Art and Religion Today." *Kenyon Review* 7, no. 4 (autumn 1945): 677–82.

Appadurai, Arjun. *Modernity at Large: Cultural Dimensions of Globalization*. Minneapolis: University of Minnesota Press, 1996.

Best, Bill, and Frances Abbott. "Tomatoes." In *The New Encyclopedia of Southern Culture: Volume 7: Foodways*, edited by John T. Edge, 274–77. Chapel Hill: University of North Carolina Press, 2007.

Bharati, Agehananda. "The Hindu Renaissance and Its Apologetic Patterns." *Journal of Asian Studies* 29, no. 2 (1970): 267–87.

Bierman, M. Lindsay. "Welcome Home." *Southern Living* 45, no. 10 (October 2010): 8.

Bourdieu, Pierre. *The Field of Cultural Production*. New York: Columbia University Press, 1993.

Bruce, Taylor, and Jennifer Ashti Cole. "25 Tips for Celebrating the Soul of the South." *Southern Living* 45, no. 9 (September 2010): 85–108.

Brundage, Fitzhugh. *The Southern Past: A Clash of Race and Memory*. Cambridge: Harvard University Press, 2005.

Cash, W. J. *The Mind of the South*. 1941. New York: Vintage 2001.

"Charleston: Citadel of the Lowcountry." *Southern Foodways Alliance*. http://www.southernfoodways.com/images/Handbook%20for%20Charleston.pdf. Accessed December 10, 2010.

Cohen, G. A. *Karl Marx's Theory of History: A Defence*. 1978. Princeton: Princeton University Press, 2001.
Davidson, Donald. "A Mirror for Artists." In *I'll Take My Stand: The South and the Agrarian Tradition*, by Twelve Southerners, 28–60. 1930. Baton Rouge: Louisiana State University Press, 1977.
———. "A Sociologist in Eden." *American Review* 8 (1937): 177–204.
Debord, Guy. *The Society of the Spectacle*. Translated by Donald Nicholson-Smith. New York: Zone Books, 1995.
Dollard, John. *Caste and Class in a Southern Town*. New Haven: Yale University Press, 1937.
Durkheim, Emile. *The Elementary Forms of the Religious Life*. Translated by Joseph Ward Swain. New York: Free Press, 1965.
Edge, John T. "Introduction." In *The New Encyclopedia of Southern Culture: Volume 7: Foodways*, edited by John T. Edge, xix–xx. Chapel Hill: University of North Carolina Press, 2007.
Egerton, John. "Founders Letter." *Southern Foodways Alliance*. http://www.southernfoodways.com/about/history.html. Accessed August 3, 2010.
———. "Grits." In *Encyclopedia of Southern Culture: Volume 2: Ethnic Life-Law*, edited by Charles Reagan Wilson and William Ferris, 494–95. New York: Doubleday, 1989.
———. "Introduction." In *Cornbread Nation 1: The Best of Southern Food Writing*, edited by John Egerton, 1–6. Athens: University of Georgia Press, 2002.
———. *Southern Food: At Home, on the Road, in History*. New York: Alfred A. Knopf, 1987.
Ferris, William. "The MoonPie: A Southern Journey." In *Cornbread Nation 4: The Best of Southern Food Writing*, edited by Dale Volberg Reed and John Shelton Reed, 153–59. Athens: University of Georgia Press, 2008.
Fish, Stanley. "Boutique Multiculturalism; Or Why Liberals Are Incapable of Thinking about Hate Speech." *Critical Inquiry* 23, no. 2 (winter 1997): 378–96.
[Hammond, James Henry.] *The Pro-Slavery Argument, As Maintained by the Most Distinguished Writers of the Southern States: Containing the Several Essays, on the Subject, of Chancellor Harper, Governor Hammond, Dr. Simms, and Professor Dew*. Philadelphia: Lippincott, Grabo, 1853.
Heller, Erich. *The Disinherited Mind: Essays in Modern German Literature and Thought*. New York: Bowes and Bowes, 1975.
Horwitz, Tony. *Confederates in the Attic: Dispatches from the Unfinished Civil War*. New York: Vintage, 1999.
Justus, Jennifer. "The Grace before Dinner." In *Cornbread Nation 5: The Best of Southern Food Writing*, edited by Fred Sauceman, 12–15. Athens: University of Georgia Press, 2010.
Krips, Henry. *Fetish: An Erotics of Culture*. Ithaca: Cornell University Press, 1999.
Kummer, Corby. "Cooking for a Sunday Day." In *Cornbread Nation 5: The Best of Southern Food Writing*, edited by Fred Sauceman, 253–56. Athens: University of Georgia Press, 2010.

LaCapra, Dominick. "Trauma, Absence, Loss." *Critical Inquiry* 25, no. 4 (1999): 696–727.

Lewis, Edna. "What Is Southern?" In *Cornbread Nation 5: The Best of Southern Food Writing*, edited by Fred Sauceman, 7–11. Athens: University of Georgia Press, 2010.

Lytle, Andrew. "The Hind Tit." In *I'll Take My Stand: The South and the Agrarian Tradition*, by Twelve Southerners, 201–45. 1930. Baton Rouge: Louisiana State University Press, 1977.

Malvasi, Mark G. *The Unregenerate South: The Agrarian Thought of John Crowe, Allen Tate, and Donald Davidson*. Baton Rouge: Louisiana State University Press, 1997.

Marx, Karl. *Capital: A Critique of Political Economy, Volume 1, Part 1*. New York: Cosimo Books, 2007.

McPherson, Tara. *Reconstructing Dixie: Race, Gender, and Nostalgia in the Imagined South*. Durham: Duke University Press, 2003.

Nora, Pierre. "Between Memory and History: Les Lieux de Memoire." *Representations* 26 (spring 1989): 7–25.

O'Brien, Michael. "Place as Everywhere: On Globalizing the American South." Keynote address presented at the "Creating Citizenship and Identities in the 19th Century South and Beyond" conference, University of Florida, Gainesville, January 15, 2009.

———. *Placing the South*. Jackson: University Press of Mississippi, 2007.

Ransom, John Crowe. *God without Thunder: An Unorthodox Defense of Orthodoxy*. New York: Harcourt, Brace, 1930.

[Ransom, John Crowe]. "Introduction: A Statement of Principles." In *I'll Take My Stand: The South and the Agrarian Tradition*, by Twelve Southerners, xxxvii–xlviii. 1930. Baton Rouge: Louisiana State University Press, 1977.

Reed, Dale Volberg, and John Shelton Reed. Preface to "Late-Night Chitlins with Momma" by Audrey Petty. In *Cornbread Nation 4: The Best of Southern Food Writing*, edited by Dale Volberg Reed and John Shelton Reed, 218–21. Athens: University of Georgia Press, 2008.

Reed, John Shelton. *Minding the South*. Columbia: University of Missouri Press, 2003.

Sumner, William Graham. *Folkways: A Study of the Sociological Importance of Usages, Manners, Customs, Mores, and Morals*. Boston: Ginn, 1907.

Thompson, Fred. "Taste of Tradition." In *Cornbread Nation 5: The Best of Southern Food Writing*, edited by Fred Sauceman, 295–96. Athens: University of Georgia Press, 2010.

Tourgée, Albion. *Bricks without Straw: A Novel*. New York: Fords, Howard, and Hulbert, 1880.

Weber, Max. *The Essential Weber*. Edited by Sam Whimster. London: Routledge, 2004.

3

Toward a Post-postpolitical Southern Studies

On the Limits of the "Creating and Consuming" Paradigm

JON SMITH

From all the references to "creating and consuming the American South" in the formal descriptions of the aims of this collection and of the August 2010 conference in Copenhagen that spurred it, it would be easy to forget that just a few years earlier the New Southern Studies had generally been a good deal less interested in such topics as "reimagining region on the world wide web," "selling southern lifestyles," and "creating and consuming southern foods."[1] As its title, "Violence, the Body, and 'The South,'" suggests, the special issue of *American Literature* in which Houston Baker and Dana Nelson gave the then-emergent field its name was concerned less with inventing southern literature or consuming southern culture than with testifying to actual physical violence. In her 2000 book *Dirt and Desire*, which Baker and Nelson cited as an exemplum of the sort of work they wanted to do, Patricia Yaeger did not just memorably declare her desire to "dynamite the rails" of old southern studies. She also called the old categories of southern literary studies—community, place, the past, etc.—"mystifications designed to overlook the complexities of southern fiction—its exploration of throwaway bodies, of a culture of white neglect, of the ways gender and racial politics work in the everyday."[2] Back then, the best and most progressive scholars did not deny that "the South" was a construct (Baker and Nelson, after all, put the phrase in quotation marks, too), but they wanted to strip away the construct like a bandage in order to reveal the oozing bodily wound beneath.

Times have changed. Yaeger and Baker and Nelson all wrote as literary studies was emerging from the 1990s, a decade when, as Hal Foster reminds us, "for many in contemporary culture, truth reside[d] in the traumatic or abject subject, in the diseased or damaged body."[3] Ten or twelve years later—after 9/11, Katrina, two wars in Iraq and Afghanistan, and the second-biggest economic failure in a century—trauma no longer seems so compellingly exotic. By the middle of the 2000s, moreover, putative white southernist concern with violated bodies seemed to have deteriorated into a parody of itself. Too often the focus seemed to shift off the bodies and onto just how bad the writer *felt* about the bodies. Rebecca Mark professed her shock that at an Emmett Till conference, none of the scholars was "keening" over his death; when an undergraduate in one of her classes asked why they were reading what Mark admitted was "about six books on Emmett Till," Mark's response (in addition to composing a prose poem) was that "we are reading these books because I love Emmett and I want everyone to know how furious and sad I am that he is dead."[4] Minrose Gwin's "Mourning Medgar" project, as its title suggests, could too often seem less about Medgar Evers than about the affective experience of white southerners of a certain age. The same was true of Michael Kreyling's 2005 essay "Teaching Southern Lit in Black and White," in which a reference to the thrown-away bodies of three civil rights workers killed in Philadelphia, Mississippi, functioned merely as an introduction to Kreyling's stated quest "to find out how much, or how little, I had learned over the decades."[5]

In any event, the "creating and consuming the American South" project seems to come out of a different tradition, one with deeper roots in the old southern studies, where the idea that "the South" is a construct has been around since at least the 1970s. Lewis Simpson wrote in 1973 that "no American writers ever worked harder at inheriting their inheritance than the Agrarians"; Michael O'Brien published *The Idea of the American South* in 1979; Richard Gray's *Writing the South: Ideas of an American Region* came out in 1986; and the '90s and '00s saw a number of works from not-exactly-radical presses arguing for ideas of the South as laboriously constructed: Kreyling's *Inventing Southern Literature* (University Press of Mississippi, 1998) and, from the long-running Southern Literary Studies series of Louisiana State University Press, Scott Romine's *The Narrative Forms of Southern Community* (1999), Suzanne Jones and Sharon Monteith's collection *South to a New Place* (2002), and Martyn Bone's

The Postsouthern Sense of Place in Contemporary Fiction (2005). By 2008 Scott Romine could rightly note that Simpson's claim "has come to seem self-evident."[6]

In revisiting these issues the present volume may be rather less interested in moving southern studies (much less American studies) forward than in bringing moments and approaches from the past decade (at least) of southern studies to the attention of southern historians. "It is now nearly a decade," wrote Brian Ward in launching the discussion portion of the conference's website, "since Houston Baker and Dana Nelson issued their call for a 'new Southern Studies' that would complicate 'old borders and terrains' and open up 'a new scholarly map of "the South,"' but it is still unclear how much southern historians have been involved with, or influenced by, or even aware of these exciting developments." (Perhaps predictably, the reactions to Ward's post from southern historians such as Karen Cox and Randall Stephens seemed less than excited, consisting largely of complaints about other fields' jargon.)[7] The present volume seems specifically interested in revisiting southern studies as we were doing it around the time of *South to a New Place*, to which Scott Romine, Martyn Bone, and I all contributed. As it harks back to a number of early-2000s scholarly works and pop-cultural phenomena, for example, the conference list of suggested topics even references Southernness perfume and the NuSouth emblem, both of which I happened to write about in my essay for *South to a New Place*. I should thus probably also be the one to point out that the perfume is no longer made, and the NuSouth clothing company shut its doors some years ago. Sometimes, moreover, the conference description seems, in its drive to finds points of commonality, to press the work of New Southern Studies figures back into older, more familiar southern studies agendas. "As James Cobb, Leigh Anne Duck and others have recently emphasized," it reads, "the creation and consumption of southern identity operates at national and global levels too." But whereas Cobb is so interested in southern identity that he wrote a history of it, Duck quite rightly finds the concept worse than useless and concludes an important essay as follows: "How might the absence of [Southern] identity alter our methods and vocabularies, and what new venues for exploration might we discover in its stead?" She calls, instead, for "Southern studies without 'The South.'"[8]

"Southern studies without 'The South'"—and, hence, without creating or consuming it—strikes me as the single most succinct definition of mainstream New Southern Studies I can imagine these days, and it puts most of us New Southern Studies scholars squarely in line not with "southern historians" but with those historians associated with the recent volume *The Myth of Southern Exceptionalism*, who argue, among other things, that ideas of "the South" get in the way of doing good history—in particular, good history of the civil rights movement. (The conference *that* volume came out of was provocatively entitled "The End of Southern History?") Put differently, in the more progressive sort of work, "the South" increasingly appears to be an unhelpful scalar unit: far better to work at a larger scale (the nation, conservatism, plantation America) or a smaller one (consumer culture in Mississippi, desegregation in Atlanta or Milwaukee). Such historians tend, for obvious reasons, not to consider themselves (much less market themselves as) "southern historians" but as urban historians, civil rights historians, and so on—and they feel not a whit of melancholy about any consequent traumatic "loss" of "southern identity."

In what follows, then, I want to do something I have resisted for nearly a decade: to argue at some length for this understanding of "New Southern Studies," and to attempt to correct some common, reductive misunderstandings of the New Southern Studies project (as, for example, merely anti-agrarian, or antinational, or even, for one southern historian, antirational). I am doing so now because I have come to realize—not least as a result of reading and rereading Michael O'Brien's January 2009 keynote talk at the second "Understanding the South" conference in Florida—that the question of our "newness" is less semantic (and hence irrelevant) than political (and hence highly relevant). My primary political concern is rooted in one suggested some time ago by Kenneth Warren: "Southernness, as a political concept, has rarely if ever portended a broader democratization of American life."[9] I would go one step further: particularly relative to "conservative" or "evangelical" or "white," "southern" increasingly seems no longer a meaningful political concept at all, and studying "southernness" may thus be a distraction from whatever political effect our academic work is likely to have. Indeed, merely acknowledging that "the South" is a construct, far from undercutting the complacencies of old southern studies, has almost always functioned to prolong them under the putatively hipper sign of the "postsouthern," where "post" in practice denotes not "after" but something like "ironic and self-aware."[10] But an ironic approach to one's ideology does not detach one from it. Instead, as

Slavoj Žižek reminds us, it licenses it, lets us enjoy it all the more in the act of pretending to disavow it:

> If there is an ideological experience at its purest, at its zero-level, then it occurs the moment we adopt an attitude of ironic distance, laughing at the follies in which we are ready to believe—it is at this moment of liberating laughter, when we look down on the absurdity of our faith, that we become pure subjects of ideology, that ideology exerts its strongest hold over us.[11]

Such is the regressive politics of the "postsouthern."

Although even now relatively few southernists—be they critics of "southern" literature or "southern" historians—seem to grasp the idea that we need to get beyond postmodernly identifying "the South" as created and consumed to actually setting aside the notion as a conceptual or identitarian tool, I still came to it somewhat later than some other scholars. It may be useful, therefore, as some readers of this volume will be historians rather than literary critics, to render my account, at first, not as an argument but as a narrative of what I learned, and from whom. I then want to question several of O'Brien's claims about the New Southern Studies, before finally challenging the conclusion of Romine's very smart book *The Real South* (2008) as a way of returning the essay to the concrete politics, such as they are, of academic writing.

When Michael Kreyling's *Inventing Southern Literature* came out back in 1998, I actually rather liked it—liked it so much, in fact, that I organized a symposium of reviews of it for the *Mississippi Quarterly*. At the time, I was trying to raise the journal's national visibility. Since we could not change our mission as "The Journal of Southern Cultures," we had to raise the visibility of southern studies—and what better way to start than by inviting major Americanists and southernists to consider, side by side, what at the time I thought was a major southernist book? Americanists would have to think about southern matters, for a change, and southernists, upon noting that one of their journals was trying to reach a broader audience, might begin to see themselves as addressing that broader audience. What could possibly go wrong?

Of course, when the reviews came in, they were much more negative than I had expected, and they were basically right. "Michael Kreyling teaches Southern literature in a Southern university," began Nina Baym in what would become our lead essay. "*Inventing Southern Literature* is for academics like himself."[12] Eric Sundquist pointed out that despite its reliance on Benedict Anderson and Eric Hobsbawm, Kreyling's book was in essence a "homegrown product," and he concluded, more gently than Baym, that Kreyling "succeeds admirably, but, one could add, with a slight sense of belatedness. After all, there probably are not too many readers left—academic readers, at any rate—who doubt that black writers and women writers should have a central place in the southern canon."[13] Ouch; double ouch coming from two of the most important American studies scholars of the previous half-century. The teachers of southern literature at southern universities, however, were only marginally kinder. Susan Donaldson noted that "southern literary historians and critics . . . have tended to repeat with startling frequency the concerns of conservative white male writers under examination," and then pointed out that Kreyling himself both observed this phenomenon and participated in it: "So pressing is his task in demystifying the inventors and inventions of 'orthodox' Southern literature—*and so compelling does he find those inventions requiring his critique*—that it is as if all his energy and effort are required simply in wrestling that 'orthodox' Southern thought, as it were, to the floor."[14] Fred Hobson argued that Kreyling "seems at times to see a neo-Agrarian around every corner, behind every bush," and that *Inventing Southern Literature* was "a thesis-driven work, and most that detracts from that thesis is omitted."[15] Asking "Why the gloom?" in Kreyling's book, Anne Goodwyn Jones answered that Kreyling's "point of view is that of the Southern white man, who stands to gain the most from perpetuating the tradition and the least from demystifying it"; like Donaldson, Jones argued that Kreyling was a little too invested in that tradition, and as a result at points his argument was "hoist on its own petard."[16]

I linger over the mixed reception of Kreyling's major work because *Inventing Southern Literature* remains a kind of touchstone for the creating-and-consuming crowd, even as it remains for more progressive scholars an emblem of just the sort of tweedy white male "professional southernism" from which it tried to distance itself. Admittedly, the important insights of Donaldson's and Jones' essays became apparent to me only years later, when I was trying to understand Kreyling's subsequent hostility to much of the New Southern Studies (the noteworthy exception being the work of younger white males still grappling with the Agrarians[17]). Years after Kreyling misread Jennifer Greeson's and Leigh Anne Duck's arguments and even motivations to a degree I initially found unfathomable,[18] returning to Donaldson and Jones would help me understand why. But the impact of Baym and Sundquist was immediate and huge. Baym's larger point—that arguing with the Agrarians was something mainstream American studies would not even *bother* doing, since *I'll Take My Stand* had always been read up at Harvard as "frank cultural pathology"—forced me (at the time, though trained as an Americanist, myself a teacher of southern literature in a southern university), along with Sundquist's arguments, to rethink my entire relation to my field(s).[19] Whatever the limits of Baym's own perspective, I wanted neither myself nor the *Quarterly* nor the field to be justly accused of belatedness or provincialism. And though I did not know it at the time, this desire was already helping animate the score or so of other scholars who, in just a few years, would come to be associated with the New Southern Studies.

At the time, however, two somewhat younger Americanists, Leigh Anne Duck and Andrew Hoberek, both recent PhDs from the University of Chicago, already had a much better sense than I did of where things needed to go. For them it was clear that even Patricia Yaeger had not gone far enough. As Duck put it in her 2001 review of *Dirt and Desire*, Yaeger

> is committed to a project that compels her to naturalize certain questions, particularly their inclusion of the word "southern." . . . It is frustrating to see such generative discussions subordinated to the importance of southern women's writing qua regional writing, an insistence that repeatedly truncates Yaeger's accounts of how the study of such writing could illuminate broader investigations into literature, history, culture, and critical methodology.[20]

In his own review, Hoberek would be more blunt: "Yaeger's aims are, perhaps, not quite so far from Kreyling's as she claims."[21] For Duck and Hoberek, the problem with Yaeger and Kreyling is not that they endorse the Agrarians' version of southern exceptionalism but that they still operate from *any* position of southern exceptionalism. To argue, then, that Yaeger or Kreyling or anyone else does "old southern studies" is not to accuse them of agrarianism (or racism or sexism) but to accuse them of assuming that "southern" offers a useful category of analysis.

And here we come to the knottiest part of my argument, because the two younger scholars (relatively speaking) most pleasing to southern studies' old guard, and not unrelatedly most interested in matters of creating and consuming, rather obviously have spent quite a lot of time arguing with the Agrarians. Scott Romine begins both his books by doing so; Martyn Bone devotes at least the first of three parts of *The Postsouthern Sense of Place in Contemporary Fiction* to the same. Reviewing the latter, Duck (once again) observes that "it is . . . surprising that this study features the Agrarians so prominently. . . . [Bone's] approach tends once more to position these avowedly reactionary thinkers at the center of southern literary criticism."[22] In my own review, I noted that "Bone often—against his better impulses—employs the terminology of a decline narrative [both Agrarian and Jamesonian] that allows conservatives in the field, the very scholars against whom Bone at points argues forcefully, to keep talking (in rather bad faith) about a Grand Old sense of place, just prefixing 'postsouthern' to things when we get into the 1970s or so."[23] An astute reader will note that, in our worry that Bone gives too much centrality to the Agrarians and hence ends up contributing to a conservative white vision "against his better impulses," Duck and I sound not unlike Donaldson and Jones in their reviews of Kreyling several years earlier. As Jones put it back then, "if the South is a construction built by white conservatives, then to stand on it while burning it down is to risk self-immolation."[24]

For the field's sake, I for one would prefer not to keep having this conversation down through the generations. Acknowledging its existence, however, usefully complicates some generalizations about the new work recently made by southern historian Michael O'Brien. O'Brien is to be commended for engaging with the New Southern Studies at all, and he has rightly identified the conservative implications of some New Southern Studies. Yet he also, I would argue, misreads both the politics and the intellectual groundings of the movement as a whole. He does so partly in a way that will be familiar to second-wave feminists: by paying a bit too much attention (as does the present essay, if only to try, like Jones and Donaldson, to correct the record) to relatively conservative white males.

In his Florida keynote O'Brien offered, by my count, four generalizations about the emergent field. First, he commends, with some qualifications, the New Southern Studies' "heterodoxy" relative to older scholars' "deep, awful fear . . . that admitting to a loss of pattern would lead to a loss of faith, to the death of God, to atheism, to disorder, and to ignorant armies clashing at night," and he praises our "lightening of the mood." For some time I found that description tremendously flattering: skeptical, funny young people taking on fearful old dogmatists is a nice narrative if you are, or believe yourself to be, the skeptical, funny young person. However, while I do indeed associate "deep, awful fear . . . of disorder" with the work of Kreyling and of Barbara Ladd—the two scholars currently pushing the idea of distinctively southern "memory" the hardest, out of explicit fear of loss of "identity" on the one hand and fear of a putative "national project of forgetting" on the other[25]—it is hard to see such fear in, say, Jones, Donaldson, or, for that matter, Hobson. It is harder still to see it in Lillian Smith or Dr. Martin Luther King Jr. O'Brien, like Kreyling and so many others, seems himself to lapse into defining "southern" thought as conservative white male southern thought. In my experience, New Southern Studies scholars possess many virtues indeed, but even those among us who consider themselves "southern thinkers" (if any of us do) have, within even that small class, no particular monopoly on fearless skepticism.

Second, O'Brien claims that in the New Southern Studies "there is a sense that the South is best understood, not by seeing it as connected to American culture and the North . . . but as one among many cultures, some in the New World, some in the Third World, some regional cultures in the developed world." This is an important charge, one crucial to his larger argument, and O'Brien is not the first well-placed southern historian to make it. At the 2004 Southern Intellectual History Circle meeting in Charleston, which O'Brien attended, Jane Dailey asserted that in our introduction to *Look Away!* Deborah Cohn and I attempt to erect a "brick wall" along the Mason-Dixon line. Both historians' claims, however, depend upon a false binarism: the idea that one must *either* tie the South to the nation *or* tie it to the global South, that noting transnational ties somehow forces one to deny national ones. Cohn and I repeatedly and explicitly reject such a binarism, arguing that "what generates the South's peculiar cultural tension is its position as a space of degrees of overlap *between*, its simultaneous embodiment of, the Yankee and the plantation."[26] Indeed, probably the most-cited sentence of our introduction describes the South as "simultaneously (or alternately) center and margin, victor and defeated, empire and colony, essentialist and hybrid, northern and southern (both in the global sense)."[27] Moreover, as their titles might suggest, Duck's *The Nation's Region* and Greeson's *Our South*—arguably the two best single-authored books in the New Southern Studies—are about nothing *but* the South's connections to, and its position within, the US national imaginary and body politic. Duck's stated aim is "to examine how the substantial cultural and institutional connections between the South and the larger nation produce and are shaped by projective fantasies"; Greeson's first sentence reads, "A concept of the South is essential to national identity in the United States of America."[28] O'Brien is on firmer ground when he cites Kathryn McKee and Annette Trefzer asking "What happens when we unmoor the South from its national harbor, when it becomes a floating signifier in a sea of globalism?" But significant portions of McKee and Trefzer's preface to their special issue of *American Literature* are composed of less cautious restatements of the introduction to *Look Away!*—here, of the part where Cohn and I ask, "What happens . . . if we look away from the North in constructing narratives of southern identity?"[29] With good reason, most of us are willing to look away (if only to regain our bearings), less willing exuberantly to cast off.

Third and crucially, O'Brien's claim about the New Southern Studies' indifference to nation follows upon a serious misconception of the intellectual roots of the overall project. "Self-evidently," he writes, "the practitioners of this discourse share the postmodernist mistrust of essence and the postmodernist trust in constructive acts of imagination and will. . . . By the same token, place is not a social premise, but a usable fiction, sometimes an un-usable one." Then comes the kicker:

> Insofar as these are postmodern literary scholars, they are less committed to the constraints of the historical imagination than was common among Southern literary critics in, say, 1960. . . . Since the fragmentary is of the postmodernist essence, if I may hazard an oxymoron, it would be inconsistent to demand consistent patterns and tight logics from the "New Southern Studies," which believes in the constitutive power of the imagination and even in playfulness.

For O'Brien, that is, our entire field—for better and chiefly for worse—is grounded in something called "postmodernism." As a result, he thinks, we feel no particular answerability to either the empirically "demonstrable" or to "tight logics"; we write out of "imagination" and "playfulness."

O'Brien's language is gentle; its thrust is not. Because logic and evidence, rationalism and empiricism, quite rightly constitute the only epistemologies that matter in scholarship, if O'Brien's chain of reasoning held, we would be no sort of scholars at all. Fortunately for us, it does not, largely because O'Brien's version of postmodernism involves something of a reactionary caricature. That postmodernism mistrusts essence is indeed self-evident. But that postmodernism "trusts in constructive acts of imagination and will" is decidedly less so. O'Brien seems here to confuse postmodernism with a remarkably hubristic and vapid form of philosophical idealism: "As I see it," he writes, "whatever Hegel and Alexander Pope may have claimed, the moral and the real are not synonymous and, for good or ill, the world is not a thing our imagination can freely construct, because we are made by the world even as we make it." No one, however, whom O'Brien cites as an influence on the New Southern Studies—neither Derrida, nor Said, nor any other major thinker after, say, the Holocaust—believes the world is such a thing. Nor does a much more obvious and immediate influence on the New Southern Studies whom O'Brien does not name, the essence-mistrusting scholar who argued,

> The South is centrally an intellectual perception . . . which has served to comprehend and weld an unintegrated social reality. . . . "The South" . . . has secured such a hold on the American mind that it is a postulate, to which the facts of American society must be bent, and no longer a deduction.[30]

That scholar is the author of *The Idea of the American South*, the thirty-one-year-old Michael O'Brien.

In fact, what the older O'Brien claims of "postmodern" thought is on one crucial point—the alleged power of the individual imagination over "the social"—the opposite of what such thinkers have tended actually to argue. The chief lesson of pretty much any postmodern scholar who has written constructively about ideology—the ideology that makes "social constructs"—over the past forty or fifty years is that ideology is nearly impossible to get "free" from. Like "late" capitalism, the "postmodern condition," as Lyotard described it some time ago, is hardly something one can imagine oneself out of; Jameson, the leading theorist of postmodernism, is most widely associated with the injunction "always historicize."

So allow me, after Jameson and perhaps even O'Brien, a rather obvious historicizing point. With the most obvious exceptions of Martyn Bone (Cornishman), Annette Trefzer (Bavarian), and Melanie Benson Taylor (Cape Cod Wampanoag), nearly everyone involved in the New Southern Studies, like no small number of the *Myth of Southern Exceptionalism* historians, grew up in the (legally integrated) southeastern United States of the '70s and '80s. Leigh Anne Duck hails from Martin, Tennessee; I grew up lower middle class in Charlottesville; Tara McPherson grew up in small-town Louisiana, where her dad coached basketball; Riché Richardson is from Montgomery, Alabama; Katie McKee grew up on a central Kentucky farm; Jennifer Greeson grew up in a suburb of Charlotte; Scott Romine comes from a house full of suburban Atlanta evangelicals. Nearly all of us were struck by the gap between "the South" as it was taught to us in college or graduate school and our own upbringings, which, different as they were, were nonetheless uniformly a great deal more determined by national culture than by regional distinctiveness. All of us grew up eating at McDonald's, attending legally integrated schools, and watching *Star Wars* and MTV and (as McKee has noted) *Sesame Street*. Contrast these really rather normal American experiences (of both time and, for most of us, social class) with the anguished confessions of relatively privileged white baby boomer southernists, such as Diane McWhorter, Jefferson Humphries, and Patricia Yaeger, about passing their formative years with "Negro" domestic servants.[31] For better or for worse, given our generation's history of growing up after the most obvious mark of southern "distinctiveness" was gone, how could we *not* be predisposed to doubt southern exceptionalism—not simply the generally celebratory exceptionalism of "southernists," but also the generally condemnatory exceptionalism of Americanists? For us, the reality-defying "constructive act of imagination and will" would be precisely to act as if we did come from a distinctive, unified "South."

As my old-fashioned historicist privileging of our own experiences over various academic and popular representations of "the South" might suggest, we are far from postmodern relativists all, and farther still from postmodern in O'Brien's intellectually weightless sense of the term. Quite the reverse: what I believe bothers most of us, whether historians or literary critics, is simply what we see as the *lack of empirical and argumentative support* for—the increasingly obviously constructed nature of—older Americanist and southernist accounts of "the South." The New Southern Studies is not some eruption of reality-defying philosophical idealism, or of rampant postmodernity (though we sometimes use contemporary theoretical terminology and would be anachronistic not to), or even of particularly brilliant skepticism. It primarily reflects the cultural milieus most of us grew up in, not the books we later read in grad school—measuring them, often skeptically, against our own experiences. It is, by and large, no more and no less than the sort of generational paradigm shift that academia periodically undergoes and will undergo again, inducing panic in the worst of the old and elation in the best of the young. I suspect that if more southern historians tried reading us in this light, they might find the going less difficult.

Yet O'Brien is right in at least one case, for one of us *is* a postmodern relativist: Scott Romine,[32] who appears to be the scholar with whom O'Brien most readily engages. When O'Brien refers to New Southern Studies' belief in "the constitutive power of the imagination and even in playfulness," he seems to be referring chiefly to Romine, who is the only one of us who refers to "play": "the deterioration of organic metaphors of culture—the garden, the body—opens culture to improvisation and play."[33] Similarly, when O'Brien writes that in the New Southern Studies, "the dissolving of boundaries, the movements of peoples, the juxtaposition and mingling of cultures, the hybridity of discourses, these are portrayed as positive developments, because they multiply choices and contingencies, and they weaken coercive authorities," he again seems to refer most obviously to Romine. Others of us write of the blurring—not dissolving, unless you are McKee and Trefzer—of boundaries, of the movements of peoples, and of hybrid discourses, but only Romine, I think, explicitly argues that these are "positive developments" *because* "they multiply choices and contingencies, and they weaken coercive authorities." "I find the bastard form of cultural nationalism infinitely preferable to its legitimate heir," writes Romine, "not least because its authoritarian praxis assumes ever gentler forms.... Better a cyber-Confederacy than a real one."[34]

This brings me to O'Brien's fourth claim, the demonstration of which takes up nearly the second half of his talk: "Globalization is not a counterpoint to nationality and not a formless sea which offers an escape from the oppressions of place, landscape, community, and nation." Here, O'Brien and I agree; indeed, I find the second half of his essay a useful corrective to some of the less careful claims advanced in American studies over the past fifteen years under the sign of the "transnational." Saskia Sassen, O'Brien's chief inspiration for this section, appears as little in the works-cited lists of transnational Americanist scholarship as she does those of the New Southern Studies (with the recent exception of Claudia Milian's *Latining America*), and that absence, as he notes, is a problem. But for all the idealisms and myopias that have plagued the larger field, I would still also note that very few of us in the New Southern Studies see globalization merely as an escape from more local oppressions. As his title *Grounded Globalism* suggests, Peacock sees emerging a happy synthesis of global and local. Most of the contributors to *The American South in a Global World*—Donald Nonini most trenchantly—grapple with the dark side of globalization. Duck, Greeson, Cohn, and I are, I have tried to show, all more interested in nation than O'Brien thinks. Once again, McKee and Trefzer, whose unfortunate casting-off metaphor O'Brien extends here, may well be on a different page.

But in *The Real South*, Romine is on a page all his own. Romine's work has always been unique in its ability to make progressive points while still charming conservatives, but at times this ability can detract from the intellectual coherence of his arguments. As I argued in my review of *The Narrative Forms of Southern Community*, Romine masterfully demonstrates the theoretical and practical impossibility of agrarian "community" in his first two pages, and he proceeds to hammer this insight home in chapter after chapter. His conclusion, however, reverses course to insist that community would still be possible, after all, if it were "extended across racial lines." Such a claim not only contradicts the preceding 90 percent of the book but also invites conservatives to assimilate such work as merely "energizing" the field by "reconceptualizing" old categories, rather than, in truth, erasing them.[35] Much the same thing happens in *The Real South*, where Romine spends a couple of hundred pages utterly demolishing clichéd and circular notions of "southern identity" with acerbic wit, only to suggest that such laughably bogus reproductions of culture are no worse than any other way of looking at "the South," because such reproduction is just how culture works.

In the remainder of this essay, I want to suggest that this drive to neutralize antagonism, far from merely constituting smart scholarly rhetoric (or simple good manners) in a field until recently dominated by a remarkable and sometimes narcissistic conservatism, reflects an underlying, rather Hobbesian political philosophy with which I want to take issue. In both Romine's books, that is, the state of nature is a war of all against all. In *The Narrative Form of Southern Community*, what "defers" such perpetual conflict is manners. "Community," he writes, "is enabled by practices of avoidance, deferral, and evasion. . . . [It] coheres by means of norms, codes, and manners that produce a simulated, or at least symbolically constructed, view of reality."[36] In *The Real South*, what defers conflict has become commodification and the Internet: "Such practices [e.g., wearing T-shirts or baseball caps expressing potentially conflicting ideas of "the South"] allow individuals and groups to get out of each other's way in relatively—I stress relatively—humane ways. Better a cyber-Confederacy than a real one."[37] The formless sea that redeems us from conflict is no longer manners but cyberspace, the virtual, postmodern capitalism itself.

The chief problem with such a model, for my purposes here, is not that, as many feminist philosophers have argued, Hobbes is insufficiently attentive to altruism and nurturing. Rather, it is that antagonism, far from being something that must be perennially deferred, is absolutely necessary to any progressive social agenda. After all, the alleged dampening effect of the Internet and of commodification cuts both ways: who would say "Better a cyber-marriage equality movement than a real one"? or "Better a cyber-movement to cut carbon emissions than a real one"? Romine's concluding hope that virtuality, commodification, and play will allow people to "get out of each other's way in relatively . . . humane ways" thus feels, like most other postmodern thinking, eerily early '90s: not merely a version of what Barack Obama gently derides in *The Audacity of Hope* as "our optimism once the Cold War ended that Big Macs and the Internet would lead to the end of historical conflict" (279–80), but also in its unwillingness to account for the necessity of conflict to attain progressive aims, a version of what political scientist Jodi Dean, considerably to the left of Obama, less gently derides as the neoliberal fantasy of the postpolitical.[38] To return to the concerns with which this chapter began, is there a way to avoid that market fantasy, a way not to abandon an earlier generation's admirable concern with politics and real bodies while avoiding the seemingly inevitable slide into a solipsistic fascination with just how very concerned one is?

I think there is such a way, but at a minimum it requires keeping Romine's cogent and masterful analysis of southern fakery while backing away from several features of the theoretical model that frames that analysis: Romine's attempt, in calling the postsouthern the "late South," to keep an "ironic distance from [the term's] own potential for eschatological grandeur"; his discomfort with antagonism; his association of the postmodern with the emancipatory; and his faith in the market.[39]

As Žižek implies, an attitude of "ironic distance" from eschatological grandeur in fact pretty much guarantees an ultimate embrace of said grandeur. The conclusion of *The Real South*, however, has difficulty even maintaining the irony. In the book's final pages, after showing the absurdity of ideas of southern authenticity, Romine nevertheless reassures (even, I think, forgives) old-school white southernists by recurring to their favorite rhetoric. The scholar who, sounding laudably like Warren, Duck, and Hoberek, notes in his introduction that a certain "hermeneutics of suspicion" is warranted toward questions of "southernness" because "stories about [culture] characteristically deploy metaphors of depth and longevity to naturalize current arrangements and practices" winds up deploying just such metaphors in his conclusion.[40] There, suspicion is replaced by comforting eschatological affirmations that "territoriality . . . isn't dead. It isn't even past," and that "we are still using regional culture as a tool to organize spaces, to build environments, and to tell stories," and that "in pushing away from the tropes of the fake South, I am still using the South as a cartographic tool," and that "the long-heralded death of southern literature hasn't materialized."[41] Setting out to describe "the late South," Romine finds instead an open tomb. Such rhetoric does not, as the Lacanians say, disrupt anyone's enjoyment, anyone's fundamental fantasy, at least among the believers on the faux-Georgian brick walks of Chapel Hill and Vanderbilt; on the contrary, in constructing a "South" impervious to deconstruction because it is always already deconstructed, it reassures old southern studies types that they are free to keep doing what they've always done, because, as "neopragmatists" such as Stanley Fish and Jane Tompkins were saying back in the '80s, at the end of the day that is all anyone can do.[42]

To put it another way, consumerist definitions of "culture"—a focus on fakes, commodities, reproductions—may exclude, almost by definition, more political aspects of civic identity, that is, precisely those aspects where antagonism serves a very positive function: not only the public sphere, but also the similarly constituted realm of academic discourse itself. In Romine's conclusion, there is room for everyone, for good ideas and bad ones, for the fresh and the stale, for the hardheaded and the sentimental, because "we may come to different Souths, but neither will be solid in fact or practice."[43] Academia, however, is not the kind of place where people just walk around wearing besloganed T-shirts. In academia, as in the wider public sphere, people do not get out of each other's way; they argue over ideas. Some ideas win, some lose. Paradigms shift; ideas that made you look like hot stuff thirty years ago make you look like embarrassing deadwood if you still hold them today—not so much because fashions and terminology change (as conservatives tend to lament) as because the flaws in arguments become apparent with time.

My final hesitation, however, may also be my biggest. It seems to me

Romine's vision of competing aggressive fashion statements and web pages is a version of the old (and also highly gendered, as scholars such Angela McRobbie were arguing from the get-go) notion of "resistance through rituals" that cultural studies got excited about back in its early days—but a version drained of the Birmingham School's exquisitely British interest in "class," perhaps even one where regional affiliation stands in the place of class affiliation. If so, there is a double problem: first, in the wake of works like Thomas Frank's *The Conquest of Cool* (1998) and Sarah Thornton's *Club Cultures* (1995), it is—or should be—hard for anyone under fifty in cultural studies to mistake this kind of cultural practice for any kind of serious "resistance" to capitalism or, in Romine's terms, any serious compensation for its deprivations. And even in that old *Resistance through Rituals* collection, John Clarke pointed out that "skinhead style does not revive the community in a real sense" (100), hypothesized that "this dislocated relation to the traditional community accounts for the exaggerated and intensified form which the values and concerns of that community received in the form of the skinhead style" (100), and ultimately labeled this kind of resistance a "'magical' or 'imaginary' one" (102). Second, issues of economic inequality tend to disappear. If you lose your job at the sock factory in Fort Payne, Alabama, because those socks are now made in the Third World, and you have to take a job at Wal-Mart because (a) you are very poorly educated and (b) there are no other jobs even for the well educated, being able to buy a "You Wear Your X" T-shirt really does not offer much in the way of compensation. (Neither, obviously, does taking your fiddle down off the wall.) What it does offer is a way of getting you not to think about the real causes of your situation.

Jodi Dean is pretty explicit about this in *Democracy and Other Neoliberal Fantasies* (2009): "Insofar as too many on the academic and typing left have celebrated isolation as freedom and consumption as creativity, we have failed to counter the neoliberalization of the economy. . . . It's easier to let the market decide."[44] It can be hard to take the enthusiasm for postmodernism now dominating some quarters of southern studies after reading Dean: "Some academics repeat terms from old battles, as if the problem of the contemporary right is its investment in essentialism and origins. . . . The prominence of politically active Christian fundamentalists, Fox News, and the orchestrations of Bush advisor Karl Rove all demonstrate the triumph of postmodernism. These guys take social construction—packaging, marketing, and representation absolutely seriously. They put it to work."⁴⁵ Worse, "enthusiasm for diversity, multiplicity, and the agency of consumers actively transforming their lifestyles unites left academics and corporate capital."⁴⁶ Welcome to the desert of the postpolitical.

What Dean and others nevertheless helpfully remind us is that postpolitics at best simply freezes us in a status quo that, while preferable to the days of slavery—or lynching, or bear baiting—has not yet erased the sorts of evil and injustice that now concern us. It is important to talk about virtual Souths, about the ways "the South" functions in the Symbolic (or even just the Imaginary) order, the way it operates as a brand, and no one does this better than Romine. But it is also important to remember that there is a world of real bodies out there, and that getting full civil rights for all, and preventing massive environmental catastrophe for most, involves getting firmly in the way of those who are working very hard to preserve the status quo, those who are even working to increase disparities that are already at their highest levels since the Gilded Age. In fighting neoliberalism's conversion of everything to brands, it is crucial to remember that other aspects of the polity—for example, a functioning public sphere, not to mention a functioning academy—are not entirely reducible to the neoliberal logic of market choice.

What, then, would a properly post-postpolitical southern studies look like? As I have been suggesting, if "southernness" no longer carries much political force, then a post-postpolitical southern studies probably has to be a "southern studies without 'the South.'" As such, it might function as a branch of American studies that, deeply informed by the insights of the New Southern Studies into national melancholy for white supremacy, or those of southern religious historians into how civil religions operate among conservatives, could talk about—and help *do* something about—national phenomena such as Fox News and the Tea Parties. It might be a reminder that a study of, say, Birmingham, Alabama, is and must be a work of American studies, not just southern studies. American studies constantly needs such reminders, but old southern studies does, too. To borrow a too-neglected American studies injunction from a decade ago: no more separate spheres!

Finally, a post-postpolitical southern studies might, I suspect, look a lot like nearly all of *The Real South*, a book I am very proud to have blurbed as "sane, funny, very smart, and cheaper than psychoanalysis." If I differ with Romine on what constitutes "the very materials out of which cultural reproduction proceeds," I very much share his impatience with those who get their jollies—sorry, derive their *jouissance*—either from ginning up anxiety over whether some essentialized South is disappearing, or from defining an essential South of, you know, family, community, foodways, memory, and the like and reveling in some authentic essence southerners allegedly have and the rest of the nation does not. Romine has worked tirelessly to cut through the malarkey and sentiment so that the rest of us can start to build something better. Finally, if I think I have generally tried to write for a different audience than Romine does, I am not insensible of how important it is that the New Southern Studies write for a range of audiences. Indeed, who today would even want a solid—a univocal—New Southern Studies?

Notes

1. "Creating and Consuming the South" list of sample topics for speakers, n.p.
2. Yaeger, *Dirt and Desire*, 34.
3. Foster, *Return of the Real*, 166.
4. Mark, "Mourning Emmett," 129, 136.
5. Kreyling, "Teaching Southern Lit in Black and White," 48.
6. Simpson, *Man of Letters*, 248; Romine, *Real South*, 5.
7. "Discussion," *Understanding the South, Understanding America*, http://understandingthesouth.wordpress.com/discussion/, accessed August 16, 2013.
8. Duck, "Southern Nonidentity," 329.
9. Warren, *So Black and Blue*, 67.
10. I have argued elsewhere that "postmodern" theory was almost instantly accommodated by the rather theory-averse old southern studies precisely because Fredric Jameson's narrative of a fall from nature into culture in *Postmodernism* (1991) is fundamentally the same as the Agrarian narrative. See Smith, review of Bone; Smith, *Finding Purple America*.
11. Žižek, *Living in the End Times*, 3.
12. Baym, review of Kreyling, 659.
13. Sundquist, review of Kreyling, 685, 687.
14. Donaldson, review of Kreyling, 667, italics added.
15. Hobson, review of Kreyling, 672.
16. Jones, review of Kreyling, 678, 681, 682.
17. Kreyling, *South That Wasn't There*, 10–15.
18. Kreyling remarkably reads Duck's takedown of V. S. Naipaul's racism in her *Look Away!* essay as a way of "gain[ing]" for the South "another Nobel laureate," failing to understand that anyone might be uninterested in a "Southern canon"; he reads Greeson as governed by "the imperative to avoid Southern literary-critical paths," as though the

kind of American studies she had been taught at Duke and Yale cared enough about those paths to bother avoiding them. Kreyling, "Toward 'A New Southern Studies,'" 9, 11.

19. Baym, review of Kreyling, 659.
20. Duck, review of Yaeger, 542.
21. Hoberek, "Reconstructing Southern Literature," n.p.
22. Duck, "Postsouthern and (Increasingly) Post-Agrarian," 300.
23. Smith, review of Bone, 373.
24. Jones, review of Kreyling, 679.
25. Kreyling, *South That Wasn't There*; Ladd, "Literary Studies," 1637.
26. Smith and Cohn, "Introduction," 7–8.
27. Ibid., 9.
28. Duck, *Nation's Region*, 3; Greeson, *Our South*, 1.
29. McKee and Trefzer, "Preface," 678; Smith and Cohn, "Introduction," 2.
30. O'Brien, *Idea of the American South*, xxii.
31. McWhorter, *Carry Me Home*, 143, 348–49; Humphries, "Introduction," x–xii; Yaeger, *Dirt and Desire*, 1.
32. In what follows, I address Romine rather than Bone, who seems about equally invested in Jamesonian ideas of the "postmodern" because his take on postmodernity is fundamentally "historical-geographical materialist"—as his emphasis on real estate and his distaste for neoagrarians' "rather airy" definition of "place" amply demonstrate (Bone, 48, 28).
33. Romine, *Real South*, 236.
34. O'Brien, "Place as Everywhere," 7–8; Romine, *Real South*, 236.
35. Smith, review of Romine; see also Ladd, "Literary Studies," 1636.
36. Romine, *Narrative Forms*, 3.
37. Romine, *Real South*, 236.
38. Obama, *Audacity of Hope*, 279–80; Dean, *Democracy*.
39. Romine, *Real South*, 2.
40. Ibid., 3.
41. Romine, Ibid., 228, 229, 229, 232.
42. Fish, "Consequences"; Tompkins, "Indians."
43. Romine, *Real South*, 237.
44. Dean, *Democracy*, 4.
45. Ibid., 9, 7.
46. Ibid., 9.

Works Cited

Baker, Houston, and Dana Nelson. "Introduction: Violence, the Body, and 'the South.'" *American Literature* 73, no. 2 (June 2001): 231–44.

Baym, Nina. Review of Michael Kreyling, *Inventing Southern Literature*. *Mississippi Quarterly* 52, no. 4 (fall 1999): 659–62.

Bone, Martyn. *The Postsouthern Sense of Place in Contemporary Fiction*. Baton Rouge: Louisiana State University Press, 2005.

Clarke, John. "The Skinheads and the Magical Recovery of Community." *Resistance through Rituals: Youth Subcultures in Post-war Britain*, edited by Stuart Hall and Tony Jefferson, 80–83. 2nd ed. New York: Routledge, 2006.

Cohn, Deborah. *History and Memory in the Two Souths*. Nashville: Vanderbilt University Press, 1999.

Dean, Jodi. *Democracy and Other Liberal Fantasies: Communicative Capitalism and Left Politics*. Durham: Duke University Press, 2009.

Donaldson, Susan V. Review of Michael Kreyling, *Inventing Southern Literature*. *Mississippi Quarterly* 52, no. 4 (fall 1999): 662–69.

Duck, Leigh Anne. *The Nation's Region: Southern Modernism, Segregation, and U.S. Nationalism*. Athens: University of Georgia Press, 2006.

———. "Postsouthern and (Increasingly) Post-Agrarian." Review of Martyn Bone, *The Postsouthern Sense of Place in Contemporary Fiction*. *Contemporary Literature* 47, no. 2 (summer 2006): 299–303.

———. Review of Patricia Yaeger, *Dirt and Desire: Reconstructing Southern Women's Writing, 1930–1960*. *Modernism/Modernity* 8, no. 3 (September 2001): 542–43.

———. "Southern Nonidentity." *Safundi: The Journal of South African and American Studies* 9, no. 3 (July 2008): 319–30.

Fish, Stanley. "Consequences." *Critical Inquiry* 11, vol. 3 (spring 1985): 435–58.

Foster, Hal. *The Return of the Real: The Avant-Garde at the End of the Century*. Cambridge: MIT Press, 1996.

Greeson, Jennifer Rae. *Our South: Geographic Fantasy and the Rise of National Literature*. Cambridge: Harvard University Press, 2010.

Gwin, Minrose. "Mourning Medgar: Justice, Aesthetics, and the Local." *Southern Spaces*. Published March 11, 2008. https://southernspaces.org/2008/mourning-medgar-justice-aesthetics-and-local. Accessed March 14, 2012.

Hobson, Fred. Review of Michael Kreyling, *Inventing Southern Literature*. *Mississippi Quarterly* 52, no. 4 (fall 1999): 670–73.

Hoberek, Andrew. "Reconstructing Southern Literature." *Postmodern Culture* 11, vol. 1 (September 2000): n.p. http://pmc.iath.virginia.edu/text-only/issue.900/11.1.r_hoberek.txt. Accessed January 22, 2012.

Humphries, Jefferson. "Introduction." In *Southern Literature and Literary Theory*, edited by Jefferson Humphries, vii–xviii. Athens: University of Georgia Press, 1990.

Jones, Anne Goodwyn. Review of Michael Kreyling, *Inventing Southern Literature*. *Mississippi Quarterly* 52, no. 4 (fall 1999): 674–85.

Kreyling, Michael. *Inventing Southern Literature*. Jackson: University Press of Mississippi, 1998.

———. *The South That Wasn't There*. Baton Rouge: Louisiana State University Press, 2010.

———. "Teaching Southern Lit in Black and White." *Southern Cultures* 11, no. 4 (winter 2005): 47–75.

———. "Toward 'A New Southern Studies.'" *South Central Review* 22, no. 1 (spring 2005): 4–18.

Ladd, Barbara. "Literary Studies: The Southern United States, 2005." *PMLA* 120, no. 5 (2006): 1628–39.
Mark, Rebecca. "Mourning Emmett: 'One Long Expansive Moment.'" *Southern Literary Journal* 40, no. 2 (spring 2008): 121–37.
McKee, Kathryn, and Trefzer, Annette. "Preface: Global Contexts, Local Literatures: The New Southern Studies." *American Literature* 78, no. 4 (December 2006): 677–90.
McWhorter, Diane. *Carry Me Home: Birmingham, Alabama: The Climactic Battle of the Civil Rights Revolution*. New York: Simon and Schuster, 2001.
Obama, Barack. *The Audacity of Hope*. New York: Crown, 2006.
O'Brien, Michael. *The Idea of the American South, 1920–1941*. Baltimore: Johns Hopkins University Press, 1979.
———. "Place as Everywhere: On Globalizing the American South." Keynote address presented at the "Creating Citizenship and Identities in the 19th Century South and Beyond" conference, University of Florida, Gainesville, January 15, 2009.
Ownby, Ted. *American Dreams in Mississippi: Consumers, Poverty, and Culture, 1830–1998*. Chapel Hill: University of North Carolina Press, 1998.
Romine, Scott. *The Narrative Forms of Southern Community*. Baton Rouge: Louisiana State University Press, 1999.
———. *The Real South: Southern Narrative in the Age of Cultural Reproduction*. Baton Rouge: Louisiana State University Press, 2008.
Rubin, Louis D. "Introduction." In *I'll Take My Stand: The South and the Agrarian Tradition*, by Twelve Southerners. Baton Rouge: Louisiana State University Press, x–xxii.
Simpson, Lewis P. *The Man of Letters in New England and the South: Essays in the History of the Literary Vocation in America*. Baton Rouge: Louisiana State University Press, 1973.
Smith, Jon. *Finding Purple America: The South and the Future of American Cultural Studies*. Athens: University of Georgia Press, 2013.
———. "Postcolonial, Black, and Nobody's Margin." *American Literary History* 16, no. 1 (spring 2004): 144–61.
———. Review of Martyn Bone, *The Postsouthern Sense of Place in Contemporary Fiction*. *Mississippi Quarterly* 59, no. 2 (spring 2006): 369–73.
———. Review of Scott Romine, *The Narrative Forms of Southern Community*. *Style* 34, no. 2 (summer 2000): 329–32.
Smith, Jon, and Deborah Cohn. "Introduction: Uncanny Hybridities." In *Look Away! The U.S. South in New World Studies*, edited by Jon Smith and Deborah Cohn, 1–19. Durham: Duke University Press, 2004.
Sundquist, Eric. Review of Michael Kreyling, *Inventing Southern Literature*. *Mississippi Quarterly* 52, no. 4 (fall 1999): 685–87.
Tompkins, Jane. "'Indians': Textualism, Morality, and the Problem of History." *Critical Inquiry* 13, no. 1 (autumn 1986): 101–19.
Warren, Kenneth. *So Black and Blue: Ralph Ellison and the Occasion of Criticism*. Chicago: University of Chicago Press, 2003.
Wilson, Charles Reagan. *Flashes of a Southern Spirit: Meanings of the Spirit in the U.S. South*. Athens: University of Georgia Press, 2011.

Yaeger, Patricia. *Dirt and Desire: Reconstructing Southern Women's Writing, 1930–1960*. Chicago: University of Chicago Press, 2000.

Žižek, Slavoj. *Living in the End Times*. New York: Verso, 2010.

———. "Melancholy and the Act." In *Did Somebody Say Totalitarianism?* New York: Verso, 2004.

II

CREATING AND CONSUMING THE SOUTH

CASE STUDIES

4

Southern (Dis)Comfort

Creating and Consuming Homosex in the Black South

E. PATRICK JOHNSON

Southerners do not talk about sex—any kind of sex. Then again, they talk about sex all of the time. How can both of these statements be true? The answer is that when southerners discuss sexuality, they use coded language that is not always discernible to the untrained ear. When southerners engage in sex talk, they often employ euphemisms to refer to sexual organs and sex acts. It goes without saying, then, that taboo sexuality, such as homosexuality, is frequently spoken about in euphemistic terms: homosexuals are referred to as "that way," "funny," and "light in the loafers." However, beyond the sometimes derogatory and sometimes playful use of language regarding homosexuality in black southern communities are vexed and apparently contradictory attitudes toward homosexuals themselves.

On the one hand, many black southerners frown upon homosexuality, most often on religious grounds. On the other hand, the black southern church is a place where one might find an inordinate number of LGBT members. While there have been no scientific studies that verify the prevalence of black queers in the church, there is abundant anecdotal evidence, as well as oral histories and even a popular novel on the subject.[1] For example, participation in the church choir is a way to at once adhere to the religiosity of southern culture while also providing opportunities to meet other black gay men. This is only one instance in which a seemingly repressive sacred space can become a site or conduit for the expression of sexual desire. What is more, homosexuals are often incorporated into the fabric of black southern social and cultural life in ways that are anathema to its religious foundations, even though that incorporation still occurs largely on the premise of "don't ask, don't tell." Much of this has to do with black communities' awareness of being under constant surveillance by whites and therefore not wanting to "air dirty laundry," especially in light of a historical legacy of stereotyping African Americans as existing outside of normative sexuality. Riché Richardson argues that the image of rural black southern masculinity in particular has been depicted as abject: "Its logic attests to the historical association of the black male body in the South with ideologies of a perverse and excessive sexuality, and to the even deeper and more complex racial and sexual pathologies that have frequently been attached to black male bodies in rural contexts."[2] Black sensitivity to being seen as sexually deviant has meant that homosexuality is often publically disavowed; homosexuality is even characterized—in an inversion of the racialized "logic" of sexual deviancy outlined by Richardson—as a "white" form of sexuality that "infiltrated" black communities.[3]

In my book *Sweet Tea: Black Gay Men of the South—An Oral History* (2008), I address these complex relationships and views between black gay southerners and their heterosexual community and family members. In fact, many of the black gay men in both urban and rural areas of the South stated that their communities embraced them as people, even if they disavowed their sexual orientation and employed the same religion they used to castigate them to also embrace them as fellow human beings. Certainly, none of the men with whom I spoke felt as if black southern people were *more* homophobic than others; indeed, in some instances, my interviewees related stories that suggested that it was more common to hear about white lesbian, gay, bisexual, and transgender (LGBT) people being disowned by fellow white southerners than it was to hear such stories about black southerners. I found black southern men who were not only living colorful lives but also engaging in a range of sexual activity that belies the myth that homosexuality in the South is repressed, restrained, or nonexistent. Indeed, the narrators of *Sweet Tea* indicate how they create and consume the South through their sexuality. In other words, they co-opt aspects of southern culture (the politics of respectability, religiosity, language) and the landscape (open fields, golf courses, farms, parks) to create not only spaces for the expression of non-normative sexuality but also communities and social networks that transgress traditional categories of work and play or gay and straight.

Whereas *Sweet Tea* gives voice to these men's lives without analysis, here I critically engage some of the stories that exemplify the ways in which same-sex encounters involving black southern men also shed light on the history of black homosexuality in the South. The predominant discourse in popular media about same-sex behavior relating to African American men centers on the "down low" (the DL). This term has its root in black vernacular speech and historically was used to refer to keeping something secretive.[4] In contemporary parlance, it has come to mean a (black) man who has sex with other men but who does not identify as gay. More importantly, public discourse concerning "down low" men centers on the fact that many of them do not disclose their same-sex encounters to their female partners, thereby exposing those partners to HIV/AIDS. While media focus on the down-low phenomenon—from the *New York Times* to Oprah Winfrey[5]—has turned all black men into "sexual suspects" and potential carriers of disease, the men I focus on here dispel the myth that all same-sex sex is underground, unloving, or unhealthy. Indeed, these men's tales are compelling because they express the men's sexual agency in ways that are not commonly associated with the South, and especially the rural South. Their sexual escapades run counter to images of the South as sexually "slow," boring, or "down low."

Creating and Consuming the City as a Site of Sexual Nonconformity

New Orleans has long held a reputation as a place that is tolerant of sexual nonconformity. However, the faces of those sexual nonconformists have generally been depicted as white. Tennessee Williams, Truman Capote, and even Ellen DeGeneres stand out as the faces of queer New Orleans, but few outsiders have heard of George Eagerson (aka "Countess Vivian"), a ninety-nine-year-old black gay local legend who lived in the Treme district. George's narrative provides a glimpse into black gay life in the 1930s and 1940s that speaks to not only a vibrant black queer subculture but also black queer ingenuity. The following interview excerpt shows how black gay lives could cut across supposedly rigid southern social boundaries of class, race, gender, geography, and sexuality.

> *Was there a gay community here in New Orleans in the '20s and '30s?*
> I did not know or realize that they had white sissies . . . We didn't see any white gay people 'cause everything was segregated. The only time you would come over here in the French Quarter would be if

you was *working*. You could come over here and scrub the floor and clean the toilet and things like that, but you couldn't say I'm going to go hang in a bar and buy me a drink or something like that.
Were there drag queens back then?

Julia Pimpay and several others ... used to ... put on dresses and dance and hustle at night.... [W]e used to call them "creepers" and they would get a trick and they would creep in the door ... and while the trick was busy doing his business, they [would] go in his pocket and steal his money.... Many ... times the person that got robbed wouldn't even go get the police, because they would be ashamed to go and tell the police that they were up there with these black hookers, if they didn't know he was a sissy; they thought it was a woman. And even if it was a real woman, they didn't want people to know that they was in there ... with these blacks. Because, you know, at that time blacks and whites wasn't close. Of course, they're not all that close now. But then, too, they were further apart than we are today.
So sometimes these were white men picking up these hookers?

Well, not sometimes, always. Always white, no black men, honey. No black men. Even the black women that hustled, they didn't fool around with them black guys.
Why? Because they didn't have any money?

That's right. That's right. You go where the money is.[6]

Here, the Countess views race queerly, queerness through class, class through race, and geography through class. His sense of a gay community in the 1920s and 1930s was filtered through racial segregation, but that segregation in turn provided a communal space for "black sissies" during his adolescence and years as a young man. When he refers to "here" in the line "the only time you could come over here in the French Quarter," he stakes a claim as a resident of an area of town once reserved for "white sissies." As an adult, now living "on the other [white] side of the tracks," his presence in the neighborhood acknowledges that desegregation happened, but without him narrating the history of desegregation in New Orleans. His body in the present time and space—"here"—is the record of that history. At the same time, the Countess also reflects the racialized class politics that mitigated one's admission to the other side of the tracks.

Work—scrubbing floors and cleaning toilets—and not leisure—getting a drink—allowed one to traverse that racial boundary.

Speaking to the racial politics of New Orleans in the early twentieth century and signifying on those same politics today, the Countess calls out the white men who supposedly do not know that they are tricking with transgender hookers, while also commenting on the socioeconomic status of black queers who become "creepers" to make ends meet. These hookers were not tricking with black men because "you go where the money is." In her history of Storyville at the turn of the twentieth century, Alecia P. Long notes that after the Civil War, New Orleans "became a tourist destination that encouraged and facilitated indulgence, especially in prostitution and sex across the color line."[7] Few historians, however, recount the city's transgression of same-gender prostitution, especially across the color line. This could be due to the fact that, as the Countess suggests, the white patrons kept such socially taboo sexual indulgences a secret; thus, they would not contact the police when swindled by one of the black transsexual hookers.

Countess Vivian was a part of a thriving black queer community in New Orleans that took advantage of the loose sexual moral codes of the city and deployed them to resist racist practices meant to undermine their very existence. At the same time, these black sexual dissidents created a supportive community around hooking that sustained them not only financially but socially as well. The Countess related that many of the "sissies" worked as cooks for wealthy whites during the day and were thus able to earn enough money to buy property that they then used for prostitution in the evening hours. These enclaves of black sissies in New Orleans' queer southern history demonstrate how class, race, gender, geography, and sexuality are imbricated in what constitutes southern life.

Creating and Consuming Southern Landscapes as Sites for Sexual Pleasure and Experimentation

The physical landscape of the South has often been identified as one of its distinguishing attributes, especially in the more rural areas, where unpaved roads, farmland, rolling hills, and marshes dictate how people interact with one another. Stephanie Camp argues that during slavery the southern landscape actually provided an opportunity for the enslaved to engage in "illicit" social activities: "Despite planters' tremendous effort, enslaved women and men routinely 'slipped away' to attend illicit parties where such pleasures as eating, dancing, drinking, and dressing were among the main amusements."[8] Employing the landscape to camouflage secular activities, especially those of a sexual nature, has its roots in slave culture but continued well after emancipation. Moreover, southerners' historical dependence on the land to grow crops to sell and provide for one's family has often determined the social and economic circumstances that in turn affect sexual and gender identification. For many of the men I interviewed, sexual experimentation occurred not inside their homes, but rather outside during work and/or play. Bob Isom, born in Baxley, Georgia, in 1940, recalls that

> My first experience of having an erection with other boys [was] in public. I say public, [because] I'd go to pick berries with about four other boys. And the older boy was with us. And we were out in this field in an old abandoned farm. . . . I must have been in ninth grade, I suppose . . . so he jacked off in front of us. And I didn't know, I'd never done that before. . . . So then I thought he had gotten ill because I never seen anybody do that and his face got all contorted. And I said, "I'm going to tell my mother that you got sick, you were playing with yourself and you got sick." He said, "Well, before you do that, you go home and try it. And after you try it, if you want to tell her, then you tell her." So I went home and tried it and I never told her. So then we did it every day after school.[9]

Bob's narrative suggests the ways in which rural "field work" occasioned opportunities for (homo)sexual experimentation. Because much of this work was not under the surveillance of an adult, youths had the freedom to discover their sexuality freely. Bob also remembers how he and his friends indulged in mutual masturbation in a tree house they had built out of pasteboard boxes deep in the woods. Again, it is the geography of the South that provides an opportunity for these young boys to create spaces to indulge their budding homosexuality. To be sure, other rural areas outside the South, such as in the Midwest, could and did provide similar opportunities for such experimentation.[10] What is unique about the southern landscape, however, is its history of functioning in multiple ways for black people—as a site of *forced* labor, yet also a refuge for sexual experimentation. Thus, black queers' orientation toward southern landscape is necessarily different from that of other inhabitants of rural areas, because of the way that history is carried in the body. Sarah Ahmed argues in *Queer Phenomenology* (2006), "If orientation is a matter of how we reside in space, then sexual orientation might also be a matter of residence; of how we inhabit spaces as well as 'who' or 'what' we inhabit spaces with."[11] The implication of Ahmed's phenomenological approach to queer desire is that black queer southerners' orientation toward the physical and sensorial landscape of the South—the scent of magnolia, the stickiness of humidity, the sight of red soil, the cry of cicadas, the sweetness of berries—all shape the body's relation to and memories of the space and therefore telegraph queer desire. Indeed, for Ahmed "spaces are not exterior to bodies; instead, spaces are like a second skin that unfolds in the folds of the body."[12] Bob's learning to masturbate while playing in a tree house is not necessarily the point so much as his relationship to that particular tree, in that particular time and space; it is this that makes his and other black queer southerners' experiences distinctive.

Unlike Bob, "Larry J.," born in Camden, South Carolina, was more than aware of the opportunities that the outdoors provided for sexual relations.

> Well, here I was a senior in high school and worked at the YMCA. Well, there was this guy that worked at the YMCA who was a football player for Camden High School. [. . .] Well, we were walking across the country club, and we get down to the little shed area and we had stopped. . . . He said, "Motherfucker, suck my dick." You know, just like a boy would say. And I said, "I don't suck on anything that I ain't gonna get full off of." And so he pulled it out. But I was like, "Wow." . . . So I went around there and I started [makes gulping sound]. I had never done that before. And he had a big dick. . . . So I was gagging on it. . . . I had no experience with doing that. And so he said, "Motherfucker, you don't know what you're doing." And so we stopped. . . . And I didn't really think much of it. Well, now mind you, I had to see him tomorrow at work. And somehow we got in the basement of the YMCA. . . . He was trying to do some anal. He was trying to screw me and no lube or nothing, you know. I mean I didn't know a thing. . . . So you know that was just becoming too risky. So we arranged to meet like later on that night at the country club . . . and mess around on one of the greens. . . . And he

was trying to, you know, penetrate. But I'm telling you, it was big. I wasn't used to this kind of stuff here. And he was trying to force it, and of course I was, you know, moving away and all this stuff. And there was no love, no kissing, no foreplay. No nothing. Not that I'd know anything about all that. Well, he gets angry.... And he started holding me tight, squeezing me, and punching. Not punching real hard but, "Motherfucker," and I was running and he was catching me and running and hitting. Not hard and not in the face, but just hitting me.[13]

Larry J. recounted various other sexual encounters in the woods near his childhood neighborhood, on the golf course, and in the basement of the YMCA. Many of these sexual encounters turned violent, with Larry J. being verbally and physically assaulted; nevertheless, he often had more than one encounter with these same men. Some might read Larry J.'s sexual encounters as examples of sex addiction rooted in sexual trauma. Given the history of sexual and physical abuse in Larry's family his seeking out these clandestine sex encounters that turn violent could be the actions of someone reliving their psychosexual trauma. Another reading, however, might suggest his enjoyment of bondage/discipline/sadism/masochism (BDSM) sex, which would explain, in part, his desire to have sex in such semipublic locations, for one dynamic of BDSM is risk—and in these places, there would be the risk of getting caught. This landscape is a site of danger and desire—the danger of physical violence that accompanies the sex, the danger (and titillation) of being discovered, and the desire to be sexually dominated. The three places that young Larry J. had sex—the shed at the country club, the basement of the YMCA, and the golf course—each provided a constructed or sculptured, as opposed to "natural," landscape to facilitate the danger/desire dyad he enjoyed. As a BDSM participant, then, Larry J. does not find liberation "in the wild" per se, but rather through the cultivated semiprivate spaces where there is always the risk (and fantasy) of being discovered. Yet each site also includes a safety valve: the degree of his sex partner's violence would necessarily be mitigated by the level of threat of discovery based on the site. An open field, for instance, would not provide the same risk of discovery that any of the three other sites would.

Larry J.'s narrative speaks to how some black southern homosexuals blur the lines between public/private, work/play, and gay/straight in their employment of the physical and psychological landscape of the South. It is important to note that these particular "work" spaces provide Larry access to a certain type of heteronormative masculine man or "trade," a gay vernacular term for a self-identified straight man who is typically on the receiving end of oral sex and the giving end of anal sex with a self-identified homosexual; in turn, the homosexual receives pleasure from providing pleasure to the trade without any emotional attachment or obligation.[14] It is notable, for example, that the football player with whom Larry J. engages in sex at work and on the golf course maintains the facade of heteronormative masculinity. The fact that he is a football player apparently precludes any presumption that he might be homosexual, which paradoxically provides him with more leverage to indulge in same-sex sex without the burden of the stigma associated with homosexuality. Within the context of his encounter with Larry J., however, it is clear that he is the more experienced of the two, as he repeatedly informs Larry J. that the latter is ignorant when it comes to performing oral sex.

With regard to the blurring of the work/play binary, Larry J. and the football player transgress the understood racial codes of "work" at the country club. Country clubs are usually thought of as exclusive suburban facilities where wealthy white men gather to socialize and play golf. Historically, access to these spaces would be off-limits to blacks as spaces of *leisure*, though they could certainly be employed at such clubs as caddies or waiters. By employing the space for homosexual sex with his trade, Larry J. undermines the established rules of work for raced bodies in a place of sport and leisure for white southern patrons. As Camp argues about enslaved women's bodies, Larry J.'s sexual escapades at the country club also reflect both "the role that [his] body played in [his white employers'] endeavors to control [his] labor" and his "resistance to that control."[15]

The Young Men's Christian Association (YMCA) is another place of work in which Larry J.'s sex acts are transgressive, especially in light of the organization's purpose of providing "a refuge of Bible study and prayer for young men seeking escape from the hazards of life on the streets," and an outlet for physical activities such as swimming.[16] But Larry's BDSM sex acts at the YMCA also transgress the boundaries of understood work ethics for blacks in the 1970s South—that pleasure or leisure are off-limits while "on the job." It is the southern landscape—both natural and manufactured—that provides these opportunities for experimentation and sexual pedagogy. The country club, the YMCA, and the golf course are not just places where Larry J. works; they are also a place to work *out*.

Creating and Consuming HBCUs as a Site of Homosex

While the first historically black college/university (HBCU) was founded in 1837 in the North (Cheyney University in Pennsylvania), the majority of HBCUs are located in the South.[17] As has been well documented, these institutions of higher education emerged in the pre–Civil War era to educate the handful of freed blacks and then expanded to accommodate emancipated former slaves who were barred from white institutions because of Jim Crow. However, it is rather less widely recognized that homosexuals have always constituted a significant portion of the student body at HBCUs and at least in some cases have received tacit tolerance. Like black churches, historically black colleges have been reluctant to publicly condone homosexuality or provide support systems for queer-identified students.[18] Part of the reason for this is the class-inflected ideology of racial uplift upon which these colleges and universities were founded.

In response to white supremacist exclusionary practices in the late 1800s and at the turn of the twentieth century, black middle-class leaders and organizations—from W.E.B. Du Bois to the women's movement within the black Baptist church—devised a discourse around the politics of respectability in order to demonstrate black humanity and intellectual and cultural equality. But as Evelyn Brooks Higginbotham notes, this political strategy was not solely directed at impressing whites; it was also used to "[condemn] what [the black middle class] perceived to be negative practices and attitudes among their own people. Their assimilationist leanings led to their insistence upon blacks' conformity to the dominant society's norms of manners and morals."[19] The results of the emergence of the politics of respectability among African American leaders was the cultivation of a set of strict codes of living that hearkened to Victorian values and ideas of social comportment. Since the acquisition of education was a premium ideal of respectability, HBCUs were a platform to cultivate the "model" black citizen. Moreover, given the pressure to counter racist images of black masculinity and sexuality as deformed and bestial, black male behavior was confined to genteel and dignified (read: white) forms of masculinity.[20] Homosexuality, of course, was anathema to such respectable presentations of masculinity and therefore condemned on not only religious grounds but also cultural ones. Indeed, as Spencer Gibbs has argued in his study of the "Morehouse Man," the hetero-masculine image of the black male student is what features most prominently in representations of HBCUs that mimic the white patriarchal lineage of the Ivy League.[21]

At least one history of queers at an Ivy League college has been written, but to my knowledge, until the publication of *Sweet Tea* there existed no scholarly treatment of the queer presence at HBCUs.[22] This dearth of scholarship and unwritten history most certainly has to do with a general complicity of silence around homosexuality on these campuses that is in keeping with black respectability politics undergirded by the religious ethos upon which many of these schools were founded. It also has something to do with some students' unwillingness to openly discuss their queer identity for fear of retribution or of being ostracized, as has happened in recent years. For example, in 2002 and 2006, Hampton University administrators denied recognition to a student group called Students Promoting Education Action and Knowledge (SPEAK), whose mission was to be a support group for LGBT students. In 2009 Morehouse passed a dress code that forbids its male students from wearing dresses, high heels, and makeup or carrying purses. These and other examples indicate a hostile environment and, paradoxically, an acknowledgment that there is a queer student presence, but one that must be confined within the boundaries of black respectability. Nonetheless, same-sex encounters at HBCUs became a common theme during my interviews with college-educated black southern gay men; despite the institutions' disapproval and disciplining stance, queer subcultures thrive.

One institution where a queer subculture purportedly flourished, especially in the 1960s and 1970s, is Southern University in Baton Rouge. "D.C.," a retired high school teacher from the Baton Rouge school system, attended Southern and was the school mascot as well as a member of several athletic teams. Now deceased, D.C. was fifty-four at the time of our interview. D.C. recalled his sexual escapades with various athletes and the homosexual culture of Southern during the late 1960s and early 1970s.

> I didn't really associate with gay people at all. I wasn't closeted, but I mean I was an athlete. . . . And my gayness was a private matter. Now, don't get me wrong. I had numerous gay experiences. I mean

plenty. In fact, there wasn't a sport that we had there that I didn't have an athlete that I was having sex with. Seriously. Serious as a heart attack. And it was all good. It was all good. I was student mascot. I traveled with the football team. There were many that were my bedmates. I mean sometimes it got a little complicated because folks would want to fight over me. [. . .] Even in my freshman year I had a roommate football player, and we were lovers. . . . We slept together every night. . . . If I thought about the number of athletes I had at Southern, or just on the football team, golly . . . I'd have to be doing some counting.

In fact, I wasn't gonna say this, but in one day, I had nine athletes. [. . .] And I only had the ninth one because he was supposed to be all of that. And they had all his buddies, this track team out there and they were daring me that I couldn't *handle* him. And so I said, "Shit, why not? One more won't hurt." And he was supposed to have me hollering and I said, "He ain't shit." I said, "That's supposed to be hurting me right there? After eight already, what can you do?" It was a lot of sex going on at Southern, yes indeed.[23]

D.C.'s account provides a glimpse into the sexual lives of black gay men at HBCUs in the South during the late 1960s and early 1970s; it also suggests an active gay subculture among the athletes. The heteronormative mask of masculinity is in keeping with the politics of respectability of black southern culture generally and at HBCUs specifically. Sports and the image of an athletic "man" provided a way for these men to adhere to the expected image of gender, on the one hand, and engage in homo-sex on the other. The close quarters of the athletic dorms provided an easy way to be intimate in ways that would not necessarily call attention to an athlete's gayness. This may be the reason why, at least publicly, D.C. and his teammates disavowed a "gay" identity, while still engaging in explicit gay sex.

The disavowal of a gay identity might also have to do with a more ambivalent relationship to identity politics than white homosexuals had at the time. While the Stonewall Riots of 1969 marked the advent of the LGBT civil rights movement, black queers did not necessarily embrace the identity and visibility politics of that movement. The politics of black respectability was not just a discourse imposed by black middle-class heterosexuals on black queers; there were instances where southern black queers actually were some of the biggest proponents of and adherents to its tenets. Often seen as arbiters of "high culture," southern black queers were rewarded with social clout and monetary gain for not only their contributions to the arts, fashion, and culture in general, but also their ability to be discreet about their sexuality. In turn, then, they were often spared from direct homophobic attacks by fellow blacks. bell hooks, who was born and raised in Kentucky, writes: "Black male homosexuals were often known, were talked about, were seen positively, and played an important role in community life.... Often, acceptance of male homosexuality was mediated by material privilege—that is to say that homosexual men with money were part of the materially privileged ruling black group and were accorded the regard and respect given that group. They were influential people in the community."[24] In his essay "Sissies at the Picnic," Roderick A. Ferguson recounts how his rural Georgian community accepted Edward Larue, a flamboyant gay man with style and flair (but who never named his sexuality), because he prepared the children in the church for the Easter Sunday program.

> He was what Mama and other black women referred to as a "pretty man." He strode down the aisle, limp-wristed with designer sunglasses, fur coat, and two-toned wing-tipped shoes. All of us knew he was "funny"; we had heard our parents say it, but that didn't seem to matter much. For they entrusted him to teach us to talk proper and sing on key. Back then, they seemed to understand that funny or not, he and men like him were part of us—little pieces in the mosaic that made up the neighborhood.[25]

This semiprivileged and protected position within the community ("semi" because the positioning did not fully endow these men with complete subjecthood) described by both hooks and Ferguson offers a more nuanced understanding of why a black queer southerner may not choose to openly identify as gay. It would seem that despite the performance of a range of masculinities—from heteronormative to effete—the *naming* of one's homosexuality was the line across which no one ventured for fear of losing his status as a respectable and good black man. For D.C. and his comrades, the repercussions of such naming might include being suspended from the team, and the loss of their public identities as hypermasculine, heterosexual athletes; for Larue, it might be banishment from the church and the loss of his stature in the community.

The narratives of D.C. and others reflect the complexity of black southern queer identities and demonstrate that regardless of an HBCU's sanctioning of homosexuality, during the 1960s and 1970s gay men created their own communities within a larger black southern student body. Sometimes gay men were (as they are now) incorporated into the fabric of student life at HBCUs, and sometimes they were (and are) cordoned off into their own discrete organizations—as in the sexual subculture of the athletic teams. Whatever the case, as sexual agents, black gay men on historically black college campuses in the South continue to thrive—openly and secretly. In fact, there are currently over a dozen HBCUs that have a student LGBT organization, thanks to a partnership with the Human Rights Campaign (HRC).[26] The experiences of graduates from these and other southern HBCUs suggest that if "a mind is a terrible thing to waste," then neither should one pass up the opportunity to have sex.[27]

Creating and Consuming a Space for HIV/AIDS Prevention

In 2004, many stories appeared in the media about the increased HIV/AIDS infection rate among African American males at HBCUs in the South. These stories coincided with the media frenzy around the down-low phenomenon. Given that black women constitute a majority of new cases of HIV infections among women, men on the DL were seen as a natural source of contagion. One of the people who became known as an "expert" and "recovering" DL brother is J. L. King, who wrote a book, *On the Down Low* (2004), which supposedly exposes the DL "lifestyle" and provides women with a "guide" for how to detect whether their man is on the DL. King's book was a financial success, due in part to his appearance on the *Oprah Winfrey Show*; one of the other guests who appeared on that episode was a young, black gay man by the name of Jonathan Perry, who is HIV-positive and attended Johnson C. Smith University, an HBCU located in Charlotte, North Carolina. Perry represents the face of HIV/AIDS in the South and offers proof that it is not just a disease affecting and infecting older men but also a younger generation.

In 2004 researchers in North Carolina released the results of a study conducted on infection rates among college students between 2000 and 2003. Seventy-three of the eighty-four newly infected male college students were black, "representing 20 percent of the state's new HIV infections among 18- to 30-year-olds."[28] As the *Chicago Tribune* reported, this trend is indicative of a larger picture of infection rates among black southerners.

> While AIDS has declined or leveled off elsewhere in the U.S., cases are rising in the South, according to a [2004] report by the Southern AIDS Coalition, which is made up of health officials in 14 states. Forty percent of the people estimated to be living with AIDS reside in the South, and an estimated 46 percent of new cases occur in the region, according to figures from several sources, including the CDC.[29]

Part of the reason for the rise in HIV infection rates among southern blacks could be the general complicity of silence around black sexuality. Rather than being open and frank about safe sex and prevention, black southerners tend to either remain silent about issues of (homo)sexuality or speak about them in stereotypical euphemisms accorded other health issues: like "sugar" for diabetes or "high blood" for hypertension, the term "sick" is used to signal someone who has AIDS. "R. Dioneaux," one of the narrators in *Sweet Tea*, is particularly strident about this point.

> I mean we can't even call it AIDS. We call it "the ninja." Oh yeah, usually the term for AIDS, "the ninja." Or they'll say, "Oooh, he's siiiick. He's siiiiiiick." And you can tell by the voice inflection, like you know what it is. I mean I'm almost waiting for somebody to say, "He has R-O-L-A-I-D-S." I'm *waiting* for that to come out, but I mean that is what we have here. A lot of dishonesty.[30]

R. Dioneaux's comments reveal his frustration about the silence around HIV/AIDS in the black South but do not tell the entire story. Several of the men I interviewed, some of whom are living with HIV, actively engage in HIV/AIDS prevention. One example is "D. Berry," a forty-seven-year-old Memphis native who has been HIV-positive for over ten years. In his story we discover the ways that black gay men in the South combat HIV/AIDS while remaining sexually active.

> I guess one of my wildest nights was three years ago, Gay Pride in Atlanta, Georgia. I was at Piedmont Park from 11:30 till 7:30 in the morning. That was the wildest thing. [. . .] I had sex with one guy, but the rest of the night, I was mainly just assisting and looking.

[. . .] Giving 'em lube, giving 'em condoms. And then one guy said, "You got one [a condom]?" And I said, "Here's some." [. . .] And he said, "Lube me up, man." And of course, I did, and I watched them screw, and it was just—oooh, there were so many people. And this went on until 7:30 in the morning.

So did you go out to sort of be a, for a lack of a better word, a counselor or, you know, to give people protection? Was that your motivation for going there?

I went out to the club, and I was going to make my way through the Park on the way home, and I went through and I met this guy and we talked and we did what we was gonna do. . . . and I was just trying to find out why everybody was just kind of walking through there and disappearing. So I kind of found a way down through the trails, and I seen it was a group over here and a group over there, and I just had the condoms and I just give 'em to 'em 'cause I always have 'em on me.

'Cause they didn't have them themselves?

If I hadn't been there they probably wasn't gonna use 'em. That was like the wildest time. Like I said, 7:30, it was still sun-up. . . . And there was a guy from Memphis on his knees, just going all the way down this line of all these guys . . . and then I went home. [. . .]

[A] lot of guys that wanna talk to me or approach me for sex, they're mainly young guys. And some of the ones that I went there with, I just kind of sit back and I'm gonna see. You put a condom there, they be like, look at it like it's a foreign object, but I make them use 'em.[31]

D. Berry's story captures the complicated and paradoxical nature of black southern gay men's relation to sex and HIV/AIDS. On the one hand, D. Berry's story buttresses the evidence that suggests that HIV/AIDS awareness and education is diminishing in the South, and that the lack of preventative measures is less about engaging sexual pleasure and more about ignorance. On the other hand, his story also demonstrates, through his own "missionary" work, that when provided with preventative tools—condoms, lube, and so on—most men will use them. Indeed, D. Berry's HIV status does not preclude him from engaging in active promiscuous sex with multiple partners or enjoying being a voyeur. From his perspective, it is not about abstinence or a loss of sexual pleasure, but more about education and prevention

Countess Vivian, D.C., Bob, Larry J., and D. Berry are just a few examples of black gay southerners who "get down" without being on the "down low." While I do not want to disparage a down-low identity, I do want to note that down-low nomenclature is not synonymous with black southern homosexuality, as folks like J. L. King would have it. The full spectrum of homosexuality exists in the South, and its expression is as wide and as varied as the range of black southerners. As Tara McPherson suggests, "[t]he South today is as much fiction... as it is a fixed geographic space."[32] In this regard, black gay men are creating multiple Souths as sexual dissidents and gender nonconformists whose sexuality is shaped not only by the history of race in the region but also by the spaces their queer bodies create and consume. Somewhere between this place as imagined and this place as lived, gay black southern men are getting down on their knees to pray while lifting their heads and their asses to the God who loves them the most.

Notes

1. See my *Sweet Tea*, especially chapter 2, "Church Sissies"; and Griffin, "Their Own Received Them Not." Popular black gay novelist E. Lynn Harris based his 2006 novel, *I Say a Little Prayer*, on the premise of what would happen if all the gays and lesbians in an Atlanta church stayed at home.

2. Richardson, *Black Masculinity and the U.S. South*, 119.

3. See, for example, Cleaver, *Soul on Ice*, 97–101, and Asante, *Afrocentricity*, 57.

4. See Smitherman, *Black Talk*, 94.

5. See Denizet-Lewis, "Living (and Dying) on the Down Low." In 2004 Oprah Winfrey devoted an entire show to the "down-low" phenomenon, while a season 5 episode of *Law and Order: SVU*, "Low Down," chronicled the life of a black lawyer who was secretly having an affair with another man, contracted HIV, and infected his wife.

6. Johnson, *Sweet Tea*, 485.

7. Long, *Great Southern Babylon*, 1.

8. Camp, *Closer to Freedom*, 61.

9. Johnson, *Sweet Tea*, 258–59.

10. See Fellows, *Farm Boys*.

11. Ahmed, *Queer Phenomenology*, 1

12. Ibid., 9.

13. Johnson, *Sweet Tea*, 280–81.

14. "Trade" is slightly different in meaning from "down-low" men in that trade typically get money or another material object in exchange for allowing the homosexual partner to perform oral sex or receive oral sex—literally, the sex act is "traded" for something. Down-low men, on the other hand, typically have an emotional attachment to the same sex that motivates their sexual intimacy; sexual encounters are also not structured around strict adherence to who gives and receives oral and anal sex. On trade, see Humphreys, *Tearoom Trade*, and for a discussion of down-low behavior, see McCune, "Out in da Club."

15. Camp, *Closer to Freedom*, 61.
16. See "The Y: Yesterday, Today, Tomorrow . . . for Good."
17. See Garibaldi, *Black Colleges and Universities*.
18. See Patton, "Perspectives on Identity," 1.
19. Higginbotham, *Righteous Discontent*, 187.
20. See Bederman, *Manliness and Civilization*.
21. See Gibbs, *Above Our Heads*.
22. See Shand-Tucci, *The Crimson Letter*, and Patton, "Perspectives on Identity, Disclosure, and the Campus Environment." Also, in May 2011, Spelman College held the first-ever summit on the topic of LGBT issues at HBCUs. See http://rodonline.typepad.com/rodonline/2011/05/spelman-hosts-first-ever-lgbt-summit-for-historically-black-colleges.html, accessed on August 11, 2011.
23. Johnson, *Sweet Tea*, 287–91.
24. hooks, *Talking Back*, 121.
25. Ferguson, "Sissies at the Picnic," 191–92.
26. HRC launched this outreach program in 2002 to transform the environment of HBCUs for LGBT students and in response to growing violence on these campuses.
27. The motto of the United Negro College Fund is "A mind is a terrible thing to waste."
28. "Black Colleges Seek to Stem HIV Cases: Stepping Up Safe-Sex Education after Spike in Infections," *MSNBC*, March 22, 2004, http://www.msnbc.msn.com/id/4556054/, accessed on August 14, 2011.
29. Dahleen Glanton, "Emerging Face of HIV: Fear of Discovery Adds to Burden," *Chicago Tribune Online*, March 30, 2004, http://chicagotribune.com/news/local/chi0403280353, accessed on August 13, 2011.
30. Johnson, *Sweet Tea*, 377.
31. Ibid., 319–20.
32. McPherson, *Reconstructing Dixie*, 1.

Works Cited

Ahmed, Sarah. *Queer Phenomenology: Orientations, Objects, Others*. Durham: Duke University Press, 2006.
Asante, Molefi. *Afrocentricity*. Trenton, NJ: Africa World Press, 1988.

Bederman, Gail. *Manliness and Civilization: A Cultural History of Gender and Race in the United States, 1880–1917*. Chicago: University of Chicago Press, 1996.

Camp, Stephanie M. H. *Closer to Freedom: Enslaved Women & Everyday Resistance in the Plantation South*. Chapel Hill: University of North Carolina Press, 2004.

Cleaver, Eldridge. *Soul on Ice*. New York: Laurel, 1968.

Denizet-Lewis, Benoit. "Living (and Dying) on the Down Low: Double Lives, AIDS and the Black Homosexual Underground." *New York Times Magazine*, August 3, 2003: 29–33, 48, 52–53.

Fellows, Will. *Farm Boys: Lives of Gay Men from the Rural Midwest*. Madison: University of Wisconsin Press, 2001.

Ferguson, Roderick A. "Sissies at the Picnic: The Subjugated Knowledges of a Black Rural Queer." In *Feminist Waves, Feminist Generations: Life Stories from the Academy*, edited by Hokulani K. Aikau, Karla A. Erickson, and Jennifer L. Pierce, 188–96. Minneapolis: University of Minnesota Press, 2007.

Garibaldi, Antonio, ed. *Black Colleges and Universities: Challenges for the Future*. New York: Praeger, 1984.

Gibbs, Spencer C. *Above Our Heads: The Making of a Morehouse Man*. New York: Hamilton House, 1999.

Griffin, Horace. "Their Own Received Them Not: African American Lesbians and Gays in Black Churches." In *The Greatest Taboo: Homosexuality in Black Communities*, edited by Delroy Constantine-Simms, 110–21. New York: Alyson Books, 2001.

Higginbotham, Evelyn Brooks. *Righteous Discontent: The Women's Movement in the Black Baptist Church, 1880–1920*. Cambridge: Harvard University Press, 1993.

hooks, bell. *Talking Back: Thinking Feminist, Thinking Black*. Boston: South End Press, 1989.

Humphreys, Laud. *Tearoom Trade: Impersonal Sex in Public Spaces*. Rev. and enlarged. New York: Aldine de Gruyter, 1975.

Johnson, E. Patrick. *Sweet Tea: Black Gay Men of the South—An Oral History*. Chapel Hill: University of North Carolina Press, 2008.

King, J. L. *On the Down Low: A Journey into the Lives of "Straight" Black Men Who Sleep with Men*. New York: Harlem Moon Press, 2004.

Long, Alecia P. *The Great Southern Babylon: Sex, Race, and Respectability in New Orleans 1865–1920*. Baton Rouge: Louisiana State University Press, 2004.

McCune, Jeffrey Q. "Out in da Club: The Down Low, Hip-Hop, and the Architexture of Black Masculinity." *Text and Performance Quarterly* 28, no. 3 (2008): 298–314.

McPherson, Tara. *Reconstructing Dixie: Race, Gender, and Nostalgia in the Imagined South*. Durham: Duke University Press, 2003.

Patton, Lori D. "Perspectives on Identity, Disclosure, and the Campus Environment among African American Gay and Bisexual Men at One Historically Black College." *Journal of College Student Development* 52, no. 1 (2011): 77–100.

Richardson, Riché. *Black Masculinity and the U.S. South: From Uncle Tom to Gangsta*. Athens: University of Georgia Press, 2007.

Rose, Alecia. *Storyville, New Orleans: Being an Authentic, Illustrated Account of the Notorious Red-Light District*. Tuscaloosa: University of Alabama Press, 1974.

Shand-Tucci, Douglass. *The Crimson Letter: Harvard, Homosexuality, and the Shaping of American Culture*. New York: St. Martin's Griffin, 2004.

Smitherman, Geneva. *Black Talk: Words and Phrases from the Hood to the Amen Corner*. New York: Houghton Mifflin, 1994.

West, Cornel. "Christian Love and Heterosexism." In *The Cornel West Reader*. New York: Basic Civitas Books, 1999.

"The Y: Yesterday, Today, Tomorrow . . . for Good." http://www.ymca.net/history/. Accessed on August 11, 2011.

5

Serpents in the Garden

Historic Preservation, Climate Change, and the Postsouthern Plantation

MICHAEL P. BIBLER

Recent critical analysis of "postsouthern" literature has revealed the ways many southern writers since the 1960s self-reflexively challenge and parody the ability of any text to represent the "real" regional space(s) it describes. Instead of pretending it is possible to depict the South mimetically, postsouthern literature knowingly (de)constructs regional identity by foregrounding images, tropes, signs, and intertextual references to what Scott Romine calls "previous imitations of place," thereby emphasizing how any understanding of "the South" and its supposed "sense of place" is inevitably created and consumed through texts.[1]

Problematically, however, postsouthernism's world of surfaces and signs can distract readers from the physical, economic, and material actualities of the southern landscape. Martyn Bone argues that while "postsouthern parody is valuable precisely because it emphasizes the extent to which the *southern* past, and southern place, have been defined primarily through literary mediations or 'images' . . . we must pay attention to the historical-geographical, material reproduction of place as real estate, and the creation, destruction, and mediation of place under capitalism generally."[2] Critics working in the field of ecocriticism make similar arguments by stressing the need to understand the tensions and connections between figurative representations of the (post-) South's natural environment, and ecological realities of climate, temperature, plant life, soil quality, and animal habitat. Christopher Rieger reminds us, "Nature is at once a cultural construct and an external reality not fully contained by human constructions," while Anthony Wilson argues that scholars who exclusively foreground signs, tropes, and "ideas" of the southern environment, instead of considering the role of natural phenomena "as dialogic participants in cultural definition," risk "occluding [nature's] significance in the formation and evolution of multiple Southern cultures."[3]

Following this ecocritical approach, this essay explores the tensions between environmentalist and postsouthern literary concepts of "place" in Scott Elliott's *Coiled in the Heart* (2003). Set outside the fictional city of Haven, Tennessee, Elliott's novel presents two interlocking narratives. The first, told in flashback, follows Tobia Caldwell's growth from childhood to maturity as he tries to come to terms with his role in the death of another boy, his new neighbor Ben Wilson, when he was seven. Jealous of Ben, the young Tobia tricked him into reaching into the nest of a cottonmouth water moccasin hidden in the stream between their houses. Over the years Tobia's guilt becomes compounded by the intense love that grows between him and Ben's sister Merritt. The novel's second narrative involves Tobia and his father's scheme to reclaim and restore forty acres of land surrounding their ancestral plantation home, "the Grand Old Caldwell Place," which was a large slave plantation originally built in 1798 but is now surrounded and threatened by the suburban sprawl outside Haven.[4] Under the corporate name "Rollback Inc.," Tobia and his father are purchasing and demolishing the suburban homes that have encroached onto the former grounds of the now much-diminished family estate. Part of their motivation is to salvage some of their family's two-hundred-year-old legacy; however, they also have an environmentalist agenda and intend to open most of the former plantation's land as a public park. Tobia summarizes this aspect of their plan in a speech to Rollback's benefactors, describing "the value of green spaces, oxygen-producing trees," and declaring "what a tragedy it would be to lose them altogether in our mad, greedy push to cover the globe in strip complexes and individually owned demi-urban bungalows, to bury the earth in asphalt and steel" (255).

However, Tobia becomes increasingly aware that Rollback cannot realistically stop the spread of sprawl and begins to imagine ways of offsetting the sprawl's physical and cultural homogenization of the southern landscape by creating a permanent niche of native trees and grasslands. His tactic is to rebrand the Caldwell Place as a site of historic preservation. The Caldwells seek to stem the capitalist development (and destruction) of their family homestead by tapping into contemporary consumers' taste for southern heritage tourism. However, the ironies involved in re-creating "historical" images of the Old South to preserve a putatively "natural" South for future re-creation become increasingly apparent to readers of *Coiled in the Heart,* and to Tobia himself. One obvious flaw in the plan is that Tobia's father imagines restoring the land to a "native greenery" (255) that existed only *prior* to the creation of the Caldwells' slave plantation, as if slavery had never been. Rollback's conceptual and political problems are inextricably linked to the Caldwell plantation's legacies of slavery and racism, and increasingly they inform Tobia's own doubts about the plan.

Ultimately, Elliott does not propose any single, easy solution to the environmental ironies and issues raised in *Coiled in the Heart.* However, the novel still reminds us that any critical examination of these problems requires us to reinsert the southern environment into debates about postsouthernism's world of floating signifiers. Moreover, when postsouthernism becomes entangled with the plantation myth, as it does in Elliott's novel, then closer attention to the natural environment becomes all the more crucial for avoiding the regressive politics of the southern past. Indeed, I conclude this chapter by extrapolating outward from the novel's meditations on the significance of place to stress the urgency of confronting the real, material threats to southern nature that the critical discourse of postsouthernism has so far tended to ignore: environmental degradation and climate change. Despite the serious dangers that climate change poses to the South, it also presents a powerful opportunity to reconnect the physical and symbolic landscapes of the (post-) South, and imagine an environmentally progressive future for the region.

Postsouthern Agrarianism

In *Coiled in the Heart,* Tobia's challenge to capitalism's transformation of southern spaces coincides with his persistent anxiety about the authenticity of southern identity. This anxiety is especially evident in his description of the sprawl around him, what he calls the "chain of chains" crisscrossing the nation.

> I drove to work every weekday morning . . . a distance of about twenty miles that used to be farm and woodland and is now covered, without a break, by the concrete, chromium, glass and neon chain of chains. . . . [I]t used to occur to me on certain mornings and nights

that if it were possible to transport someone seamlessly, in a millisecond, and without warning to another chain of chains in another American city a thousand miles or more away and this person were asked to identify, quickly, where he was, gauging only from the collection of shopsigns he could see out the car window, he would have not the slightest idea where he was. (80–81)

In Tobia's view, whatever was unique about the region's natural landscape and its culture has been replaced with national and global franchises. Where references to the South remain, they are even more distressing to Tobia because they seem to parody the notion of regional authenticity, as in the gay-owned restaurant "Dan 'n Dave's," whose owners are a couple also named Dan and Dave: "[The] restaurant's sign and logo (a silhouette of two buckskin-clad pioneers holding hands) suggest a fictional homosexual union between Daniel Boone and Davy Crockett" (53). When Tobia notes that this controversial image of Boone and Crockett has "created a rift in the usual place," he means the rift between people who enjoy the restaurant's ironic take on heteronormative masculinity and those who despise it. However, he might as well mean the rift in "place" itself: Dan 'n Dave's is a site where the figures of Tennessee's pioneers have become denaturalized signifiers of a culture available for consumption on all levels, not least in the dishes offered on the restaurant's menu. Dan 'n Dave's signposts the territory of the postsouthern, where anything that announces itself as "southern" is ultimately a simulacrum. Tobia readily understands that it's "all in good fun, and . . . layered thickly in irony," yet he still finds the restaurant "a little unsettling for its out-of-control mock-authenticity" and admits that it "embarrasses" him (53).

To counteract the "unsettling" feeling created by postsouthernism's "mock-authenticity," as well as the fear that Rollback might be just as inauthentic as Dan 'n Dave's—a fear that is evident throughout the novel, though never stated explicitly—Tobia tries to conjure a South, as well as a southern identity for himself, that dodges the forces of consumption by staying rooted in nature.

> I wanted to learn to properly love the land I felt I should have known so much better than I did. I vowed to rediscover, for myself, the broken connection between the production and consumption of food. I would plant a garden; I would get some chickens and a cow, some pigs. . . . I was . . . feeling the gnaw of a colossal emptiness. I

wanted to take up my own lost cause, to make an eddy for myself against . . . the overhyped myth of progress. (82)

Tobia's struggle against the "emptiness" he feels at the heart of the "overhyped myth of progress" offers another allusion to the book's title, which comes from a key passage in Jean-Paul Sartre's *Being and Nothingness*: "Nothingness lies coiled in the heart of being—like a worm."[5] Anxious about this "emptiness" and the "broken connection" between production and consumption, Tobia imagines a form of salvation in returning to an agrarian past. He reiterates this desire when scorning honky-tonk singer Buck Kelly's claim to be "pure redneck," because Buck has "never worked on the land": "I feel like reminding Buck and everyone else at the table that the original rednecks were yeoman farmers, beloved of Jefferson, gracefully, artfully living close to the land. . . . I want to let them know this is my lost cause—to die as Tobia-Yeoman-Farmer" (163). Tobia's use of the phrase "lost cause" in the last two quoted passages exposes his own investment in a particular mythology of the South. Yet his attempts to *literalize* this image of the South by restoring the countryside and building a subsistence farm with his father also suggest that the material dimensions of his plan are something more than strictly mythological.

Ironically, Tobia's reading habits underscore this idea that working with the land encompasses more than the reproduction and consumption of culture in the form of tropes and signs. His library includes "all the works of Wendell Berry, *I'll Take My Stand* among others" (75). Of course, as writers and readers rather than actual farmers, the original "Twelve Southerners" were often accused of being merely academic or armchair Agrarians. Moreover, Berry's political ideas about race and southern regionalism do not neatly line up with the Twelve Southerners' politics, despite their shared interest in agricultural life. Nevertheless, we recognize that Tobia would be drawn to *I'll Take My Stand* and Berry's books because of their meditations on the moral and environmental benefits of finding a balance between industrial society and an agrarian self-sufficiency that cannot be wholly commodified.[6] Yet, by taking this idea of the yeoman farmer from a southern intellectual and literary tradition spanning (though by no means seamlessly) from Jefferson to Berry, "Tobia-Yeoman-Farmer" is no less self-consciously immersed in (and manipulative of) selective signs and stories of "southernness" than are the owners of Dan 'n Dave's. Still, by planting trees and rebuilding the farm, Tobia is doing more than just performing and projecting a virtual image. Put another way, he seeks to go beyond Buck Kelly's performative, stylized version of the redneck by reconnecting with the land and a lived experience of agrarianism. Here the novel reminds us that physical interaction with nature cannot be simulated. The Caldwells' plan to remake the plantation into an environmental haven is an attempt to recover some of the materiality of place and to revalorize it as something that cannot be completely mediated through language, culture, or commodification.

Elliott signals this gap between nature and cultural mediations of nature in a lesson Tobia learns about the difference between a snake and a serpent. Once out of college, Tobia starts working with a herpetologist named Henley Dempster, who tells him:

> A snake is just an animal—a slithering, cold-blooded reptile.... But a *serpent*, now, a *serpent* is more than just a snake. The serpent has greater meaning.... Snakes become serpents through the stories we tell. They become serpents when they're given a cultural depth, the symbolism and extra po-tency [sic] we weave for them—myth, legend, folktale, religion, sign, symbol.... We cannot see the snake without it suggesting something of the serpent. (191)

Elliott here parses the difference between the material elements of nature and the layers of cultural signification attached to these elements. The natural *snake* and the cultural *serpent* can never be fully separated, yet there is also much to be gained by learning to distinguish between them, as in Tobia and Henley's slow discovery of an antitoxin to the venom of cottonmouths—something that could obviously never be gleaned from a cultural study of serpents.

Southern Environmental Exceptionalism

Elliott's exploration of the gaps and inconsistencies between nature and culture can be extended from snakes to the complex entity we call "the South" by considering nature's influence on the creation of southern cultures since the days of European colonialism. Lewis P. Simpson maps a long tradition of southern exceptionalism that is grounded in the natural environment, beginning with colonial writers who portrayed the South as a natural "paradise" and imagined the colonists participating in a divine "errand" to cultivate, perfect, and exploit the fruits of this fertile landscape. J. V. Ridgely echoes this narrative of history, arguing that European settlers in the southern colonies demonstrated an "exuberance" about southern nature and established "a strong agrarian point of view" in their writing that contrasts fundamentally with the Puritan settlers' portrayal of New England as a "wilderness."[7] This exceptionalist equation between the South and nature has shaped much of the canon of southern writing right up to the present, mainly in the form of nostalgic pastoral literature but also in the shape of the southern "anti-pastoral."[8] However, southern environmental exceptionalism is perhaps nowhere more clearly expressed than in historian U. B. Phillips' *Life and Labor in the Old South* (1929). Philips begins the book by linking every component of southern history and culture back to the distinctiveness of the region's "weather," where the heat and humidity "fostered the cultivation of the staple crops, which promoted the plantation system, which brought the importation of negroes, which not only gave rise to chattel slavery but created a lasting race problem. These led to controversy and regional rivalry for power, which produced apprehensive reactions and culminated in a stroke for independence. Thus we have . . . the Confederate States of America."[9] For Phillips, the southern climate is the lone spark igniting the entire evolution of southern history and identity.

Phillips failed to subject this exceptionalist narrative to substantial critical scrutiny. Yet precisely because it is oversimplified, his account best reveals how a nature-centered version of southern exceptionalism elides the actual complexities of southern landscapes and climate zones. Indeed, for all the South's reputation (and narration) as an idyllic and temperate place, recurring droughts, hurricanes, floods, fires, and extreme heat can quickly make the southern environment difficult and inhospitable. For example, scientific data gathered from tree rings in 1998 have revealed that when the English established the Roanoke colony in 1585, they did so in the midst of the worst drought to affect the region in the last eight hundred years. When settlers established Jamestown in 1607, very nearly succumbing to the same fate as their Roanoke predecessors, they did so during a seven-year drought that turned out to be the worst in 770 years.[10] This is inauspicious timing, to be sure, but it also serves to emphasize how, despite all scientific evidence to the contrary, even the very first European narratives about the place we now call "the South" selectively glorified the climate as a positive force conducive to colonization.

Early in the region's colonial history, white writers tried to craft a symbolic image of the environment that the actual environment sometimes exposed as limited or false. Discussing William Bartram's 1791 description of the Georgia Sea Islands, Monique Allewaert demonstrates how, "in spite of [Bartram's] effort to describe the southern lowlands as a temperate space, the tropical, the useless, and the cataclysmic continually set him off course." However, those difficult regional ecologies also contributed to resistant identities and communities among enslaved Africans and their descendants: "Plantations did not offer an abstract nature that could be made into symbols for revolution; rather, their ecology contributed to revolution."[11] Like Allewaert, Jon Smith argues that the South shares much in common with the Caribbean by "resist[ing] figurations of identity-bestowing American 'wilderness' simply because it is *hot*: swampy, snaky, roiling with deadly, engulfing agency." Although Smith comes dangerously close to asserting a different kind of southern exceptionalism based on the region's liminal position between northern and tropical climes, he reveals how southern writing often tries to come to terms with these contradictory ideas attached to the physical landscape. Smith notes that "one often finds in U.S. southern literature . . . a certain stammering as it attempts to negotiate between the discourses" usually associated with "American" ideologies on the one side and "Caribbean" ideologies on the other: "spirit and body, mountains and coast, temperate and tropical, sublime global-northern wilderness and marvelously real global-southern jungle."[12] The tropical elements of the southern environment not only disrupt attempts to create an exceptionalist model of the "American South"; they also facilitate the creation of alternative cultures and alternative Souths. Smith's chapter in this volume builds on this consideration of the material and political factors that undercut exceptionalist notions of (post)southern literatures and cultures. Though he does not dwell on environmental factors, there are many ways that our critiques of postsouthern cultural consumption are aligned.

Historian A. Cash Koeniger's influential essay "Climate and Southern Distinctiveness" offers a compelling example of the value of paying greater attention to the complex interplay between the material actualities of southern spaces and discursive representations of (post)southern cultures. Drawing from an interdisciplinary range of scholarly research, Koeniger avoids Phillips' environmental determinism and essentialism while still showing how "climate has played a larger role in shaping southern distinctiveness than contemporary historians are prone to acknowledge." While Koeniger is careful not to claim that climate has directly determined "a distinctive southern personality type," he charts a number of ways that climate has helped shape mannerisms and behavior patterns long identified in U.S. culture as distinctly "southern." He explains how the South's patterns of warm and cold weather typically affect human physiology and psychology, how the South's heat and humidity have caused "indirect pathological consequences" by spreading diseases, and how the warm seasons have historically influenced farming, industry, urban development, and leisure activities.[13] It is hard to deny Koeniger's fundamental claim that some elements of culture can be seen as responses to, or perhaps, rather, outgrowths of, the micro- and macro-environments in the geographic place we call "the South."

The ties between contemporary southern cultures and the environment are harder to identify, not least because air conditioning and climate control have radically changed southerners' daily interactions with the natural world. Historian Raymond Arsenault famously argued that when air conditioning "engulfed" the South between the 1950s and the mid-1970s, it significantly diminished the region's cultural specificity. In Arsenault's view air conditioning brought changes to health, life expectancy, education, architecture, business, and population, especially the massive influx of nonsoutherners; and these changes, combined with other historical forces, effected "the erosion of several regional traditions," particularly southern folkways: "In escaping the heat and humidity, southerners have weakened the bond between humanity and the natural environment. In the process, they have lost some of what made them interesting and distinctive."[14] As Koeniger saw it, however, air conditioning's cultural impact has been minimal: "[O]ne suspects that most of climate's cultural consequences will persist to some degree, as customs or habits, into the age of climate control. Originally produced, at least in part, by physical environment, they have become part of the cultural environment. They have evolved into folkways that are taught by example."[15]

Both Arsenault and Koeniger invoke fairly monolithic and stereotypical versions of southern culture that flatten the differences between subregional, racial, class, and gendered formations of community and identity. But what is most revealing is their agreement that, after World War II, separation from the natural environment became a dominant characteristic in the definition of southern culture itself. Put another way, these two articles suggest that there is a striking historical context connecting postsouthern literature's emphasis on the immateriality of culture with the change in how southerners have interacted with the physical environment since the second half of the twentieth century. In a world of climate control, it makes sense that southern writers became increasingly skeptical about the concept of place and the very notion of the real. Yet as these histories of environmental influence remind us, the material realities of place can never be wholly disregarded. Postsouthernism is by no means the fatal, final outcome of the South's "surrender" to climate control. Nor is the natural environment something that can only be imagined nostalgically as a "place" that has been derealized or deterritorialized in postsouthern culture. Instead, as I argue below, as long as parts of the region continue to be affected by major droughts and hurricanes, it becomes abundantly, tragically clear that the physical nature of place still matters.

The Plantation vs. Climate Change

Elliott's inclusion of the plantation within a simultaneously postsouthern and ecocritical literary project is fairly unique. Although Tobia self-consciously echoes some of Berry's ideas in his embrace of subsistence farming and the figure of the yeoman farmer, the foundations of Rollback are decidedly more aristocratic, because they depend on the preservation of the plantation at the park's center. As Tobia's father exclaims at the "reclamation party" celebrating the project's move into its final stage, "We *will* be keeping the house and the acreage that has been in our family for the better part of two hundred years. . . . The rest will be, as I said, a park for everyone to use, regardless of race, color, or creed" (257). The environmentalism of their project is less a model of activism and more an example of historic preservation, the creation of an oasis nestled in the postsouthern sprawl of Haven, Tennessee. Furthermore, despite their quasi philanthropy in letting anyone use the park, the Caldwell men cling to an old model of white proprietorship that limits the social and ecological impact of their experiment. Their plan is inherently reactionary, because they restrict their environmentalism to a mere forty acres instead of imagining a change in the lives of all the other inhabitants of this postsouthern world.

Here *Coiled in the Heart* also differs from other recent texts that try to balance ecological awareness with an exploration of southern whiteness: most notably, Larry Brown's *Joe* (1991) and Janisse Ray's *Ecology of a Cracker Childhood* (1999), which both focus on environmental issues linked to white southern poverty. In his analysis of these books, Jay Watson concludes that "any conservationist ethos worthy of the name in the South must include the pursuit of economic justice for the many casualties of the region's extractive industries and exploitive labor arrangements."[16] However, rather than judging Elliott's novel by Watson's standards, it is crucial that we understand the anxieties and doubts that Tobia struggles with as he strives to preserve his family plantation. Elliott is ultimately trying to consider the possibilities for southern environmentalism from a different perspective than Brown, Ray, and even Berry. His focus on the limitations embedded within that different perspective is what makes his novel especially rich for an ecocritical analysis.

What gives Tobia most trouble is the legacy of his family's slaveowning past. His mind stalls every time he tries to confront it.

> Even in my grandfather Thomas's day, when my father grew up here, there were a thousand acres. Still longer ago, our ancestors planted cotton and hemp. They had an overseer to look after hundreds of slaves. This still amazes me. There were slaves here. Sometimes, walking the property I feel their presence and hear their whispers and remember that it was not long ago in the course of time, that they lived and worked and suffered here. . . . It's difficult to believe; there were humans working this land for my ancestors who my ancestors thought they owned. Here. On this land. Not all that long ago. My thinking goes only so far before awe hits rewind. (51)

The significance of this passage lies in the presentation of slavery's unresolved legacy as an impasse that traps Tobia's thought processes in a circular loop. We also see Tobia's emotional and mental paralysis regarding his family's history of slave ownership at the reclamation party, when his speech is interrupted by a Native American activist, John Redbear, and the head of the local branch of the National Association for the Advancement of Colored People (NAACP), Brandon Campbell, who challenge the Caldwells to "go all the way," beyond preservation to reparations, by giving the land back to either the Indians or the descendants of the Caldwell slaves (255). Tobia's father becomes defiant, but Tobia freezes with conflicting responses.

I'm torn, afraid to say anything at all. Afraid if I open my mouth I'll say something drastic like, "Yes, take the land. It's yours. You're right. Tear down our house. You, John, were here first. If we believe the current thinking, your people lived as peaceful stewards of the land. And you, Brandon, your people were taken from your African homeland and brought here to work the land without pay for the great profit of my ancestors while they stood by sipping whiskey. You deserve it. Yes. Have it." On the other hand, I'm equally concerned I'll hear myself say something out of character like, "Off our land! Get trucking! Both of you! Out of my line of sight before my daddy and I whup the living shit out of you like our ancestors did before us and you know good and well we still can! This ain't no university! Now get before we put shot in your tails!" (256–57)

Although Elliott acknowledges the crimes of the southern past and their continuing influence on the present, Tobia's ambivalent reactions are extreme, as the odd change in his dialect suggests. However, instead of having Tobia either succumb to white guilt or embrace an aggressive form of white pride, Elliott chooses to foreground the stalemate between Tobia's conflicted feelings. For Tobia, the South either is a future of postsouthern environmental degradation and endless sprawl or involves hitting the rewind button—undertaking small, reactionary projects that, in trying to roll back time, become implicated in a history of inequality, trauma, and shame. Elliott wants readers of Tobia's narrative to see the problems inherent in both ways of thinking.

Tobia's inability to move past his family's involvement in the histories of southern oppression is more than just a personal failing that echoes his guilt over Ben Wilson's death as a child. He also finds it impossible to make Rollback socially and politically neutral because of the ideologies of race and individualism that are inextricably linked to the southern plantation. One major flaw of this project derives from the enduring "proprietary ideal" that Bone, following Paul Conkin, identifies at the heart of the Agrarians' "sense of place." This proprietary ideal privileges private ownership of the land and compromises the Agrarians' presentation of southern place as "a rural, self-sufficient and nigh-on precapitalist locus focused upon the small farm, operating largely outside the cash nexus, and absent large-scale land speculation."[17] Elliott tries to get around this tension between capitalist proprietorship and precapitalist agrarianism by portraying the redesigned Caldwell estate as something that exists within, rather than purely in opposition to, a postmodern capitalist economy. But in doing so, Elliott only reveals how impossible it is to untangle the connections between the capitalist proprietary ideal and the romanticization of southern "place." The plantation's park space is meant to offer a temporary refuge for anyone hoping to escape the sprawl, yet Tobia has funded this project through his early investments in Pinkmellon Computers, making the project hopelessly complicit with what it is meant to counteract. Moreover, Tobia is clear that the Caldwell Place will never become a place that belongs to everyone.

There are further problems tied to Tobia's plantation-based proprietary ideal. First, Tobia's conflation of the Caldwell plantation with the farm model ignores the discrepancies between the two agricultural systems—discrepancies that dogged the Agrarian project that Tobia seeks to emulate.[18] Second, historian Lynn A. Nelson has shown that even when southern planters tried to practice environmental conservation on larger plantations, those efforts always served "the white male [land owner's] desire for personal autonomy." Nelson shows that while "[i]nvesting in conservation proved to be a sound business and ecological strategy," most planters abandoned agricultural reforms because of "their dream of possessive individualism—to live independent, prosperous, and secure on their own farms."[19] The ideal of living self-sufficiently on the plantation—especially with a self-contained workforce of slaves and then tenants—limited planters' willingness and ability to invest in larger programs meant to fix ecological problems such as soil erosion that extended beyond the boundaries of their individually owned estates. The possessive individualism at the heart of the planter's identity was a barrier to ecological sustainability, because environmentalism requires wider human collaboration in a space far larger than one fenced-in plantation. By dressing up the restored plantation as a park, Tobia's Rollback does nothing to jettison such possessive individualism, or proprietary idealism. While Elliott tries to consider how the unresolved legacies of Native displacement and African slavery undercut Tobia's venture, the historic preservation of the plantation remains deeply problematic, because it implicitly preserves a pre–Civil War form of whiteness defined by individual ownership of private property and mastery over the land (and people). As an attempt to preserve a version of the southern past rooted in nature, Rollback precludes the kind of progressivism that would realistically ameliorate post-southern sprawl or aid the creation of a more equitable and just society.

On another level, the conceptual and political impasses that Tobia faces stem from the *figurative* construction of the plantation as the cornerstone of southern regionalism. As Simpson explains, planters readily incorporated chattel slavery into their conception of the Anglo-European "errand into paradise." Although they acknowledged fears that slavery posed a threat to the social order, Simpson shows how planters insisted on "the metaphor of the plantation as a pastoral social order, in which the chattel is the gardener."[20] Writers in the post–Civil War South elevated this image of the plantation-as-garden into a full-blown mythology, as Lucinda H. MacKethan explains: "Through the works of writers like Joel Chandler Harris and Thomas Nelson Page, the Old South received new life; the plantation regime was vindicated and its pleasant rural peace held up as an alternative to the confusion of the materialistic New South."[21] Although Elliott tries to avoid the reactionary politics of Harris and Page, MacKethan's description could just as easily refer to his text as to theirs. This similarity suggests that the problems in Tobia's plan stem as much from *literary* models of the plantation as they do from historical ones. If Tobia must confront the ideologies of race and private property that undermine his attempt to remake the plantation into a place of natural preservation, Elliott as author must confront the figurative tropes and literary precedents that challenge his efforts to use the plantation to imagine a new form of agrarianism for the postmodern South.

This literary-historical dilemma becomes most apparent at the novel's end, when Tobia considers different possible futures for himself and Merritt, who is about to reenter his life after a long separation. One alternative that he imagines is living a heroic life with Merritt in "some desert hellzone" where they are "made strong by the way people need us." Another is to remain "on the Old Caldwell Place going backward, learning to be agrarian, to be yeoman farmers" (292). But the possibility he finds most alluring is making "a clean break and a new start far away from the old house and its ghosts. . . . We could go away and never come back like couples in nineteenth-century Romantic poems. . . . Or maybe it's just me on the road, speeding away from everyone, everything here. Clean slate. The final incarnation—Tobia-the-Cleansed-of-Past? Now would be the time" (292–93). These metafictional fantasies are seductive yet still problematic, because they are such blatantly *literary* endings: even the wildest notion of freedom is mediated by previous fictions.[22]

Ultimately, however, Elliott's goal is not to construct a utopian vision of the future so much as to explore the various pitfalls involved in any attempt to strike a balance between southern ecologies and postsouthern models of literature and culture. Consequently, he avoids imposing any narrative closure and concludes *Coiled in the Heart* with an open-ended suggestion of natural catastrophe. In the novel's last line, Tobia's reunion with Merritt becomes blurred with the suggestion that an earthquake is under way: "We each take a step toward the other. A shudder runs through the earth" (293). Here, besides the cliché of feeling the earth moved by love, Elliott is referring back to scenes from earlier in the novel in which characters invoke the potential recurrence of earthquake activity along the New Madrid fault that runs through Tennessee. An elderly friend of the Caldwell family, Fenton Monroe, is obsessed with the New Madrid earthquakes of 1811 and 1812, the latter of which was one of the largest earthquakes ever recorded in the contiguous United States, creating new lakes in Tennessee and even changing the course of the Mississippi River. Fenton is convinced that the next big quake is due at any moment. Moreover, as Merritt signals a new possibility for Tobia to leave his family's past behind—to form a romantic partnership that goes against the script of family loyalty and the traditional structure of southern plantation fiction, in which the heir of the plantation moves his new bride into the ancestral home—the earthquake operates as a metaphor for a final rupturing of southern environmental exceptionalism that, as I have shown, is itself a cultural fiction. The earthquake represents a violent way to move beyond the stalemates and impasses tied to the southern past by leveling them and forcing a new start. Unable to resolve the different interpretations of the past's relationship to the present, Elliott utilizes the earthquake as a third possibility: a natural deus ex machina that might just break the tendency of Tobia (and white southerners more generally) to keep turning back to a romantic vision of a pastoral past.

However, considered in more historicist terms, an earthquake is hardly the best way of signaling a sudden rupture with the southern past. The novel suggests that fixing the South's cultural wrongs requires a change in our understanding of southern nature, because nature was exploited to support the possessive individualism of plantation whiteness and the violent injustices of slavery and racism. Yet the history of the New Madrid fault indicates that a new quake would not force the radical reconceptualization of nature that Elliott seems to hope for. While people would still have to renegotiate their relationship to a changed landscape, the earthquake would not change nature itself; it would not keep people from reclaiming and rebuilding the older mythologies of the southern garden, as suggested by the fact that the Grand Old Caldwell Place survived the first quake and, according to Fenton, will surely survive another one. The earthquake might drain a lake or flatten a suburb, but "the South" as a cultural entity will likely endure much as it was before. Still, a change to the physical environment of southern nature itself—or at least the threat of a change—might open new possibilities for breaking the ties between nature and southern exceptionalism. If it were possible to change the idea of the "southern garden" from something beautiful and constant to something fragile and endangered—threatened not only by capitalism but also by climate change—then we might be able to find a new conceptualization of nature that, following Elliott's suggestion, could move us beyond both reactionary neo-Agrarianism and the creative destruction of postsouthern sprawl.

The threat of climate change has already become evident over the last two decades. In 2006, to accommodate rising average temperatures, the Arbor Day Foundation redrew the U.S. Department of Agriculture's 1990 map of hardiness zones for plants (figure 5.1). Based on average annual minimum temperatures, these zones explain what kinds of plants can thrive in the ground throughout the year. The difference between the two maps is thus important to gardeners, but it also carries symbolic importance. For example, the new map tells us that the southern magnolia can now survive as far north as southern Pennsylvania, raising questions about whether any *cultural* shifts might follow this northward drift of southern heat and plant life. One environmental force that did change the cultural fabric of the South is Hurricane Katrina. Although it should be considered a human-made disaster as well as a natural one, because of the levee failures in New Orleans, Katrina was one of the largest, most powerful, and fastest-forming hurricanes in recorded history, and it contributed substantially to the astounding 29 percent drop in New Orleans' population between 2000 and 2010. While there is no definitive proof that global warming contributed to the storm's ferocity, there is scientific agreement that a rise in temperatures may cause greater intensity in, and

Differences between 1990 USDA hardiness zones and 2006 arborday.org hardiness zones reflect warmer climate

Zone Change
- +2
- +1
- no change
- -1
- -2

1990 Map

2006 Map

After USDA Plant Hardiness Zone Map, USDA Miscellaneous Publication No. 1475, Issued January 1990

National Arbor Day Foundation Plant Hardiness Zone Map published in 2006.

Zone

2 3 4 5 6 7 8 9 10

© 2006 by The National Arbor Day Foundation®

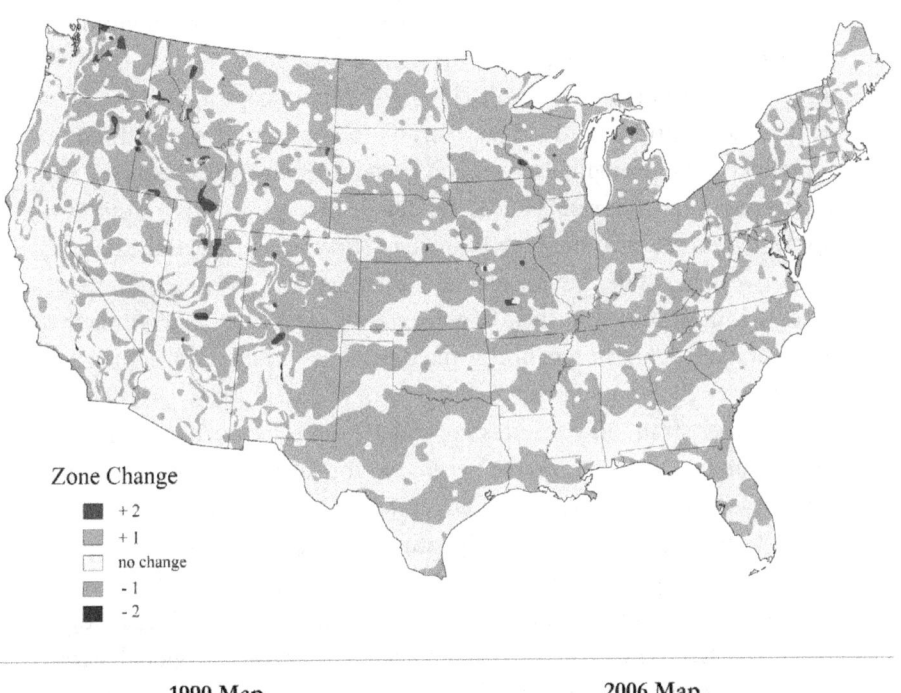

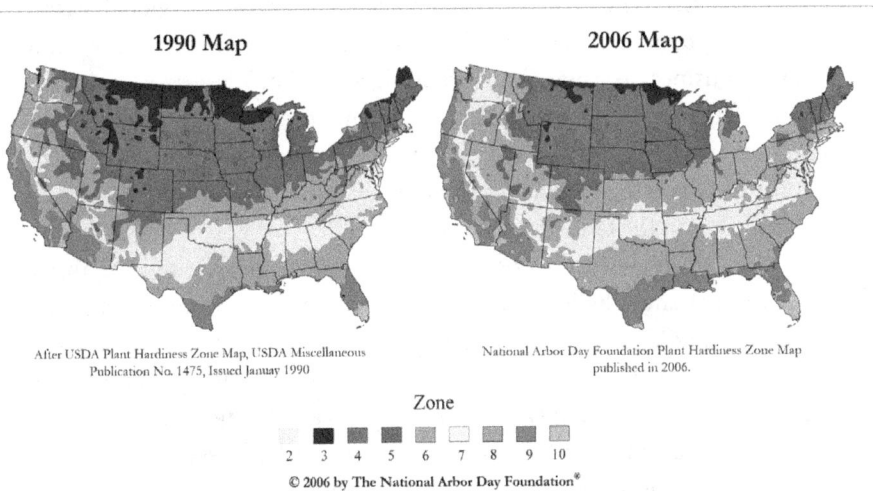

Figure 5.1. In 2006, to accommodate rising average temperatures, the Arbor Day Foundation redrew the U.S. Department of Agriculture's 1990 map of hardiness zones for plants. Courtesy of the Arbor Day Foundation 20144 under CCC license.

frequency of, hurricanes, spelling danger for all the southern states in the hurricane zone.[23]

Major *political* changes in the South have also occurred as a result of environmental changes. In 2007 and 2008, the Southeast experienced the worst drought since 1895, when drought indicators were first used. In some of the localities hardest hit, the physical landscape altered substantially as lakes, ponds, and streams shrank to almost nothing or dried up completely. The drought also sparked a legal battle between Georgia and Tennessee over water rights to the Tennessee River. The basis for this lawsuit rested on an error made in 1818 when surveyors mapped the boundary between the states but accidentally included a sliver of the Tennessee River within Tennessee instead of Georgia. This was not the first time that Georgia had sought to regain this portion of the river, but it returned to this issue in 2008 because the rapid growth of Atlanta over past decades put a greater strain on the state's natural resources. Suburban sprawl has exacerbated drought conditions because of the increased demand on water supplies, as has the spread of concrete roads and parking lots, which prevent rainwater from adequately saturating the ground and moving to underground aquifers. Finally, a major drought in Texas in 2011 sparked record numbers of wildfires across the state, prompting the climatologist James Hansen to remark: "Climate change—human-made global warming—is happening. It is already having noticeable impacts. . . . If we stay on with business as usual, the southern U.S. will become almost uninhabitable."[24] Even if these droughts had nothing to do with global warming, their severity still attests to the fact that as temperatures rise, maps of the South are changing, and southerners will have to begin rethinking their relationship to the land and environment.[25]

Together, new histories of the southern environment and the threat of climate change challenge any lingering notion that the South is or was a stable paradise of permanently fertile soils and consistently temperate seasons. Such new histories also reveal how the narrative of southern environmental exceptionalism is a deeply problematic, nostalgic construction that locates the prelapsarian "southern garden" deep in the past of the slave plantation. As Elliott's novel acknowledges, invoking an image of a pastoral landscape that existed prior to the development of modern society means invoking a particular history of the South that is defined by Indian removal, African slavery, and postbellum racial segregation.

Coiled in the Heart shows that efforts to restore this idealized notion of ecological balance in the region always risk recurring to a romantic vision of an agrarian South that is politically regressive. Any romantic wish to "get back" to an idyllic southern nature might also become freighted with the unintentional wish to "roll back" to pre–Civil War ideals of possessive individualism and racial exploitation.

The turn toward postsouthern parody in contemporary literature might help limit such nostalgia by reminding readers that narratives of southern exceptionalism are, ultimately, nothing more than narratives— that the natural world at the heart of southern history is a cultural construction with minimal grounding in the material actualities of nature. Yet postsouthernism also threatens to hinder southern environmentalism by privileging the symbolic over the material. Some aspects of southern cultures *are* tied to the physical landscape, and too much emphasis on symbols and signs can limit the possibilities for recognizing and confronting the material threats of overdevelopment and climate change facing the South today. Shifting the discursive representations of nature from the past to the future, and away from pastoral utopianism to something more nuanced and occasionally even apocalyptic—as Elliott does in the novel's ominous suggestion of a looming earthquake—could help redress the limitations of postsouthern literature while also avoiding the trap of cultural nostalgia. Instead of portraying a healthy and balanced southern environment as something that has been lost, or that southerners have lost touch with in their air-conditioned homes and cars, environmentalists might start emphasizing that ecological stability is something that has *never* existed in the South, at least since colonization, because plantation agriculture always distorted and interfered with the natural vagaries of the climate. Instead of imagining the balance between human society and the natural world as something that must be recovered, southerners should rather treat that balance as something the South has yet to see, as something that people living in the South must build and maintain. The place for a utopian southern nature is in the future, not the past, and visualizing such a radical break from the past would help southerners avoid nostalgia for institutions like the southern plantation and begin building new possibilities for unprecedented forms of social and environmental justice.

Notes

1. Romine, "Where Is Southern Literature?," 40.
2. Bone, *Postsouthern Sense of Place*, 46.
3. Rieger, *Clear-Cutting Eden*, 8; Wilson, *Shadow and Shelter*, xi.
4. Elliott, *Coiled in the Heart*, 8; hereafter cited by page number in the text.
5. Sartre, *Being and Nothingness*, 21.
6. For a discussion of the Agrarians' attention to nature, see MacKethan, *Dream of Arcady*, 128–52. For a discussion of Berry's environmentalism, see Smith, *Wendell Berry and the Agrarian Tradition*. For a discussion of Berry's relationship to the original Twelve Southerners, see Murphy, *Rebuke of History*, 255–72.
7. Simpson, *Dispossessed Garden*, 15; Ridgely, *Nineteenth-Century Southern Literature*, 3, 4, 15.
8. For discussion of southern pastoral, see Rieger, *Clear-Cutting Eden*, 2–7; MacKethan, *Dream of Arcady*, 4; and Grammer, *Pastoral and Politics in the Old South*. For a discussion of southern "anti-pastoral," see Simpson, *Dispossessed Garden*, 65–100; and Grammer, "A Thing against Which Time Will Not Prevail," 30–32.
9. Phillips, *Life and Labor in the Old South*, 3.
10. Stahle et al., "The Lost Colony and Jamestown Droughts," 564.
11. Allewaert, "Swamp Sublime," 341, 350.
12. Smith, "Hot Bodies," 117–18.
13. Koeniger, "Climate and Southern Distinctiveness," 26, 21, 31–37.
14. Arsenault, "End of the Long Hot Summer," 613, 616, 622.
15. Koeniger, "Climate and Southern Distinctiveness," 37.
16. Watson, "Economics of a Cracker Landscape," 513.
17. Bone, *Postsouthern Sense of Place*, 5. Janet Fiskio critiques Berry's emphasis on land ownership in "Unsettling Ecocriticism."
18. Though most of the authors in *I'll Take My Stand* celebrated the small farm, the plantation was still central to their visions of agrarian southern culture. See Young, "Not in Memoriam, but in Defense," 337.
19. Nelson, *Pharsalia*, 25, 27.
20. Simpson, *Dispossessed Garden*, 17, 23.
21. MacKethan, *Dream of Arcady*, 10.
22. Tobia's postapocalyptic vision echoes earlier novels about environmental degradation and destruction such as Whitley Strieber and James Kunetka's *Warday* (1984) and *Nature's End: The Consequences of the Twentieth Century* (1986), or Walter J. Williams's *The Rift* (1999), which also imagines a new earthquake occurring on the New Madrid fault line. The final vision of Tobia lighting out on his own clearly alludes to Mark Twain's *Adventures of Huckleberry Finn* (1885) and Jack Kerouac's *On the Road* (1951).
23. Krupa, "New Orleans' Official 2010 Census Population"; Berger, "Hurricane Study."
24. Romm, "NASA's Hansen."
25. Dewan, "Georgia Claims a Sliver of the Tennessee River"; Copeland, "Drought Spreading in Southeast"; Lovaas, "Report: Sprawl Compounds Water Crisis"; and Hollis, "Southeast Drought Going into Record Books."

Works Cited

Allewaert, Monique. "Swamp Sublime: Ecologies of Resistance in the American Plantation Zone." *PMLA* 132, no. 2 (2008): 340–57.

Arsenault, Raymond. "The End of the Long Hot Summer: The Air Conditioner and Southern Culture." *Journal of Southern History* 50, no. 4 (November 1984): 597–628.

Berger, Eric. "Hurricane Study Puts Less Blame on Global Warming." *Houston Chronicle*, May 18, 2008. http://www.chron.com/disp/story.mpl/front/5789245.html. Accessed May 26, 2014.

Bone, Martyn. *The Postsouthern Sense of Place in Contemporary Fiction*. Baton Rouge: Louisiana State University Press, 2005.

Copeland, Larry. "Drought Spreading in Southeast." *USA Today*, February 11, 2008. http://www.usatoday.com/weather/drought/2008-02-11-drought_N.htm. Accessed November 30, 2011.

Dewan, Shaila. "Georgia Claims a Sliver of the Tennessee River." *New York Times*, February 22, 2008. http://www.nytimes.com/2008/02/22/us/22water.html. Accessed May 26, 2014.

Elliott, Scott. *Coiled in the Heart*. New York: Bluehen Books, 2003.

Fiskio, Janet. "Unsettling Ecocriticism: Rethinking Agrarianism, Place, and Citizenship." *American Literature* 84, no. 2 (June 2012): 301–25.

Grammer, John M. "A Thing against Which Time Will Not Prevail: Pastoral and History in Cormac McCarthy's South." *Southern Quarterly* 30, no. 4 (1992): 19–30.

———. *Pastoral and Politics in the Old South*. Baton Rouge: Louisiana State University Press, 1996.

Hollis, Paul L. "Southeast Drought Going into Record Books." *Southeast Farm Press*, February 6, 2008. http://southeastfarmpress.com/news/southeast-weather-0208/. Accessed May 26, 2014.

Koeniger, A. Cash. "Climate and Southern Distinctiveness." *Journal of Southern History* 54, no. 1 (February 1988): 21–44.

Krupa, Michelle. "New Orleans' Official 2010 Census Population Is 343,829, Agency Reports." [New Orleans] *Times-Picayune*, February 3, 2011. http://www.nola.com/politics/index.ssf/2011/02/new_orleans_officials_2010_pop.html. Accessed May 26, 2014.

Lovaas, Deron. "Report: Sprawl Compounds Water Crisis in Drought-Stricken Cities." National Resources Defense Council press release, August 28 2002. http://www.nrdc.org/media/pressreleases/020828.asp. Accessed May 26, 2014.

MacKethan, Lucinda H. *The Dream of Arcady: Place and Time in Southern Literature*. Baton Rouge: Louisiana State University Press, 1980.

Murphy, Paul. *The Rebuke of History: The Southern Agrarians and American Conservative Thought*. Chapel Hill: University of North Carolina Press, 2001.

Nelson, Lynn A. *Pharsalia: An Environmental Biography of a Southern Plantation, 1780–1880*. Athens: University of Georgia Press, 2009.

Phillips, Ulrich Bonnell. *Life and Labor in the Old South*. 1929. Columbia: University of South Carolina Press, 2007.

Ridgely, J. V. *Nineteenth-Century Southern Literature*. Lexington: University Press of Kentucky, 1980.

Rieger, Christopher. *Clear-Cutting Eden: Ecology and the Pastoral in Southern Literature.* Tuscaloosa: University of Alabama Press, 2009.

Romine, Scott. "Where Is Southern Literature? The Practice of Place in a Postsouthern Age." In *South to a New Place: Region, Literature, Culture,* edited by Suzanne W. Jones and Sharon Monteith, 23–43. Baton Rouge: Louisiana State University Press, 2002.

Romm, Joe. "NASA's Hansen: 'If We Stay on with Business as Usual, the Southern U.S. Will Become Almost Uninhabitable.'" *Think Progress,* September 29, 2011. http://thinkprogress.org/romm/2011/09/29/332369/nasa-hansen-the-southern-u-s-will-become-almost-uninhabitable/. Accessed May 26, 2014.

Sartre, Jean-Paul. *Being and Nothingness: An Essay on Phenomenological Ontology,* translated by Hazel E. Barnes. London: Methuen, 1957.

Simpson, Lewis P. *The Dispossessed Garden: Pastoral and History in Southern Literature.* Athens: University of Georgia Press, 1975.

Smith, Jon. "Hot Bodies and 'Barbaric Tropics': The U.S. South and New World Natures." *Southern Literary Journal* 36, no. 1 (fall 2003): 104–20.

Smith, Kimberly K. *Wendell Berry and the Agrarian Tradition: A Common Grace.* Lawrence: University Press of Kansas, 2003.

Stahle, David W., Malcolm K. Cleaveland, Dennis B. Blanton, Matthew D. Therrell, and David A. Gay. "The Lost Colony and Jamestown Droughts." *Science* 280, no. 5363 (April 24, 1998): 564–67.

Watson, Jay. "Economics of a Cracker Landscape: Poverty as an Environmental Issue in Two Southern Writers." *Mississippi Quarterly* 55, no. 4 (fall 2002): 497–513.

Wilson, Anthony. *Shadow and Shelter: The Swamp in Southern Culture.* Jackson: University Press of Mississippi, 2006.

Young, Stark. "Not in Memoriam, but in Defense." In *I'll Take My Stand: The South and the Agrarian Tradition,* by Twelve Southerners, 328–59. 1930. New York: Harper Torchbook, 1962.

6

Creating and Consuming "Hill Country Harmonica"

Promoting the Blues and Forging Beloved Community in the Contemporary South

ADAM GUSSOW

Although I recognize the risks attendant on what follows, this essay offers a contemporary case study in the creation and consumption of "southern culture" in which, of necessity, I feature quite prominently. Academics (and humanities academics in particular) are used to standing back from the action, arms folded, rhetorics of suspicion at the ready—especially if the action involves collecting money from customers, paying wages to subcontracted employees, and creating a brand-name event with significant growth potential. That sort of enterprise smacks of capitalist bad faith and the profit motive, and most of us try not to dirty our hands in that way, much less offer a narrative of our sullying. Indeed, this very essay, as Jon Smith has taught me to see, might be understood as an insidious sort of brand positioning, the transnational marketing of a self-consciously "homegrown" southern product to a reading audience of southernists who just might help spread the word.[1] Still, I think there is something to be gained by working both sides of the fence: walking you through the event-planning, profit-accruing process as I experienced it but also leavening that account with moments of embedded reflection and further thinking-through that became possible only after the tents had been folded.

I am going to describe Hill Country Harmonica, an event that I organized, publicized, produced, and performed at in the spring of 2010—an adventure on the supply side of Mississippi blues tourism, as it were. I am also going to try, as the participant-observer that I was, to work through several key issues that emerged. I use the word "adventure" as a way of indicating that I have a day gig as a professor, not as a way of suggesting that the staging of such an event was child's play or an exercise in middle-class romanticism. Hill Country Harmonica involved significant financial risk on my part and a great deal of hard work. But that, as we all know, is the song that capitalists always sing in order to salve their uneasy consciences and justify their hefty profits.

I am going to foreground race in this essay, and for an obvious reason: I am a white man who plays, and professes, the blues, and the event I put on was an interracial collaboration on Deep South soil. It involved white people and black people working together in various ways—serving and learning from each other, profiting from each other's labor, representing each other to a consuming public—and the precise meaning of that word "together" is what concerns me, especially in light of the Mississippi location in which Hill Country Harmonica took place. Mississippi is not a place with a notable track record of just and equitable personal and business relationships between white folks and black folks. Before I speak about all that, and about the event itself, I need to offer a little personal history.

When I first moved from New York City to Oxford, Mississippi, in 2002 to take a teaching job at the University of Mississippi, I was a scholar in transition. Although a chief focus of my research for the prior eight years had been blues culture in the South and the shaping role that violence—especially white violence against black folk—had played in that culture, I came to Mississippi determined to shift my focus toward more hopeful themes. This shift was spurred by a two-year immersion in New Age religion, especially Tibetan Buddhism and a book called *A Course in Miracles*, one that followed on the heels of a minor heart attack I'd suffered several years earlier. After arriving in Mississippi, I spent my first several years at the university researching a new book—or what I intended to be a book—on the theme of racial reconciliation. I ended up losing interest in it, and for a curious reason: I got married. More specifically, I fell in love with and married an African American woman from Dallas, and the two of us had a son. The project of actually living a reconciled life—dancing the dance of an interracial marriage and the raising of a biracial son in the contemporary South—turned out to be far more compelling, as least for me, than the writing of a scholarly study about the subject.

I begin with this personal confession as a way of being honest about the ground on which I stand and out of which my perspective on contemporary southern life emerges. As a scholar trained in African American studies and the father of a black boy in Mississippi, I am deeply committed to the project of creating racial justice in the world my family inhabits. I know too much about the decades of invisibility, mockery, and misunderstanding that confronted African American cultural contributions, as well as the violence inflicted on African Americans themselves as they pursued their long-deferred dream of full citizenship, not to care about such things. By the same token, as a contemporary southernist, a working blues musician, and a partner in an interracial marriage, I know how important it is to be attentive to transracial alliances, unexpected paradoxes, and lived particulars of race and culture that may not dovetail with familiar racial scripts. In this respect, I am particularly moved by Tara McPherson's words in *Reconstructing Dixie*. McPherson asks that we attend to "a small minor chord of southern history, those moments of commonality, sameness, humanity, across racial lines. It is important to recall this history, not because what a tiny percentage of white southerners achieved in the name of antiracism in any way approximates the labor of black southerners toward that end, but because we need models of commonality across difference, of shared traditions, of productive alliance."[2]

What I offer here, then, is a contemporary case study in the creation and consumption of southern culture, one in which the phrase "productive alliance" encompasses both the profit motive and a commitment to racial justice. Even as I do so, I am aware that history teaches us to be skeptical about those who would presume to align those two motivations—an alignment shamelessly endorsed by this essay's subtitle: "Promoting the Blues and Forging Beloved Community in the Contemporary South." Beloved community, as the Reverend Martin Luther King, Jr. defined the term, is characterized by a condition in which a group of people, and especially a group of blacks and whites, recognize and embrace the fact that they are "caught in an inescapable network of mutuality, tied in a single garment of destiny."[3] When worldly profit enters the picture, however, mutuality has a way of being corrupted in the direction of instrumentality. Although plantation paternalism in the Old South and the postwar Mississippi Delta led some slaveowners and bossmen to speak about taking care of "their Negroes," the sort of care they were talking about always ultimately revolved around possession, control, and extraction of surplus wealth. The sort of genuinely just and equitable mutuality referenced by King was very rarely in evidence back then—although occasional exceptions must have occurred, as McPherson urges us to acknowledge. Anybody familiar with the history of the blues, in any case, will be well aware of the economic exploitation that was suffered by those who played and listened to the music in pre–civil rights Mississippi, and by the violence that kept this exploitation in place. A desire to escape from the dollar-a-day dead end of cotton-field sharecropping is a constant theme in the autobiography of Mississippi bluesman Honeyboy Edwards; a secondary theme is the shameless ease with which he could be picked up by local lawmen on the flimsiest of vagrancy charges and forced to labor, unpaid, on one prison farm or another.[4]

One of the most powerful evocations of this bad old Mississippi—the Mississippi that spurred its residents to sing sad, restless, escape-oriented music—can be found in the autobiography of Danny Barker, a black New Orleans banjo player who worked his way through the state as a young man with pianist Little Brother Montgomery. "Just the mention of the word Mississippi amongst a group of New Orleans people," insisted Barker, "would cause complete silence and attention. The word was so very powerful that it carried the impact of catastrophes, destruction, death, hell, earthquakes, cyclones, murder, hanging, lynching, all sorts of slaughter. It was the earnest and general feeling that any Negro who left New Orleans and journeyed across the state border and entered the hell-hole called the state of Mississippi for any reason other than to attend the funeral of a very close relative—mother, father, brother, wife, or husband—was well on the way to losing his mentality, or had already lost it."[5]

Mississippi has changed a great deal since those dark, bluesy days. In 1954, for example, a white supremacist organization calling itself the White Citizens' Council was formed in Indianola, a Delta town, in order to orchestrate so-called massive resistance to the school desegregation mandated by the Supreme Court's *Brown v. Board of Education* decision. Yet only fifty years later, groundbreaking ceremonies were held in Indianola for the B. B. King Museum and Delta Interpretive Center, an institution whose stated mission is to tell King's "life's story of hardship, perseverance, talent and humility as a way to further the arts, youth development, and racial reconciliation in the Mississippi Delta and beyond."[6] That sort of reversal—an African American blues performer celebrated in 2004 as a representative Delta hero rather than denigrated as a second-class citizen—is a heartening thing, and not to be taken lightly. But progress in matters of racial justice is uneven. Is it possible to make money with the blues in the post–civil rights South and do so in a way that does justice to Dr. King's dream of beloved community? This was the challenge that confronted me, a novice blues promoter, as I attempted not just to talk the talk but to walk the walk in contemporary Mississippi.

Curiously enough, the prelude to my first experience promoting Mississippi blues was my frustration with another blues promoter, whom I'll call Vince. Between 2006 and 2009, I served as a coach—a kind of teacher/performer—at a number of blues harmonica instructional retreats that Vince put on. Vince is a spirited, friendly, quirky white guy from a blue state out West. He's a good player and an inspiring teacher who holds the curious honor of having sold more blues harmonica instructional books—millions of them—than anybody else in the world. I enjoyed being a part of his team, and the money was certainly good; the hours were long, but the work was rewarding, and the sense of community that developed between coaches and campers during his five-day events was and remains memorable. Still, after I'd worked a handful of his camps in St. Louis, Jacksonville, Dallas, and Virginia Beach, I noticed a curious thing about his coaches and the backing bands he provided: they were always, and without exception, white. Now, it is true that in the contemporary world of blues harmonica, the preponderance of fans and students are white, as are most of the touring pros. Still, as a trained African Americanist, I almost reflexively think about issues of inclusion, representation, and economic justice. Who has a voice here? Who is getting paid? Since most of the pioneering figures of blues harmonica were African American, and since Vince and his campers ceaselessly invoke their names—Little Walter, Big Walter, Sonny Boy Williamson, Sonny Terry, Junior Wells—it seemed strange that Vince had never managed to include an African American teacher or musician on his free-floating staff. So without explicitly pointing this out, I began occasionally emailing him the names of prospective black coaches whom I knew to be at least as qualified as I was, and—in the case of Billy Branch and Phil Wiggins—notably more qualified. Maybe he was open to the idea but hadn't done the research. One premise of affirmative action is that those in charge, unless pushed to do otherwise, tend to hire people they know, people with whom they feel comfortable. I was engaged in a gentle kind of affirmative action: deliberately trying to broaden the range of people from whom Vince was selecting his coaching staff, nudging him in the direction of inclusiveness.

Vince put me off. He always found a reason not to hire the people I suggested. Yet he kept putting on his workshops in Clarksdale, Mississippi, in the heart of the Delta. He wouldn't hire several local black harp players I'd steered him toward, but he would hire me, because, he said, I was "local." I'd shake my head and complain to my wife. "It's weird," I'd say. "His campers are coming to Mississippi because of the black people who created the music right here, and guys like Terry Bean are still creating the blues *right here*, but he won't hire Terry. That's weird." I didn't want to say "That's racist," because I like Vince, and he's certainly not the kind of overt bigot the word "racist" was invented to describe. I suspect that he thinks of himself as antiracist, in fact; and in some ways that's an apt characterization. A handful of black registrants have shown up at his workshops over the years, and he seems delighted and flattered by their presence. He just didn't want to put black people on his payroll, teach the blues side by side with them, and share power with them. That was the only conclusion I could draw from his all-white roster of employees and his continuing nonresponse to my suggestions.

My wife finally tired of my complaints. "Why don't you put on your own event?" she said. "Hire the people you want." Then she said something that startled me and called my bluff: "Your ideals aren't real until you put them into action." It's easy to complain about other people's racial bad faith; it's harder to enact your own vision of how the world could be. So I decided to act. At this point, another disclosure is required: although a concern with racial justice was one of my motivations, it wasn't the only one. Nor was a hunger to maximize profit what drove me—although *some* concern with profit was part of the mix. Hill Country Harmonica was born in December 2009 when I shared an idea with one of my fellow pros: that it would be fun, and potentially lucrative, to convince a bunch of blues harmonica players from various points on the compass to come to Mississippi for a tribal gathering the following spring—a long weekend of clinics, concerts, and jam sessions. I knew that Mississippi held considerable mystique for blues fans from outside the region, in part because I had sensed the mystique myself the moment I moved down from New

York. Although my commitment to critical thinking led me to view this mystique skeptically, I also relished the idea of *working* the mystique for a change, now that I could claim to be a naturalized citizen of the state. The mystique has a legitimate basis, it must be acknowledged, in the creative output of the extraordinary number of African American blues greats, including Robert Johnson, Muddy Waters, Sonny Boy Williamson, and B. B. King, who were born or resided in the Delta. How to explain why so many musical artists, and such powerful, visceral, influential sounds, flowered here? People have always made pilgrimages to such places and imbued them with near-religious significance. But the Mississippi blues mystique is also grounded in the enduring fascination—especially among cloistered urbanites, and often facilitated by cinematic representations of Mississippi blues culture—of a fantasized Deepest South made up of endless cotton fields stretching to the horizon, a prison farm complete with an overseer on horseback and prisoners in stripes and leg irons, and a backwoods juke joint: hell on Earth backed by a hell of a good time, with a soundtrack courtesy of *O Brother, Where Art Thou?*, *Mississippi Burning*, and *Crossroads*.

Contemporary Mississippi differs in most respects from that Bad Old Mississippi, in part because the agonies of the civil rights years really did have a transformative effect. Yet the mystique of Mississippi-as-Bluesland, leavened by a shudder of phantasmic danger, has lingered. More than that: the mystique has been shaped quite deliberately over the past decade by the development of blues tourism, an industry that links business leaders, small-scale entrepreneurs, state government, and educators in a community of interest. With the help of a Mississippi Blues Commission and the installation of more than one hundred "Mississippi Blues Trail" markers, an explosion of local festivals, and the continuing efforts of the Mississippi Development Authority Tourism Division, the state has energetically sought to rebrand itself in the national imaginary. In his study of blues tourism in the Delta, communications scholar Stephen A. King argues that Mississippi, once thought of as a "death place" associated with lynching and other forms of white racist brutality against black folk, has transformed itself into "the birthplace of the blues," whitewashing the harsher elements of its own past so that mythic rather than properly historicized understandings of blues musicians' lives tend to predominate.[7] Hell on earth for black folk has faded to sepia, for better or worse, so that a hell of a good time for everybody—but especially white blues tourists—can blossom. The sovereign state of Mississippi accrues cultural capital; those talented, shrewd, or well financed enough to ride the blues juggernaut make a profit.

To make my own supply-side dream of Mississippi blues a reality, I was forced from the start to navigate the conflicting demands of historical accuracy and consumer desire, which is another way of saying that where the blues are concerned, mystique is good for business. Lest I be accused of bad faith, I should note that blues performers themselves often exploit the music's mythic overtones to their own advantage. Two of the first performers I hired, Terry "Harmonica" Bean and Bill "Howl-N-Madd" Perry, are black Mississippians from the hill country; the moniker portions of their names—the "stagey" side, if you will—remind us that a successful life as an economic actor in the blues world is often assisted by an element of self-created legend, the calculated performance of a recognizable blues identity. I have been friends with Terry and Bill since I moved to Mississippi; I've absorbed a certain amount of the local style. If they were working this angle, why shouldn't I?

I decided to call my event "Hill Country Harmonica," and I quickly added the subtitle "A North Mississippi Blues Harp Homecoming." I wanted to take advantage of the fact that my prospective customers were at least vaguely familiar with both the hill country sound of R. L. Burnside and Junior Kimbrough, and the rock-tinged version of that sound propagated by the younger, white-led North Mississippi Allstars. The word "homecoming" was purely aspirational: if I built the damned thing, I hoped they would come, at least in sufficient numbers so that I broke even. I also wanted to engage prospective attendees on a subliminal level, combining the idea of a tribal gathering for blues harp players with some dimly remembered idea—taken, I suspect, from Tyler Perry's *Madea's Family Reunion*—that summertime in the South is where extended families, especially black families, gather their northward-migrant cousins back into the family bosom.

I went further than this: I deliberately exploited the pastoral imagery that I've been helping my Southern Studies students at the University of Mississippi to recognize and critique when it shows up in the form of achingly nostalgic songs like Buddy Jewel's "Sweet Southern Comfort." When I built a website for Hill Country Harmonica, I chose the most intensely green, expansive, morning-in-Mississippi header that I could find. I wanted my prospective customers, whom I imagined to be cooped up in their cold northern garrets, to yearn so badly for the South's soft, warm embrace that they could hear Mississippi roosters crowing in the hill country dawn.[8] It would be fair to say that I had begun to sense a tension between my scholarly commitment to the pursuit of truth and a businessman's instinctive desire to use all the tools at his disposal. Racial justice and beloved community are *very good things*, but I needed to get paid, too. The blues business, like any business, is about creating desire for a product, and myths are a powerful tool for inciting desire. I might have felt considerably more cognitive dissonance had my new identity as fledgling blues promoter not meshed almost seamlessly with my longstanding self-identification as a struggling blues performer—underpaid, nobody's fool, and doggedly determined to get over.

The most curious thing about Hill Country Harmonica, as concept and product, is that there is virtually no tradition of blues harmonica in North Mississippi. With the exception of Johnny Woods, who played with Mississippi Fred McDowell, even scholars of blues harmonica are hard-pressed to name another African American mouth organist who hails from the region. All the Mississippi-born greats, including Sonny Boy Williamson, Howlin' Wolf, and James Cotton, come from the Delta, not the hills. (Big Walter Horton comes from Horn Lake, twenty miles south of Memphis, which lies just outside both regions.) So my event was founded on a paradox that might, in the hands of a different sort of businessman, have been soft-pedaled or disavowed. What I did—because my academic training leads me to take a positive pleasure in exploring such paradoxes—was create a page on the event website in which I offered a primer on hill country blues and highlighted this curious absence of the harmonica from the region's otherwise distinctive blues tradition.[9] In other words, I juxtaposed the invented tradition of "hill country harmonica" with its own lack of firm grounding: a classic deconstructive move.

I knew that many of my prospective clients would skip quickly over such semischolarly fine print. For them, the phrase "hill country harmonica" was likely to conjure up a phantasm like the late Otha Turner, an indomitable old blues elder, sitting out on his back porch and wailing on a harp as he gazed off across the rolling green countryside. Now the truth, as everybody in North Mississippi knows, is that Otha didn't play harmonica. He whittled his own fifes out of hill country cane. Nor did he wail the blues; he tooted them. He helped keep alive the venerable hill country tradition of fife-and-drum music, and his great-granddaughter

Sharde carries on the tradition now that he has gone. I posted a photo and video on the website that made all this clear, along with videos of R. L. Burnside, Junior Kimbrough, and several younger artists who cover their songs. There *is* no tradition of hill country harmonica, I stressed, except the one I had invented. But invented traditions need ancestor figures, too, and if Otha Turner and his North Mississippi brethren had earned places of honor in various overheated out-of-state imaginations, I could live with that. Ancestor figures are good for business; I had made no misleading claims. Or so I told myself, even as my scholarly conscience took notes for whatever future moral accounting I'd be forced to make. At what point, for example, did the profit-pursuing process of creating a website and populating it with representations of African American ancestor figures become the postmodern equivalent of the paternalist instrumentality through which white plantation owners shepherded "their Negroes" through the labors of an agricultural year? *That* question, those phantasmic echoes, alarmed me—or would have, had I dared to ponder the point amid the hustle and bustle of my own entrepreneurial spring planting season.

If what I am exploring here is the complex process through which one particular contemporary southern brand began to work its way into the public sphere and engage its prospective audience, then what I will call brand iconics—the creation and manipulation of visual representations and symbols of the brand—is a crucial element of that process. One reason I settled on "Hill Country Harmonica" was that it effortlessly acronymed into HCH. In the fast-paced, corporatized, texting-maddened world we inhabit, with its LOL's, WTF's, and KFC's, acronyms not only save time but also create subcultural bonding, distinguishing those in the know from . . . well, from the four or five people in the world who still don't know that KFC abbreviates "Kentucky Fried Chicken." The acronym HCH was quickly picked up, in any case, by the steady trickle of paid-up participants who began chattering on the forum I had created on the event website.

By this point I had accumulated a partner: Jeff Silverman, a bulky, fast-talking, Bronx-born Jewish consultant in the auto sales field who happened also to be a retired U.S. Army sergeant. He was blunt, shrewd, sensible, and tireless. He knew little about the South, but he was a raving fanatic about all things harmonica. "I love it!" he barked into the phone when I first shared my vision. "Mississippi! The harmonica! The Delta!

The blues! We can't lose! It'll be twice as big next year." I interrupted him. "The, ah . . . the Delta is an entirely different part of the state," I said. "I'm talking about an event in the hill country. Up in the hills. The Delta is dead flat and it's sixty miles from here." "Whatever," he said. "The Delta, the hills. I'm cool with it. It's all Mississippi to me."

The truth was, I had been in some confusion myself about Mississippi's geography before moving to the state. I could hardly blame Jeff for collapsing the territory into one undifferentiated blues-drenched world. Indeed, I was counting on some of our prospective attendees to do the same thing. This helps explain why I was both chagrined and amused when he emailed me a PDF file of the event poster. The image, which would be splashed all over our publicity and would decisively brand us in the public mind, was the creation of Douglas (not his real name), an Army buddy of Jeff's who had a day gig as a curator/restorer in the U.S. Capitol Building, but whose piquant design sense called up the ghosts of Haight-Ashbury in 1968. If the South, as Leigh Anne Duck has argued, is "the nation's region," a place into which the rest of America projects various sorts of fantasies, and if the Mississippi Delta, in James Cobb's phrase, is "the most southern place on earth," then it was somehow fitting that our art director, gazing down at Mississippi from his perch at the figurative heart of American national power, should have confected such a surreal, fact-challenged—and totally groovy—tableau. What he did was make the two most iconic "blues highways" in the Delta, Highways 61 and 49, into the backdrop for our hill country event, along with a sign reading "crossroads." He had borrowed that image from a photo that shows up when you Google image-search the words "Mississippi blues." The photo itself was taken in Clarksdale at a spot by now familiar to local folk and blues tourists alike, a nondescript urban intersection where civic boosters decided in the late 1990s to make some money off the Robert-Johnson-and-the-Devil myth by erecting a sign-festooned sculpture that decisively branded that location as *the* place where Johnson traded away his soul back in the 1930s, even though there is absolutely no evidence to back up this claim. Neither those highways nor that crossroads had any geographic or historical reason for being associated with Hill Country Harmonica. They were located eighty-five miles from our venue, in an entirely distinct part of the state. Yet there they were: some Delta booster's pre-fab gothic legend shoehorned by a starry-eyed Yankee art director into my own dubious exercise in myth creation. This is how contemporary southern culture, or at least some of it—the iconic image for a Mississippi-based blues event—is made. Now the image would be broadcast worldwide on the Internet and consumed hungrily—or so we hoped.[10]

A small-time blues impresario is required to wear many hats. Not only was I handling all negotiations with the venue and our performers; not only would I be teaching, performing, MCing, and stage-managing the event; but, as we entered the final week's countdown, I carried my pitch to our regional audience with a personal appearance on Memphis TV. WREG's "Live at Nine" is a one-hour morning show on the CBS affiliate; it features a black male host and a white female host who banter intimately in the Regis-and-Kathie-Lee style. It exemplifies, not just in its hosts but in the range of local folk it puts on display, a familiar form of mass-mediated contemporary southern interracialism. Given the racial tensions that still animate Memphis's political culture more than forty years after Martin Luther King Jr.'s assassination, "Live at Nine" functions as a sort of southern urban pastoral, a regularly scheduled but fleeting taste of post-racial utopia, featuring—as pastorals do—lots of childhood-innocence stuff (groups of school kids doing cute things), pretty maidens (black and white models strutting the latest fashions), and pipers piping (musical groups). The musical groups are often integrated: a reflection of Memphis's singular role as a spawning ground for soul, blues, gospel, and rock 'n' roll and a scene of continuing musical interchange, but also, I suspect, a way of deliberately staging images—multicultural panoramas of hardworking musicianship—that reinforce the interracialist premise of the show's twin anchorpersons.

My own appearance, thanks to my sideman, meshed seamlessly with the show's ethos. My sideman was Brandon Bailey, a young African American harmonica player from the projects of south Memphis whose acquaintance I had made several years earlier when he posted comments on my YouTube instructional video about the J. Geils Band's harmonica instrumental "Whammer Jammer." Brandon may have a classic blues pedigree—born in St. Louis, raised in Memphis, with a great-grandfather who used to play harmonica—but his most overt aesthetic influence, apart from me, is a white Canadian performer, Son of Dave, who used the distinctly contemporary technique of "looping" to create one-man performances, including a song called "Hellhound," which Brandon has covered in several recent recordings. I had visited Brandon in Memphis after our initial email exchange; I had coached him to victory in a citywide "Star Search" competition; and I had invited him to sit in on several of my gigs. I had also written him several letters of recommendation and offered suggestions on emailed drafts of literature papers he was writing at the University of Memphis, where he maintains a 3.8 GPA as a pre-med and is pursuing his goal of becoming a pediatric oncologist. He, in turn, had gifted me not just with a new harmonica case, but with a tiny stomp-pedal that had spurred me to become a one-man band. When Hill Country Harmonica came along, I happily hired him to teach and perform. A pair of blues nerds, each of us has decisively shaped the development of the other's musical visions. In some sense, our partnership exemplifies Dr. King's dream; Brandon and I are indeed "caught in an inescapable network of mutuality, tied in a single garment of destiny." This dynamic was subtly but decisively underlined as our ensemble performance on the "Live at Nine" set concluded and the black male and white female host walked onstage to chat us up. No velvet ropes separating the races at *this* rhythm and blues concert! Here instead was the New South dramatizing itself as the conspicuous erasure of racial division and discord: a quartet-sized beloved community—or the convincing simulacrum of such a community—making a space for playful banter, a product to be pushed, and a little music.[11]

The venue in which Hill Country Harmonica took place and the owners of that venue are another crucial part of the story. Foxfire Ranch, located in Waterford, Mississippi, about twenty miles north of Oxford, is an eighty-acre horse farm owned by an African American couple, Bill and Annie Hollowell. Bill is a retired U.S. Army lieutenant colonel who coaches schoolchildren part-time; Annie is a fixture at the front desk of the registrar's office at the University of Mississippi. For the past three years, the Hollowells have been attempting to reinvigorate a longstanding tradition of Sunday evening blues parties in the Mississippi hill country—a tradition that had sputtered to a halt in the late 1990s after the death of Junior Kimbrough, and the fire that burned down his world-famous juke joint a year later. Bill built an outdoor pavilion on the high ground of his spread and wired a soundstage; he hires local blues performers to play the 5–9 shift. Annie cooks lots of soul food and dishes it out to a sporadic flow of cash customers. Business has been slowly building. On Sunday evenings at Foxfire, from late spring through early fall, the Hollowells are stewards of the blues, providing a venue in which local working-class black folk, students from the university, and the occasional European or

Japanese tourist can mingle. In their own quiet way, the Hollowells have been working to dissolve the lingering legacy of segregation and create a free-floating beloved community, all in the service of a modest profit.[12] They are one face of the blues tourism industry in contemporary Mississippi: not yet an established stop on the Blues Trail established by the Mississippi Development Authority Tourism Division, but very much hoping to become one.

I had attended several of these blues parties each summer, and I knew that Foxfire Ranch was the ideal venue for Hill Country Harmonica. I visited Bill on a chilly January day, tromped through the mud with my son in tow, and, before I left, sealed the deal with a handshake. "We'll work with you," Bill said. The figure he quoted me for two days' use was fifty dollars below the figure I had come prepared to offer; I threw in the extra fifty. Although I could have asked for some play in the Hollowells' food, wine, and beer sales during the weekend, I suggested preemptively that they should take it all—easily doubling or tripling the business they did on any normal Sunday—and I suggested that we split the cover charge fifty-fifty for local trade in the evenings. Bill smiled and said, "Done." On the basis of that handshake, Jeff Silverman and I went to work. For the next three and a half months, with a planned budget of more than $10,000 and several thousand dollars already paid out as deposits and plane tickets, we did everything we could to put Hill Country Harmonica, and Foxfire Ranch, in the public mind. Besides the poster, the website, and my TV appearance, we had also invested money in print, radio, and Internet ads, while working Facebook, YouTube, and other social media. By the time we reached May 15, with only one week to go, it had become clear that we were close to achieving our best-case scenario: advance purchases had already put us in the black, and we were likely to make a profit of several thousand dollars each. At this point we had a conference call with the Hollowells (at their request) that threatened to derail the entire event. Since we had been open with them about the numbers of attendees we were expecting, as a way of facilitating their planning, and since they could read on the website that we were charging $150 per attendee for the weekend intensive, they had done the math and decided that they deserved an additional part of our action. They wanted to renegotiate.

It was more complicated than that, of course; such things always are. The driving force behind the renegotiations was Annette Hollowell, Bill and Annie's daughter: a recent graduate of the University of Mississippi law school, a social justice crusader on the Gulf Coast, and in this case an advocate for a father whose generosity, Annette seemed to feel, was threatening to get him ripped off, since the price he had suggested and I had agreed to was, she told us on the phone, only two-thirds of the normal Foxfire weekend rental fee. This fact was new to me, but it struck me as irrelevant, a low blow, since the Hollowells would be making a healthy profit on the food-and-drink end, and in any case I had merely accepted, and slightly increased, the fee Bill had initially suggested. More importantly, I knew from several of Bill's recent emails that traffic had spiked on the Hollowells' website as a result of Jeff's labors and my own. Hill Country Harmonica was already promising to be, in purely business terms, the best thing that had ever happened to Foxfire Ranch.

The conversation between Annette, Jeff, and me became brittle; mother Annie didn't say much, and Bill said almost nothing. The blues—an aching feeling compounded of money-grievance, personal betrayal, a sense of rules being changed and the carpet being yanked—suddenly blossomed. The ghosts of Mississippi's racial past flared to life and hovered in plain view, trying to find purchase in the brave new world of contemporary Mississippi, a world where racial scripts sometimes mutate in unexpected ways. Here I was, a local blues musician working my butt off and being treated like a sharecropper at the settle by the big landowner who held all the chips and could change the rules so I got nothing! Then again, here were Jeff and I, two carpetbagging white Yankee capitalists—a Jew and a half-Jew!—trying to profit handsomely by exploiting the inexperience and generosity of black southern landowners!

So which script was in effect?

Race was certainly at issue in all this, but it wasn't determinate, and for a curious reason: Annette and I were *both* interracially married. Marriages between white men and black women are not unheard of in contemporary Mississippi, but they remain fairly rare. The fact that she and I were, in a manner of speaking, living parallel lives, meant that, tense as things got on the phone, it was impossible for us to simply write each other off as wholly motivated by conventional racial scripts—or at least that was how it seemed to me when I reflected on it later.[13] Here, once again, were the constituent elements of King's vision: Annette and her family, my own family and I, were all "caught in an inescapable network of mutuality, tied in a single garment of destiny." I had met Annette's husband. Bill and Annie had met my wife and child. After the first time we'd visited Foxfire,

Annie had made a point of giving me a big hug every time we crossed paths on campus. If the Hollowells and I were not exactly family, we were something more than business associates. We were fellow travelers in the world of contemporary southern interracialism. Some of the pain arising between us now was rooted in the fact that a business dispute had routed the relaxed intimacy we had previously enjoyed. Although the five of us managed to address a host of other production issues briskly and effectively during our phone conversation, we ended with the central issue unresolved. We agreed to speak the following evening.

Sometimes this sort of impasse, with imprisoning racial scripts hanging heavy in the air, leads to an irreparable breach. Sometimes things can be worked out through dialogue, reparation, forgiveness: the hard, necessary work of racial reconciliation. Sometimes, if you're lucky and you've kept channels of communication open, grace enters the picture and effortlessly sets things straight.[14] The following evening, grace was present and our problems seemed to have solved themselves. No large concessions were required on either side, merely sensible adjustments. The feeling-tone of the conversation had, it seemed to me, a palpable admixture of beloved community reclaimed: a sense that we all had so much to gain here, as friends as well as stakeholders, that none of us had a desire to go down the path we had ended up on the evening before. Although the interracial kinship dynamics that I noted earlier were, I think, a part of this turnaround, two other elements were clearly in play. One was the profit motive at its most naked and beneficent: if we kept our cool and found a way of moving forward as friends, we were *all* going to make enough money to dwarf the relatively small sums we were dickering over. Foxfire Ranch, too, stood to gain a great deal of favorable publicity of a sort that could only help its long-term business prospects. The other element, curiously enough, was the military connection: both Bill and Jeff were retired soldiers. I had made a point of noting this as we began our initial conversation, and I pointed it out again at the beginning of Day 2. "I'm sure a couple of Army guys can work it out," I said. Friendly banter ensued between the lieutenant colonel and the sergeant, and pretty soon everything was copasetic. Contemporary southern culture—a Mississippi blues event struggling to be born, a Mississippi blues venue struggling to survive—was rescued by an appeal to a shared affiliation with the military branch of the American nation and the workings of entrepreneurial capitalism. William Faulkner's bad old Mississippi, a place where the past isn't dead, or even past, had been given a good beat-down. The five of us emerged from the shadows energized, chattering excitedly about the work that remained to be done before our guests showed up. Hill Country Harmonica was now officially incoming.

The final tally was impressive. HCH 2010 drew one hundred full-price attendees and twenty-five significant others from thirty U.S. states and seven foreign countries. The musicians, black and white, delivered inspired performances, and we paid most of them more than the contracted amount. As the event roared toward its Sunday evening conclusion, Annie Hollowell hugged my wife and exclaimed, "Your husband has put us on the *map!*" I shared her euphoria. Jeff and I had given her and Bill the fullest house they'd ever enjoyed; they'd given us the perfect home for this event. We'd all gotten paid. Our registrants raved about the weekend in post-event surveys, and although several complained about the warm, humid weather, and one, surfeited with Annie's pork BBQ and fried catfish, complained about the lack of vegetarian options, the majority insisted they would return the following year. If this sounds like a happy ending—well, yes, I guess it does. Those occasionally happen, even in what's left of Faulkner's Mississippi, the land where the blues began, and all those other clichés.

Afterword

Within six months of HCH 2010, Vince hired Terry "Harmonica" Bean to teach and perform at his next Clarksdale workshop. Hill Country Harmonica returned to Foxfire Ranch in 2011 and 2012. After a pause to catch their breath in 2013 and 2014, Jeff and I recently spoke with the Hollowells, and all parties are excited about bringing Hill Country Harmonica back on line in 2015. Sharde Thomas and the Rising Star Fife & Drum Band continue her grandfather Otha Turner's legacy—a two-day blues picnic in late August—and she has recently expanded the franchise to include a July 4 picnic as well. Bill and Annie Hollowell continue to minister to the local blues trade.

Notes

1. Smith, "Race, Civic Branding, and Identity Politics," 2–8.
2. McPherson, *Reconstructing Dixie*, 29.

3. King, *Strength to Love*, 72.

4. Edwards, *The World Don't Owe Me Nothing*, 36–39, 45, 47.

5. Barker, *A Life in Jazz*, 71.

6. Gussow, "Where Is the Love?," 158. The quoted language was found on the B. B. King Museum website when in fall 2010 I researched the conference presentation on which this essay was based, but it has since been changed. The mission statement now reads: "The mission of the B. B. King Museum and Delta Interpretive Center, a 501(c)(3) nonprofit organization, is to empower, unite and heal through music, art and education and share with the world the rich cultural heritage of the Mississippi Delta. The vision is to inspire hope, creativity, and greatness." See http://www.bbkingmuseum.org/mission (accessed May 26, 2014).

7. King, *I'm Feeling the Blues Right Now*. King's study, which I refereed in manuscript for the University Press of Mississippi, was published in 2011.

8. The *Hill Country Harmonica* website can be found at http://www.hillcountryharmonica.com/home.html. Accessed May 26, 2014.

9. See *Hill Country Harmonica*, http://www.hillcountryharmonica.com/hillcountryblues.html. Accessed May 26, 2014.

10. The Hill Country Harmonica 2010 poster can be viewed here: *Hill Country Harmonica*, http://www.hillcountryharmonica.com/photos_2010.html. Accessed May 26, 2014.

11. The video can be viewed on *YouTube*: http://www.youtube.com/watch?v=Gf4D2kVUg-A. Accessed May 26, 2014.

12. The Foxfire Ranch *Facebook* page can be found at https://www.facebook.com/foxfireranch2008. Accessed May 26, 2014.

13. According to US Census statistics and the 2008 American Community Survey, Mississippi had the fastest growth in interracial marriages between 2000 and 2008 but still ranked forty-ninth in overall percentage of mixed marriages. See Casey Gane-McCalla, "Interracial Marriage Still Rising, but Not as Fast," *NewsOne*, May 26, 2010, http://newsone.com/nation/casey-gane-mccalla/interracial-marriage-still-rising-but-not-as-fast/comment-page-1/. Accessed May 26, 2014.

14. See Rice, *Grace Matters*.

Works Cited

Barker, Danny. *A Life in Jazz*. Edited by Alyn Shipton. 1986. New York: Oxford University Press, 1988.

Cobb, James C. *The Most Southern Place on Earth: The Mississippi Delta and the Roots of Regional Identity*. New York: Oxford University Press, 1994.

Duck, Leigh Anne. *The Nation's Region: Southern Modernism, Segregation, and U.S. Nationalism*. Athens: University of Georgia Press, 2006.

Edwards, David Honeyboy. As told to Janis Martinson and Michael Robert Frank. *The World Don't Owe Me Nothing: The Life and Times of Delta Bluesman Honeyboy Edwards*. Chicago: Chicago Review Press, 1997.

Gussow, Adam. "'Where Is the Love?': Racial Violence, Racial Healing, and Blues Communities." *Southern Cultures: The Fifteenth Anniversary Reader*, edited by Harry L. Watson and Larry J. Griffin. Chapel Hill: University of North Carolina Press, 2008.

King, Martin Luther, Jr. *Strength to Love*. 1963. Philadelphia: Fortress Press, 1981.

King, Stephen A. *I'm Feeling the Blues Right Now: Blues Tourism in the Mississippi Delta*. Jackson: University Press of Mississippi, 2011.

McPherson, Tara. *Reconstructing Dixie: Race, Gender and Nostalgia in the Imagined South*. Durham: Duke University Press, 2003.

Rice, Chris P. *Grace Matters: A True Story of Race, Friendship, and Faith in the Heart of the South*. San Francisco: Jossey-Bass, 2002.

Smith, Jon. "Race, Civic Identity, and Branding in the 21st-Century South." Unpublished manuscript. Courtesy of the author.

7

Pride at Preservation Hall

Tourism, Spectacle, and Musicking in New Orleans Jazz

ANNE DVINGE

In the second episode of the first season of the HBO series *Treme*, jazz trombonist Antoine Batiste (played by Wendell Pierce) rolls his eyes when offered a gig at a bar on Bourbon Street. For Batiste, Bourbon Street is a site of faked authenticity, a staged, static version of the New Orleans jazz tradition that he treasures. However, the fellow musician telling Batiste about the gig (sousaphonist Matt Perrine as himself), as well as his old trombone teacher (played by rhythm and blues man Deacon John Moore), responds that there is nothing to be ashamed of—there is "pride on Bourbon Street." They insist on the authenticity and dignity of the music, and on the strength of the New Orleans jazz tradition over its apparent commodification. In the first episode of *Treme*'s second season, Delmond Lambreaux (Rob Brown), the New York–based jazz musician and son of New Orleans Indian chief Albert Lambreaux (Clarke Peters), storms off in anger after two New York colleagues deride New Orleans jazz and Preservation Hall as "caught in [a] tourist economy, like a minstrel show." Even though Delmond himself has chosen the New York bebop scene over New Orleans jazz and his father's fierce adherence to that tradition, he bristles at these outsiders' judgment of his hometown's jazz culture as hokey and anachronistic. Lambreaux junior insists on its validity and authenticity by stating that "it's a living tradition . . . I call up New Orleans in every note I play."[1]

The tension between consumerism and authenticity that exists in the creation and consumption of New Orleans jazz is the paradoxical product of the highly successful branding of the Crescent City as the birthplace of jazz. This branding has emerged from a complex nexus of marketing and tourism, as well as tradition and heritage. Even a quick browse through various travel guides and websites promoting New Orleans as a tourist destination confirms the connection: along with Mardi Gras and Cajun culture, live music and jazz in particular are mentioned as among the top attractions in New Orleans.[2] Recent guide books cite jazz culture as evidence of the indomitable spirit of New Orleans' recovery following Hurricane Katrina, while in 2010 the official New Orleans tourism website featured a video on the front page in which trumpeter and singer Jeremy Davenport beckons the viewer, "Come out and play."[3] Jazz is promoted as the soundtrack of New Orleans. However, New Orleans' musical culture is woven deep into the fabric of New Orleans history and culture. As Helen Taylor points out elsewhere in this volume and in her 2010 essay "After the Deluge," Katrina prompted an outpouring of creative energy and narratives of rebirth, with music repeatedly figured as key to the soul of the city.[4]

Despite the city's crucial role in the creation of jazz at the turn of the twentieth century, today's association between jazz and New Orleans stems mainly from the work of record collectors in the 1940s who rediscovered the tradition of early jazz, classifying it as "hot" in opposition to "sweet" or more commercially oriented dance music. Prior to the 1940s, jazz was not generally recognized locally as a heritage worth preserving, but the effort of the "hot" collectors to revitalize and sustain New Orleans-style jazz generated a revival that swept through the jazz world on both sides of the Atlantic. In particular, New Orleans jazz came to be associated with authenticity and origins: it has often been claimed by musicians, writers, and filmmakers as the only pure and original form of jazz and, by extension, as the source and center of the one true American art form.[5] Thus, jazz in New Orleans has become a complex signifier of not only a particular "southern" lifestyle that is marketed to visitors and essential to residents but also the greater American (jazz) tradition.

As the two scenes from *Treme* suggest, ideas of New Orleans jazz as a source of cultural tradition and a site of commodification for tourism have coexisted uneasily. Yet both ideas have also been interrogated as dubious constructs. Traditionalist histories of jazz have been criticized for constructing a neat evolutionary model of the music deriving from its "roots" in New Orleans that can then be inscribed into a consensus-based imagining of jazz as "America's classical music."[6] Furthermore, as Bruce

Raeburn argues, to create a "usable jazz history," the original hot collectors imposed a purist model "that precluded an accurate interpretation of the past"—that is, a past of multiple cultures, and the creolization of those cultures. Such collectors also "tended to undervalue the nature of New Orleans as a system of performance practices grounded in experimentation and variegation."[7] Helen Regis has juxtaposed such performance practices with the second lines staged in the French Quarter. Regis criticizes those second lines as a product of the increased commodification of African American culture, and part of a larger pattern in postindustrial society where cities become "sites of cultural consumption." For Regis, these French Quarter parades and shows are staged and static, aimed solely at tourists, and have nothing or little to do with the living practice of jazz culture in the city more broadly.[8] From this perspective, then, the French Quarter is merely an inauthentic backdrop for debased jazz tourism. However, as Connie Atkinson has pointed out, New Orleans musicians are engaged in forms of negotiation with the tourist industry, using music to address "issues of political, social, and economic identity, as well as creativity and ownership."[9] Thus, the issues of creation and consumption in New Orleans jazz culture are intertwined in complex ways.

In my own encounters with New Orleans jazz in the French Quarter, I have certainly come across the air of marketing hype and consumerism. However, I have also experienced jazz played with such passion and skill that it transcends simple dichotomies of tourism versus living art form, or consumerism versus authenticity. Through a close reading of the quintessential site of the marriage between traditional jazz revivalism and tourism, Preservation Hall, this essay argues that the French Quarter also offers strategies and moments for a more progressive understanding of both the music and its function. My analysis is based partly on readings of jazz historiography, cultural history, and ethnomusicology, and partly on personal observations made during several visits to Preservation Hall in the spring of 2010. Through the process that Christopher Small calls "musicking," Preservation Hall articulates complex relationships between form, practice, and symbolic space. The question of jazz music's function also complicates the notion that New Orleans and jazz constitute an ontological signifier of American identity.

The Creation, Creolization, Revival, and Recognition of Jazz in New Orleans, 1890s–1961

Hurricane Katrina's devastating impact in September 2005 displaced New Orleans' jazz musicians and destroyed important archives and collections of jazz memorabilia. However, it also intensified an ongoing discussion about the cultural importance of New Orleans and jazz. In the aftermath of the hurricane, there was a marked rise in the national media's attention toward both the city and its jazz culture.[10] *Down Beat Magazine* ran a special issue on New Orleans in November 2005 in which Wynton Marsalis signified on the city's status as not merely a southern city but a repository for the nation's sprit and memory: "When you take New Orleans from America, our soul equation goes down. Our city will come back, but it will take the entire country."[11] By contrast, Ben Jaffe, the current director of Preservation Hall, emphasized connections with the past, claiming that "New Orleans is a city that has remained pure, free from modern advances in culture and changing etiquette. [. . .] Old World charm and decadence drip from the heavy black iron rails of the city's gates and walls."[12] While Marsalis insists that New Orleans is essentially American (or rather, that America is essentially New Orleansian), Jaffe evokes the city's European links as implicitly a disavowal of modern American culture.

Such differing perceptions of New Orleans and its jazz tradition suggest the ambivalence that surrounds the music and its racial, cultural, and economic implications; they exemplify the tensions that have been and continue to be present in the marketing and commodification of New Orleans. These tensions also reflect the South's complex status as simultaneously the crucial locus of American history and a distinct and separate region—what literary scholars Leigh Anne Duck and Jennifer Greeson have respectively termed "the nation's region" and "internal other."[13] As historian James C. Cobb has noted, the South's regional distinctiveness was imagined in opposition to what came to be seen as the normative Northeast as early as immediately after the Revolutionary War.[14] New Orleans' ambiguous Americanness also derives from its location in a state that first entered the Union in 1812, the prior colonial history of which produced French, Spanish, and African influences that made the city more culturally diverse than other parts of the South and the nation. Thus, New Orleans can be utilized to represent the foreign, the regional, *and* the national ideal of the "melting pot." I am less interested in which New

Orleans is "real" than in how such competing conceptions of the city have been created and consumed regionally, nationally, and transnationally.

When tourism first became a possible source of significant income for New Orleans, the city was promoted in terms of that "Old World charm" and romantic foreign past still cited by Jaffe in 2005. As Anthony Stanonis points out in *Creating the Big Easy* (2006), rather than promoting the city as full participant in the modern United States, business and political leaders opted for an urban image that cast the city as a relic, a leftover still mired in French Catholic traditions.[15] "Paris-in-the-wilderness" was an early moniker, and, as Helen Taylor demonstrates, this image has continued to reverberate: in the nineteenth century it changed to "the American Paris," and as recently as the 1990s the city was still referred to as "America's European Masterpiece."[16] New Orleans' "Europeanness," Taylor argues, derives from on one hand a certain focus on the sensual pleasure of the body, such as food and music, and on the other from a sense of history as a tangible presence, which "sets it apart from postmodern hyperreality."[17] As such, New Orleans has held a continued fascination for both European and American visitors, who in turn produce and reproduce this image of the city in travel literature, fiction, drama, and art. Taylor points to the role jazz plays in today's imaginings of New Orleans as a repository of authenticity.[18] Yet jazz was not initially perceived as an asset to New Orleans tourism: its hybrid origins as well as its overt modernity presented an image that was too jarring to the representations of French antiquity that were usually privileged by city boosters and artists alike.

New Orleans is also a port city through which goods, people, and cultures have flowed, creating a profoundly modern and hybrid society. As Charles Hersch points out in *Subversive Sounds: Race and the Birth of Jazz in New Orleans* (2007), the environment that facilitated jazz derived partly from French Louisiana's more malleable racial categories and its relatively moderate approach to slaves' retention and expression of their African cultural heritage.[19] Hersch argues that in particular the use of the term *Creole*, as a "catch all term for those of mixed race, as long as the white part of the mixture was not American," blurred racial boundaries and "challenged race-based thinking because it rested on culture rather than biology." As such, "rather than an innate or inherited identity, Creoleness was something one performed."[20]

In jazz research, the term *creole* first appeared in 1959, in a two-part essay by Ernest Borneman for the *Jazz Review*. Borneman, who had been part of the revivalist movement in the late 1930s and 1940s, questioned the assumption that jazz arose out of New Orleans "by an act of spontaneous creation." Instead, Borneman suggested, jazz had its roots in an Afro-Latin/Latin-American music, "the music of French and Spanish speaking Negroes and Creoles—a music very much more complex than the first recorded examples of jazz."[21] The direct Afro-Caribbean musical characteristics later faded, leaving behind what piano man and early jazz originator Jelly Roll Morton referred to as the "Spanish tinge," such as various Latin rhythm patterns. Borneman's pioneering argument for the recognition of the Caribbean and creole roots of jazz was eventually extended by such researchers as Thomas Fiehrer and Christopher Washburne. Washburne in particular makes a convincing argument for the pervasiveness of the *clave* rhythm in jazz:

> The frequency of these rhythms in early jazz suggests that the Caribbean influence was so tied to its developmental stages that the rhythms became part of the rhythmic foundation of jazz. . . . Their absence in other African-American styles not as closely associated with New Orleans as jazz—such as work songs, field hollers, spirituals, gospel, and some blues traditions—attests to the unique nature of New Orleans and the influence its ethnic diversity had on the music that was made there.[22]

However, the flexibility of racial and ethnic identities that creole cultures implied and performed—not least in jazz—produced deep anxieties in New Orleans. One of the most famous objections to jazz, and in particular the idea of New Orleans as its place of origin, appeared in the 1918 *New Orleans Times-Picayune* editorial, "Jass and Jassism."

> On certain natures sound loud and meaningless has an exciting, almost an intoxicating effect, like crude colors and strong perfumes, the sight of flesh or the sadic pleasure in blood. To such as these the jass music is a delight. [. . .] In the matter of jass, New Orleans is particularly interested, since it has been widely suggested that this particular form of musical vice had its birth in this city—that it came, in fact, from doubtful surroundings in our slums. We do not recognize the honor of parenthood. [. . .] Its musical value is nil, and its possibilities of harm are great.[23]

Although those "certain natures" mentioned in the editorial are not explicitly defined by race, the connections made between jazz, primitivism, sexualized behavior, and the suspect city "slums" strongly imply a racialized anxiety about New Orleans' identity. As Hersch points out, these anxieties were not confined to white society, as both black and Creole communities rejected jazz on the grounds of respectability.[24]

Still, newspaper editorials are not necessarily an expression of public opinion, and, as Raeburn points out, the reactions to jazz in New Orleans were as varied as elsewhere in the United States. Some readers of the *Picayune* came to the music's defense.[25] During the 1920s, a younger generation increasingly found jazz to be "all the rage," and it was accepted into middle-class society at dance parties and restaurants. Small jazz bands started performing at debutante balls as well as restaurants and society clubs.[26] Thus, the music and the musicians transcended racial and class lines—at least to the extent of being better paid and accepted as a source of entertainment in white middle-class society. It remained the case, however, that jazz accrued little cultural capital among the city's arbiters of taste. As jazz critic and early hot collector Charles Edward Smith noted, although "the people of New Orleans enjoyed and sustained the music," the music itself never got more than "a passing nod from the local guardians of culture."[27]

During the 1930s, the small combos that characterized early New Orleans jazz were overshadowed by the big swing bands that rose to national fame. The style of the musicians who played in the small orchestras became outdated, and those musicians once again found themselves struggling to make a living. Other factors also contributed to the decline of jazz in New Orleans. The Great Migration ensured the dissemination of jazz to the rest of the United States, but as Mark Souther points out, "by World War II, New Orleans had the smallest proportion of African Americans of any major Southern city, paving the way for a dilution of black cultural forms." In addition, the Great Depression and World War II put a damper on the general thirst for revelry, as well as venues' inclination and/or ability to pay musicians. Instead, the radio and the jukeboxes took over to such an extent that when Sterling Brown arrived in New Orleans in 1942, he noted with evident disappointment that "New Orleans gave jazz to the world; the world parcelled bits of it back over the turn-table and the air-waves."[28]

An organized and conscious effort to celebrate and preserve New Orleans jazz did not arise until the revival of the 1940s, led by hot collectors from outside the city. The trend of collecting hot records began almost as soon as jazz reached a mainstream audience in the 1920s, and a small group of white male Ivy League students started seeking out the rare and obscure (and thus purportedly less commercial) recordings of early jazz. It became a more widespread pastime in the 1930s, and as the community of hot collectors grew, so did the need for better and more in-depth information.[29] Only so much could be gleaned from album covers, which had not yet evolved into small works of art with accompanying liner notes. Hence, collectors began making pilgrimages to the Crescent City, where they found an underappreciated music and struggling musicians. A small number of devotees either stayed in or returned to the city, playing an important part in the revival of the music in New Orleans.

This revival of New Orleans jazz may be understood in terms of Josh Kun's concept of *audiotopia*. Kun proposes that "music functions like a possible utopia for the listener," where "almost-places of cultural encounter" map the music's social and cultural space, and thus potentially remap the listener's own social and cultural geography.[30] The Ivy League students listening to early recordings of New Orleans jazz were met with and transported to an audiotopia that suggested a creolized cultural, social, and musical space. Now as then, attempts to realize the utopian potential in such an (imagined, aural) scenario contain the possibility of creating new social spaces that allow differential social relationships. However, two sets of factors endanger the potential for social change in such spaces. The first set contains the socioeconomic-political realities of racial and ethnic difference (such as segregation) in New Orleans and beyond, as well as the role of the marketplace, and the difficulty any imagined space may have in effecting real change in these areas. The other set of factors relates to the processual nature of both creolization *and* utopias. *Creolization* is a term that not only denotes racial ambiguity but also continuously undergoes semantic shifts; meanwhile, utopia is that which must necessarily be perpetually deferred or else become frozen in impossible perfection. Thus, to insist on creating and maintaining a utopian, creolized space is not just to contradict oneself; it also risks ossifying notions of creolization through romanticized ideas of purity and authenticity.

The difficulty in negotiating such complex terrain has encumbered various attempts to create a new social and cultural space for jazz in New Orleans. The first jazz organization in New Orleans to self-consciously promote and sustain the city's music was founded in 1944. Named the National Jazz Foundation (NJF), it was governed by a twofold impetus toward revival and official recognition: the NJF declared its aim to "maintain a lively interest in jazz music" and to establish a jazz museum.[31] However, as the name implies, the NJF's approach was not exclusively concerned with New Orleans jazz, and the foundation soon focused on mainstream swing, possibly as an attempt to cater to popular taste (and the marketplace) but with the result that it lost its focus along the way. The NJF folded in April 1947, and a more purist and localized endeavor began in February 1948. The New Orleans Jazz Club (NOJC) took seriously its commitment to the local music culture, seeking to create employment for musicians. The NOJC's constitution vowed to "afford a common meeting ground for lovers of jazz. To preserve, stimulate, encourage and retain New Orleans jazz, primarily, and also all the ramifications and forms thereof. To help foster and advertise all creators of New Orleans music."[32] Like the NJF, the NOJC aimed to establish a jazz museum, again with greater emphasis on New Orleans and its musicians. The museum became a reality in November 1961, and its collection is today housed at the Louisiana State Museum's Old Mint building.[33] As Raeburn points out, the establishment of the museum, along with the jazz archive at Tulane University, marked the "arrival" of jazz as an officially sanctioned source of city pride and identity and provided formal "recognition of the city's multiracial musical heritage." Even the *Times-Picayune* ran an editorial that celebrated the entry of jazz into the hallowed halls of culture.[34]

The Creation and Consumption of Authenticity at Preservation Hall, 1961–2011

In June 1961 Preservation Hall was established on the basis of what had started in the mid-1950s as a series of informal musical gatherings at the Associated Artists Studio, a gallery owned and run by E. Lorenz "Larry" Borenstein. According to Borenstein, he had opened the gallery on St. Peter Street in 1952 but found that running it conflicted with his desire to go out for live music around town. Instead, he started inviting musicians to come by for "rehearsals" (so labeled to avoid trouble with the unions) that were open to audiences by invitation only.[35] However, double doors opening on to St. Peter Street and the location next to the bar Pat O'Brien's encouraged passersby to drop in under the pretext of looking at the art, sit down for a while to listen, and place some money in the "kitty" on their way out. As William Carter notes, people were not encouraged to stay for hours, and the band would often repeat tunes over the course of the session. This set a praxis that continues to this day. As both the interest in the music and the audiences grew, the gallery and Borenstein attracted negative attention, especially because the sessions were often racially integrated. As one Judge Babylon was reported to have said, the city did not "want any Yankees coming to New Orleans mixing cream with our coffee."[36]

The continued anxiety among locals (or at least white officials) over the racially hybrid dimensions of jazz may partially explain why most of the people behind the Preservation Hall initiative were not natives of New Orleans. Borenstein was originally from Milwaukee, while the first managers of Preservation Hall, Ken Mills and Barbara Reid, were from San Francisco and Chicago respectively. Allan and Sandra Jaffe, who ran the hall after Mills and Reid, had arrived from Pennsylvania in 1960. These "outsiders" were the ones who felt compelled to sustain the traditional New Orleans jazz idiom. To be sure, the bars in the French Quarter had begun to see the money-making potential in hosting live jazz music, but it was felt that this purely monetary interest did not serve the music well.[37] Once Mills took over from Borenstein, Preservation Hall functioned on a strictly noncommercial basis, running on kitty donations only. The anticommercial sentiment was also reflected in some of the names that were suggested for the hall at 726 St. Peter Street: "Authenticity Hall," "Perseverance Hall," and finally "Preservation Hall."[38]

The implication that the authentic and the commercial are mutually exclusive is located within a romantic discourse about the purity of art unsullied by the demands of the marketplace. It has little basis in the historic reality of jazz music as a form of popular entertainment, or its ongoing function in New Orleans everyday life in the form of jazz funerals and second lines. However, as jazz musicians and fans have sought wider recognition of jazz as an original and "high" art form, the romantic discourse of authenticity has increasingly been adopted, culminating in the "jazz is America's classical music" paradigm that has solidified since the late 1980s. At Preservation Hall, the management's typically romantic distinction between base commerce and the "preservation" of authentic, traditional New Orleans jazz meant that, ironically, a lack of income came close to endangering the concert schedule. When Allan and Sandra Jaffe took over the Hall in the fall of 1961, they initially had to work full-time jobs to sustain the music. Eventually, taking the music—and brand—of Preservation Hall on tour beyond New Orleans provided the financial basis for the St. Peter Street venue itself. Starting in 1963, Allan Jaffe built a large roster of musicians (large enough to set up different band configurations so that one or two could be on the road while others were playing at the Hall) and started touring on a regular basis, both nationally and internationally.[39] Already on the second tour, in August 1963, the band traveled as far as Japan, playing all over the country for three months and selling out every single concert, performing to an estimated 320,000 people.[40] Other touring schedules encompassed South America, the United Kingdom, and continental Europe, as well as, in 1979, a State Department–sponsored tour of the Soviet Union not unlike the kind of Cold War cultural diplomacy undertaken by William Faulkner during the 1950s and discussed by Deborah Cohn elsewhere in this volume.[41] These tours served the double function of providing an income for the Hall while continuing to disseminate the music to a worldwide audience, in the process contributing to the ongoing creation and consumption of New Orleans jazz beyond the city and the South.

Preservation Hall is situated in a historic building on St. Peter Street in the French Quarter. The structure, built in Spanish style with its simple facade and wrought iron balcony, dates back to 1750, though in fact the majority of the current building was rebuilt after a fire in 1816 destroyed a number of houses on St. Peter Street.[42] Despite the humble exterior, it is difficult to miss Preservation Hall on a performance night: the line starts to build two hours before the first scheduled set, and it does not peter out until after the last set. Once guests enter through the gates of the carriage house, there is a mad rush for the eight narrow benches that serve as the only real seating in the house. Those concertgoers who linger in the carriageway or were too far back in the queue have to either sit on the floor in front of the benches or stand behind them in a tightly packed crowd.

The room is bare save for the setup for the musicians and a few paintings and signs on the walls. All colors are brown and sepia. There is no air conditioning, just a couple of fans that on a hot and humid night only stir the heavy air a little. Nor is there any sale of any form of beverages. This is not a bar, where the music functions as entertainment and perhaps even becomes secondary to the socializing and drinking that bars usually facilitate. Rather, the space clearly signals that the music is the primary event, and that it is to be experienced without any distractions. It is not dissimilar to the sort of space found at living history museums or a side room at a modern art museum showing a movie about the current artist or artwork on a thirty-minute loop.[43] The cumulative effect is of a space where the music becomes an artifact that we are encouraged to admire and appreciate.

According to musicologist Christopher Small, the design of a space reflects assumptions about the sort of behavior and relationships that are supposed to be performed inside, as well as ideals of human relations on a larger scale.[44] In this respect, Preservation Hall sends out a mixed or at least complex signal. The humble exterior on one hand signifies that what takes place inside is not of grand significance (compared, for example, to Jazz at Lincoln Center's residence in the Time Warner Building in New York City). On the other hand, the basic, even minimalist, design speaks of a "pure" experience, unpolluted by commercial or other extra-musical concerns. The sepia color scheme signifies vintage, the absence of amplification suggests authenticity, and the whole museum-like setup encourages a sharp distinction between (active) performers and (passive) audience.

However, Preservation Hall is also something more and different than a museum that "preserves" traditional New Orleans jazz in amber. In its representation of the city's musical tradition, it takes on the character of what French historian Pierre Nora refers to as "lieux de mémoire"— realms of memory. These are sites of embodied memory where the material, the functional, and the symbolic coexist.[45] Nora defines them as "vestiges, the ultimate embodiments of a commemorative consciousness that survives in a history which, having renounced memory, cries out for it."[46] Nora's observation that realms of memory are hybrid places, combining the eternal and the temporal, seems particularly apt for Preservation Hall. The deliberately unrestored vintage feel of the building and the lack of modern comforts encourage the notion that the place has been around since the halcyon days of New Orleans jazz, while drawing too on the discourse of antiquity about the city's "Old World" architecture. Yet the music's temporal aspects—in terms both of the moment of performance and of jazz's broader identity as a musical form that originated at a specific and relatively recent point in time—destabilize any tendency to locate Preservation Hall in the purely archival.

Here, one might consider Michel Foucault's coupling of time and heterotopia. On one hand, Preservation Hall reflects the "indefinitely accumulated time [of] museums"; on the other hand, it embodies the "transitory, precarious time in the mode of the festival."[47] Kun's conception of audiotopia paraphrases Foucault's heterotopia, as when he deems audiotopias "sonic spaces of effective utopian longings where several sites normally deemed incompatible are brought together, not only in the space of a particular piece of music itself, but in the production of social space and the mapping of geographical space that music makes possible as well."[48] Similarly, the music and the performances at Preservation Hall disrupt the rules of behavior that the space, as well as its position as a site of tourist consumerism, seems to dictate.

"Sing with Me Now": Ideal Relationships and Collective Improvisations at Preservation Hall

The immediate impression of a museum-like demarcation between performers and audience is reversed by the cramped nature of Preservation Hall, which entails that audiences share the concert space with the performers. There are seats along the side of the stage, and those seated on the floor in front of the musicians not only risk being knocked in the head by a trombone slide, but also cannot remain (literally or metaphorically) distant consumers: the music and musicians are up close and very personal. On the nights that I attended Preservation Hall during spring 2010, the audience's demographic makeup was dominated by tourists, with a notable predominance of French visitors. Almost all of the audience, from whatever country, would have been conventionally defined as "white." In terms of age, there was a slight tendency toward the forty-plus demographic, but it spanned the generations. This is not a typical jazz audience, but a mix of jazz lovers and tourists with no jazz experience or preferences.

Thus, when the music first starts, the audience takes a little while to get into "the swing of things," so to speak. Some will know to clap on two and four, while others will happily clap on one and three unless they are taught otherwise. Since this is (partly) a pedagogic venture, the band directs and regulates not only the clapping, but also sing-alongs and call-and-response sequences. Also, those members of the audience who are returning customers know the routines and will lead the way. On one of the nights I attended, Shannon Powell & the Preservation Hall Stars were performing, and Powell launched into a lengthy explanation of the form and cultural meaning of a New Orleans funeral march. In many ways, all of this fits with the preservation ethos, enlightening and educating the audience about the music. The songs in the repertoire are mostly tried and tested classics from within the tradition: "Exactly like You," "St. James Infirmary," "Li'l Liza Jane," and, the pièce de résistance, "What a Wonderful World." However, "Li'l Liza Jane" is provided with a funky second-line beat and becomes a communal affair as Powell moves into the crowd, urging everyone to sing along in harmony. Meanwhile, "What a Wonderful World" is rescued from sheer corniness by heavy signifying from the band, as when the singer grabs a dollar bill from the kitty and wipes his sweaty forehead while singing the title words and looking pointedly out into the crowd. This wry reference to Preservation Hall's position in a tourist economy is reaffirmed in a sign on the wall behind the musicians that announces costs: "Traditional requests $2.00," "Others $5.00," and "The Saints $10.00." The sign acknowledges the overuse of "The Saints" as a New Orleans anthem, but it also dismantles hierarchies of canon and tradition by the insertion of the highly ambiguous category of "Others."

Central to an understanding of what goes on in Preservation Hall is the insight that the music is not separate from the moment of performance, but integral to it. Moreover, the performance involves not only the musicians and their instruments, but also the audience and the physical space. There is no hint of the living museum's classic strategy of reenactment; no sense of dutiful but uninspired tourist-centered performance. Forget static, narrow, and even purist definitions of what jazz is or is not: the sounds coming from the band are too swinging, too filled with passion, humor, and knowledge to be staid and stable. This is not a museum artifact or easy entertainment, but a living, breathing artistic practice—at least for a moment. Some of those tourists I talked to seemed to have had their appetite for music sharpened and were heading to another gig; others had gotten the symbolic jazz experience they came for and were ready for another aspect of their New Orleans vacation. Meanwhile, musicians joked among themselves and talked of what second lines would be coming up on Sunday.

The transcending force that allows Preservation Hall to be something more than a museum, a concert hall, or just a simple music venue is "musicking." In transposing the noun *music* to the present participle verb *musicking*, Small emphasizes an understanding of music not as an object but as an activity. Musicking is something we do and participate in, rather than a separate entity we may possess as a commodity. Furthermore, as an activity, musicking implies a social rather than an individual meaning: it functions as a "human encounter" that "provides us with a language by means of which we can come to understand and articulate [ideal] relationships and through them to understand the relationships of our lives."[49] If we consider the relationships that are posited and performed at Preservation Hall as forms of musicking, the desire to keep the music alive and to pass it on seems essential. But something else is at play as well: an oppositional relationship between the ways the space and the performance embody that desire. The physical space insists on a relationship between audience and the music that is based on passive appreciation, reverence, and consumption, whereas the more ephemeral performance embodies a relationship of active participation, humor, and improvisation. In the process, the performance transcends both the physical and socioeconomic space, disrupting the rules of behavior that these dictate.

The reason for this is to be found in matters of form and practice. A central element in New Orleans traditional jazz—the one that you will most frequently find missing in watered-down or static versions of the music—is the collective improvisation. In (almost) all jazz, improvisation is key, but from swing up through bebop to modern jazz, this praxis takes the form (with variations and greater subtleties than I can go into here) of alternating between the group playing the melody and harmonies together, and a soloist taking off while the rhythm section accompanies and makes the occasional riff or musical comment. In New Orleans, traditional jazz developed from the melody being passed from one instrument to the other, but by the 1920s a lead (e.g., trumpet or vocal) would be playing the melody, with variations through syncopating and paraphrasing. Simultaneously, the clarinet and/or the saxophone may be improvising countermelodies, with the trombone and rhythm section providing the rhythmic foundation—all coming together in a collective improvisation.[50] Longer solos will be taken, but it is this sound—what Olly Wilson refers to as a "heterogeneous sound ideal," with dense overlapping textures—that most clearly defines this music.[51]

There are several important implications to this praxis. One points to jazz improvisation as a deeply inclusive and relational act, not only in the way the musicians must relate to and include one another, but also in the sense of different sonic identities. This might involve an individual musician and his instrument, or a harmonic or rhythmical pattern derived from different cultures and traditions, thereby entering into a relationship of creolized sound. A second implication is that this heterogeneity also reflects the origins of the music and provides us with a counternarrative to the idea of jazz as "America's classical music." A third and final implication is that the collective reaches beyond the bandstand, out to the audience and even further, as it implies improvisatory human relationships in and of the world.

Any national, cultural, or musical purism that attempts to corral jazz music into a neatly linear history, or make it act as a metaphor for the greater American melting pot and democracy, collapses under closer scrutiny. This sort of music and history cannot easily be contained in a neat exhibition of a musical artifact. It must therefore explode such a framework to create an audiotopia, an identificatory "contact zone" of "both sonic and social spaces where disparate identity-formations, cultures, *and* geographies historically kept and mapped separately are allowed to interact with each other as well as enter into relationships whose consequences for cultural identification are never predetermined."[52] Through its complex origin and continually creolized present, New Orleans jazz functions as an audiotopia in the greater American soundscape.[53]

There is no doubt that the setting of Preservation Hall taps into the touristic consumption of New Orleans, bound up with ideas about the city's Old World origins and its marketing as the site and source of jazz. Still, staged or not, the level of musicianship and commitment to the music resists easy dismissal as "commercialized," "inauthentic," or "nostalgic." The relationships between space and performance at Preservation Hall are complex and heterogeneous. In the momentary transformation of Preservation Hall through a process of musicking that encompasses both the performers and the audience, we see the potential of this supposedly old-fashioned music to reinvent and reappropriate the jazz tradition, as well as the geographical and symbolic space that the Hall inhabits. Thus, in contrast to Nora's nostalgic jeremiad for the loss of "true memory" and rituals, the performative moment enacted in every twenty-minute session at Preservation Hall embodies ritual and living memory. This relational act of musicking prevents Preservation Hall from being either a hermetically closed *lieu de mémoire* or a purely heterotopic site, separate from other sites. Sure, consumption is at play here, but so are creative flow, conversation, and cultural polyphony.

Notes

1. See *Treme*, season 1, episode 2; and *Treme*, season 2, episode 1.
2. See, for example, *Lonely Planet New Orleans*, with an image of Preservation Hall under the headline "Introducing New Orleans"; the guide also features a whole chapter devoted to the New Orleans Jazz & Heritage Festival, which supposedly "sums up everything that would be lost if the world was to lose New Orleans" (Karlin, *Lonely Planet New Orleans*, 2, 50). It is also noteworthy that *Frommer's New Orleans* guidebook featured jazz musicians on the cover in 1997, 2001, 2003, 2004, 2006, 2008, and 2010.
3. The video is no longer available at http://www.neworleansonline.com but can be viewed at http://vimeo.com/872674, accessed October 28, 2011.
4. Taylor, "After the Deluge," 487–88; "Recovering through a Cultural Economy," in this volume.
5. Raeburn, *New Orleans Style*, 4.
6. DeVeaux, "Constructing the Jazz Tradition," 25–26, 31. This idea of jazz gained currency in the mid-1980s with Grover Sales' book *Jazz: America's Classical Music* (1985) and William Taylor's 1986 article of the same title. It subsequently became part of a concerted effort to shift jazz from the margins to the center of American culture. As I have argued at length elsewhere, this strategy risks narrowing the definitions of jazz to fit perceived canonical standards, and marginalizing music that is not seen as immediately or obviously "American." See Dvinge, *Between History and Hearsay*, especially 223.
7. Raeburn, *New Orleans Style*, 7, 9.
8. Regis, "Blackness and the Politics of Memory," 753, 769.
9. Atkinson, "Shakin' Your Butt for the Tourist," 155.
10. A news search on LexisNexis, using the terms "jazz" and "New Orleans" in "Headline and Lead," and searching only newspapers with article location set to the U.S., brought the following results: 8/1/2004–8/1/2005: 816 hits; 8/1/2005–8/1/2006: 1,797 hits.
11. Ouellette, "New Orleans Special Report," 38.
12. Jaffe, "New Orleans Special Report," 42.
13. Duck, *Nation's Region*; Greeson, *Our South*, 1.
14. Cobb, *Away down South*, 2–7.
15. Stanonis, *Creating the Big Easy*, 196–97.
16. Taylor, *Circling Dixie*, 93.
17. Ibid., 99.
18. Ibid., 107ff. As Taylor also demonstrates in her book, the appreciation of New Orleans jazz came initially (and continues to this day) from overseas, particularly France and Britain.
19. Hersch, *Subversive Sounds*, 10, 17–18.
20. Ibid., 21–22.
21. Borneman, "Creole Echoes I," 13, 14.
22. Washburne, "Clave of Jazz," 75. See also Fiehrer, "From Quadrille to Stomp."
23. Reprinted as "Location of Jass," in Walser, *Keeping Time*, 7–8.
24. Hersch, *Subversive Sounds*, 67–69.
25. Raeburn, *New Orleans Style*, 220–21.
26. Ibid., 222–23.

27. Smith, "Land of Dreams," 268.
28. Souther, "Making the 'Birthplace of Jazz,'" 44, 40.
29. Stephen Smith lists Charles Edward Smith's article "Collecting Hot" in *Esquire*, February 1934, as one of the catalysts of a wider movement. See Smith, "Hot Collecting," 289.
30. Kun, *Audiotopia*, 2–3.
31. Raeburn, *New Orleans Style*, 236.
32. "The Jazz Club Story," *The Second Line Archive*, http://www.nojazzclub.org/V06.S.htm, accessed April 7, 2011.
33. See the Louisiana State Museum Jazz Collection, http://lsm.crt.state.la.us/collections/jazz.htm, accessed April 5, 2011.
34. Raeburn, *New Orleans Style*, 247–48.
35. Carter, *Preservation Hall*, 115.
36. Ibid., 125, 116.
37. See Raeburn, *New Orleans Style*, 255.
38. Carter, *Preservation Hall*, 148.
39. Raeburn, *New Orleans Style*, 256.
40. Carter, *Preservation Hall*, 234.
41. See Cohn, "Southern Regionalism and U.S. Nationalism in William Faulkner's State Department Travels," in this volume. The State Department tours were part of the official cultural diplomacy or soft power policy of the United States during the Cold War. See also Von Eschen, *Satchmo Blows Up the World*, for a comprehensive account of the jazz tours.
42. Carter, *Preservation Hall*, 28–29.
43. The band plays only short sets of between twenty and twenty-five minutes, after which the audience is encouraged, although not ordered, to circulate back out and let those waiting outside or in the carriageway in.
44. Small, *Musicking*, 29.
45. Nora, *Realms of Memory*, 14.
46. Ibid., 6.
47. Foucault, "Of Other Spaces," 26. For a more in-depth discussion of the relationships between musical performance, time, and heterotopia, see Dvinge, "Keeping Time."
48. Kun, *Audiotopia*, 23.
49. Small, *Musicking*, 9–10, 13–14.
50. Monson, "Jazz Improvisation," 115.
51. Wilson, "Black Music as an Art Form," 3.
52. Kun, *Audiotopia*, 23.
53. Ibid., 12.

Works Cited

Atkinson, Connie. "'Shakin' Your Butt for the Tourist': Music's Role in the Identification and Selling of New Orleans." In *Dixie Debates: Perspectives on Southern Cultures*, edited by Richard H. King and Helen Taylor, 150–64. London: Pluto Press, 1996.

Borneman, Ernest. "Creole Echoes—Part I." *Jazz Review* 2, no. 8 (1959): 13–15.
———. "Creole Echoes—Part II." *Jazz Review* 2, no. 10 (1959): 26–27.
Carter, William. *Preservation Hall: Music from the Heart*. New York: W. W. Norton, 1999.
Cobb, James C. *Away Down South: A History of Southern Identity*. New York: Oxford University Press, 2005.
DeVeaux, Scott. "Constructing the Jazz Tradition: Jazz Historiography." *Black American Literature Forum* 25, no. 3, Literature of Jazz issue (1991): 525–60.
Duck, Leigh Anne. *The Nation's Region: Southern Modernism, Segregation, and U.S. Nationalism*. Athens: University of Georgia Press, 2006.
Dvinge, Anne. *Between History and Hearsay: Imagining Jazz at the Turn of the 21st Century*. PhD diss., University of Copenhagen, 2007.
———. "Keeping Time—Performing Place: Heterotopia and Jazz in Candace Allen's *Valaida*." *Journal of Transnational American Studies* 4, no. 2 (2012). http://escholarship.org/uc/item/79w3r5ck. Accessed January 10, 2013.
Fiehrer, Thomas. "From Quadrille to Stomp: The Creole Origins of Jazz." *Popular Music* 10, no. 1 (1991): 21–38.
Foucault, Michel. "Of Other Spaces." *Diacritics: A Review of Contemporary Criticism* 16, no. 1 (1986): 22–27.
Greeson, Jennifer. *Our South: Geographic Fantasy and the Rise of National Literature*. Cambridge: Harvard University Press, 2010.
Herczog, Mary. *Frommer's New Orleans 2010*. Hoboken, NJ: John Wiley and Sons, 2009.
Hersch, Charles. *Subversive Sounds: Race and the Birth of Jazz in New Orleans*. Chicago: University of Chicago Press, 2007.
Jaffe, Ben. "New Orleans Special Report: What Does It Mean to Preserve New Orleans?" *Down Beat: Jazz, Blues & Beyond* 72, no. 11 (2005): 42.
Karlin, A. *New Orleans, City Guide*. Oakland: Lonely Planet, 2009.
Kun, Josh. *Audiotopia: Music, Race, and America*. Berkeley: University of California Press, 2005.
Monson, Ingrid. "Jazz Improvisation." In *The Cambridge Companion to Jazz*, edited by Mervyn Cooke and David Horn, 114–32. New York: Cambridge University Press, 2002.
Nora, Pierre. *Realms of Memory, Rethinking the French Past*. New York: Columbia University Press, 1996.
Ouellette, Dan. "New Orleans Special Report: Jazz Community Begins Massive Musician Relief Efforts." *Down Beat: Jazz, Blues & Beyond* 72, no. 11 (2005): 38–39.
Raeburn, Bruce Boyd. *New Orleans Style and the Writing of American Jazz History*. Ann Arbor: University of Michigan Press, 2009.
Regis, Helen A. "Blackness and the Politics of Memory in the New Orleans Second Line." *American Ethnologist* 28, no. 4 (2001): 752–77.
Small, Christopher. *Musicking: The Meanings of Performing and Listening*. Hanover, NH: University Press of New England, 1998.
Smith, Charles Edward. "Land of Dreams." In *Jazzmen*, edited by Frederic Ramsey and Charles Edward Smith, 265–85. New York: Harcourt, 1939.

Smith, Stephen W. "Hot Collecting." In *Jazzmen*, edited by Frederic Ramsey and Charles Edward Smith, 287–99. New York: Harcourt, 1939.

Souther, J. Mark. "Making The 'Birthplace of Jazz': Tourism and Musical Heritage Marketing in New Orleans." *Louisiana History: The Journal of the Louisiana Historical Association* 44, no. 1 (2003): 39–73.

Stanonis, Anthony J. *Creating the Big Easy: New Orleans and the Emergence of Modern Tourism, 1918–1945*. Athens: University of Georgia Press, 2006.

Taylor, Helen. *Circling Dixie: Contemporary Southern Culture through a Transatlantic Lens*. New Brunswick: Rutgers University Press, 2001.

———. "After the Deluge: The Post-Katrina Cultural Revival of New Orleans." *Journal of American Studies* 44, no. 3 (2010): 483–501.

"The Jazz Club Story." http://www.nojazzclub.org/V06.S.htm. Accessed April 7, 2011.

Treme. Season 1, episode 2. First broadcast April 18, 2010 by HBO. Directed by Jim McKay, written by David Simon and Eric Overmyer.

Treme. Season 2, episode 1. First broadcast April 24, 2011 by HBO. Directed by Anthony Hemingway, written by David Simon, Eric Overmyer, and Anthony Bourdain.

Von Eschen, Penny M. *Satchmo Blows Up the World: Jazz Ambassadors Play the Cold War*. Cambridge: Harvard University Press, 2006.

Walser, Robert. *Keeping Time: Readings in Jazz History*. New York: Oxford University Press, 1999.

Washburne, Christopher. "The Clave of Jazz: A Caribbean Contribution to the Rhythmic Foundation of an African-American Music." *Black Music Research Journal* 17, no. 1 (1997): 59–80.

Wilson, Olly. "Black Music as an Art Form." *Black Music Research Journal* 3 (1983): 1–22.

8

Recovering through a Cultural Economy

New Orleans from Katrina to Deepwater Horizon

HELEN TAYLOR

New Orleans has long been a cosmopolitan center of world culture. Its close transatlantic—especially French and Spanish—cultural links and influences are enriched and complemented by African and Caribbean fusions. Its particular colonial and demographic history has given it a global profile and ensured longstanding artistic relations with Europe and Africa. However, this history also sets New Orleans apart from almost all Protestant U.S. cities and has led to both demonization of its sensual delights and neglect by successive administrations of its severe socioeconomic problems.

The disastrous events following hurricanes Katrina and Rita in August and September 2005 brought all of this into sharp focus. Despite Katrina veering away from the city just before making landfall, the levees broke and swaths of the city flooded. At least two thousand people died, and many disappeared; the city's infrastructure was devastated; and its population (especially African American) was drastically reduced. In the 2010 U.S. Census, the city's numbers were shown to be one-third less than they were in 2000, with a post-Katrina toll showing a fall in the black population from 67 percent to 60 percent of the total population, with 118,000 fewer black residents in the city.[1]

Less than five years later, in April 2010, a new disaster struck the Gulf Coast area. An explosion occurred on the Deepwater Horizon drilling rig in the Gulf of Mexico. Eleven rig workers were killed, and the resulting oil spill, lasting from April to July, polluted the coasts of four Gulf states. The spill from the Deepwater Horizon catastrophe was sixteen times that of the 1989 *Exxon Valdez* disaster in Alaska. The scale of the spill prompted a ban on new deepwater drilling in the Gulf and led to hundreds of lawsuits being submitted by fishing and seafood interests, the tourism industry, restaurant owners, and other groups. Moreover, a major lawsuit was filed on behalf of the federal government against a group of corporations headed by London-based BP (owner of the oil and gas prospect on which Deepwater Horizon was located) and Geneva-based Transocean (the multinational offshore drilling contractor that owned Deepwater Horizon). Such legal actions were grim proof that the calamitous side-effects of globalized corporate capitalism were now threatening the very livelihood of New Orleans and its environs.

That said, the voices of doom predicting the demise of the Crescent City after Katrina have been challenged by an optimistic and energetic movement both within and beyond the city to bring displaced residents home, and to revive and renew the city. Among the movement's most notable strategies has been the showcasing of New Orleans' diverse cultures by grassroots and professional groups of poets and novelists, visual artists, dramatists, chefs, sportsmen and women, and carnival organizers. This most recent reconstruction of New Orleans is proceeding through the re-creation and aggressive promotion of the city's cultural industries for consumption by not only returning U.S. and international tourists, but also a wider global audience that encounters New Orleans' cultures in traveling and mediated forms.

New Orleans in Context, before and after Katrina

Between the years 2005 and 2010, Louisiana was at the center of political, social, and economic events on a global scale. The aftermath of Katrina was so poorly administered by the federal and state governments, as well as national and local organizations, that it cost George W. Bush his remaining credibility and national support, leading to the Republicans' resounding defeat in the 2008 presidential election. Katrina also revealed to the world's media the ugly face of a racially and culturally divided city and nation. While the Deepwater Horizon oil spill had a short-term negative effect on New Orleans' restaurant culture and visitor numbers, it has had a huge impact on the profits and ambitions of one of the world's major oil companies; indeed, it has shaken the entire oil industry so profoundly that safety procedures and standards are now under stricter scrutiny, and

President Obama refused permission for further drilling off Alaska. The Gulf states most affected by both Katrina and the oil spill—Louisiana, Mississippi, and Alabama—have never received so much international media attention, although, as Natasha Trethewey reminds us, the focus on New Orleans has tended to overshadow the devastation done to other parts of the Gulf Coast.[2] Images of post-Katrina New Orleans acquired an iconic status that—like those of New York after the 9/11 attacks—have become key reference points for the era. To cite only one resonant example of how such political, social, and economic events have reverberated in not only U.S. but also transnational culture, the radical British graffiti artist Banksy has spent considerable time in New Orleans, leaving his "tags" across the most devastated areas of the city (images that have been glassed over for posterity).

Yet long before Katrina, there was a sense within southern Louisiana generally, and New Orleans in particular, that those great waters surrounding it—the Gulf, the Mississippi, and Lake Pontchartrain—may swallow it up one day. The desperate hedonism of "Laissez les bons temps rouler" bears this out, and a preoccupation with imminent disaster pervades writings, photography, films, and publicity/advertising materials that depict the state and city by turns as gothic, romantic, tragic, and mythic.[3] Many geographers and ecologists have foreseen disasters on the scale of Katrina, and there is no lack of commentators and artists who have noted the delicate balance of the eco-structure within and surrounding the city. Following Katrina, Rita, and Deepwater Horizon, not to mention the near-disaster of Hurricane Gustav in 2008, voices of doom have predicted the demise of this physically sinking, demographically shrunken city, at the mercy of not only natural disaster, but also local corruption, federal neglect, multinational oil companies' carelessness, and the inefficiency of the Army Corps of Engineers.[4]

Nevertheless, New Orleans is a city of stubborn and often miraculous survival. In its almost three centuries of existence, it has been devastated by fire, flood, and plague; it has changed hands, architectural styles, racial and ethnic mixtures, economic fortunes, and social and political cultures. Its colonists and citizens have adjusted, sometimes bloodily, to each major shift, partly because of strong loyalty and commitment to a city of many cultural pleasures. New Orleans is a consumer's delight, one of the United States' oldest tourist towns, a place where people of all nationalities and races have found a haven, a creative space renowned for public spectacle, and (as E. Patrick Johnson reminds us elsewhere in this book) a site of multiple pleasures of the flesh. In the last century, its unique and extraordinarily influential music has been at the core of these pleasures. Since Katrina, internationally celebrated musicians and cultural figures have fought to keep the city alive and to relocate its musicians after many of them lost their houses and whole neighborhoods. Besides music, the city's cinema, visual arts, literature, published testimony, and oral histories have reminded the world of New Orleans' rich multicultural, postcolonial history and have drawn journalists, tourists, and visitors to celebrate it.

In a book published four years before Katrina, *Circling Dixie: Contemporary Southern Culture through a Transatlantic Lens* (2001), I described New Orleans as the single best example of a U.S. southern city that has profound historic and creative links with Europe, and that reverberates as a cosmopolitan center of world culture. New Orleans' uniquely eclectic colonial history, not least its hybrid demographic makeup, has generated important artistic relations with Europe and Africa. A mixture of French, Spanish, African, and Caribbean histories and cultures, the city is often described in terms of Atlantic culture: 'Paris in the Wilderness,' "the American Paris," and (in Gwendolyn Midlo Hall's much-repeated phrase) "the most African city in the United States."[5] This "cultural palimpsest of three colonial empires," as Berndt Ostendorf has described it, is celebrated as the "authenticity well" of jazz; the "spiritual home" of the best-known American dramatist, Tennessee Williams; the "sister city" of Liverpool; and the city with long-established musical, literary, culinary, and tourism partnerships and links across the Atlantic. Recently, French Atlantic critics and historians such as Bill Marshall have complicated and enriched our understanding of the city's French and French-Caribbean heritage.[6]

It is clear from the extraordinary impact of the New Orleans Saints football team's January 2010 victory in Superbowl XLIV that the confidence and morale of cities rely on far more than their economic status. In dire circumstances and following great crisis, people's need for communal celebration and creative expression are as important as other material needs. The "Who Dat Nation" celebration of this first win by the Saints (the oldest professional team in the city) was a great boost to a demoralized city. Strangers of all races embraced and celebrated together in a packed French Quarter. A friend who is a native New Orleanian told me, "The whole city levitated a bit."

It is the city's celebrated culture—especially its music and food—to which local government officials, tourist chiefs, cultural figures, and grassroots organizers alike have looked to propel the city's regeneration. The importance of New Orleans' culture to its sociopolitical economy has long been understood, but in the wake of the economic devastation wrought by Katrina, it has taken on even greater significance. Furthermore, the (re)creation and promotion of the city's cultures for consumption by tourists, and post-Katrina attempts to retain and attract native-born and nonlocal members of a broad creative community, place New Orleans within a wider national and transnational competition to brand global cities as thriving cultural economies.

Recovery and the Creative Economy after Katrina

Although once a major port, and still operating as such with container traffic, the city's postindustrial artistic and cultural heritage and reputation are now its greatest economic and social assets. As Maria-Rosario Jackson argues, in New Orleans, "[a]rt and culture were understood as an economic driver and an important asset of the city long before scholars and planners around the country expressed any interest in cultivating a creative economy or building a creative city."[7] In recent years, a global trend has emerged for arts-led urban economic development and regeneration. Festivals and productions of art, music, literature, and film are increasingly important in capturing the tourist market, and reviving or creating a profile for places in economic decline or the sociocultural doldrums. Urban branding, in cities as disparate as Dubai and Liverpool, Berlin and Memphis, has been led by art initiatives and cultural strategies—even though some of these initiatives have been fragmented or halted by global and national economic depression. Richard Florida's controversial book *The Rise of the Creative Class* (2004) argued for the importance of a new creative class in determining the economic success of U.S. cities; Florida claimed that attracting creative and talented people into cities ensures their economic survival and prosperity. Even though Florida's list of successful cities did not include any in the Deep South (his examples include Seattle, Boston, and Los Angeles), his formula for the creative city might well be applied to post-Katrina New Orleans.

Even before Katrina, New Orleans began producing official reports that complemented Florida's focus on the importance of the creative class and cultural production to contemporary urban economies. On August 25,

2005, just before the hurricane struck, Louisiana's Department of Culture, Recreation and Tourism issued a report entitled *Louisiana: Where Culture Means Business* as part of its strategy to promote the economic value of culture to New Orleans' global branding. The report cited culture as the second-largest state industry after transportation and shipping. Revised hastily after Katrina and Rita, a second version published on September 20, 2005 is entitled *Louisiana Rebirth: Restoring the Soul of America*. The need to strengthen cultural networks and catalogue the city's cultural assets was noted as laying "the groundwork for rescue and recovery."[8] More commercially savvy and internationally focused than before the hurricanes, the cultural regeneration program has been delivered through an Arts District called "Prospect 1. New Orleans"; the building of homes for local musicians; tourism packages; music initiatives; festivals such as the Tennessee Williams Literary Festival and JazzFest; and coordinated plans for film, oral history, and literature.

In another official report prepared before Katrina but published only in February 2007, the Department of Culture, Recreation and Tourism emphasized the state's "economic asset that other states can only dream of: a deeply rooted, authentic culture." The report argued that with more workers employed in cultural industries than any other Louisiana state sector apart from health care, the "road map to greater prosperity" lay in growing "the economic engine that is the state's cultural economy."[9] Although one might blanch at such a flagrant yoking of culture to economics, it should be emphasized that the commercial exploitation of purportedly "authentic culture" has a long history in the South generally (see W. Fitzhugh Brundage's opening essay in this volume), and in New Orleans more specifically (see Anne Dvinge's analysis of New Orleans jazz in the preceding chapter). By the time of the report's publication, in the wake of Katrina, there was all the more reason to identify—and invest hope as well as capital in—the idea of culture as the city's driving force, and perhaps even its salvation.

New Orleans as a Global City of Culture in Transatlantic Context: Venice and Paris

One prominent trend in the promotion of New Orleans' culture, both before and after Katrina, is an emphasis on its links to European cities and cultures. In the wake of Katrina and the competition for tourists among various global cities, such links do seem more resonant than ever—though sometimes for ironic reasons. While it may seem gratuitous to note that the main onshore activity surrounding the Deepwater Horizon oil spill was located in Venice, Louisiana (decimated only five years earlier by Katrina), there are many parallels to be drawn between the fragile eco-structure and political shenanigans of Venice, Italy, and the post-Katrina situation in New Orleans and Venice, Louisiana. Both New Orleans and Venice, Italy, are precariously constructed sinking cities run by compromised (if not corrupt) regional governments, clinging to a tourism-led economy against many climatic and economic odds. Just as one cannot turn a corner in the twisted streets of Italy's Venice without bumping into fashion photo shoots and hordes of tourists enjoying carnivals, music and street performance, so New Orleans has endured largely because it remains a site of consumerist desire and fantasy, from music and cultural festivals to ersatz voodoo. Romanian-born, New Orleans–based Andrei Codrescu is among those commentators who have identified parallels between New Orleans and Venice, comparing their "beauty and tenuousness . . . love of music, art, and carnival." However, Codrescu also notes that while the world has been preoccupied by the problem of ensuring the survival of Venice, New Orleans has been relatively neglected. Codrescu further complains that his adopted city is the victim of "big oil and global warming," and thus its neglect is an indication of a global myopia about the whole planet's survival.[10]

The Italian Venice was undoubtedly the inspiration for "Prospect 1. New Orleans," the citywide art exhibition organized in November 2008 by respected curator Don Cameron. It was described by the *New York Times* as "something magical . . . a merging of art and city into a shifting, healing kaleidoscope," mingling "so-called site-specific art and portable art objects whose meanings are expanded by their settings" with "a tour of the city's rich past, recent trauma and often struggling arts organizations." Though failing to hit his own audience targets, Cameron boasted that the Venice-style biennale brought forty-two thousand visitors and $23 million to the city in an eleven-week run that involved many international as well as local artists.

Paris is another common point of reference throughout New Orleans' history—not surprisingly, given Louisiana's French colonial heritage. The French capital has long been idealized as a site of pleasure, romance, and exoticism, all qualities with which the Big Easy has also been associated.

These associations have continued since Katrina, as city boosters attempt to reiterate traditionally successful ways of promoting New Orleans to tourists. The fact that both Paris and New Orleans have also experienced politically and racially turbulent histories is conveniently forgotten in this soft-focus comparison. Many post-Katrina commentators have noted the desire of city and federal governments to erase all trace of the "down and dirty" elements of African American culture—those associated with drugs, crime, poverty, and violence, and which many whites would prefer to see vanish forever from urban life. The historical tendency to compare New Orleans to Paris, and to figure the Crescent City as "America's European Masterpiece," seems to have become implicated in this troubling erasure of black life and culture. For example, a month after hurricanes Katrina and Rita hit New Orleans, the October 3 edition of *Newsweek* ran an article on this post-hurricane city "starting over," describing the ambitious "Operation Rebirth" aimed at creating a new "vital center." A local developer, Pres Kabacoff, spoke about re-creating New Orleans as "'an Afro-Caribbean Paris,'" tearing down the poor black Iberville housing projects near the tourist haven of the French Quarter in order to "transform Canal St. into a dense, 'Parisian' haven."[11] Turning their backs on the idea of New Orleans as a mixed-class, multiracial gumbo of peoples, commercial figures saw the opportunity to rebuild it as a largely Europeanized city of frivolity and consumption—the very things that Americans tend to associate with the City of Light. Despite the gesture to "an Afro-Caribbean Paris," Kabacoff's plans signaled the proposed erasure of yet another layer of New Orleans' multicultural and mixed-class history. The Iberville projects were built on land occupied for two decades by the notorious prostitution area Storyville, which was knocked down in the 1930s by embarrassed and profit-hungry city fathers. In recent years, the projects (constructed during the 1940s) had become a drug- and crime-ridden area inhabited by poor blacks who were seen as a major threat to the safety of the neighboring tourist area, Vieux Carré. Evidently some city officials and developers saw the devastation of the city's built landscape by Katrina as an opportunity to erase such troublesome, majority black neighborhoods through some creative destruction of their own.

One of the chilling facts about those lost citizens who were bundled onto federal buses sometime after the city flooded is that there is only fitful knowledge of what happened to them: a multigenerational group of indeterminate number (though mainly African American) who had no homes, insurance, or work to return to and had to accept enforced relocation in large cities like Houston and Baton Rouge. Disgraceful treatment by the federal government drove New Orleans residents to establish new links—or reestablish old ones—beyond the nation's border, especially in France and other European countries. In their anger at federal neglect, New Orleanians repeatedly defined their city as non-American. The 2006 Mardi Gras rallying cry, "Buy us back, Chirac!" together with the widely adopted fleur-de-lis tattoo, offered a rather different perspective on the city's connections to France than those advanced in Kabacoff's plans to redevelop the post-Katrina city along the lines of Paris.

Cultural Responses to Post-Katrina New Orleans: Memory, Mourning, and Music

Of the many cultural responses to the city's traumatic recent history, some of the most celebrated and widely disseminated have come from television and film. The city has attracted new film productions such as Werner Herzog's *Bad Lieutenant* (2009), starring sometime city resident Nicolas Cage. Other films and television series have derived directly from the Katrina catastrophe: Spike Lee's highly critical HBO television documentaries, *When the Levees Broke: A Requiem in Four Acts* (2006) and its sequel *If God Is Willing and da Creek Don't Rise* (2010), as well as the HBO series *Treme* (2010), set three months following Katrina in a traumatized city with half the population displaced elsewhere, homes and neighborhoods abandoned. *Treme* especially was seen as a major coup and commercial boost for New Orleans: it focused on the rich subcultures of the city's music and cuisine, even as it delivered sharp criticism of the response by federal and local authorities to Katrina's impact on the city's most vulnerable residents. The April 2010 issue of *Offbeat*, a free magazine that promotes Louisiana music and culture, featured an article about *Treme* in which journalist Alex Rawls noted that local "interest in *Treme* is more than just the desire to see our reality reflected on big and small screens. Tourism has been down since Katrina, and business leaders think the show will become an ad for the city . . . and . . . stimulate the economy. Almost every group has some stake in *Treme*'s success, something the production knows very well."[12]

Treme featured (as themselves) Dr. John, Kermit Ruffins, Allen Toussaint, and Terence Blanchard and explored the struggles of African American trombonist Antoine Batiste (played by Wendell Pierce) to make a living in a town of flooded bars and clubs with depleted audiences. Produced by David Simon and Eric Overmyer (fresh from their success with *The Wire*) and scripted by David Mills, an award-winning writer who previously worked on *ER* and *NYPD Blue*, *Treme* was a critical and popular success, with a second series commissioned as the first got under way. Nicholas Lemann, an exiled New Orleanian, observed approvingly, "Underneath its culturally celebratory surface, *Treme* succeeds in conveying, with patience and humanity, quite a lot of the grinding cruelty of life in postKatrina New Orleans," though Lemann also argues that the series' "tight cultural frame" prevented it from allowing the viewer to understand the underlying causes of the Katrina disaster.[13]

Beyond the popular and critical success of *Treme*, both in the United States and abroad, there have been many fine responses to the horror and political scandal of the Katrina tragedy. Within the city itself, professional and first-time poets, painters, photographers, and rappers gave voice to their own experiences of the storm, and to their anger at the politicians and others they felt had failed them in their hour of need. The disaster certainly put New Orleans on the global cultural map. In terms of Florida's thesis, New Orleans' infrastructural and economic recovery—however uneven and precarious—was kick-started by cultural groups and creative individuals, as well as a large and energetic body of "voluntourists," many of whom have subsequently settled in the city. The voices of New Orleans' citizens have borne witness to and kept alive its history, culture, and memories of a catastrophic time. The use of this testimony in film, fiction, music, drama, carnival, and personal display cheered the city's deeply traumatized citizens, boosted the internal and tourist economy, and gave new pride to citizens and those forced to resettle permanently elsewhere.

New Orleans culture is the site where its politics is played out, given expression and meaning for citizens. Inevitably, the city's most famous form of expressive culture—music—has played a particularly prominent role in this process. Bruce Boyd Raeburn, curator of Tulane University's William Ransom Hogan Archive of New Orleans Jazz, noted the habitual disinclination of New Orleans musicians to write and perform topical songs about disaster—to use music "to mitigate the harsh realities endemic to a city that finds itself perennially in harm's way." However, as Raeburn and music journalist John Swenson observed, both immediately before and since Katrina some of the city's musicians, such as Tab Benoit and Don Vappie, became involved in addressing political and environmental issues through recording and performance.[14] In January 2005, eight months before "the federal flood," a group of musicians had assembled as the Voice of the Wetlands All-Stars, creating an album to educate the public about the dangers of the region's wetlands' erosion; the album appeared in September 2005, "ironically overshadowed by the very calamity it was attempting to warn people about," and sounding like—in Cyril Neville's words—"just another hurricane record."[15] Pointing out that Katrina "exposed the fallacy of the city's 'good time' ethos," Raeburn notes the paradoxical need for the recovering city to find inspiration for renewal in the very musical culture within black neighborhoods that were devastated.[16] He also recalls that the hurricane of 1915 and the 1927 flood led to new musical fusions—the rural/urban Sam Morgan Jazz Band (recorded in 1927) and the rural black Creole/urban blues sound that became zydeco.

Swenson argues that New Orleans' legendary musicians, including Allen Toussaint (in collaboration with Elvis Costello), Terence Blanchard (for Spike Lee's *When the Levees Broke*), Dr. John, Irma Thomas, and Michael G. White, have all written and played some of their best music since Katrina.[17] Most of the city's famed musicians who could afford to return (Dr. John, Harry Connick Jr., Etta James, and others) helped finance and thus sustain the post-Katrina musical culture, with Allen Toussaint claiming that the disaster was "not only a drowning but a baptism."[18] Even White, a jazz archivist as well as a performer, who suffered the devastating loss of his entire music archive, noted the "deeper passion in my playing these days," as well as the fact that "New Orleans jazz has never seemed more important to me than it does now."[19] Indeed, that familiar refrain of New Orleans songs, going home ("Sweet Home New Orleans," "Ain't Got No Home," "Walkin' to New Orleans"), has been given new resonance after Katrina through hurricane-themed albums by familiar figures such as Dr. John and the Marsalis brothers; the widespread delight and relief at the rescue of Fats Domino and the restoration of his house and studio, as well as Fats' decision to stay in the city; the new Musicians' Village built in the Upper Ninth Ward; and the donation of instruments to players who had lost all in the flood. The once-schmaltzy Louis Armstrong song "Do You Know What It Means to Miss New Orleans?" has, since Katrina, acquired in cover versions and performances an angry and sardonic tone.

As Benjamin Morris relates, on the second anniversary of Hurricane

Katrina's landfall, the French Quarter saw a long procession of brass-band musicians marching down the streets in silence, holding their instruments at their sides. That day, August 26, 2007, residents carried banners saying, "Imagine a Silent NOLA," and distributed a leaflet asking, "Can you imagine a New Orleans without music? We hope not. But since the levees broke, it's getting harder for musicians to stay here." The leaflet called on citizens to support live music and buy CDs, urged political leaders to employ local musicians in a sustainable manner, and implored hotels and tourist venues to pay musicians their asking rate—as well as pressing professional musicians to play for that rate.[20] Of what Kevin Fox Gotham terms the "holy trinity" of New Orleans (history, music, and food), the greatest of the three—music—is just about keeping its head above water, despite the scattering of the city's musicians to other cities and the flourishing of their careers elsewhere.[21]

One heterogeneous group of musicians has kept a sharp eye on the political and racial aspects of the Katrina debacle. In the months following the storm, New Orleans hip-hop artists from the poorest projects, who were temporarily rehoused throughout the South in cities such as Houston and Miami, released chants and call-outs with titles such as "My FEMA People," "F*** Katrina," and "What Is Your FEMA number?" The New Orleans vernacular hip-hop, "bounce," produced independent underground compilations on YouTube or MySpace, as well as live performances and wild parties. Many rappers and bounce artists (such as DJ Jubilee, Mia X, Sissy Nobby) provided powerful and witty critiques of the ways their city had been neglected and mistreated by politicians. Bounce artists addressed shout-outs to depopulated or razed projects—"From the Magnolia to the Melpomene to the Calliope." This phenomenon has been given prominent cultural attention; it featured at length in the second season of HBO's *Treme* (2011), and in 2010 the Ogden Museum of Southern Art held a temporary exhibition on its originators. Three years later, Tulane University's Amistad Research Center (which specializes in African American history and culture) decided to add New Orleans hip-hop and bounce music to its collections.[22]

The prospect of a music-free New Orleans is so unthinkable that is has served to focus minds on the historic and future significance of the birthplace of jazz and—in recent years—politically engaged hip-hop and bounce. Indeed, deathly silence, signifying the absence of cultural richness, has been a refrain in many cultural tributes to and testimonies from the post-Katrina city. Similarly, the adjective "vanishing" recurs in articles and books about the whole coast and city hinterland.[23] The possibility that the entire city might disappear into the waters of the Mississippi or Gulf of Mexico, leading to the loss of an "authentic" and complex New Orleans, has increasingly become a trope in New Orleans-focused poetry, fiction, and drama.[24] The project of recovery involves difficult processes of mourning, coming to terms with loss, accepting the different phases of adjustment to major change, and beginning to create a narrative to make sense of events. Cultural production is vital in this process and in New Orleans has become a source of comfort and support for many citizens—through not only music, but also personal memoir, democratic exhibitions, essay and photographic collections, websites of memory and commemoration, and much more. The evidence of people's own senses and personal witness seemed more important than ever; individuals' visual, olfactory and aural testimony were offered as both historical source and marker of the much-cited "authenticity" that would challenge the undoubted falsity and obfuscations of official sources.

Culture and Conflict

In the last two decades, figures such as Susan Sontag, who in 1993 directed Samuel Beckett's *Waiting for Godot* at the Youth Theatre in besieged Sarajevo, and Daniel Barenboim and Edward Said, who in 1999 established their West-Eastern Divan, an Arab–Israeli young people's orchestra, have used artistic collaborations to bring different peoples together and help transform relations in conflict zones. In 2007 *Godot* was also produced outdoors in New Orleans' Ninth Ward by the Classical Theater of Harlem. Within the United States, the aftermath of the 9/11 attacks on the World Trade Center has provided another valuable model for post-Katrina testimonies. As oral historians Alan B. Stein and Gene B. Preuss suggest, people can be "active participants in their own historical drama." For example, in the visual arts, the NOLA RISING campaign encouraged everyone, however untutored, to display publicly works of art "for the purpose of rebuilding and restoring the human spirit in our city." As Stein and Preuss put it, "How investigators, lawmakers, and the public wade through the mountains of oral witness to evaluate what went wrong during and after Katrina will inform their decisions as they make plans for future responses"—for all Americans, a "weav[ing of] this tragedy into their collective history."[25]

If the role of New Orleans musicians in articulating the experience of Katrina and its aftermath is unsurprising, writers too have produced a plethora of powerful—and often critical—narratives. Codrescu is only one of many commentators who have described the post-Katrina period as one of war. *Times-Picayune* journalist Chris Rose has described how he underwent a metamorphosis on August 29, 2005, from journalist to "war correspondent." As with wartime experience, for a long time people became obsessed with recording memories and experiences of loss of life, loved ones, and homes, amidst a postwar landscape of decay, damage, and appalling sights and smells. It may be that this "war correspondence" has gone a long way to save the city. As people's testimonies—emerging in photographs, paintings, installations, autobiography, and other forms— tell of the first days and weeks following the breach of the levees, the very weight of cultural expression gave a resounding riposte to the indifferent silence of a federal and state government at a time of greatest need. Nor is the "war" analogy an exaggeration, given that the fallout from Katrina became imbricated with the War on Terror. This is powerfully depicted in *Zeitoun* (2009), Dave Eggers' book-length account of the post-Katrina experiences of Abdulrahman Zeitoun, a Syrian-American resident of New Orleans who was arrested and detained for suspected terrorism without rights or dignity in a Guantanamo Bay–style makeshift jail at the city's Greyhound station.

While Eggers' *Zeitoun* has become a widely acclaimed bestseller, it is important to emphasize that it emerged from the grassroots project Voices of Witness, a "series of books that use oral history to illuminate human rights crises." Voices of Witness staff interviewed residents of New Orleans, including Abdulraham Zeitoun, "about their lives before, during, and after the storm," and published those oral histories in a volume entitled *Voices from the Storm* (2005). Only then did the internationally renowned Eggers expand the "vivid narrative" of Abdulrahman and Kathy Zeitoun into book form.[26] According to Eggers' take on events, Abdulrahman Zeitoun had already seen his situation in terms of war after the storm but before his arrest when reflecting on the sight of a body floating in filthy water near his home as an "image . . . from another time, a radically different world. It brought to mind photographs of war, bodies decaying on forgotten battlefields."[27] The broader story of Zeitoun's shattered faith in American democracy, and his Baton Rouge–born wife, Kathy's, post-traumatic stress disorder, emerged over the course of many meetings with Eggers, who donated the book's royalties to the Zeitoun Foundation for rebuilding New Orleans and supporting various human rights organizations.[28]

Despite the embattled and horrific nature of many such experiences, Codrescu observes, "I think what other people find hard to understand is just how much New Orleanians love their city."[29] This is part of a New Orleans exceptionalism—a feeling that the city is unique and utterly irreplaceable—that has helped save it from the despair and indifference that can face an urban site in terrible straits or decline. Such fierce passion for the city emerges in much recent writing. One of the best examples is *Blood Dazzler,* Patricia Smith's 2008 poetry collection dedicated to her granddaughter, husband, and "the people of the Gulf Coast, who redefined faith." The collection envisages the hurricane as a monstrous, malignant female force seeking to devour and destroy ("Scarlet glare fixed on the trembling crescent, / I fly"), drawing on mythologies of natural forces and the way New Orleanians explain evil and suffering in terms of voodoo. Smith captures poignant vignettes of people dying unaided in their flooded homes, outside the Convention Center in the heat, and in a nursing home; she also satirizes the ineptitude of Michael Brown, boss of FEMA, and George Bush's guitar playing while New Orleans drowned ("I understand that somewhere it has rained").[30]

This creative response to Katrina and imaginative reinvention of New Orleans has taken place not only within the city or nation but also from transnational perspectives. The city's renowned musicians have played at benefit concerts and premier venues across the world, and Katrina has featured in television and radio documentaries as well as creative productions. For instance, in London, Jonathan Holmes's play *Katrina: A Play of New Orleans* (2009) offered a model of active engagement in, rather than passive consumption of, a tragic narrative. Drawing on the testimonies of people who lived through the crisis and focusing especially on six individuals' remarkable stories, *Katrina* functions, according to Holmes, in such a way that the audience becomes "a collective of witnesses . . . to a form of public hearing of untold stories . . . [and] a kind of collaborator in their authorship."[31] Thus, the usual "scenes" of a play become a series of "storeys" on which those narratives are constructed, *Katrina* taking the audience physically through a building that is intended to represent the real-time experience of the storm and its aftermath. The theater company for which Holmes wrote and directed his play is the London-based Jericho House, a "nomadic venue" that brokers alliances between music, theater, and installation art and focuses on themes of hospitality, refuge, and urban life. The audience was moved through the various scenarios and places relevant to the disaster, following key characters who formed a chorus of voices and experiences that culminated in a classic New Orleans jazz funeral and a cacophony of voices and music for Virgil, the classically named musician whose body was literally dragged through the waters of the flood and whose neglect and humiliation embodied the scandalous treatment by the authorities of the dispossessed.

Armageddon or Rebirth: The Cultural and Creative Future of New Orleans

The growing importance of cultural heritage and tourism to many countries and cities has changed the way disaster, climate change, and sustainability are configured, and the demographic, racial, and social transformation and evolution of particular places and spaces are reshaped. Creative industries and the cultural economy now constitute a significant element of many countries' gross domestic product, and in times of downturn and recession, let alone crisis, are receiving greater prominence. This has certainly been the case in New Orleans since Katrina. As in the Depression, focus on and investment in cultural events and organizations are vital in terms of the creation of historical record and memory, as well as offering artistic commemorations of terrible human experience. Derrick Price points to the parallels between representations of suffering and destruction in Farm Security Administration magazine-based documentary photography from the 1930s and those within photojournalism about Katrina and its aftermath now adorning walls and galleries within and beyond New Orleans.[32]

The initial rather uncritical use of collective memories of Katrina will need to sediment down from "crisis research," where the gathering of stories "works [too quickly] at the intersection of grief and history," into something more considered.[33] Archives, university collections, research projects, and organizations such as the Louisiana Endowment for the Humanities will need to create more coherent and objective histories and deliver authoritative verdicts on popular myths such as the "deliberate bombing" of the levees by the Army Corps of Engineers in order to divert floodwaters into the Ninth Ward and away from wealthier parts of the city. Since Katrina there is also a new determination to recognize and memorialize publicly the city's political history. A monument was erected at the intersection of Press and Royal Streets, site of Homer Plessy's boarding a whites-only East Louisiana railroad car, which led to the infamous 1896 *Plessy v. Ferguson* Jim Crow laws. As has been the case in New Orleans during calmer times, public spaces and deserted buildings are being seen as a new kind of sociopolitical theater, the city's ravaged wards rendered a vast creative cultural playground and site of politically charged engagements—reminders that this city has been at the center of many battles of national and international significance.

The experience of Katrina forced people to confront issues of survival in new ways. Historian Marline Otte sees survivors' testimonies in cultural terms, describing the "deep caesura in their lives," and the way they "strove to reclaim the choreography of their lives" through oral testimony, the widespread adoption of the fleur-de-lis as both fashion statement and political motif, and the extraordinary wave of body tattooing—especially of the fleur-de-lis and the acronym "NOLA"—to heal recent traumas.[34] The rescue from destroyed homes of small mementoes (a daughter's high school diploma, the house altar) signals the importance of tangible icons of a significant family life—the very things that survivors of disasters from the Holocaust to the 2011 Japan earthquake and tsunami have treasured as validations of destroyed lives that were well lived. There are politically charged markers of the storm, not only by a world-famous artist like Banksy, but also by the Levee.org-sponsored historic marker on the 17th Street Canal Floodwall, noting the site of the largest and most important drainage canal that gave way to drown hundreds of residents. The marker concludes its inscription with a reminder:

> In 2008, the US District Court, Easter District of Louisiana placed responsibility for this floodwall's collapse squarely on the US Army Corps of Engineers: however, the agency is protected from financial liability in the Flood Control Act of 1928.[35]

Locals and historians alike look to comparable tragedies in the past, to try to understand the present.

It is hard to predict the future for New Orleans. At this juncture, it is impossible to gauge the extent of the latest environmental and economic shocks deriving from the Deepwater Horizon disaster. Taking the long view, one can say with some certainty that the combined effect of the 1927 Mississippi River floods (to which the 1928 Flood Control Act was a response), the resulting disastrous redirection of the river, the faulty building of levees that could not withstand even a Category 3 hurricane like Katrina, and the damage to the ecosystem by oil companies' miles of pipework and then explosion and leaks has rendered the future of the Crescent City ever more perilous. Now New Orleans also faces formidable challenges from global warming, the imperfect nature of post-Katrina levee reconstruction, the corrupt and lax nature of the powerful oil companies and subsidiaries lining Louisiana's coastline, a lack of focused political will at national and local level to rebuild properly, a large violence and crime problem, and a destabilized and insecure population.

Kevin Fox Gotham predicted one of three possible futures for the city: first, a twenty-first-century Pompeii ("Armageddon for the culture," as one pianist put it); second, a Disney theme park or Las Vegas–style entertainment destination; and third, "a phoenix-like rebirth of local culture that will animate and reinvent local heritage."[36] It is still unclear which of these will characterize a city where at one point there were as many "disaster tourists" taking the "Misery Tour" of the Lower Ninth Ward as convention-attending midwestern dentists and businessmen getting drunk on Bourbon Street, and where for the first time the city considered television network sponsorship of the Mardi Gras festivities.

Nevertheless, cities depend on their people's loyalty and civic pride, as well as creative entrepreneurs and energetic incomers. Hopeful signs include the redevelopment occurring in parts of the city; musicians returning to live and play in reopened clubs and bars; the success of *Treme*; and creative responses from international writers and artists. The popular response to Katrina has demonstrated how passionately native citizens, new settlers, and tourists alike cling to an ecologically fragile city renowned for its unique cuisine, music, architecture, and parades, as well as its eroticism, sexual transgression, and hedonism. Celebrities such as Brad Pitt have given a high profile to the post-Katrina recovery, as have fundraisers organized for the city in both 2005 ("Shelter for the Storm," broadcast across twenty-nine U.S. channels, raising $30 million for Katrina recovery efforts) and 2010, when show business heavyweights such as Robert Redford and Sting co-organized a two-hour telethon on CNN's *Larry King Live* show to raise money for organizations helping Gulf Coast families and wildlife rescue and conservancy. Rose quotes the words of an enthusiast: "If there was no New Orleans, America would just be a bunch of free people dying of boredom."[37]

Although there is a danger of corporate packaging and cleaning up of the down and dirty (and the loss of music-generating neighborhoods remains a major problem), the arts and culture and sensual pleasures for which the city is renowned are being revived and restyled in order to secure the city's economic and social future, and to consolidate its reputation as a globally valued "creative city." In the worst-case scenario, the oil companies' ravages, climate change, and future natural disasters, combined with federal and local neglect and indifference, may yet complete Katrina's unfinished business of draining New Orleans of its social and economic lifeblood. In the best-case scenario, the creative regeneration of the city may also produce a new narrative that shifts focus away from doom-laden visions, and toward cultural vitality and revival.

Notes

The author wishes to take this opportunity to thank Martyn Bone for his considerable editorial help with this essay.

1. See Robertson, "Smaller New Orleans after Katrina."
2. See Trethewey, *Beyond Katrina*. Trethewey describes asking audiences at readings around the country what they remember when they hear the words "Hurricane Katrina": "Almost all of them say 'New Orleans.' . . . Almost never does anyone answer 'The Mississippi Gulf Coast'" (*Beyond Katrina*, 2).
3. See Taylor, *Circling Dixie*, chapter 4.
4. See, for example, Barry, *Rising Tide*; Hartman and Squires, *There Is No Such Thing as a Natural Disaster*; and Tidwell, *Bayou Farewell* and *The Ravaging Tide*.
5. Hall, "Formation of Afro-Creole Culture," 59.
6. Ostendorf, "New Orleans: A Caribbean Metropolis of the Senses," 2; see also Marshall, ed., *France and the Americas* and *The French Atlantic* (chapter 5, "Common Routes to New Orleans").
7. Jackson, "Rebuilding the Cultural Vitality of New Orleans."
8. The revised DCRT report is quoted in Morris, "Culture après le Deluge," 290–91.
9. Louisiana Department of Culture, Recreation and Tourism, "Louisiana: Where Culture Meets Business," 2, 3.
10. Codrescu, *New Orleans, Mon Amour*, 263.

11. Kabacoff quoted in Thomas and Camp-Flores, "Battle to Rebuild," 38.
12. Rawls, "HBO's *Treme*."
13. Lemann, "Charm City, USA."
14. Raeburn, "They're Tryin' to Wash Us Away," 817; Swenson, *New Atlantis*, 3–11.
15. Swenson, *New Atlantis*, 16, 11.
16. Raeburn, "They're Tryin' to Wash Us Away," 812, 813.
17. Swenson, *New Atlantis*, 47, 158–60, 204.
18. Quoted by Hill, "About Allen Toussaint."
19. White quoted in Otte, "The Mourning After," 828.
20. Leaflet distributed at a silent second-line rally, August 26, 2007, quoted in Morris, "Culture après le Deluge," 15.
21. Gotham, *Authentic New Orleans*, 20.
22. See Cohn, *Triksta*; Solnit and Snedeker, *Unfathomable City*, 121–26; and Hobbs, "New Digital Archive."
23. See Knapp and Dunne, *America's Wetland*, and Lockwood and Gary, *Marsh Mission*.
24. See Taylor, "After the Deluge," for a discussion of literary responses.
25. Stein and Preuss, "Oral History, Folklore, and Katrina," 39, 56.
26. See Eggers' account of the "process and methodology" of producing *Zeitoun*, 345.
27. Eggers, *Zeitoun*, 158.
28. The Zeitoun story became more complicated in 2012 when Abdulrahman Zeitoun was charged with attempting to murder his wife. He was subsequently acquitted but arrested again in May 2014. He and his wife may well prove to be two of the highest-profile examples of post-Katrina trauma victims. See Martin, "Zeitoun, Famed Hurricane Katrina Protagonist, Arrested Again."
29. Codrescu, *New Orleans, Mon Amour*, 266.
30. Smith, *Blood Dazzler*, v, 12, 36.
31. Holmes, "Introduction," *Katrina*, n.p.
32. Price, "FSA and Katrina," unpaginated.
33. Stein and Preuss, "Oral History, Folklore and Katrina," 56, 40.
34. Otte, "Mourning After," 831.
35. Photograph sent to the author by Connie Zeanah Atkinson, August 27, 2010.
36. Gotham, *Authentic New Orleans*, 2–3.
37. Rose, *1 Dead in Attic*, 154.

Works Cited

Barry, John M. *Rising Tide: The Great Mississippi Flood of 1927 and How It Changed America*. New York: Simon and Schuster, 1997.

Codrescu, Andrei. *New Orleans, Mon Amour: Twenty Years of Writings from the City*. Chapel Hill: Algonquin Books of Chapel Hill, 2006.

Cohn, Nik. *Triksta: Life and Death of New Orleans Rap*. 2nd ed. London: Random House, 2006.

Eggers, Dave. *Zeitoun*. New York: Penguin and Hamish Hamilton, 2009.
Florida, Richard. *The Rise of the Creative Class: And How It's Transforming Work, Leisure, Community and Everyday Life*. New York: Basic Books, 2004.
Gotham, Kevin Fox. *Authentic New Orleans: Tourism, Culture, and Race in the Big Easy*. New York: New York University Press, 2007.
Hall, Gwendolyn Midlo. "The Formation of Afro-Creole Culture." In *Creole New Orleans: Race and Americanization*, edited by Arnold R. Hirsch and Joseph Logsdon, 58–97. Baton Rouge: Louisiana State University Press, 1992.
Hartman, Chester, and Gregory D. Squires, eds. *There Is No Such Thing as a Natural Disaster*. London New York: Routledge, 2006.
Hill, Michael. "About Allen Toussaint." *Nonesuch Records*. www.nonesuch.com/artists/allen-toussaint. Accessed December 2, 2011.
Hobbs, Holly. "New Digital Archive of Hip Hop and Bounce in New Orleans." *Southern Spaces*, December 9, 2013. http://www.southernspaces.org/blog/new-digital-archive-hiphop-and-bounce-music-new-orleans. Accessed April 8, 2014.
Holmes, Jonathan. *Katrina: A Play of New Orleans*. London: Methuen, 2009.
Jackson, Maria-Rosario. "Rebuilding the Cultural Vitality of New Orleans." In *After Katrina: Rebuilding Opportunity and Equity into the New New Orleans*, a report published by the Urban Institute, February 15, 2006. www.urban.org/publications/900927.html. Accessed December 2, 2011.
Knapp, Bevil, and Mike Dunne. *America's Wetland: Louisiana's Vanishing Coast*. Baton Rouge: Louisiana State University Press, 2011.
Lemann, Nicholas. "Charm City, USA." *New York Review of Books*, September 30, 2010. http://www.nybooks.com/articles/archives/2010/sep/30/charm-city-usa. Accessed December 2, 2011.
Lockwood, C. C., and Rhea Gary. *Marsh Mission: Capturing the Vanishing Wetlands*. Baton Rouge: Louisiana State University Press, 2011.
Louisiana Department of Recreation and Tourism. "Louisiana: Where Culture Meets Business, a Strategic Plan for Louisiana's Cultural Economy." February 2, 2007.
Marshall, Bill. *The French Atlantic: Travels in Culture and History*. Liverpool: Liverpool University Press, 2009.
———. *France and the Americas*. 3 vols. Oxford and Santa Barbara: ABC-CLIO, 2005.
Martin, Naomi. "Zeitoun, Famed Hurricane Katrina Protagonist, Arrested Again." *NOLA.com/The Times-Picayune*, May 17, 2014. http://www.nola.com/crime/index.ssf/2014/05/zeitoun_post-katrina_famed_pro.html. Accessed May 29, 2014.
Morris, Benjamin Alan. "Culture après le Deluge: Heritage Ecology after Disaster." PhD thesis, University of Cambridge, 2010.
Ostendorf, Berndt. "New Orleans: A Caribbean Metropolis of the Senses." Unpublished paper, Southern Studies Forum conference, Paris, 2009.
Otte, Marline. "The Mourning After: Languages of Loss and Grief in Post-Katrina New Orleans." *Journal of American History*, 94, no. 3 (December 2007): 828–36.
Price, Derrick. "The FSA and Katrina." Unpublished paper, Society for the Study of Southern Literature conference, New Orleans, April 2010.

Raeburn, Bruce Boyd. "'They're Tryin' to Wash Us Away': New Orleans Musicians Surviving Katrina." *Journal of American History* 94, no. 3 (December 2007): 812–19.
Rawls, Alex. "HBO's *Treme*: To Tell the Truth." *Offbeat*, April 1, 2010. http://www.offbeat.com/2010/04/01/hbos-treme-to-tell-the-truth/. Accessed January 15, 2012.
Robertson, Campbell. "Smaller New Orleans after Katrina, Census Shows." *New York Times*, February 3, 2011. http://www.nytimes.com/2011/02/04/us/04census.html?pagewanted=all&_r=0. Accessed May 26, 2014.
Rose, Chris. *1 Dead in Attic*. New Orleans: Chris Rose Books, 2005.
Smith, Patricia. *Blood Dazzler*. Minneapolis: Coffee House Press, 2008.
Smith, Roberta. "Kaleidoscopic Biennial for a Scarred City." *New York Times*, November 4, 2008, C1.
Solnit, Rebecca, and Rebecca Snedeker. *Unfathomable City: A New Orleans Atlas*. Berkeley: University of California Press, 2013.
Stein, Alan H., and Gene B. Preuss. "Oral History, Folklore, and Katrina." In *There Is No Such Thing as a Natural Disaster*, edited by Chester Hartman and Gregory D. Squires, 37–58. London New York: Routledge, 2006.
Swenson, John. *New Atlantis: Musicians Battle for the Survival of New Orleans*. Oxford: Oxford University Press, 2011.
Taylor, Helen. "After the Deluge: The Post-Katrina Cultural Revival of New Orleans." *Journal of American Studies* 44, no. 3 (August 2010): 483–501.
———. *Circling Dixie: Contemporary Southern Culture through a Transatlantic Lens*. New Brunswick: Rutgers University Press, 2001.
Thomas, Evan, and Arian Camp-Flores. "The Battle to Rebuild." *Newsweek*, October 3, 2005, 38.
Tidwell, Mike. *Bayou Farewell: The Rich Life and Tragic Death of Louisiana's Cajun Coast*. New York: Random House, 2003.
———. *The Ravaging Tide: Strange Weather, Future Katrinas, and the Coming Death of America's Coastal Cities*. New York: Free Press, 2006.
Trethewey, Natasha. *Beyond Katrina: A Meditation on the Mississippi Gulf Coast*. Athens: University of Georgia Press, 2010.

III

Creating and Consuming the South in Transnational Contexts

9

Creating a Multiethnic Gulf South

Vietnamese American Cultural and Economic Visibility before and after Katrina

FRANK CHA

The Gulf South has built its reputation as a popular destination for tourists on its confluence of cultures: visitors can experience African American, Creole, and Cajun influences in cities such as New Orleans, Baton Rouge, Biloxi, and Gulfport. What surprises many who visit the contemporary Gulf South is the considerable presence of Vietnamese Americans who first settled in the region during the 1970s. Confronted with the unfamiliarity of living in a foreign country, Vietnamese refugees imbued their new surroundings with their own cultural traditions and transformed once dilapidated communities into vibrant neighborhoods built on the collective experiences of displacement and survival.

However, the widespread devastation resulting from Hurricane Katrina in August 2005 threatened to displace Vietnamese Americans once again as the damage to homes and businesses forced residents in the Gulf South away from the communities that they grew to embrace and call home. Moreover, the failures of local and federal officials in the months immediately following the storm further marginalized Vietnamese Americans already accustomed to being overlooked by regional and national policymakers alike. Such failures also exposed more clearly than ever before cultural misperceptions about the Gulf South Vietnamese that threatened to obscure and erase the cultural and economic contributions that they had made to the region for over thirty years. Put simply, the Gulf South Vietnamese were poised to become a forgotten community.

Many locals, as well as those following the recovery process worldwide, were therefore surprised by the swift response of the Vietnamese Americans determined to rebuild their neighborhoods. Despite the dangers of unsafe structures, looting, and the health hazards posed by storm debris, many in the predominantly Vietnamese areas of New Orleans East and East Biloxi returned to their homes and businesses in the weeks after Katrina. Their goal was to not only rebuild their communities, but also establish a stronger cultural and economic presence that would reaffirm their sense of belonging in the Gulf South. Yet for Vietnamese Americans living in New Orleans and Biloxi, the wider political and cultural debates concerning the post-Katrina recovery process failed to acknowledge their needs and goals. Too often perceived as an insular immigrant community by local and federal officials, Vietnamese Americans found themselves on the outside looking in at the official rebuilding process. Nevertheless, the ethnic community that had worked to become an integral part of the Gulf South insisted on playing a more prominent role in shaping what M. B. Hackler refers to as the "discourse of cultural policy" in the post-Katrina era.[1] While many Vietnamese Americans living in southern Louisiana and coastal Mississippi do not explicitly identify themselves as southerners, they are actively re-creating the Gulf South by embedding their ethnic culture into the economic, social, and physical landscape of the region. The refashioning of public and private spaces to reflect the strong Vietnamese American presence in cities like New Orleans and Biloxi represents both a means of increasing ethnic pride among residents and a self-conscious effort to create and promote an increasingly diverse and globalized Gulf South identity for both locals and tourists.

This essay focuses on the ways in which Vietnamese Americans have attempted to establish an economic and cultural influence in the Gulf South. In particular, it considers New Orleans East and East Biloxi, two communities with a sizeable Vietnamese American population, as spaces that continue to undergo significant transformations as residents, civic leaders, and entrepreneurs attempt to rebrand and re-create these neighborhoods as cultural destinations. The political and economic setbacks experienced in the aftermath of Katrina helped to galvanize Vietnamese Americans and inspire new projects that would increase their cultural visibility at a time when they were in danger of being overlooked. While the stories of their perseverance and determination during the recovery process stoked the "model minority" myth often associated with Asian

Americans more generally, the Vietnamese American residents of New Orleans East and East Biloxi have striven to reinvent themselves as a socially conscious and politically assertive community that plays a proactive role in the cross-racial, (multi)cultural regeneration of the Gulf South. Vietnamese Americans in Louisiana and Mississippi have worked to create an alternative historical narrative that both iterates their own ethnic group identity—initially derived from transnational migration but increasingly rooted in the Gulf South region—and interrogates established but obviously outmoded models of southern identity. This revisionist narrative focuses not just on the successes and achievements of Vietnamese Americans across the Gulf South, but also on the collective needs of communities in the region.

Creating Community before Katrina: Economic and Religious Spaces

The development of Vietnamese communities in south Louisiana and coastal Mississippi has deviated from the settlement trends of most Asian immigrants who came to the United States in the years following the passage of the 1965 Hart-Celler Act, which eliminated national-origins quotas. Cities have long been the preferred destination for contemporary immigrants. Larger metropolitan areas provide a greater number of low-skilled jobs that do not require English-language proficiency and often possess established ethnic communities. Though the Gulf South lacked existing ethnic enclaves like Little Saigon in Orange County, California, the region did attract Vietnamese refugees, due to its subtropical climate, affordable housing, and the availability of jobs in the seafood industry. By the late 1970s refugees had settled in cities across the Gulf South, transforming once low-income neighborhoods into lively communities of culture and commerce.

New Orleans East and East Biloxi emerged as two of the most prominent Vietnamese American communities in the Gulf South. Home in the 1960s to employees of the nearby Michoud NASA assembly facility, during the early 1970s Versailles and Village de l'Est—located about twelve miles east of downtown New Orleans—became low-income and approximately 90 percent African American neighborhoods as middle-class whites moved out of the city and into the surrounding suburbs.[2] Similarly, East Biloxi was a low-income neighborhood predominantly populated by African Americans when Vietnamese refugees first arrived in the 1970s.

The first Vietnamese came to Biloxi to work on shrimping boats and in canning factories, as many had experience from growing up in fishing villages in South Vietnam. The strong Catholic presence in cities such as New Orleans also attracted Vietnamese refugees to the Gulf South. Nearly one-fourth of the Vietnamese who arrived in the United States after 1975 were either practicing Catholics or attendees of Catholic services in Vietnam.[3] With the help of religious and refugee assistance organizations such as the United States Catholic Conference (USCC), the Catholic Social Services Migration and Refugee Services, and the Refugee Center of Biloxi, Vietnamese refugees in both cities worked to attain economic self-sufficiency and create a sense of community and belonging.

However, many longtime Gulf residents, especially white shrimpers, were ambivalent about the growing economic and cultural influence of Vietnamese refugees. Lingering frustrations over American involvement in Vietnam, coupled with poor shrimping seasons in the 1980s, created racial tensions between white and Vietnamese shrimpers. At times these conflicts erupted into physical violence, including the well-documented 1979 incident in Seadrift, Texas, where a white shrimper was killed during an altercation with two Vietnamese fishermen.[4] While tensions remained high, by the late 1990s Vietnamese and white shrimpers were working together to help the weakened Gulf South seafood industry compete with increasing foreign competition. Established in 2003, the Southern Shrimp Alliance (SSA) created a cooperative partnership between white and Vietnamese American shrimpers to combat what they viewed as unfair business practices by foreign seafood companies. The alliance's explicit identification of Vietnamese Americans as part of the *southern* shrimping industry is significant, given the volatile relationship between early Vietnamese refugees and white shrimpers in the late 1970s. The SSA website prominently displays quotes by Vietnamese shrimpers to underscore the important role that they play in protecting and strengthening the Gulf's seafood industry.[5] This emergent partnership between Vietnamese American and white shrimpers epitomizes the growing effort to recast the Gulf South shrimping industry as a multiethnic enterprise and has helped to legitimize Vietnamese Americans as vital to the health of the region's economy and culture more broadly.

Vietnamese Americans in Louisiana and Mississippi have created a strong ethnic presence in their respective neighborhoods. For residents and business owners in the Versailles and Village de l'Est neighborhoods of eastern New Orleans, embedding Vietnamese culture into the physical landscape represents a critical means of establishing a strong economic and culture presence. Several Vietnamese businesses, including grocery stores, restaurants, pharmacies, and beauty salons, line New Orleans East's three main thoroughfares (Chef Menteur Highway, Michoud Boulevard, and Alcee Fortier Boulevard). Most businesses utilize signs written in both English and Vietnamese; some use signs solely written in Vietnamese. While these signs serve a specific economic purpose (attracting Vietnamese customers), they also play a critical role in terms of establishing a strong communal identity centered on ethnic solidarity. The prominent use of Vietnamese markings reveals the ways in which immigrants as well as second- and third-generation Vietnamese Americans appropriate the local landscape as a means of preserving cultural practices and traditions brought over from Vietnam. While businesses come and go, the significant presence of economic spaces geared toward Vietnamese customers, goods, and social services suggests an increasingly transnational identity in New Orleans.

Religious spaces have also helped to assuage first-generation refugees' feelings of dislocation and to establish a sense of community by providing a central gathering location where residents can partake in shared cultural practices. As Christopher Airriess suggests, the refugees' rural background and history of religious persecution represent major influences on "space and place construction in the adaptation process."[6] Churches and temples have been the focal point of strong communal networks that link refugees through their shared experiences of displacement and help them preserve long-held cultural practices. In particular, New Orleans' Catholic churches became and remain a central communal space for the city's Vietnamese population. Centrally located on Dwyer Boulevard, which runs through the Versailles and Village de l'Est neighborhoods, the Mary Queen of Vietnam (MQVN) Catholic church quickly became the epicenter of the Vietnamese community in New Orleans. Minh Zhou and Carl Leon Bankston note that the church's location reflects its "institutional centrality to the community."[7] The MQVN church serves as a place of worship, social gathering spot, and symbolic marker of belonging for the approximately 6,300 parishioners. Architecturally adorned with both religious and cultural elements, the church and surrounding structures serve—like the storefront signs—as material markers of the strong Vietnamese presence in New Orleans.

Residential sections of Versailles and Village de l'Est also incorporate cultural markers that establish the neighborhoods as markedly Vietnamese spaces. Street signs and road markers reveal a synthesis of long-established, rooted New Orleans and recently arrived, routed Vietnamese cultures. Michel de Certeau suggests that the use of proper names imbues specific places with a "poetic geography on top of the geography of the literal, forbidden, and historical order of movement"; these simple geographic markers help "carve out pockets of hidden and familiar meanings" for residents and visitors.[8] In New Orleans East, renamed road signs constitute a poetic geography that physically and symbolically re-creates Vietnam, even as it refashions the local historical geography. Vietnamese-inspired roadways have developed alongside storied avenues such as St. Maxent Street (the name of which references French colonial history—a history that Vietnam shares with Louisiana), incorporating the collective memories of the Vietnamese immigrants into the local landscape.[9] Street names such as Saigon Drive and My-Viet Drive, which translates to "Vietnamese American," represent another appropriation of the local landscape that works to reestablish Versailles and Village de l'Est as transnational spaces. In *The Southern Past* (2005), historian W. Fitzhugh Brundage contends that throughout southern history, from Confederate monuments to civil rights museums, infusing material objects and places with "commemorative significance" has helped "combat the transitory nature of memories."[10] This regional process continues today but in transnational form as New Orleans East's streets become literal intersections of cultures, experiences, and histories, embedding Vietnamese culture into the historical memory of the city and solidifying a place for Vietnamese immigrants in the contemporary Gulf South.

East Biloxi's physical landscape similarly reflects the cultural traditions of its Vietnamese American residents and entrepreneurs. As in New Orleans East, so too in East Biloxi religious and economic spaces have enabled Vietnamese refugees and immigrants to continue their everyday practices despite their forced migration. Although shrimping provides jobs for those who possess limited English language skills and little to no formal education, a number of Vietnamese immigrants have recognized the need to develop small businesses to provide new economic opportunities for Vietnamese residents. The Oak Street Corridor, a one-mile stretch of homes and businesses located off Biloxi's main strip of beach resorts and casinos, emerged during the 1980s as the central location for activity, with its numerous businesses and religious spaces that catered to Vietnamese residents. Prior to Katrina the majority of the stores on Oak Street centered on Vietnamese goods and services and helped introduce both locals and tourists to Vietnamese culture: Biloxi residents and visitors began to venture to East Biloxi to purchase Vietnamese produce and eat a bowl of pho. The religious spaces in East Biloxi that reflect the Vietnamese community's strong Catholic and Buddhist heritage include the Vietnamese Martyrs Catholic Church and the adjacent Chua Van Duc Buddhist Temple. These buildings serve as central gathering spaces for Vietnamese American residents, the majority of whom are practicing Catholics or Buddhists.[11] As Evelyn Nieves notes, for many of the Buddhists who left Vietnam in search of a new home in the United States, the temple was a symbol of their strength and a "sign that they belonged" in East Biloxi's (predominantly Catholic) Vietnamese immigrant community.[12]

A Natural and Human-Made Disaster: Political Empowerment and Social Activism

Hurricane Katrina was devastating for numerous predominantly Vietnamese American neighborhoods in south Louisiana and coastal Mississippi, especially New Orleans East. Situated between Lake Pontchartrain and the Mississippi River Gulf Outlet, the seventy-five-mile channel that runs from the city's ports to the Gulf of Mexico, New Orleans East suffered some of the worst damage, as the massive storm surge caused levees in the community to breach in multiple places. Many New Orleans East homes and businesses were destroyed, while others required considerable repairs. In Biloxi a twelve-foot storm surge pushed casino barges and commercial fishing boats onshore and leveled homes and businesses. Though it sits a few miles inland, East Biloxi sustained considerable damage as the once active commercial lots were severely flooded. The storm temporarily displaced hundreds of residents who fled farther inland, while others left the city altogether for cities such as Houston.

For many of the older immigrants living in Louisiana and Mississippi, Katrina and its aftermath reawakened the feelings of dislocation that resulted from their abrupt departure from Vietnam. Having already been forcefully displaced by the war, many Vietnamese refugees and immigrants questioned whether this latest catastrophic event would result in another lost sense of home and place. Yet these immigrants also expressed their deep attachment to the Gulf South, a sentiment that drove them to quickly return to their storm-damaged communities and begin the rebuilding process. Vietnamese Americans were the largest and fastest group to return to New Orleans en masse, as nearly 50 percent of Versailles and Village de l'Est residents moved back just weeks after the storm. Residents rallied around the strong sense of community that helped them first establish themselves in the United States in the 1970s. Father Vien The Nguyen, who served as priest of MQVN Church from 2003 to 2010, explains that the Vietnamese have only become more attached to New Orleans "when they feel that the community is threatened."[13] Vietnamese Americans living in Biloxi share similar sentiments, as the desire to reclaim and redevelop their damaged homes and businesses prevailed in the aftermath of the storm. Thao Jennifer Vu, a Vietnamese refugee from Gulfport and a counselor for the community-building organization Mercy Housing and Human Development, notes that while Vietnamese residents understood that rebuilding would be a difficult undertaking, the Gulf South "is home and it will always be home."[14]

While Katrina's physical destruction was catastrophic, the social and political challenges that emerged during the rebuilding process posed the greatest challenge to the Gulf South Vietnamese. Local and federal government officials were hesitant to allocate critical funds to rebuild sections of the city that were considered beyond repair. In New Orleans, lower-income neighborhoods like the Lower Ninth Ward and Village de l'Est were specifically identified as low-priority areas because officials believed that the majority of residents in these communities would choose not to return and rebuild.[15] One of the main sticking points that hampered rebuilding efforts in New Orleans was what to do with the estimated 7.2 million tons of storm debris that littered the city. As the amount of trash continued to grow, mayor Ray Nagin quickly called for the construction of a new landfill that would be located less than two miles from the most concentrated residential and business areas in New Orleans East. The proposed Chef Menteur Construction & Demolition Debris (C&D) Disposal Facility was planned to help expedite rebuilding efforts by removing 2.6 million tons of debris from across the city. City council members were reluctant to approve the project, because they wanted more time to learn about residents' concerns and the environmental impact of the landfill. Despite growing opposition, Nagin moved ahead with the landfill plans, and in April 2006 trucks began dumping storm debris at the Chef Menteur C&D Facility. Village de l'Est and Versailles were on the verge of becoming a literal wasteland.

Concerned about the potential dangers that the storm debris posed to nearby homes and businesses and frustrated by the lack of opportunities to offer their input on the landfill plans, Vietnamese Americans in New Orleans East came together to protest the new dumping site. Community leaders enlisted the help of local environmental and health activists who argued that the landfill's close proximity to residential areas created a toxic environment for local residents. Because of its hasty construction, the Chef Menteur facility lacked key environmental safeguards. Without safety features such as protective linings, hazardous materials, including cleaning products and mold, posed the danger of seeping into the surrounding soil and waterways, which supported residential and commercial vegetable gardens. Furthermore, the landfill threatened to pollute the nearby twenty-three-thousand-acre Bayou Sauvage, the nation's largest urban wildlife sanctuary. The landfill threatened to endanger not only nature but also the culture and economic livelihood and culture of New Orleans East's Vietnamese community.[16]

The debates over the Chef Menteur landfill and its impact on the future of the Versailles and Village de l'Est neighborhoods exposed the political and cultural barriers that segregated the Vietnamese from the rest of New Orleans in the aftermath of Katrina. Residents and community leaders believed that the needs of Vietnamese Americans were being ignored. Father Nguyen argues that "the paradigm of the powers that be in Louisiana is still between black and white," leaving Vietnamese Americans "voiceless" and "invisible."[17] Nguyen's comments suggest that a white–black racial binary continues to influence and even determine social and political decisions in the contemporary Gulf South. The lack of Vietnamese Americans holding government positions and the difficulties that government officials encountered in hiring translators compounded the challenges facing Vietnamese Americans during the rebuilding process. Furthermore, many older Vietnamese immigrants were wary of government officials, whom they viewed as outsiders unfamiliar with Vietnamese customs. First-generation immigrants were also unaware of the resources offered by local nonprofit organizations and federal agencies like the Federal Emergency Management Agency (FEMA). Despite the efforts to cultivate and strengthen New Orleans East through new social service programs, community-based organizations, and business ventures, many city officials perceived Vietnamese Americans as an insular community solely invested in their own recovery.

Yet the groundswell of community activism and economic revitalization in Versailles and Village de l'Est in the years following Katrina revealed that city leaders had failed to recognize that the Vietnamese American community wanted to become more politically and socially engaged. The conflicts surrounding the Chef Menteur landfill inspired residents in New Orleans East to play a more assertive role in shaping the social, economic, and environmental policies that impacted their neighborhoods and daily activities. Moreover, they worked to establish new relationships with those outside of their ethnic group in hopes of creating a stronger, more unified community. Joining forces with African American community leaders and environmental activists, Vietnamese Americans staged several protests to call attention to the potential dangers that the site posed to residents. As Eric Tang demonstrates, political challenges following Katrina strengthened the relationship between Vietnamese Americans and African Americans in New Orleans East. Tang notes that "representatives from both communities would support each other on the political front" as Vietnamese Americans and African Americans worked together to demand "greater state accountability" and access to "concrete resources."[18] The fight against the landfill also garnered attention from local and national media outlets, becoming the focus of the 2009 PBS documentary *A Village Called Versailles* and challenging the perception of Vietnamese Americans as politically passive and socially disengaged. Father Nguyen notes how Vietnamese residents recognized the need to become more politically active: "we saw the city government as impeding our way of life."[19] The large-scale mobilization of residents eventually persuaded Nagin to allow the contract for the landfill to expire in August 2006, a major victory for New Orleans East. This public display of social and environmental activism served as a harsh criticism of the city's established political leadership and paved the way for a more socially and environmental conscious Vietnamese community.

From Margin to Center: Sustaining and Promoting Vietnamese Culture

As Vietnamese Americans discovered, survival in the post-Katrina era has involved the physical work of rebuilding homes and businesses, renewed efforts to develop community-based programs, and interracial as well as interethnic partnerships that would spotlight their contributions to the city's cultural and economic identity. The political challenges and cultural misunderstandings that emerged during the rebuilding process became a catalyst for fresh attempts to increase civic and cultural pride within the ethnic community. Much as the first immigrants who settled into New Orleans East in the 1970s worked to establish a solid cultural and economic foundation, those who returned to the city after Katrina have been focusing on community outreach and entrepreneurial ventures to show longtime residents, newcomers, and tourists that New Orleans' Vietnamese have played and continue to play a critical role in the creation and re-creation of the Crescent City.

Community leaders view the preservation and promotion of Vietnamese culture as a central aspect of reinventing New Orleans East as a socially and politically active community. As Helen Taylor suggests in the preceding chapter in this volume, the city's culture is a vital source of sustenance and revenue "in the wake of the economic devastation wrought by Katrina."[20] Having witnessed the ways in which ethnic cultural traditions helped provide residents with a sense of hope and community during the recovery process, New Orleans resident Huynh Bui argues that "our culture is the most important thing, we have to build up our culture." Social organizations and business owners in Versailles and Village de l'Est hope to attract visitors to their neighborhoods through the creation of community-sponsored events and public spaces that acknowledge and affirm the cultural contributions that Vietnamese Americans have made to the city.[21] The MQVN church serves as an important site of cultural development: religious services help to reinforce a sense of communal solidarity, and call attention to the spiritual traditions that link Vietnamese Americans to other communities in the city.[22] In May 2006 church parishioners and community leaders founded the Mary Queen of Vietnam Community Development Corporation (MQVN CDC) to promote and strengthen civic and cultural pride among New Orleans East's residents. Neighborhood events such as Mid-Autumn Festival (one of the most important holidays in Vietnamese culture, centering on family and children) and church services, as well as the construction of recreational spaces and cultural centers, have enabled the organization to "preserve and promote [Vietnamese Americans'] unique diversity."[23]

One of MQVN CDC's larger goals is to build a "Viet Village" to reinforce ethnic pride and rebrand New Orleans East as a cultural destination for locals and tourists. The construction of a Vietnamese-inspired public space represents a self-conscious effort by residents to further promote their ethnic culture to the broader New Orleans community. The Viet Village would allow Vietnamese Americans to further incorporate their stories and experiences into the already diverse historical narrative of the Crescent City. Vietnamese architectural designs and cultural activities would provide tangible markers of the residents' ethnic heritage and illustrate how Vietnamese Americans "make a contribution to the city."[24] A major component of the project is the construction of a twenty-eight-acre Viet Village Urban Farm that would be located directly across from the MQVN church. Gardening is an important activity for Vietnamese Americans, particularly among older immigrants who implemented growing methods they learned in Vietnam in their own private home gardens. Growing traditional Vietnamese produce such as bitter melons functions not only as a hobby but also as a form of "cultural promotion and preservation."[25] The concept of a community-run farm "builds on a long tradition of productive gardening and farming" in both Vietnam and New Orleans East and serves to reaffirm and promote a tangible form of Vietnamese culture.[26] Organizers hope to integrate traditional Vietnamese gardening techniques with farming practices that focus on sustainability: incorporating green practices would allow residents to preserve long-held traditions while raising environmental consciousness within the community.

The Viet Village Urban Farm would generate revenue for the community by allowing residents to sell their produce to local vendors, residents, and tourists. The farm would also help supplement the Vietnamese Farmers' Market, which has been a staple of the community since the mid-1980s. Residents gather on Alcee Fortier Boulevard every Saturday morning to sell products ranging from lemon grass to Vietnamese baked goods. Primarily centered on older immigrants who have grown produce in their own backyard gardens for years, the market now includes over twenty vendors. John Besh, the prominent New Orleans chef and James Beard Award winner, regularly supplies his six local restaurants, which primarily focus on Cajun and French cuisine, with produce grown by Versailles and Village de l'Est residents. He utilizes the Vietnamese Farmers' Market because "these are people who can deliver" when local businesses need the best products.[27] Organizers and vendors hope that the presence of high-profile New Orleanians such as Besh will help make the market as popular as well-known markets such as the Crescent City Farmers Market that operates in neighborhoods across the city.

Cultural preservation projects taking shape in the Gulf require an improvement of the relationship between younger, American-born Vietnamese and older immigrants. Residents in New Orleans and Biloxi acknowledge that a generational and cultural gap had opened up within the Vietnamese American community before Katrina. Minh Nguyen, a community youth leader born and raised in New Orleans, suggests that the younger, U.S.-born residents could not relate to the older immigrants because they "did not experience what [the first-generation Vietnamese Americans] experienced" as refugees.[28] Growing up surrounded by poverty and crime and daunted by the recovery process, many younger Vietnamese Americans believed that there were few incentives to remain in New Orleans East after Katrina. For some the experiences of living in other regions after being displaced by the storm reinforced their desire to move away from the city. Meanwhile, older refugees felt that American-born Vietnamese teens failed to embrace their ethnic heritage and their cultural past. Father Nguyen notes that older residents viewed the youth as "those who've lost their roots."[29]

The tragedies surrounding Katrina compelled older immigrants and younger, American-born Vietnamese to work past their cultural differences in order to strengthen and showcase the economic and cultural vitality of the Gulf South Vietnamese. Struggling to make sense of the complex logistics surrounding the rebuilding efforts, older immigrants turned to second- and third-generation Vietnamese Americans who possessed stronger English language skills and a greater understanding of the tools and resources offered by local and federal organizations for assistance during the recovery process. They believed that younger Vietnamese residents were more connected to the region's political and social affairs and represented a valuable asset to the re-creation of their communities. Meanwhile, younger Vietnamese Americans sought to learn from their elders, who had previously experienced the hardships of a sudden and forced displacement. Those who had been born in the United States recognized that the perseverance of older refugees who first moved to the country in the late 1970s and early 1980s could serve as a model of survival for future generations of Vietnamese Americans living in the Gulf South.

Second- and third-generation Vietnamese Americans who spearheaded the efforts to stop the construction of the Chef Menteur landfill became the core of advocacy and outreach projects aimed at rebranding New Orleans East as a cultural destination and politically conscious community. The Vietnamese American Young Leaders Association of New Orleans (VAYLA NO), founded by Minh Nguyen, emerged out of the landfill debate as a means of ensuring that younger residents stay involved in the community. The overwhelming support and mobilization of residents in the wake of the landfill fight reinvigorated youths who recognized the need to honor and continue the hard work done by their parents who transformed New Orleans East's low-income neighborhoods into a livable space for immigrants. Nguyen has developed VAYLA NO as a youth-oriented group that encourages younger Vietnamese residents to become economic and civic leaders of the New Orleans East community. The organization provides meeting spaces and mentoring programs and organizes special events geared toward youth culture, such as talent shows and dances. More importantly, VAYLA NO is working to restore younger Vietnamese Americans' connection to and affection for the neighborhoods in which they grew up. In Vietnamese the organization's acronym means "Home Is New Orleans," a symbolic statement of the group's sense of belonging in the Gulf South.[30] Despite the challenges of rebuilding, many Vietnamese American teens in New Orleans East are embracing the roots that connect them to the Gulf South and their Vietnamese heritage. Minh Nguyen notes how Katrina was "both painful and a blessing," as the devastation and the subsequent rebuilding efforts allowed him to reflect on the larger history of Vietnamese Americans living in New Orleans.[31] Witnessing the strong desire of first-generation immigrants to rebuild their homes and businesses helped persuade him and other younger Vietnamese Americans to reestablish a link to their ethnic culture, and to work on improving the economic and social conditions in Versailles and Village de l'Est.

Younger Vietnamese Americans in Mississippi also play a prominent role in the efforts to reinvent the Gulf South's Vietnamese as an increasingly civic-minded and socially active community. After living in cities like Chicago and Houston, Magalie Albert, a twenty-six-year-old businesswoman and community activist, felt compelled to return to her hometown of D'Iberville, Mississippi, to help increase the political and cultural visibility of Vietnamese Americans in the region. She explains that while many of the younger Vietnamese "hated this place" while growing up, because it lacked social and economic opportunities, they returned after Katrina having recognized that the region's Vietnamese community "makes you feel at home [and] comfortable." Albert hopes that Vietnamese Americans will learn to look beyond their individual needs and work together to "build a community where we want our kids to grow up in." Organizations led by younger Vietnamese residents such as Gulf Coast Reach (formed by Albert in 2009) work to unite Vietnamese and non-Vietnamese residents through communal activities that celebrate coastal Mississippi's diverse cultures. Programs such as food festivals and sports tournaments help Vietnamese residents become more involved in citywide matters and break down racial and ethnic divisions. Creating social, economic, and religious networks across Mississippi and Louisiana serves as a means to raise the prominence of the Gulf South's Vietnamese American community and the region more generally. Some residents suggest that communal events and increased multiracial and multiethnic cooperation will help portray the Gulf Coast as a unique southern tourist destination not solely centered on the casinos and beachfront resorts. Ginni Tran, a thirty-year-old Vietnamese American born and raised in Ocean Springs, Mississippi, suggests the need for Biloxi to distinguish itself from other beach and gaming destinations like Panama City, Florida.[32] She hopes that the efforts to build up Biloxi's cultural spaces will help visitors view the Gulf Coast as "more of a historical site" that offers activities and experiences outside of the gaming industry.[33] Broadening the region's economic and cultural identity would help, as Albert suggests, "make the coast somewhat more visible on the map" and strengthen its reputation as a crucial part of the South's tourism industry.[34]

Community outreach programs in New Orleans and Biloxi are also working to produce new economic and cultural networks that help Vietnamese Americans integrate into the larger Gulf South community. These groups hope to spotlight the shared experiences and values that unite residents regardless of their racial or ethnic affiliation. Rachel Luft suggests that the impetus for many of the social movements that emerged in the Gulf South after Katrina was to spotlight and eradicate the longstanding economic and social disparities that encumbered racial minorities. These community organizations "likened the displacement, impoverishment, and service deprivation of hurricane survivors to the chronic conditions of racialized poverty."[35] In New Orleans East, MQVN CDC was one of the first organizations specifically dedicated to the needs of the Vietnamese community, many members of which had limited access to basic needs such as health care, education, and housing.[36] The church-affiliated group has also focused on improving the relationship between residents in New Orleans East and the rest of the city through projects aimed at increasing interracial cooperation. These plans include a new charter school in Versailles and establishing partnerships with citywide groups such as Louisiana Economic Development and the United New Orleans Planning program.[37]

The collaborative efforts that bring together New Orleans' Vietnamese and non-Vietnamese residents suggest that the post-Katrina sense of community in New Orleans East will center on regional rather than racial and ethnic identity. Cynthia Willard-Lewis, an African American former city council member who from 2002 to 2010 represented the district that included Versailles and Village de l'Est, explains how her Vietnamese American constituents are "fighting to stay united and connected" by working with non-Vietnamese residents.[38] By emphasizing the shared goals of improving education, health services, and the local economy, community organizers are working to establish multiracial and multi-ethnic coalitions that strengthen New Orleans' reputation as a culturally diverse but unified city. Similar efforts are taking place in Biloxi, where community leaders encourage Vietnamese residents to focus more on collective than individual needs. In the months after Katrina, national and regional organizations such as Boat People SOS, the National Alliance of Vietnamese American Service Agencies, and Hope Community Development Agency (CDA) worked to establish meaningful relationships with Gulf Coast Vietnamese Americans by providing translators and holding information sessions on business development and health services. These groups work to bolster activism among Vietnamese Americans while also creating a stronger communal identity defined by collective action.

While community outreach organizations help Vietnamese Americans in the Gulf South mobilize and assert their collective voice in the rebuilding efforts, economic sustainability and growth also play a crucial role in increasing their influence over political and cultural processes in the post-Katrina era. Since their arrival in the late 1970s, Vietnamese immigrants and their U.S.-born families have relied heavily on the expansion of Vietnamese-owned businesses for their survival. The devastation of Katrina reinforced the need to increase the economic presence of Vietnamese Americans, as residents seek to rebrand their neighborhoods as viable locations for new businesses. In New Orleans East, community leaders and entrepreneurs initiated the Viet Village Collective Marketing Campaign to promote Vietnamese-owned businesses to both local residents and tourists. Organizers have used a variety of methods to promote the economic strength of the community, including the publication of a business directory, the display of company banners along main thoroughfares, and meetings with developers to attract new businesses to the area.[39] Local Vietnamese Americans hope that these projects will attract new customers and draw attention to the cultural impact that the Vietnamese have had and continue to have on the city.

Economic recovery in Biloxi has been slow but steady as Vietnamese residents who returned confronted a poor job market as well as soaring insurance rates for businesses and homes. Such problems have caused some longtime residents to move further inland to cities like D'Iberville, located on the other side of Back Bay. A number of the commercial lots along Oak Street remain vacant because of increased operational costs. Local residents who depended on the Oak Street Corridor as their source of Vietnamese goods and services have had to travel farther away, to cities like New Orleans, to find businesses that catered to their needs.

A significant consequence of Katrina that has both facilitated and hampered the economic recovery and growth of Vietnamese communities in coastal Mississippi is the increased emphasis on the gaming and tourism industry. Casinos have been a staple of the local economy since 1991, when the state government permitted offshore gambling barges to park along the coastlines. In an effort to create jobs and reinvigorate tourism after Katrina, onshore casinos were permitted, leading to a surge in the number of gaming establishments along Biloxi's main thoroughfare. City officials hoped to reestablish Biloxi as a leading tourist destination in the Gulf South. While some residents welcomed the construction of new gaming and resort properties, many within the Vietnamese community were skeptical. Anxiety over higher property costs, and fears that casinos could potentially overtake their properties, frightened displaced residents from returning and calling the city home. In May 2007 Harrah's Entertainment Inc. and singer Jimmy Buffett announced plans to open a new $700 million Margaritaville Casino and Restaurant along the waterfront. The new resort was to be the largest single private investment in Biloxi since Hurricane Katrina. Some residents viewed the construction of new casinos as a crucial step toward economic recovery for coastal

Mississippi's Vietnamese community. Casino and resort projects would create new jobs at a time when employment opportunities were limited. In the years following the storm, younger Vietnamese Americans, who possessed greater English language skills, were able to find work through the city's existing casinos as dealers, restaurant servers, and hotel staff members. However, despite the possibility of new employment opportunities, several Vietnamese residents were concerned that the new casinos and resorts would force existing business owners out of the neighborhood and drive away potential investors who hoped to open new stores. Plans for the Margaritaville resort allocated a portion of the Oak Street Corridor for the construction of the new casino, a move that would limit the amount of retail space in East Biloxi for Vietnamese entrepreneurs. Trinh Le, a community empowerment coordinator at Hope CDA, notes how plans for the new casino and resort "really scared some Vietnamese folks off."[40] Vietnamese entrepreneurs feared that efforts to reinvigorate Biloxi's gaming and tourism industry would do so at the expense of locally owned small businesses, and that the proposed casinos would literally and symbolically overshadow the central space of Vietnamese commerce and culture.[41]

While community leaders and entrepreneurs continue to debate how the expansion of Biloxi's gaming and tourism industry will impact the city's Vietnamese community, many are in agreement that the Oak Street Corridor should not center on one ethnic group but rather reflect the region's changing demographics. Trinh Le notes how community leaders and entrepreneurs hope to rebrand East Biloxi as an "International District on Oak Street" that would feature an array of businesses, social services, and gathering spaces that showcase the cultural diversity of the neighborhood. This new iteration of the Oak Street Corridor would provide an economic boost to local businesses by attracting tourists to the area and revitalize East Biloxi through collaborative projects such as beautification programs, cultural events, and small business forums that unite Vietnamese Americans, African Americans, and the growing number of Latinos who have moved to the city after Katrina.[42] Many Vietnamese Americans in Biloxi hope to improve their relationships with those outside of the ethnic community as a means of creating a strong support network of residents, business owners, and city politicians. Jack Nguyen, a longtime Biloxi business owner and resident, notes that many of the city's Vietnamese are now "working to put their cliques together" and focus their efforts on the *"whole* community."[43] Rather than perpetuating an ethnocentric model, Vietnamese Americans like Nguyen hope to rebuild East Biloxi as a more inclusive place. The efforts to spotlight racial and ethnic diversity represent a critical means of reestablishing the neighborhood as a culturally significant destination. As Magalie Albert explains, communal solidarity is a crucial means of raising the cultural, economic, and political visibility of Gulf South residents, "so the next time a hurricane hits again, they [will] know us."[44]

The 2008 congressional election of Ahn "Joseph" Cao, a Vietnamese refugee who came to the United States shortly after the fall of Saigon, suggests relations between local-born southerners and Vietnamese immigrants have improved since the 1970s. A Republican without an extensive political background, Cao found himself not only the first Vietnamese American to serve in Congress but also the voice of a New Orleans congressional district predominantly made up of Democrats and African Americans.[45] While the experiences of multiple displacements, racism, and natural disasters have presented unprecedented challenges for Vietnamese Americans living in south Louisiana and coastal Mississippi, they continue to display a strong commitment to the Gulf South through their efforts to rebuild and strengthen their communities in the twenty-first century. The development of new businesses, cultural events, and civic organizations underscores their cultural resilience as well as their attachment to a place that Vietnamese immigrants transformed into a thriving community when they first arrived almost forty years ago. The widespread damage caused by Katrina and the 2010 Deepwater Horizon oil spill has forced the Gulf South's Vietnamese to reinvent themselves once again. But the unforeseen economic and political challenges that emerged from these recent disasters also helped to generate a renewed investment in civic responsibility and communal solidarity. Residents in cities such as New Orleans and Biloxi are working with one another as well as those outside of their ethnic community to ensure that their collective voice is heard in matters pertaining to the economic and cultural revival of the Gulf South. Furthermore, the post-Katrina rebuilding and revitalization projects are becoming crucial historical records of an ethnic community that has often been overlooked by both locals and tourists. Vietnamese Americans living in southern Louisiana and coastal Mississippi are preserving and commemorating their own experiences of loss and displacement, acts that help broaden our understanding of not only

Vietnamese Americans, but also the Gulf South more generally. Rather than functioning as an alternative historical narrative of the region, the efforts to maintain and promote Vietnamese culture in the post-Katrina era represent an attempt to celebrate the history of multiracial and multiethnic exchange that has been a central aspect of the Gulf South's past and present.

Notes

1. Hackler, "Louisiana's New Oil," 5.
2. See Tang, "Gulf Unites Us."
3. Bankston, "Vietnamese-American Catholicism," 42.
4. See Ha, "Troubled Water."
5. See http://www.shrimpalliance.com, accessed May 26, 2014.
6. Airriess, "Spaces and Places," 184.
7. Zhou and Bankston, *Growing Up American*, 98.
8. Certeau, *Practice of Everyday Life*, 105, 98.
9. St. Maxent Street is named after Gilbert Antoine de St. Maxent, a former French military officer who became a wealthy businessman and politician in New Orleans.
10. Brundage, *Southern Past*, 6.
11. Approximately 65 percent of Vietnamese Americans in the United States are Catholic, while 35 percent are practicing Buddhists.
12. Nieves, "Center of Solace."
13. Nguyen, interview by Shelborne.
14. Vu, interview by author.
15. Shaftel, "Ninth Re-Ward."
16. Eaton, "New Landfill."
17. Nguyen, interviewed by Shelborne.
18. See Tang, "Gulf Unites Us."
19. Nguyen quoted in Lashinsky, "New Orleans."
20. Taylor, "Recovering through a Cultural Economy," in this volume.
21. Shaftel, "Ninth Re-Ward."
22. According to the 2006 *Official Catholic Directory*, over 490,000 practicing Catholics live in the greater New Orleans area.
23. Quoted in "About Us" section of the MQVN CDC website, http://www.mqvncdc.org, accessed March 7, 2013.
24. Ibid.
25. Schwartz, "Making Groceries," 130.
26. Viet Village Urban Farm," MQVNCDC website, http://www.mqvncdc.org/page.php?id=18, accessed March 7, 2013.
27. Peck, "In New Orleans' Vietnamese Community."
28. Nguyen quoted in *Village Called Versailles*.
29. Ibid.

30. Nguyen, interview by author.
31. Ibid.
32. While Florida laws prohibit land-based casinos, companies like SunCruz provide gaming venues in the form of casino cruises that operate out of cities that include Panama City and Jacksonville. These ships sail to areas outside of the state's territorial waters in order to bypass gambling restrictions. In January 2014 the Florida state senate submitted new proposals that would allow for the construction of casino resorts in Miami-Dade and Broward counties. See Klas, "Senate Bill Would Expand Gambling."
33. Tran, interview by author.
34. Albert, interview by author.
35. Luft, "Beyond Disaster Exceptionalism," 507.
36. Shortly after Katrina, MQVN CDC helped develop a temporary housing site comprising almost two hundred trailers.
37. MQVN CDC projects include partnerships with the Tulane University Medical School and the Deep South Center for Environmental Justice. See "Projects" section of the MQVN CDC website at http://www.mqvncdc.org/index.php, accessed March 7, 2013.
38. Willard-Lewis quoted in Leong et al., "Resilient History," 778.
39. "Projects." MQVN CDC website.
40. Le quoted in "Harrah's to Open Biloxi Margaritaville Casino."
41. Harrah's Entertainment backed out of the partnership, but Buffett secured new investors and opened the Margaritaville Casino and Restaurant in May 2012.
42. See Thomas, "Biloxi Vietnamese."
43. Nguyen quoted in ibid., emphasis mine.
44. Albert, interview by author.
45. Cao's 2010 reelection bid failed: he lost to Democratic State Representative Cedric Richmond.

Works Cited

"About Us." *Mary Queen of Viet Nam Community Development Corporation.* http://www.mqvncdc.org/index.php. Accessed November 28, 2010.

Airriess, Christopher A. "Spaces and Places of Adaptation in an Ethnic Vietnamese Cluster in New Orleans, Louisiana." In *Immigrants outside Megalopolis: Ethnic Transformations in the Heartland*, edited by Richard Jones, 163–87. Lanham: Lexington Books, 2008.

Albert, Magalie. Interview by author. August 12, 2009.

Bankston, Carl L. III. "Vietnamese-American Catholicism: Transplanted and Flourishing." *U.S. Catholic Historian* 18, no. 1 (winter 2000): 36–53.

Brundage, Fitzhugh. *The Southern Past: A Clash of Race and Memory.* Cambridge: Harvard University Press, 2005.

Certeau, Michel de. *The Practice of Everyday Life.* Translated by Steven Rendall. Berkeley: University of California Press, 1984.

Corley, Cheryl. "Immigrant Neighborhood Fights Katrina Dump." *NPR.org*, May 12, 2006. http://www.npr.org/templates/story/story.php?storyId=5400944. Accessed March 7, 2013.

Eaton, Leslie. "A New Landfill in New Orleans Sets Off a Battle." *New York Times*. May 8,2006. http://www.nytimes.com/2006/05/08/us/08landfill.html?pagewanted=all&_r=0. Accessed March 7, 2013.

Ha, Thao. "Troubled Water." *Southern Exposure* 33, nos. 1–2 (2005): 51–57.

Hackler, M. B. "'Louisiana's New Oil': Planning for Culture on the New Gulf Coast." In *Culture after the Hurricanes: Rhetoric and Reinvention on the Gulf Coast*, edited by M. B. Hackler, 3–16. Jackson: University Press of Mississippi, 2010.

"Harrah's to Open Biloxi Margaritaville Casino." *Reuters*, May 15, 2007. http://www.reuters.com/article/2007/05/15/us-harrahs-margaritaville-idUSN1540833720070515. Accessed May 26, 2014.

Klas, Mary Ellen. "Senate Bill Would Expand Gambling While Adding New Regulations." *Tampa Bay Times*, February 24, 2014. http://www.tampabay.com/news/politics/stateroundup/senate-bill-would-expand-gambling-while-adding-new-regulations/2167196. Accessed April 8, 2014.

Lashinsky, Adam. "New Orleans: An Immigrant Community Thrives." *CNN.com*, August 10 2007. http://money.cnn.com/2007/08/10/magazines/fortune/no_vietnamese.fortune/. Accessed March 7, 2013.

Leong, Karen J., Christopher A. Airriess, We Li, Angela Chia-Chen Chen, and Verna M. Keith. "Resilient History and the Rebuilding of a Community: The Vietnamese American Community in New Orleans East." *Journal of American History* 94, no. 3 (December 2007): 770–79.

Luft, Rachel E. "Beyond Disaster Exceptionalism: Social Movement Developments in New Orleans after Hurricane Katrina." *American Quarterly* 61, no. 3 (September 2009): 499–528.

Nieves, Evelyn. "A Center of Solace for Families: Storm Takes Community Back to Its Beginnings, but Buddhist Temple Offers Hope." *Washington Post*, September 9, 2005. http://www.washingtonpost.com/wp-dyn/content/article/2005/09/08/AR2005090802141.html. Accessed July 14 2009.

Nguyen, Minh. Interview by author. December 8, 2010.

Nguyen, Vien. Interview by Elizabeth Shelborne, May 22, 2006, Wilson Library Special Collections, University of North Carolina, Chapel Hill, Chapel Hill, NC.

Peck, Renee. "In New Orleans' Vietnamese Community of Village de l'Est, Gardening Is a Way of Life." *Nola.com*, September 27, 2008. http://blog.nola.com/reneepeck/2008/09/in_new_orleans_vietnamese_comm.html. Accessed May 26, 2014.

Schwartz, Jeffrey. "Making Groceries: Food, Neighborhood Markets, and Neighborhood Recovery in Post-Katrina New Orleans." In *Cultures after the Hurricanes: Rhetoric and Reinvention on the Gulf Coast*, edited by M. B. Hackler, 107–38. Jackson: University Press of Mississippi, 2010.

Shaftel, David. "The Ninth Re-Ward: The Vietnamese Community in New Orleans East Rebuilds after Katrina." *Village Voice*, February 21, 2006. http://www.villagevoice.com/2006-02-21/news/the-ninth-re-ward/. Accessed March 7, 2013.

Tang, Eric. "A Gulf Unites Us: The Vietnamese Americans of Black New Orleans East." *American Quarterly* 63, no. 1 (March 2011): 117–49.
Thomas, Danielle. "Biloxi Vietnamese Say Poor Economy Equals Local Population Rise." *WLOX*, May 10, 2009. http://www.wlox.com/story/10336767/biloxi-vietnamese-say-poor-economy-equals-local-population-rise. Accessed March 7, 2013.
Tran, Ginni. Interview by author. August 11, 2009.
"Viet Village Urban Farm." *Mary Queen of Viet Nam Community Development Corporation*. http://www.mqvncdc.org/page.php?id=18. Accessed March 7, 2013.
A Village Called Versailles. Directed by S. Leo Chiang. Walking Iris Films, 2009. DVD.
Vu, Thao Jennifer. Interview by author. August 11, 2009.
Zhou, Minh, and Carl Leon Bankston. *Growing Up American: How Vietnamese Children Adapt to Life in the United States*. New York: Sage Foundation, 1998.

10

A "Southern, Brown, Burnt Sensibility"

Four Saints in Three Acts, Black Spain,
and the (Global) Southern Pastoral

PAIGE A. MCGINLEY

> A Jew and a Protestant turn out a Catholic opera about Spain in the sixteenth century and in the course of writing that music I came into practically total recall of my Southern Baptist upbringing in Missouri.
>
> Virgil Thomson, in Watson, *Prepare for Saints*

On February 8, 1934, an organization called the Friends and Enemies of Modern Music presented an opera at the Avery Memorial Building, a new modernist wing of the Wadsworth Atheneum, in Hartford, Connecticut. *Four Saints in Three Acts* starred a celebrated cast of African American singers, many of them members of Eva Jessye's famous Harlem choir. A group of rising modernist stars, all of them white, made up the production team: Gertrude Stein wrote the libretto; Virgil Thomson composed the music; John Houseman directed; Florine Stettheimer designed sets and costumes; and Frederick Ashton choreographed the dance sequences. While not holding an official role on the production team, Stein's close friend Carl Van Vechten, an impresario and enthusiast of Harlem's cultural scene, was among the opera's biggest backers and promoters. The *New York Times* reported on the "curious nature" of *Four Saints*, describing "a libretto that avowedly did not make sense, an all-Negro cast impersonating Spanish saints, cellophane scenery and a text whose stage directions had been set to music as well as the lines—all this attracted considerable publicity to the world premiere."[1] Musically indebted to the

Figure 10.1. A shop window plays on the title of *Four Saints in Three Acts*. Photograph by Carl Van Vechten. Yale Collection of American Literature, Beinecke Rare Book and Manuscript Library, New Haven, Connecticut. Permission granted by the Carl Van Vechten Trust.

works of European modernists, as well as to U.S. hymns and folksongs, the opera mounted a series of static tableaux, linked together by Ashton's exuberant dance sequences, that featured the black cast in campy costumes that ranged from angel wings to nightclub spangles. The opera had not four, but dozens of saints; not three, but four acts. There was no readily apparent narrative, but in the months to come, the opera would be widely celebrated for Stein's confounding prose; its most widely quoted lyric was "pigeons on the grass alas."

The anticipation surrounding the production was so great that dozens of members of New York's elite traveled to Hartford in specially chartered railcars to witness the world premiere at the Atheneum. Everett "Chick" Austin, the museum's director, simultaneously hosted a Picasso retrospective, the first of its kind in the United States; the intelligentsia roamed the exhibition halls during the opera's two intermissions. Two weeks later, *Four Saints in Three Acts* opened in New York, where it ran for just over two months. While the opera itself received mixed reviews, it was a popular sensation, so much so that department stores on and off Fifth Avenue chose the opera as a theme for their window displays on Easter Sunday. Radio and print publicity spread word of the production to a national audience; on one occasion the cast performed on the *March of Time* radio broadcast and sped back to the theater, escorted by a special police convoy, arriving just in time for their curtain.[2] The opera, in combination with the publication of *The Autobiography of Alice B. Toklas* (1933), vaulted Stein to full-blown celebrity in her home country. After living in Paris for three decades, she and Toklas embarked on a wildly popular lecture tour throughout the United States; they saw the opera for the first time on its Chicago tour in November of 1934.

When asked to describe the development of the opera, Thomson replied that he and Stein aimed to create "an allegory for [our] lives as artists." According to Thomson's biographer Anthony Tommasini, this allegory required an appropriate "metaphorical setting."[3] Stein and Thomson settled on sixteenth-century Catholic Spain as the setting of *Four Saints* and chose St. Teresa of Ávila and St. Ignatius as their onstage representatives. Why did Stein and Thomson choose *Spanish* saints as their allegorical stand-ins? Tommasini suggests they did so because Italian and medieval saints were "overdone"; Stein and Toklas' honeymoon trip in Ávila may also have played a role.[4] While these elements may indeed have been at play, the Spanish setting of an opera that featured an all-black cast reveals a matrix of global southern relations and exchanges; through a dizzying set of equivalences and substitutions, *Four Saints in Three Acts* put the (global) South on a modernist stage.

The black cast of *Four Saints*, which preceded *Porgy and Bess* by a full year, was certainly cause for much of the popular sensation, even though black performers were not rare on New York stages. In addition to an established tradition of African American participation in musicals, musical revues, and the Harlem club circuit, performers such as Paul Robeson and Sissieretta Jones had already made a name for themselves as concert singers with operatic repertoires, and Theodore Drury's Grand Opera Company had been presenting operas with racially mixed casts since the first decade of the century. Still, the reaction to *Four Saints*' combination of an African American cast with baroque operatic modernism exposed the lack of a comprehensible framework for popular and critical understanding among white audiences. The black press, generally speaking, responded positively to the production, with the *Amsterdam News*, the *Afro-American*, and the *Chicago Defender* focusing on the opportunities

Saints provided for Harlem's most educated and experienced singers, including Beatrice Robinson-Wayne, Edward Matthews, and the Eva Jessye choir. Some of the singers expressed pleasure at being able to perform a new kind of role. Thomas Anderson noted, "We wanted to prove that black people didn't have to only sing 'Massa's in the Cold, Cold Ground,' and then fall on our knees and wave our hands about."[5] Profoundly impacted by the Great Depression, these Harlem-based artists were not only employed in a high-profile production but also paid for rehearsals—a signal advance.

In recent years scholars have interrogated Stein and Thomson's collaboration, particularly Thomson's decision (of which Stein approved) to cast African American performers in a piece that did not—at least in its libretto—touch on themes of slavery, plantation life, or the rural U.S. South. The casting of black performers in a work that, musically and narratively, did not address "blackness" in any direct way distinguished the opera from the many contemporary black-cast musicals and revues that—by turns both earnest and parodic—endeared themselves to uptown Harlem and midtown Broadway audiences with their decorative fantasies of plantation life. For some critics and scholars, *Saints'* casting is of little significance. However, musicologist Lisa Barg has astutely argued that treating the casting of black performers as "merely supplemental" to an analysis of *Four Saints* not only neglects the performance dimension of the work but also implies that the casting was immaterial, a "superficial skin that can be stripped away to reveal the 'real' (white) work."[6] Like Barg, Barbara Webb places the casting choice at the center of her analysis of the opera, arguing that it reveals the primitivist exoticism that drove modernist artists like Stein and Thomson.[7] There has been, however, relatively little critical attention paid to the intersection between the casting and the racialized *geographies* the opera evokes. This neglect is particularly surprising when we consider Stein's own repeated evocation of *landscape* in her writings about the theater. Employing Stein's landscape dramaturgy as an interpretive lens enables an exploration of the presence of "the South" on the stage of *Four Saints*. Though at times oblique, the opera's staging of an imagined version of the U.S. South locates the work within a long tradition of theatrical stagings of the region, from Tom shows to plantation musicals, from the songs of Stephen Foster to the spectacular shows of the Cotton Club. In its design and staging, then, the opera was much closer to the southern-themed shows of its day than is often acknowledged.

In particular, *Four Saints in Three Acts* resonated deeply with audiences familiar with *The Green Pastures* (1930), an enormously successful black-cast musical of the period, and one that also took up religious themes. *Four Saints* not only staged transatlantic modernism but also, especially in certain scenes, theatrically echoed the pastoral South that *The Green Pastures* had staged. Examining this oddly indirect operatic creation of the U.S. South for consumption by a largely white New York audience reveals a skewed logic of substitution—what I call "transitive blackness"—that shaped the absent presence of the South in *Four Saints in Three Acts*.[8] By superimposing one "southern" landscape (an imagined U.S. South, racialized as "black") on another (a southern European country, Spain, also figured as primitivist and "black"), the opera brought together landscapes of the circum-Atlantic rim and the global South.

To observe the presence of "the South" in *Four Saints* as both characteristic of circum-Atlantic modernist performance and an expression of a globalized U.S. South is also to recognize the centrality of movement, travel, migration, and diaspora to a more complete understanding of the opera. Furthermore, such a focus on circum-Atlantic performance and global-southern cultural formations serves to challenge Eurocentric approaches to modernist production. Instead, *Four Saints* foregrounds, to quote Joseph Roach, "the centrality of the diasporic and genocidal histories of Africa and the Americas, North and South."[9] Indeed, *Four Saints* was intrinsically circum-Atlantic insofar as it was deeply dependent on a black diasporic imaginary *as well as* on the contributions of black artists. More than that, though, *Four Saints* thematically and formally staged the global flows, migrations, and exiles of both the Middle Passage and the contemporary migration of black Americans to New York from the rural South. At the same time, however, the opera indulged in problematic fictions of the U.S. South as an ahistorical place of racial difference and pastoral reverie.

Recently, New Southern Studies scholars Jessica Adams, Michael Bibler, and Cécile Accilien have built on Roach's pioneering formulation by combining a circum-Atlantic framework with a focus on the U.S. South in order to examine circum-Caribbean cultures of performance. My analysis of *Saints* brings the Black Atlantic into conversation with the global South, recognizing that theatrical representations of a mythical U.S. South have historically been shot through with transnational associations, journeys, and imagery.[10] Already in 1934 *Four Saints* embodied that idea of the U.S. South more recently articulated by Sharon Monteith as not "a unitary phenomenon but a participant in a metageography of interrelated multiple Souths."[11] The presence of "interrelated multiple" southern landscapes in *Four Saints* underscores the transnational bonds between places throughout the global South—places linked by not only histories of circum-Atlantic slave markets, but also perceptions of phenotype and "race." Read through a global-southern lens, *Four Saints in Three Acts* highlights these "interrelated multiple Souths," even while it also shows the problematic equivalences (U.S. South = Spain = black = primitive) that such an approach can invite.

Landscape Dramaturgy: Blackness, Spain, and the U.S. South

"*Four Saints in Three Acts* became the crossroads of Harvard and Harlem, Paris and New York, the Upper East Side and Broadway's theatre district."[12] In his account of *Four Saints*' creation, historian Steven Watson cements the opera's relation to the capitals of transatlantic modernism. But if we think specifically in terms of the Steinian category of landscape, many imagined communities of the global South also come into view, including Haiti, Spain, West Africa, and the U.S. South. The opera's "crossroads," then, were not only the cultural capitals of Europe and New York City, but also the circum-Atlantic sites of diasporic migration and relocation that prompted modernist racial fantasies about the primitive and exotic Other.

"In *Four Saints*," Gertrude Stein wrote, "I made the Saints the landscape."[13] Scholars Elinor Fuchs, Una Chaudhuri, Bonnie Marranca, and Marc Robinson have identified Stein's theater-as-landscape dramaturgy as one of the most deeply influential of the twentieth century, a modernist innovation that has guided a great deal of postmodern theatrical production.[14] Stein's landscape dramaturgy spatialized the theatrical experience and rejected realism's emphasis on psychological character and Aristotelian narrative. Instead, the static experience of a landscape vista replaced the dramaturgy of temporal progression, creating what Robinson has called "an intransitive idea of dramatic action."[15] Made "nervous" by "the emotional time of the play," which was always ahead of or behind the emotional experience of the spectator, Stein attempted to evade what she called "syncopated time" by staging theatrical landscapes of the continuous present.[16] While these landscape plays may have eschewed the narrative qualities associated with Aristotelian drama, Stein's concept of landscape was not exclusively theoretical. "A certain kind of landscape induces plays," Stein wrote, and, as Fuchs notes, the interchange between geographic landscapes and plays as/of landscape frequently oscillates throughout Stein's work.[17] So, while Stein's landscape dramaturgy was formal and conceptual, in certain works from her literary and theatrical oeuvre—*The Geographical History of America* (1936) and *Four Saints in Three Acts*, for example—her landscapes appear strikingly literal, particular to land mass, to geography, and to perceived national or regional character. The combination of landscape dramaturgy and the evocation of actual geographic landscapes is evident in *Four Saints in Three Acts*, where representations of Spain, the U.S. South, and Harlem are superimposed upon each other in stage image after stage image. However, before we directly examine *Four Saints*' oblique representation of the U.S. South, we must travel through another site of the global South: "black" Spain.

For Stein, Thomson, and Van Vechten, Spain's "blackness" served as a malleable tool, one that on the one hand implicitly justified the casting and on the other drew the perceptual experience of the audience *away* from Spain, and toward the United States. The result was a logic of transitive substitution that generated theatrical equivalences between Spaniards and U.S. southerners, "Moors" and African Americans. Many eighteenth- and nineteenth-century operas—*Carmen* being the most notable—set their stories in Spain, imagining it as a site of primitivism, sexual intrigue, and excessive passion. From the sexual conquests of Don Giovanni to the picaresque wanderings of Don Quixote, Spain served as a celebrate locale of heightened, operatic theatricality. Meanwhile, many black-cast musicals and revues, particularly those directed and produced by whites, staged the United States' own rural South as a site of primitive blackness. The conflation of the Spanish setting and the African American cast in *Four Saints* thus denoted not only the opera's Americanness, but also its southernness.

Conjoined by histories of Atlantic conquest and trade in human flesh, Spain and the U.S. South were conceptually, pseudo-scientifically, and popularly linked in the 1920s and 1930s. Rhetorical and pseudo-scientific constructions of "race"—especially whiteness—discursively produced the United States as a nation that, like Spain, was a "European" (read: white, western) nation that contained the racial Other within its borders. Although Paul Gilroy cogently argues that "'race,' ethnicity, nation, and culture are not interchangeable terms," early-twentieth-century social scientists thought differently.[18] *Four Saints'* problematic racial logic—one that racialized Spain as "black" and (globally) "southern"—was not particular to Stein and Thomson but instead reflected and extended late nineteenth- and early-twentieth-century racialist social science and its zeal for classifying and reclassifying the so-called races of Europe. Such classifications echoed and extended the ways in which—as Roberto Dainotto demonstrates in his comparative literary study *Europe (in Theory)* (2007)—eighteenth- and nineteenth-century thought, guided by Montaigne and Hegel, rhetorically divided Europe into the civilized, Christian North (the Germanic and Scandinavian nations) and the pagan, savage South (the Iberian Peninsula, Italy, Greece).[19]

In the United States, the embrace of eugenics, genetics, zoology, and anthropology during the early twentieth century fed and was fed by a growing anxiety about immigration and migration, resulting in the further consolidation of whiteness as a racial category of superiority. Two American writers in particular were especially concerned with racial categorization in Europe, and its implications for the growing cultural and ethnic diversity of the United States. For these authors and their adherents, Spain's history of cultural contact with Northern Africa marked it as nearly African itself. Describing the "Mediterranean race" of southern Europe as "the long skulled Negroes of Africa," Madison Grant's influential *The Passing of the Great Race* (1916) conflated Italians, Spaniards, and Greeks into a racialized category of "black." This conflation was enabled by histories of cultural contact between the peoples of the Iberian Peninsula and Northern Africa, and it was clumsily enacted on the stage of *Saints*. Lothrop Stoddard's *Racial Realities in Europe* (1924) capitalized on anxiety over demographic shifts; his virulent prose aimed to prevent internal migration and immigration to the United States by illuminating the unbridgeable—and hierarchical—gaps between "races." Like Grant, Stoddard identified Spain as biologically "Negroid." Between them, Grant and Stoddard portrayed the Iberian Peninsula as white but not white, European but not European. In doing so, they promulgated an idea of Spain as *both* self-identical (to Europe) and Other (to Europe). This paradoxical position is captured by Dainotto's observation, "A modern European identity begins when the non-Europe is internalized—when the south, indeed, becomes the sufficient and indispensable *internal* Other: Europe, but also the negative part of it."[20]

Absorbing and reflecting the racialist thought of Grant and Stoddard, Thomson and Stein correlated the blackness of southern Europe with that of the southern United States. For Stein and Thomson, the landscape of Spain could operate as the "appropriate metaphorical setting" for their allegory of themselves as American artists, because it was a space of Otherness that was not truly Other, a space in which the Other was oneself, incorporated into the national culture. Like other visual, literary, and performance artists of the twentieth century, Stein and Thomson figured an imagined South that, as Leigh Anne Duck and Jennifer Greeson have both explored, relied heavily on coordinates of spatial and temporal alterity within the nation. Like Dainotto, Greeson uses the phrase "internal other" to describe U.S. literary figurings of what she calls "our South." Both Duck and Greeson illuminate a process of (in Greeson's phrase) "thinking geographically *with hierarchy*": because Spain was seen as the "internal other" of Europe, and because the U.S. South functioned as what Duck calls "the nation's region," (black) Spain could be figured in *Four Saints* as a fruitful allegorical parallel with the (black) U.S. South.[21] The imaginative association of African Americans with the South, as an uneasily contained form of Otherness within the nation's cultural and geographical borders, had a particular power during a period of massive African American internal migration—a demographic process that both titillated and threatened whites and brought the people, music, foodways, and daily practices of the South—"the sufficient and indispensable *internal* Other"—northward.

Nested within this intertextual web of associations from "black" Spain to black musicals, *Four Saints* staged a black South that was mobile and, implicitly, global. Both Stein and Thomson rhetorically linked Spain to the United States in the years preceding the opera's production. For Stein, Spain was characterized by its "blackness." After a visit to Granada, she wrote, "Women there wear black more often than colors, the earth is dry and gold in color, the sky is blue almost black, the star-light nights are black too or a very dark blue and the air is very light, so that every one and every thing is black. All the same I like Spain."[22]

A frequent tourist to Spain, Stein wrote often about both the nation and its people, attributing to them so-called primitive qualities. Pablo Picasso was Stein's closest Spanish friend; describing his affinity for African art, she claimed that what "was naïve and exotic for Matisse was for Picasso, a Spaniard, a thing that was natural, direct, and civilized." For Stein and others, the Spanish artist embodied the quintessential modern primitive.

Of their friendship, she remarked: "I was alone in understanding him, perhaps because I was expressing the same thing in literature, perhaps because I was an American and, as I say, Spaniards and Americans have a kind of understanding of things which is the same."[23] The triangulation of the American, the Iberian, and the African emerges in one of Picasso's most famous works: his *Portrait of Gertrude Stein* presents her as an Iberian-American hybrid. Stein sat as Picasso's model for many weeks in 1904; after a long struggle, Picasso painted out Stein's head, leaving the portrait unfinished. Two years later, after returning from a trip to Spain, Picasso painted the head as an Africanized Iberian mask, influenced by ancient Iberian reliefs he had seen at the Louvre. In *The Autobiography of Alice B. Toklas,* Toklas quotes Picasso, who says of Stein's portrait that "everybody says that she does not look like it but that does not make any difference, she will."[24] Referring not only to their friendship, but also perhaps to Picasso's supposed primitivism, Chick Austin wrote to Stein during the preparations for the premiere of *Four Saints* in Hartford, informing her of the simultaneous Picasso retrospective, and describing it as "particularly appropriate to the occasion." Two artists each divided between two countries, Picasso and Stein's friendship triangulated with an idea of Iberian blackness that, for each of them, enabled the development of their modernist aesthetics.

For his part, Thomson made a direct comparison between African American and Spanish music in the year before *Four Saints'* premiere, implicitly justifying the casting of black performers on musical grounds: "Coming from Paris to the United States is like going from Paris to Spain. [. . .] What popular music! What melodic precision, sharp and spectacular and elegant! What richness and fancy in the harmonic accompaniment! [. . .] In Spain it lives on in Moors and gypsies. The passion behind it is erotic and picturesque. . . . In America it belongs to the Negroes, is equally exotic, almost more picturesque; and the Negro remains the master of it. "[25]

One of the most enthusiastic proponents of Spanish music was Stein and Toklas' close friend Van Vechten. Multiple scholars have observed Van Vechten's affection for and participation in black cultural forms, as well as his cultural and social "expeditions" to Harlem. Less noted but no less impassioned was Van Vechten's affinity for Spanish culture. In *The Music of Spain* (1920), Van Vechten cited Nietzsche's words of praise for the imagined Spanish soundscape of Bizet's *Carmen*:

The music is cheerful, but not in a French or German way. Its cheerfulness is African; fate hangs over it, its happiness is brief, sudden, without pardon. I envy Bizet for having had the courage for this sensibility which had hitherto no language in the cultivated music of Europe—for this more Southern, brown, burnt sensibility [. . .]. How soothingly the Moorish dance speaks to us. How even our insatiability for once gets to know satiety in this lascivious melancholy![26]

While contemporary musicologists, most notably Susan McClary, have singled out Nietzsche's praise of *Carmen* for its racialism and racism, Van Vechten unequivocally claimed, "I humbly subscribe to all of Nietzsche's outpourings." *The Music of Spain* goes on to make several brief but unsubstantiated references to the "elemental" relationship between Spanish and African American music.[27]

The link between Spain and the United States did not only occur on a discursive or contextual plane. In its score and scenario, *Four Saints in Three Acts* musically and visually superimposed the landscapes of Spain and the U.S. South. Musically, Thomson's score most often resembles nothing so much as works by early-twentieth-century European modernist composers. However, *Saints* also contains many musical references to regional musical histories of the United States: vaudeville tunes, military marches, nursery rhymes, and, most obviously, a brief moment in the first act in which the entire cast breaks into the first line of the tune of "America." This sonic interruption punctuates the complex intersection of landscape, performer, and text that characterizes the opera. Instead of composing new music to Stein's words, Thomson directly inserted the melody of "America"/"God Save the Queen" into the score, creating an obvious and audible transatlantic reference to the United States and Europe—as sung by African Americans depicting sixteenth-century Spanish saints. In the third (but, contrary to the opera's title, not the last) act of *Four Saints*, Thomson's score makes brief but direct reference to Spanish musical stereotypes, as percussive castanets punctuate Stein's text. Later in this same act, the organ music of the American carnival that serves as one of the opera's musical themes recurs, but with the addition of stereotypical Spanish sounds, as Thomson transforms the organ theme into a "tango." When the carnival music reappears as a tango, it has already been heard several times in its original form throughout the opera. When the theme music recurs in act III, the organ's part is the same as before, pounding out its monotonous, waltzy theme. Yet this time the listener is startled out of her expectations by the strings' intrusion on the organ's resolute rhythm, sinuously moving into a tango that does not fully drown out the organ but coexists with it; the waltz and the tango move together in ¾ time, suggesting a rich and complex conflation of Euro-American musical traditions and dance practices with a "Spanish" tango. Thomson's modification of the tango from an Argentine/Afro-Cuban form to a Spanish one is telling in its own right, pointing to the histories of colonialism, conquest, and diaspora that haunt all circum-Atlantic performance forms. Reviews frequently referred to the tango scene of *Saints* as a highlight of the performance and evidence of the talent and sophistication of choreographer Frederick Ashton. Florine Stettheimer's costumes, with their tiered full-bodied skirts, suggested a sexualized *Carmen* revival. The choreography of tango was danced by an African American performer, whose blackness, deployed by Stein and Thomson as transitive, made legible multiple national landscapes and subject positions.

"Doing Nothing" on the Move: Southern Pastoral in *The Green Pastures* and *Four Saints in Three Acts*

Innovative as Stein's landscape dramaturgy was, it shared a great deal in common with a much more conservative form, the pastoral. "Can it be," Fuchs asks, "we've been so fascinated with Stein's cubism, that we haven't seen her pastoralism?"[28] Marrying the fragmented narratives and simultaneity of modernism to the pleasantries and slower pace of the rural pastoral, Stein's works very much reflected her life: deeply immersed in the modernism of European capitals, but doing her most productive work outside them. She prized above all else her summer visits to Bilignin, France, with its landscapes that "induced" her plays. As she collaborated on *Saints* with Thomson, she instructed him directly: "Make it pastoral, in hills and gardens."[29] While Jane Palatini Bowers has noted that Stein saw landscapes as "an expression of national character," we also must consider how the pastoral was a particularly *regional* American form and that, by invoking the pastoral, Stein deliberately turned to a tradition that was inextricably linked to literary, artistic, and theatrical representations of the U.S. South.[30] This link to pastoral theatricals, particularly the black-cast musical *The Green Pastures*, foregrounds the absent presence of the South at the heart of *Four Saints in Three Acts*.

The uses and abuses of the southern pastoral promulgated a racial logic that linked nostalgia to the Old South's economies and hierarchies of chattel slavery. As Saidiya Hartman has eloquently argued, the organicity of the pastoral form, and the happy song of the slave contained therein, props up the fiction that slavery was a mutually beneficial arrangement between master and slave. In particular, pastoral depictions of African American leisure were offered as evidence of contentment with slavery.[31] While Hartman focuses on antebellum cultures of performance such as blackface minstrelsy, we would do well to heed her arguments when considering the black-cast musicals and musical revues of the early twentieth century. The performers of these works, conscious of the demands of white audiences, the economic and social limitations on black expression, and the racist performances that preceded their entrance onto the stage, navigated a complex dance of accommodation and resistance, collusion and parody. These musicals and musical revues at the Cotton Club and other locales that catered primarily to white audiences frequently represented the rural South as an unchanging verdant paradise. However, "mak[ing] it pastoral," especially when employing an African American cast, also sometimes involved indulging the pastoral's racial fictions, especially its celebration of black life as leisure. In refusing to recognize the histories of slave labor, the pastoral's southern scene became a nostalgic site of prelapsarian harmony—and, not coincidentally, an imagined sanctuary from the economic and migratory demands of modern life. Stein herself struck this nostalgic pose, mourning the modern hustle of Cambridge, Massachusetts, in contrast to the pleasures of the "dreamy South." Waxing rhapsodic about Baltimore, where she studied at Johns Hopkins, and whose African American community she rendered in her story "Melanctha," she wrote, "It is disheartening to come back to Cambridge after a week of the delicious, dreamy South. Baltimore, sunny Baltimore, where no one is in a hurry and the voices of the negroes singing as their carts go lazily by, lull you into drowsy reveries."[32]

This description of the "delicious" South as a site of laziness correlates with Stein's aesthetic preferences for a landscape play where "doing nothing" was the ultimate aesthetic goal. She claimed of *Four Saints*, "I said that what was most exciting was when nothing was happening."[33] Indeed, most of the opera took place in stillness; Maurice Grosser organized the scenario around a series of tableaux, most of which featured the saints posing and "doing nothing." These tableaux featured the saints in various leisure activities: painting a giant Easter egg or picnicking in the grass, scenes that, as we shall see, recall the fish-fry leisure of *The Green Pastures*. These static scenes of leisure and non-action, though certainly a formal goal for Stein, who reviled the "syncopated time" of dramatic action, also point to her embrace of the pastoral. Duck's *The Nation's Region* (2006), an examination of southern literary modernism's exploration of different temporal registers, provides a useful lens through which to read Stein's regionalist modernism. The "drowsy reverie" that characterized other artistic imaginings of "the South" functions here not only as modernist experiment, but also as a static chronotopic foil to a *national* liberal temporality of linear progression—a dramaturgy of emplotted *action*.[34]

Amalgamating nightlife costumes with Steinian libretto, *Four Saints in Three Acts* straddled an aesthetic dividing line between the black-cast musical revue and modernist opera; it was not quite purely the first (because of its score) or the second (because of its casting). Contributing to this generic confusion was the work's New York premiere in a venue that frequently presented comedies and musicals, rather than in the Metropolitan Opera House. While *Four Saints* is discussed today as opera, audiences and critics of the period frequently described it in relation to popular black musicals of the day. These black-cast musicals—among them *In Dahomey* (first produced in 1903), *Plantation Revue* (1922), *From Dixie to Broadway* (1924), and *The Green Pastures*—often explicitly engaged themes of race, place, and migration, while frequently depicting the rural South as a blissful, nostalgic site. This did not go unnoticed by a *New York Times* reviewer of 1927's *Africana*, who sardonically described how the production featured "the usual romantic songs about the hypothetical delights of a Dixie paradise."[35] The Plantation Club, a cabaret theater decorated with watermelon lights and a southern-themed stage set, opened in New York in 1922 and was wildly popular for years.[36]

Such theatrical representations of the rural South resonated powerfully in New York, which was in the midst of an enormous demographic shift, propelled by the influx of hundreds of thousands of black southerners. These migration patterns transformed the terrain of race relations in the nation's largest city, and the new arrivals from the black South became, by turns, New York's most unwelcome residents and most embraced trendsetters. European immigrants to northern cities in the 1920s and 1930s, though frequently seen as "black" or racially Other, were gradually absorbed into a category of constituted whiteness, while blacks became the racial Other for the nation as a whole, not just the South. Simultaneously, the fascination with the Old South—and with black southerners—reached new heights among white audiences in New York, and throughout the nation. This fascination, though, involved some degree of fear and antipathy. Matthew Guterl describes the twinning of Negrophobia and Negrophilia during this period: "Only after the Great Migration of African Americans in the 1920s would the Southern tradition of Negrophobia become the dominant mind-set of the 'world city' of Manhattan."[37] Attending black musicals and revues that represented fantastical landscapes of the rural South enabled white New Yorkers to observe and encounter black New Yorkers, often safely distanced by the orchestra pit. Many of these works frequently employed racial and regional stereotyping for both humorous and narrative purposes. This tradition generated a set of expectations for audiences of *Four Saints*, some of whom suggested that the modernist opera about sixteenth-century Spanish saints should include elements such as fish fries or African drumming.

No one work was more influential to the opera's production and reception than the smash hit *The Green Pastures*, to which it both directly and indirectly referred. The musical, with a choir conducted by Hall Johnson, was adapted and directed by Marc Connelly, ran for 640 performances, and won the Pulitzer Prize for Drama in 1930 (in 1936, a film version was released by Warner Brothers and became extremely successful). Recounting Bible stories—of Adam and Eve, of Noah and the Flood, and the Exodus from Egypt—with a cast of black characters, *The Green Pastures* was widely popular among both black and white audiences. On the one hand, the work, whose performers were celebrated by James Weldon Johnson for their "capacity to get the utmost subtleties across the footlights, to convey the most delicate nuances of emotion, to create the atmosphere in which the seemingly unreal becomes for the audience the most real thing in life," was a watershed in black performance, a play that broke out of the format of musical revue and minstrelsy-derived comedy.[38] On the other hand, the work could be—and in some cases was—read as restaging the racial logics of the theatrical pastoral, an aspect of the musical that *Four Saints in Three Acts* seems to reproduce.

The Green Pastures also had a modernist pedigree: its sets were designed by Robert Edmond Jones, whose expressionistic designs for Eugene O'Neill and other American dramatists garnered him a lasting spot in the history of theatrical design. Jones' merging of an iconic southern landscape with the Elysian Fields is captured in the stage directions for the second scene:

> The chorus is being sung diminuendo by a mixed company of angels. That is they are angels in that they wear brightly colored robes and have wings protruding from the backs. Otherwise they look and act like a company of happy negroes at a fish fry. The scene itself is a pre-Creation Heaven with compromises. [...] a live oak tree [...] is up left. The tree is leafy and dripping with Spanish moss.[39]

Like *Four Saints in Three Acts*, part of *The Green Pastures* is set in heaven, albeit a heaven where fish fries dominate. The landscape of the rural South is superimposed upon that of paradise, resulting in a theatrical pastoral that stages the pleasures of black southern life and narrates the stories of the Bible through the eyes of a child. The final act of *Four Saints* is also staged in heaven, a correlation that inspired one reviewer to write, "The person who goes to see and hear Gertrude Stein's opera ... must be ready to see it all through naïve and childlike eyes, and to find gold lace and pink cellophane clouds a true representation of heavenly glory, as *Green Pastures* saw it in terms of a fish fry and angels who dusted and swept."[40] This particular review is representative of the many letters and reviews that spoke of *The Green Pastures* and *Four Saints* in the same breath: the musical became a touchstone for understanding the opera.

The climactic scene of *Four Saints in Three Acts* was a theatrical echo of a nearly identical scene in *The Green Pastures* and makes evident the opera's indebtedness to—and campy quotation of—the musical. Toward the end of *Four Saints*, movement interrupted the stillness of the tableaux of "doing nothing," and the scene that followed directly referenced the diasporic history of black Americans. The "procession scene," as it came to be known, diverged radically from the frontal orientation of the still tableaux, and the entire cast processed across the stage, their bodies at ninety degrees to the proscenium and the audience, for a lengthy four minutes. This procession represented both a wedding and a funeral, and Ashton's choreography gave (as he described it) "the impression that [the cast] was moving the whole time but actually they were only swaying backwards and forwards, then every now and again they took one step." Stein herself had suggested this procession, and it was one of the most enthusiastically praised scenes of the production.[41] Representing the exile of the Israelites from Egypt with a black cast, the Exodus scene of *The*

Green Pastures employed a nearly identical stage image. The musical featured its entire cast processing from stage left to stage right, its bedraggled men, women, and children carrying banners aloft—an image that *Saints* would repeat a few years later. The celebrated actor Richard Harrison, who played the character of "De Lawd," overcame the geographic limitations of the stage by utilizing a relatively novel piece of technology that made his journey seem endless: a treadmill sunk into the stage floor. The scene made a broad cultural impression and was described by a reviewer in *Opportunity* as a "thrilling scene" and an "admirably conceived picture."[42] Furthermore, the scene was an emotional high point of *The Green Pastures*, likely because the representation of Exodus by a black cast could not help but gesture to the Middle Passage—as well as the contemporaneous northward migration of black Americans. This emotional depiction of potent "overlapping diasporas" produced a "sea of handkerchiefs" in the audience.[43]

Embracing the pastoral tradition of rural timelessness as well as modernism's love of movement and simultaneity, *Four Saints in Three Acts* interrupted its tableaux of stillness with an extended—and emotionally potent—depiction of diasporic movement, theatrically quoting the Exodus scene of the black-cast *The Green Pastures*. The landscapes of the global South, from Spain to the U.S. South, oscillated throughout *Four Saints in Three Acts*. On a formal level, the opera proposes a movement among Stein's landscapes of black diaspora, staging the South as what Kathryn McKee and Annette Trefzer have called a "porous space through which other places have always circulated."[44] But while the African American performers of *Four Saints* enabled its conceptual staging of movement, migration, and diaspora, their own personal journeys *off*stage may have contributed to the mobile modernism of the opera. Harrison's parents had escaped from slavery via the Underground Railroad, and the actor himself made most of his living as a touring performer; Eva Jessye, the director of *Four Saints*' choir, was a recent arrival to New York from Kansas, by way of Baltimore. Of course, Stein and Thomson were also from outside the city; in creating "an allegory for our lives as artists," they aligned their own travels with those of the African American diasporic journeys represented onstage. Cosmopolitan urbanites though they were, Stein and Thomson kept their focus trained not on the city, but on the rural scene that they had ostensibly left behind, as Thomson's reference to "total recall" of his Missouri youth in the epigraph to this essay makes evident. Stein too was

Figure 10.2. Procession scene, *Four Saints in Three Acts*. Yale Collection of American Literature, Beinecke Rare Book and Manuscript Library, New Haven, Connecticut.

always looking *out* of her chosen city of Paris: to Baltimore, to Bilignin, to supposedly timeless pastoral landscapes that escaped the syncopation of urban time, with its jazz music and industrial noise.

Though Stein strives for a continuous present in her plays, her invocation of the pastoral in *Four Saints in Three Acts* takes up the posture of nostalgia. A triumphant production that signaled a new moment in American theatrical modernism, *Saints* also—if indirectly—staged the centrality of black culture, black artists, and racial formations to the idea and practice of modernism. In its citation of multiple Souths, from the U.S. South to southern Europe (especially Spain), to the global South (including Africa), *Four Saints* theatrically staged a global southern turn. It did so, however, by indulging stock notions of racial characteristics and by advancing a theatrical logic of transitive blackness that used phenotype to flatten out difference. Though it invited attention to circum-Atlantic flows and overlapping diasporas, the opera's invocation of nostalgia, stereotype, and transitive blackness exposes the limits of its own global-southern turn; moreover, it may suggest potential risks of the similar turn in the

New Southern Studies today. While the recent scholarly examination of transnational or global "Souths" has been most often figured as a progressive shift away from more nationally or regionally bound frameworks of analysis, *Four Saints* shows us not only that the global South has long been invoked, but also that global or transnational frameworks are not necessarily always detached from the racialist or nationalist thinking that such a turn often seeks to debunk.

Notes

1. "Activities of Musicians," X6.
2. Downes, "Stein-Thomson Concoction," X6.
3. Tommasini, *Virgil Thomson*, 125.
4. Ibid., 160.
5. Watson, *Prepare for Saints*, 252.
6. Barg, "Black Voices/White Sounds," 124. Racist attitudes about the "naturalness" of black performers also informed the casting of *Four Saints*. Thomson claimed to have cast African American singers because of their abilities to sing Stein's text "without being troubled by self-consciousness because of its apparent senselessness, as white singers, perhaps already inured to operatic and textual traditions, could not do" ("Broadway Greets New Kind of Opera," 22).
7. See Webb, "Centrality of Race."
8. My use of the term "transitive" here gestures not only to the idea of transit or movement, but also to the transitive property of mathematics: If a = b, and b = c, then a = c. Such transitive logic, I suggest, governs the significations accorded to the black performers in *Four Saints*. For Stein and Thomson, if Spain = black, and black = U.S. South, then Spain = U.S. South.
9. Roach, *Cities of the Dead*, 4.
10. See Adams, Bibler, and Accilien, eds., *Just below South*.
11. Monteith, "Southern like US?," 67.
12. Watson, *Prepare for Saints*, 7.
13. Stein, "Plays," 2.
14. Fuchs, *Death of Character*, 92–96; Fuchs and Chaudhuri, "Land/Scape/Theatre and the New Spatial Paradigm"; Marranca, *Ecologies of Theatre*; Robinson, *Other American Drama*.
15. Robinson, *American Play*, 188.
16. Stein, "Plays," xxix.
17. Stein, *Everybody's Autobiography*, 202; Fuchs, *Death of Character*, 94.
18. Gilroy, "There Ain't No Black in the Union Jack," 154.
19. Dainotto begins his book with an account of Italy's entry into the European Union and the anti-South backlash that followed; a pejorative acronym found its way into the press: PIGS (Portugal, Italy, Greece, Spain).

20. Dainotto, *Europe (in Theory)*, 4.
21. Greeson, *Our South*, 1, 6; see also Duck, *Nation's Region*.
22. Stein, *Gertrude Stein on Picasso*, 11.
23. Ibid., 22, 23.
24. Stein, *Autobiography of Alice B. Toklas*, 14.
25. Thomson, "Forecast and Review," 107–8.
26. Quoted in McClary, *Georges Bizet: Carmen*, 118.
27. Van Vechten, *Music of Spain*, 141.
28. Fuchs, *Death of Character*, 95.
29. Thomson, "Forecast and Review," 91.
30. Bowers, "Composition That All the World Can See," 130.
31. Hartman, *Scenes of Subjection*, 52–53.
32. Stein, *Everybody's Autobiography*, 43.
33. Ibid., 283.
34. See Duck, *Nation's Region*, 1–11.
35. "*Africana* a Swift Negro Musical Revue."
36. Brown, *Babylon Girls*, 207.
37. Guterl, *Color of Race in America*, 13.
38. James Weldon Johnson, *Black Manhattan*, 218.
39. Connelly, *Green Pastures*.
40. Murray, "Gertrude Stein Opera Premiere February 8."
41. Ashton, quoted in Harris, "Original *Four Saints*," 128–29.
42. *Opportunity* 8 (May 1930), clipping (page numbers missing) in James Weldon Johnson and Grace Nail Johnson Papers.
43. Phillips, "Green Pastures Recalled." The phrase "overlapping diasporas" comes from Lewis, "To Turn as on a Pivot."
44. McKee and Trefzer, "Preface: Global Contexts, Local Literatures," 679.

Works Cited

"Activities of Musicians," *New York Times*, February 18, 1934, natl. ed.: X6

Adams, Jessica, Michael Bibler, and Cécile Accillien, eds. *Just below South: Intercultural Performance in the Caribbean and U.S. South*. Charlottesville: University of Virginia Press, 2007.

"*Africana* a Swift Negro Musical Revue." *New York Times*, July 12, 1927, 29.

Barg, Lisa. "Black Voices/White Sounds: Race and Representation in Virgil Thomson's *Four Saints in Three Acts*." *American Music* 18, no. 2 (2000): 121–61.

Bowers, Jane Palatini. "The Composition That All the World Can See: Gertrude Stein's Theatre Landscapes." In *Land/Scape/Theatre*, edited by Elinor Fuchs and Una Chaudhuri, 121–44. Ann Arbor: University of Michigan Press, 2002.

"Broadway Greets New Kind of Opera." *New York Times*, February 21, 1934, natl. ed., 22.

Brown, Jayna. *Babylon Girls: Black Women Performers and the Shaping of the Modern*. Durham: Duke University Press, 2008.

Connelly, Marc. *The Green Pastures, a Fable*. New York: Farrar and Rinehart, 1929.
Dainotto, Roberto. *Europe (in Theory)*. Durham: Duke University Press, 2007.
Downes, Olin. "The Stein-Thomson Concoction." *New York Times*, February 25, 1934, natl. ed., X6.
Duck, Leigh Anne. *The Nation's Region: Southern Modernism, Segregation, and U.S. Nationalism*. Athens: University of Georgia Press, 2006.
Fuchs, Elinor. *The Death of Character: Perspectives on Theater after Modernism*. Bloomington: Indiana University Press, 1996.
Fuchs, Elinor, and Una Chaudhuri. "Land/Scape/Theatre and the New Spatial Paradigm." In *Land/Scape/Theatre*, edited by Elinor Fuchs and Una Chaudhuri, 1-7. Ann Arbor: University of Michigan Press, 2002.
Gilroy, Paul. *"There Ain't No Black in the Union Jack": The Cultural Politics of Race and Nation*. Chicago: University of Chicago Press, 1987.
Greeson, Jennifer. *Our South: Geographic Fantasy and the Rise of National Literature*. Cambridge: Harvard University Press, 2010.
Guterl, Matthew. *The Color of Race in America, 1900-1940*. Cambridge: Harvard University Press, 2001.
Harris, David. "The Original *Four Saints in Three Acts*." *Drama Review* 26, no. 1 (spring 1982): 101-30.
Hartman, Saidiya. *Scenes of Subjection: Terror, Slavery, and Self-Making in Nineteenth-Century America*. New York: Oxford University Press, 1997.
Johnson, James Weldon. *Black Manhattan*. New York: Da Capo Press, 1930.
Lewis, Earl. "To Turn as on a Pivot: Writing African Americans into a History of Overlapping Diasporas." *American Historical Review* 100, no. 3 (1995): 765-87.
Marranca, Bonnie. *Ecologies of Theatre: Essays and the Century Turning*. Baltimore: Johns Hopkins University Press, 1996.
McClary, Susan. *Georges Bizet: Carmen*. Cambridge: Cambridge University Press, 1992.
McKee, Kathryn, and Annette Trefzer. "Preface: Global Contexts, Local Literatures: The New Southern Studies." *American Literature* 78, no. 4 (2006): 677-90.
Monteith, Sharon. "Southern like US?" *Global South* 1, no. 1 (2007): 66-74.
Murray, Marian. "Gertrude Stein Opera Premiere February 8." Wadsworth Atheneum Museum of Art Archives, Hartford, CT.
Phillips, John. "Green Pastures Recalled." *American Heritage* 21, no. 2 (1970). http://www.americanheritage.com/articles/magazine/ah/1970/2/1970_2_28.shtml. Accessed February 2, 2011.
Roach, Joseph. *Cities of the Dead: Circum-Atlantic Performance*. New York: Columbia University Press, 1996.
Robinson, Marc. *The Other American Drama*. Cambridge: Cambridge University Press, 1994.
———. *The American Play: 1787-2000*. New Haven: Yale University Press, 2010.
Stein, Gertrude. *The Autobiography of Alice B. Toklas*. 3rd ed. New York: Vintage, 1990.
———. *Everybody's Autobiography*. New York: Random House, 1937.
———. *Gertrude Stein on Picasso*. Ed. Edward Burns. New York: Liveright, 1970.

———. "Plays." In *Last Operas and Plays*. Ed. Carl Van Vechten. Baltimore: Johns Hopkins University Press, 1995.
"Stein Opera Sung By All-Negro Cast." *New York Times*, February 9, 1934, natl. ed., 22.
Thomson, Virgil. "Forecast and Review." *Modern Music* 10 (1933): 107–8.
Tommasini, Anthony. *Virgil Thomson: Composer on the Aisle*. New York: W. W. Norton, 1997.
Van Vechten, Carl. *The Music of Spain*. London: Kegan Paul, Trench, Trubner, 1920.
Watson, Steven. *Prepare for Saints: Gertrude Stein, Virgil Thomson, and the Mainstreaming of American Modernism*. New York: Random House, 1988.
Webb, Barbara. "The Centrality of Race to the Modernist Aesthetics of Gertrude Stein's *Four Saints in Three Acts*." *Modernism/Modernity* 7, no. 3 (2000): 447–69.

11

Southern Regionalism and U.S. Nationalism in William Faulkner's State Department Travels

DEBORAH COHN

In November 1950 the *New York Times* heralded the announcement that William Faulkner had been awarded the Nobel Prize for Literature with an editorial that declared that the writer's "field of vision is concentrated on a society that is too often vicious, depraved, decadent, corrupt. Americans must fervently hope that the award by a Swedish jury and the enormous vogue of Faulkner's works in Latin America and on the European Continent . . . does not mean that foreigners admire him because he gives them the picture of American life they believe to be typical and true. . . . Incest and rape may be common pastimes in Faulkner's 'Jefferson, Miss.' but they are not elsewhere in the United States." The prize, the editors declared, surely must have been awarded for works such as *The Sound and the Fury*, *Light in August*, and *The Hamlet*, and could not have been meant for "the author of *Sanctuary*, the father of that illegitimate horror, 'No Orchids for Miss Blandish.'" Nevertheless, the editorial begrudgingly concluded that "Faulkner is a great artist and deserves the award, and the United States can be proud that one of its artists has earned the Nobel prize again."[1]

For the editors of the *New York Times*, Faulkner's fiction and, implicitly, the U.S. South were, to use Richard Gray's term, aberrations from the national norm.[2] For Faulkner himself, though, as for many of his readers, the relationship between region and nation was not oppositional but, rather, intertwined. The focus of this essay is the interplay between constructions of the post-Nobel public "Faulkner" as "southerner" (and therefore not representative of "American life"), as "American," and as representing "all humanity," as well as the international reception and consumption of these images of "Faulkner" and "the South" through his role as representative (in many senses) of the United States during his travels as a goodwill ambassador for the U.S. Department of State. Ever the reluctant traveler, and generally quite uncomfortable with the public role foisted upon him following his receipt of the Nobel Prize, Faulkner often sought on his official trips to efface himself by creating and projecting an image of himself as "southern" that was predicated on stereotypes of a rural and nonintellectual community. In turn, his interlocutors abroad, including both local audiences and his embassy hosts, read him through the lens of his pose, but also in light of preconceived ideas of "the South" and of "southernness" that risked turning his diplomatic missions into games of smoke and mirrors rather than ventures at mutual understanding. This is also a tale about the sublimation of Faulkner the regionalist into Faulkner the nationalist and Cold Warrior whose official travels and pronouncements on race relations in the United States played directly into the State Department's battle against communism.

The *New York Times* editorial in many ways epitomizes the prevailing attitudes in the United States toward the writer during what was a pivotal moment in the process of what Lawrence Schwartz has called "creating Faulkner's reputation." Faulkner built his reputation on works based in the U.S. South and only gradually was able to move away from being considered a "regional" writer to being viewed as an "American" writer. Schwartz details how in the late 1940s and 1950s Faulkner's reputation was retooled by critics such as Malcolm Cowley, Irving Howe, Robert Penn Warren, and others. Transforming the received notion of Faulkner as a southern nationalist with limited appeal in both the literary establishment and among a broader public, these critics reconfigured Faulkner as a "writer with universal appeal," a moralist whose work spoke to the human condition in general terms.[3]

Such readings of Faulkner fit in nicely with contemporaneous, Cold War interpretations of Faulkner in both Western and Eastern Europe that tended to depoliticize and universalize his fiction.[4] As the Nobel Prize award accelerated the rise in Faulkner's reputation, so the critics' emphasis on the universal implications of the writer's work—what Faulkner himself called "the old universal truths lacking which any story is ephemeral and doomed"—made him attractive to the State Department as a cultural emissary with wide appeal.[5] This radical reinvention of Faulkner's reputation was part of a shift in the broader artistic establishment that was emblematic of what Volker Berghahn calls the "emergent totalitarianism paradigm":[6] a struggle to defend artistic freedom—conceived of as both synecdoche and symbol of democracy—from the "subjugati[on of] art to the dreary dictates of a totalitarian political ideology" associated with the communist countries.[7] During the postwar years, abstract expressionism, jazz, and modern dance were celebrated and subsidized by U.S. government agencies, because their refutation of realism and mimetic representation was seen as emblematic of the freedom of expression—and, by extension, freedom in general—enjoyed by artists in the United States. As Schwartz has argued, Faulkner's rise to fame in the United States took place within this context. It was also tied into the promotion of a depoliticized literary modernism cast as "an instrument of anti-Communism and an ideological weapon with which to battle the 'totalitarianism' of the Soviet Union." There was also a corresponding "shift in literary culture away from social concerns and from any criticism that tended to weaken or thwart United States interests."[8]

Faulkner and the State Department I: Performing "Southernness" Abroad

As a Nobel Prize winner, Faulkner's very person attested to the height of U.S. cultural achievement. Perhaps just as importantly, his complex, modernist style (like that of Jackson Pollock in abstract expressionism and Louis Armstrong in jazz) was figured as expressing artistic—and, by extension, democratic—freedom, as well as opposition to the rigid social realist doctrine underpinning officially sanctioned Soviet politics and art. Moreover, Faulkner's own rhetoric throughout his post-Nobel public pronouncements on freedom and democracy was deeply intertwined with that of the totalitarianism paradigm. This tendency was exemplified by his Nobel acceptance speech, with its concern about the question "When will I be blown up?" Tellingly, the Nobel speech was described by one State Department official as voicing "the free world's challenge to all forces that would enslave the human spirit"; the official further observed that it "has been quoted on the floor of Parliament, in both Houses of Congress, etc., etc., as a [n]oble summing-up of free man's determination to stay free."[9] Beyond the literary content or supposedly universal appeal of Faulkner's speech, then, the State Department cannily latched onto its advocacy of democracy—a move that was fairly symptomatic of its approach to the writer and his public performances over the next few years.

The State Department also took note of how Faulkner was one of the "stars" of the 1950 Nobel festivities.[10] Officials calculated that, given his international popularity, he would be welcomed enthusiastically abroad. In 1954 they asked him to attend the International Congress of Writers in Brazil.[11] Faulkner's presence was meant to "further the interests of the U.S." by both showcasing U.S. cultural accomplishments and pouring oil on the water of political tensions between the U.S. and Brazil.[12] Although the trip was marred by his drinking, a side trip to Peru and an impromptu stop in Venezuela proved to be very successful, prompting the State Department to call on him several more times to serve as a goodwill ambassador. Between 1955 and 1961, Faulkner made official visits to Japan, the Philippines, England, France, Germany, Italy, Greece, Iceland, and, again, Venezuela. Many of these countries were chosen to allow the U.S. government to bolster the nation's image in "strategic" areas during the Cold War. Faulkner's unusually congenial interactions with international audiences and journalists, as well as his vocal support for democracy, proved to be quite effective at winning over international populations and periodicals that had harbored anti-U.S. sentiment.

The 1950s and 1960s were an era of U.S. government funding of public diplomacy programs, many of which were based on cultural exchanges. Such programs sought to promote U.S. cultural achievements and democratic values abroad and were inspired by the belief that greater understanding of the cultural production of other countries would ultimately benefit national security. Postwar mass communications research indicated that the diffusion of political ideas was particularly effective through so-called opinion leaders, respected community members with the means to disseminate their ideas widely and to therefore "exert significant influence on their peers' opinion formation."[13] Faulkner's travels were coordinated by the State Department's International Educational Exchange Service, which over the years has sent thousands of artists and intellectuals abroad. As a writer with massive appeal among the cultural elite, the general public, and thus also the media, Faulkner had the potential to reach both "opinion makers" and the popular classes.

Michael Kreyling has observed, "The needy causes of southern literature, the Department of State, and other official cultural interests loaded the author with claims of 'Faulknerian' wisdom that the writer often found beyond his desire or inclination to fulfill."[14] Never the extrovert, Faulkner was reluctant to suffer through the formal functions and social obligations that comprised the bulk of official visits, and he responded to these pressures with a complex dialectic of self-invention and self-concealment. As Kreyling details, these were strategies that the writer had been perfecting throughout his life, but he drew on them ever more frequently after receiving the Nobel Prize, when the "absolutely private person and the public figure" collided as he was thrust into the international spotlight.[15] On his State Department travels, a favorite strategy for self-concealment involved invoking stock, even stereotypical, images of the South and of southerners as rural and removed from highbrow culture. Thus, when faced with requests to go on State Department missions or with queries about his work, the man who was dubbed in *Newsweek* the "most unapproachable and unpredictable personality" in the United States[16] often hid behind the mask of a regional identity by casting himself as a "farmer who wants to write," or a "countryman who simply likes books."[17] Consider, for example, the trip to receive the Nobel Prize in December 1950. Although it was not an official visit, Faulkner's initial refusal to travel to Stockholm almost caused an international incident that was resolved only following the interventions of the U.S. ambassador to Sweden, the secretary of state, and several other State Department officials. Faulkner's excuse for not going to Sweden was that he was a farmer and had to stay home and take care of his cows. The excuse met with little sympathy from the Swedish ambassador to the United States, who was a farmer himself.[18] Ultimately Faulkner capitulated and went to Sweden, where he ended up discussing farming with the king.[19]

At times Faulkner referred to himself as a "farmer of the South"; on other occasions he termed himself an "American farmer."[20] Faulkner was drawing on two topoi here—that of the southern agrarian, and that of the Jeffersonian yeoman farmer.[21] Peter Nicolaisen considers the representation of rural Yoknapatawpha County in Faulkner's work to be "a far cry from the agrarian order either Thomas Jefferson or his latter day disciples at Vanderbilt contemplated." Faulkner nevertheless seemed to harbor a "wish, almost against better knowledge, to believe in the beneficence of an agrarian order." This wish was evident in what Nicolaisen sees as the "Jeffersonian tradition of thought" in Faulkner's fiction of the 1940s, and in his posturing as a farmer.[22] For Lothar Hönnighausen, the posture had an additional, instrumental, purpose, providing the writer with a "pose as a nonintellectual, nonliterary person" that served to lessen the expectations of his interlocutors. At the same time, though, "the mask of farmer and that of horseman are related, both emerging as manifestations of the pastoralism with which many contemporary writers and artists responded to the changes and challenges of modernism."[23]

Faulkner's masks thus wove together contrary and contemporaneous notions of "southernness." On the one hand, he played on notions of the South as backward, unrefined, and simple: the legacy of the years when the U.S. South was, in Franklin D. Roosevelt's formulation, the nation's "number one economic problem." On the other, he also cultivated the image of the southern gentleman farmer that still determined preconceptions of the South and its literature. In 1960 Caroline Gordon observed that "after the Civil War there was a school of literature foisted on us by Northern publishers. They demanded moonlight and magnolias and a lot of people furnished it to them and that idea stuck in people's heads ever since. If a Southerner writes a novel now, whoever is reviewing for the *New York Times* will make a point of saying it isn't moonlight and magnolias." The moonlight, magnolias, and "white columns" that Gordon identifies in this passage are elements of the aristocratic South that Faulkner's poses invoked.[24]

Faulkner's State Department contacts as well as his international audiences responded to this strategy, interpreting the writer's behavior in light of both his pose and these preconceived (and mutually contradictory) notions of southernness. In fact, an embassy dispatch following his Nobel Prize acceptance speech noted that the press in Sweden was "apparently surprised by his courtly and gracious manners. Obviously Mr. Faulkner's references to his farming had led people to expect a rough diamond of the 'hillbilly' variety."[25] U.S. professor Gay Wilson Allen, who witnessed Faulkner's taciturn behavior during his stay in Japan, was led "to wonder if he were not, after all, the Mississippi farmer and not the great novelist we had proclaimed him to the Japanese." Allen ultimately concluded, though, "The real man, who sustained the artist within, was the self-effacing 'farmer' answering questions in Nagano. He was as simple, unaffected and innately friendly as his Deep South neighbors."[26] By setting off his second reference to "farmer" in quotation marks, Allen here seems to suggest that he has seen through the pose, but his enumeration of the qualities of Faulkner's "Deep South neighbors" raises the question of whether he was not, after all, taken in by the writer's ruse. Then there was Madeleine Chapsal, the French journalist who in 1955 described colleagues trying to interview Faulkner in Paris as running "into a wall . . . built of the most exquisite but the most obdurate politeness—the special politeness we in France think of as the attribute of certain Americans brought up in the South."[27] Descriptions like those of Allen and Chapsal, as well as multiple USIS (United States Information Service) and State Department reports over the years describing Faulkner as "gracious," "charming," and "courtly," suggest that the writer's interlocutors abroad—whether foreign or hailing from the United States—read him through a paradigm that construed him not only as a southern agrarian, but also as a southern gentleman, which is precisely what one of his State Department contacts called him at one point.[28]

Faulkner and the State Department II: The Cold Warrior

Whereas "southernness" was a pose, a strategy through which Faulkner dealt with social and literary obligations, Cold War nationalism was the modus operandi that dominated Faulkner's political pronouncements on his State Department trips. For all of Faulkner's reluctance to travel, the writer was, in his own way, a patriot, and he understood the importance that the State Department placed on his service. Numerous USIS reports describe how he pushed himself—quite successfully—to be charming. As one official wrote following his 1961 trip to Venezuela, "'I don't think any other living North American could have affected the minds and hearts of Venezuelans as he did during his two weeks here. . . . The most hardened press elements, the politically unsympathetic, all fell before his charm and his unwavering integrity.'"[29] Indeed, reports from this trip also noted that journalists had taken to calling him "el hombre simpático" (the nice man)—an assessment of Faulkner's personality that their U.S. counterparts would never have agreed with.[30] Faulkner also proved adept at navigating delicate political situations and was tenacious about putting forth a good image of the United States. All of Faulkner's State Department trips took place in the wake of the 1954 *Brown vs. Board of Education* ruling, which had explicitly identified the negative impact that the nation's segregation policies had abroad during the Cold War, so it was not surprising that he often faced questions about racism in the United States from his audiences. As he told one group in Japan, "I love my country enough to want to cure its faults and the only way that I can . . . is to shame it, to criticize."[31] And so he did, interweaving his praise for the United States and its democratic system with references to the South's situation and unflinching criticism of the nation's racial problems that in the end served both to heighten his appeal and to improve the image of the United States abroad.

Faulkner's 1955 trip to Asia and Europe is especially significant because, in addition to the multiple occasions when he was promoted—or promoted himself—as a Cold Warrior, there were several instances when this role entailed if not exactly a performance of "southernness," then certainly the invocation of the U.S. South as a site where the United States' difficulties with race were cast in sharp relief. The writer's representation (in multiple senses) of the United States on this trip was thus inflected and undergirded by his constructions of the region. As I have discussed elsewhere, the writer's 1954 trip to Latin America was part wild success and part debacle, with embassy staff in Brazil working overtime to contain the damage caused by his drinking.[32] Faulkner made the trip, which took place in the wake of the U.S.-backed coup d'état in Guatemala as well as in the midst of political and economic tensions with Brazil, because his State Department contact, Muna Lee, a fellow Mississippi native and writer, appealed to his sense of patriotism. As Lee later noted, Faulkner undertook the trip—which centered on his participation, along with that of Robert Frost, in the International Congress of Writers in São Paulo— "because the Department put it to them as an important contribution to inter-American cultural relations. They are going to South America because they believe that they serve their country by doing so. That is also the view of the Department of State."[33]

The trip, which took place just three months after the Brown decision was handed down, provided Faulkner with several opportunities to speak out against racism: he declared his "repugnance for racial discrimination" to an audience in Peru,[34] and told another in Brazil that race was "'one of the preeminent problems on this continent.'"[35] Faulkner generated positive publicity for both himself and the United States in Peru and Venezuela, where he made short stops; the success of his stay in Brazil, however, was compromised by his drinking, which kept him from interacting with audiences and kept his embassy hosts on high alert and doing damage control. Despite the mixed results of this particular trip, Faulkner himself was keenly aware of the political usefulness of such cultural diplomacy. He wrote to one official upon his return to the United States, "I know now something of the problems the U.S. has to cope with in Latin America, and the problems which the State Department has to face in order to cope with them." He promised to make himself available to the State Department as needed.[36]

The opportunity came soon enough: in 1955 Faulkner was asked by the State Department to participate in an annual seminar in Nagano on U.S. literature. The seminar had been organized by the State Department three years earlier as a means of "improv[ing] the status of American literature in Japan and the quality of its instruction in the universities."[37] Prior to the Second World War, U.S literature had not been widely taught in Japanese universities, and there were few faculty members with expertise in the field. The postwar years, however, brought a rise in interest in U.S. culture that, in turn, sparked an increase in student interest in U.S. literature. With the seminar, whose goals included "conduct[ing] a first-class cultural event that will add to the prestige of all the Embassy's cultural activities in Japan," and "bring[ing] together Japanese and Americans... where they can... develop a feeling of mutual respect," the USIS saw an opportunity that was at once academic, cultural, and political.[38]

Faulkner's work was well known in Japan. According to Kiyoyuki Ono, the Japanese had been surprised by Faulkner's being awarded the Nobel Prize, for they viewed his works as sensationalistic. As happened in the United States as well, though, the award prompted a reconsideration of his work, and Japanese publishers quickly began to issue translations.[39] By 1955 many of these were in print, and his work had been taught in universities by Fulbright professors and at previous Nagano seminars, so his nomination for the seminar was welcomed by the Japanese. Faulkner spent almost two weeks in Nagano, as well as several days in Tokyo and Kyoto. He interacted directly with hundreds of people—diplomats, intellectuals, students, and the general public—and gave press conferences that reached many more. In his sessions at Nagano, as well as on his other stops, Faulkner fielded questions about his work and requests to "tell about the South": about racism and the situation of African Americans in the United States, as well as his perception of changes stemming from the *Brown vs. Board of Education* decision. He engaged with these directly, criticizing the United States' double standard on racism in his assertion that if Americans are to "talk to other people around the world about freedom, let us practice it... so nobody can say, 'Well, you talked to us about freedom, look at your own country.'"[40] At the same time, though, he emphasized on numerous occasions that his work spoke not just of the

U.S. South, or even just of the United States, but, in keeping with the ideas articulated in his Nobel Prize speech, of humanity in general. While his universalizing message helped him to build bridges with his audience, this sublimation of regional and national origins also worked to unite people under a common banner—humanity—which he viewed as a key step in resisting the advance of communism.

Faulkner was also frequently asked for his impressions of Japan and of similarities between Japan and the U.S. South. According to Joseph Blotner, his answers spoke to "the idea of the family and the process of recovery after a devastating military defeat and occupation."[41] Contemporary politics came up, too, and Faulkner's patriotism shone through in his answers, which, in the words of his embassy host in Japan, G. Lewis Schmidt, hit "hard against Communism, Socialism, and any form of radicalism in general, defending Democracy as the best system yet devised by man for all of its faults."[42] This is evident in Faulkner's essay, "To the Youth of Japan," which he wrote during his trip, and in which he compared the postbellum U.S. South and postwar Japan. Here, Faulkner suggests that a shared history of war and loss allows (white) southerners to sympathize with what he perceives as a sense of hopelessness among Japanese youth. Faulkner predicted that "good writing" would arise in the aftermath of military defeat, as it had in the U.S. South, in the form of "a group of Japanese writers whom all the world will want to listen to, who will speak not a Japanese truth but a universal truth." There is a sleight of hand here: Faulkner presents a specific example of comparative historical consciousness (U.S. southern and Japanese experiences of defeat in war) as "universal." This slippage is, moreover, compounded when Faulkner subsumes an ideological (i.e., anti-communist) position under the rhetoric of "universality." He argues that the "universal truth" to be articulated by Japanese writers would itself be both a function of and a testament to democracy, for it would be rooted in

> freedom in which to hope and believe. . . . And that Freedom must be complete freedom for all men; we must choose now not between color and color . . . nor between ideology and ideology. We must choose simply between being slave and being free. . . . We think of the world today as being a helpless battleground in which two mighty forces face each other in the form of two irreconcilable ideologies. I do not believe they are two ideologies. I believe that only

one of them is . . . a political state or ideology, because the other one is simply a mutual state of man mutually believing in mutual liberty, in which politics is merely one more of the clumsy methods to make and hold good that condition in which all man shall be free. A clumsy method. . . . But until we do find a better, democracy will do.[43]

Faulkner's statement is deeply imbued with the rhetoric of the "totalitarianism paradigm" that pits the freedom enjoyed by democratic societies against a vision of stifling Soviet authoritarianism, all the while denying that democracy is an ideology at all. At the same time, it is interesting to note the alignment of the nation and region in this piece: on the one hand, Faulkner's description of the (white) South's experience of defeat and its aftermath slides seamlessly into a description of the United States' Cold War battle, whereas the "peculiar institution" of slavery with which the region was so long associated is distilled here into a metaphor and figure for communism. Harilaos Stecopoulos has argued, "To locate Dixie in Japan was at once to connect two different races and two populations whose refusal to accept the dictates of liberal modernity rendered them alien to the United States."[44] Yet at the same time, the connection of the United States with Japan also allowed Faulkner to invoke the nations' common humanity and shared search for a "universal truth"—a rhetorical move that disguised ideology as "universality" as a means of bringing the former wartime enemies together in support of the democratic system.

Faulkner seemed to have made a tremendous impression on the Japanese. The U.S. Mission in Tokyo's assessment that Faulkner's "contributions to USIS efforts will be among the most lasting contributions ever made by any one individual in any given country" was a statement that was echoed by many of his hosts over the years.[45] From Japan, Faulkner traveled to Manila. The idea, first deployed in Japan, of a shared tragedy as offering a means through which peoples could come to understand one another became a leitmotif in his travels through the Philippines as well. At the same time, Faulkner himself was both created for and consumed by the Filipino public as a figure whose importance transcended the boundaries of the South and the United States alike. As one newspaper reported, Faulkner and the world he created were "American," but his work showed that "the act of creation has no origin and that the creator belongs to all humanity."[46] This sublimation of regional and national origins echoed Faulkner's own universalizing and supposedly nonideological language—part of the rhetoric of U.S.-led resistance to Soviet Communism—as he worked to unite people under a purportedly common humanity. Faulkner's own political pronouncements in the Philippines further advanced the message of shared interests and shared beliefs: in addition to proclaiming the death of McCarthyism, Faulkner asserted, "We, in my country, know that the Filipino is a friend: we know that there is a mutual dependence between our two nations, our two peoples . . . we would defend that friend—all people—who believe as we believe."[47] Faulkner's meeting with the president of the Philippines, Ramon Magsayay, an ally of the United States and a firm opponent of communism, conveyed a similar message and was widely covered in the local press.

Audiences in the Philippines warmed to Faulkner because of what they saw as his sincerity and wit. They appreciated his willingness to criticize the United States, and the fact that he encouraged them to write in Tagalog as well as English. In a testament to his popularity, posters at the University of the Philippines showing his famous map of Yoknapatawpha County disappeared as soon as they were hung, only to reappear in student dormitory rooms.[48] Blotner describes Faulkner on this visit as "conscientiously working at his self-chosen double role: to speak for himself as an individual artist, and to speak for his country as a representative of part of its culture. . . . The more he traveled, apparently, the more the conviction grew upon him that America needed all the friends it could get, both at home and abroad, and he would do his best to that end."[49] Faulkner's best was considerable, and he received superlative write-ups in newspapers that otherwise tended to be critical of the U.S. and its policies. The *Philippines Herald*, for instance, wrote that "Faulkner's writings represent, perhaps, the vexed American soul seeking to communicate the lasting spiritual values it has experienced to the hearts of other free men in other parts of the world. As ambassador of that American spirit in letters, Faulkner commands the reverent attention of all humanity, as much for the greatness of his literary craft as for the validity of the experiences of the human American soul depicted in his novels."[50] For the *Herald*, then, the writer was a metonym of both U.S. culture and the nation itself: his writings represented the "vexed" and "human American soul" and its "spiritual values," and he himself was cast as "ambassador of that American spirit in letters"—a fusion of the national and the universal that echoed both Faulkner's own rhetoric and that of the officials promoting his visits. Thus did the writer's visit come to be seen by U.S. officials as a textbook example of how, as John A. Malley at the U.S. Embassy in Manila put it, "cultural exchange can help create a climate of respect in the small but articulate circle of journalists, writers, and intellectuals among whom unfortunately are some of the severest critics of American mores and policies."[51]

After Manila, Faulkner traveled through Europe. Emmett Till's murder in Mississippi in August 1955 took place during Faulkner's stay in Rome, and the United Press contacted the writer for a comment. Faulkner issued a statement, which was distributed widely by the United Press and the State Department, and which revealed his sense that the incident was a litmus test of the survival of his home state, of the U.S. South, and of the (white) United States. "When will we learn," Faulkner asked, "that if one county in Mississippi is to survive it will be because all Mississippi survives? That if the state of Mississippi survives, it will be because all America survives? And if America is to survive, the whole white race must survive first?"[52] Much could be said about this statement, but I would like to foreground its underlying slippage, which intertwines the destinies of the state, the region, and the nation. At the same time, it speaks to Faulkner's view of the national and international implications of racism in the United States during the Cold War. How, he continues, "can we hope to survive the next Pearl Harbor, if there should be one, with not only all peoples who are not white, but all peoples with political ideologies different from ours arrayed against us—after we have taught them (as we are doing) that when we talk of freedom and liberty, we not only mean neither, we don't even mean security and justice and even the preservation of life for people whose pigmentation is not the same as ours?" In many of Faulkner's speeches and comments at this time, and especially on his trips for the State Department, "freedom" was synonymous with "U.S.-style democracy." The racial division that Faulkner sees as underlying and undermining the United States' possibilities for survival bleed here into an ideological division that likewise threatens the nation's well-being, precisely by countering the image of democracy that it put forth to the world. What Faulkner saw as necessary, then, was finding a way to bring the races together under the umbrella of democracy, for "if we Americans are to survive, it will have to be because we choose and elect and defend to be first of all Americans to present to the world one homogeneous and unbroken front, whether of white Americans or black ones or purple or blue or green."[53] For Faulkner, racism threatens to destabilize democracy, and can be exploited by communists as evidence of U.S. hypocrisy about "freedom"; as such, it must be subsumed under a greater, shared cause, lest all Americans—whether white or black "or purple or blue or green"—risk becoming "red."

From Rome, Faulkner traveled to Munich, Paris, and then Reykjavik. Embassy officials here noted that his visit received more publicity, "of a more favorable kind, than any other American brought to Iceland under the visiting artists program, and there is good reason to believe that he had a very wholesome effect on the thinking of all Icelanders." He had a similar impact on the "opinion molders," such as the "university circles, which often have been peculiarly subject to influences cool or even hostile to the United States." Of particular interest to USIS was the writer's assertion during an interview about the U.S. military presence in Iceland.

> I understand why you are cautious in your behavior toward the foreign army and are not too enthusiastic about having it here. But neither of our nations is responsible for the circumstances that cause American forces to be here. And people must remember that they are not here under the auspices of the United States, but the North Atlantic Treaty Organization. . . . Is it not better to have American forces here in the name of freedom, than a Russian one in the name of aggression and violence, as in the Baltic States?

Faulkner thus sought to mollify Icelanders by reframing the U.S. presence not as representing national power, but, rather, as a necessary part of the battle of democracy versus communism that was a common cause for the two nations. The USIS was buoyed by the effect that he had on "developing Icelandic respect for American culture and, less directly, the policies of the United States Government. . . . The extent to which he altered anyone's views is impossible to measure, but if anyone could alter them it was this shy, modest man, commanding the enormous reservoir of respect and good will that was demonstrated every day during his stay in Iceland. . . . Nothing could be more effective in giving Icelanders a broader, more comprehensive view of the United States, the American people's deep interest in the freedom of the human spirit, and American friendship toward Iceland."[54]

Faulkner returned to the United States in mid-October, after almost three months abroad. It was the most ambitious, and exhausting, of his trips for the State Department. The questions, and challenges, that the writer faced during the course of his tour, as well as the responses that he chose to give, speak to many different constructions of "Faulkner" and, by extension, of "the South" and "the United States" that coexisted and competed at the time. They speak to the ramifications of *Brown vs. Board*, and to the pivotal role of race, and racism, in international constructions of both region and nation. Finally, Faulkner's experiences offer insight into the creation of a Cold War discourse that hid ideological battles behind a mask of "universality" and "humanity" as part of a widespread effort to rally populations both domestic and international behind the cause of U.S.-style democracy.

To be sure, studying Faulkner as a U.S. patriot on the international public stage provides us with only a limited vantage point on an extremely complicated figure. There is a marked discrepancy between the sweeping, binary political pronouncements that he made on these trips and the critiques of capitalist democracy that are evident in his Cold War fiction, which dates from roughly the same years as his travels for the State Department. As Noel Polk observes, Faulkner was quite critical of the United States in that period, although "he did indeed support the notion that America, with all its problems, offered better alternatives for individual achievement than the Soviet Union."[55] Polk, Nicolaisen, Richard Godden, Richard Gray, John T. Matthews, and other scholars have discussed Faulkner's concerns about the growth of military-industrial capitalism as expressed in *A Fable* (1954), as well as his more general distrust of the establishment, and of those who govern it. In turn, the Snopes trilogy offers, as Matthews observes, a strong critique of commodification, class conflicts, and the entrenchment of injustice and inequality in U.S. imperial capitalism. Matthews argues that in *The Mansion* (1959), "Faulkner uses the vulnerabilities of the South to criticize capitalist Cold War certitudes. He insists that the South, as the forgotten subtext of national failure, exploitation, and hypocrisy, contradicts American pride in itself as the land of freedom, equal opportunity, and justice. The prevailing contemporary view of the South as the nation's *problem* functions critically for Faulkner as the country's Achilles heel."[56] This view of the U.S. South as a "check" on triumphalist visions of the United States sharply counters the fusion of nation and region proclaimed by Faulkner when abroad, and even anticipates historian C. Vann Woodward's comparativist thesis that the (white) South's "experience of military defeat, occupation, and reconstruction" diverged from notions of U.S. exceptionalism, but was "shared by nearly all the peoples of Europe and Asia."[57]

Polk suggests that Faulkner's whitewashing of his skepticism about democracy in his public statements may be seen as fulfilling "a performative ritual of public pronouncements under the cultural terms of which, having agreed to make a public comment . . . one cannot make a comment that violates the terms of the occasion."[58] I would certainly agree that this dynamic is at play in Faulkner's public statements throughout the official trips discussed in this essay. Following Kreyling, one might suggest that the expectation of wisdom led audiences to create and consume Faulkner as an expert on both the U.S. South and the United States (an expectation that Faulkner sometimes met, but from which he sometimes fled by inventing himself as a farmer who could not be expected to meet such lofty ideals). At the same time, Faulkner did exhibit a deep-seated patriotism that manifested itself as an eagerness to do his best to promote freedom (qua democracy) in general and the United States in particular. Perhaps there is also a grain of truth to Blotner's suggestion that Faulkner's "advocacy of American-style democracy . . . demonstrated that if his trips had created an effect upon his foreign hearers, they had also had a profound effect upon him as well."[59] My sense is that ultimately both Polk and Blotner are right, and that the performative dimension of Faulkner's work that the former identifies is key: Faulkner seemed to get caught up in the moment when on site, and his patriotism took over, only to recede when he was back at home and immersing himself in his fiction, or when facing the prospect of another official trip. Cold Warrior or not, then, the conflicting views of democracy offered by Faulkner as writer and Faulkner as cultural diplomat speak to a figure who must be viewed from more than one perspective, and who cannot be reduced to the function that the Department of State wanted him to serve.

Notes

I am indebted to the following people for thoughtful feedback as well as opportunities to present my research, which have been invaluable to me: Martyn Bone, Richard Gray, Peter Hulme, Liam Kennedy, Richard King, John T. Matthews, Brian Ward, and Noel Polk, whose mentorship is deeply missed. I have been granted permission to quote from materials in the Special Collections Department, University of Virginia Library, and the Center for Faulkner Studies, Southeast Missouri State University. I am particularly grateful to Regina Rush at the University of Virginia Library for all of her assistance over the years.

1. "Nobel Bedfellows."
2. See Gray, *Southern Aberrations*.
3. Schwartz, *Creating Faulkner's Reputation*, 200.
4. See, for example, Nicolaisen and Göske, "William Faulkner in Germany"; Pitavy, "Making of a French Faulkner"; and Schneider, "William Faulkner and the Romanian 'Criticism of Survival.'"
5. Faulkner, *Essays, Speeches, and Public Letters*, 120.
6. Berghahn, *America and the Intellectual Cold Wars in Europe*, 115.
7. Wilford, *Mighty Wurlitzer*, 101.
8. Schwartz, *Creating Faulkner's Reputation*, 201.
9. Philip Raine, memo to Mr. Riley, June 22, 1954, Blotner Papers, Brodsky Collection, Center for Faulkner Studies, Southeast Missouri State University, Box 9, Folder 11 (henceforth, "Blotner Papers").
10. U.S. Embassy, Stockholm, to the Department of State (DS), Washington D.C., December 21, 1950; 090.5811/12-2150; Central Decimal Files, 1950–1954; General Records of the DS, Record Group 59 (RG 59); National Archives at College Park, College Park, MD (NARA).
11. Regarding Faulkner's 1954 and 1961 trips to Latin America, see my "Combating Anti-Americanism."
12. Raine, memo to Mr. Riley, June 22, 1954, Blotner Papers, Box 9, Folder 11.
13. Robin, *Making of the Cold War Enemy*, 83.
14. Kreyling, *Inventing Southern Literature*, 129.
15. Ibid., 137.
16. Emerson, "William Faulkner," 48.
17. "Famed Writer Observes Japanese Writers Now More Comprehensible," *Evening News*, August 24, 1955, Hal Howland–William Faulkner Papers, 1954–1976, Accession #11615, Special Collections Department, University of Virginia Library, Charlottesville, Va. (henceforth, "Howland–Faulkner Papers"), Newspaper Clippings re: William Faulkner (1955 Aug.–Sept.), Folders 1 and 2; Faulkner, *Selected Letters*, 384.
18. Erik Boheman, letter to Faulkner, November 21, 1950, Blotner Papers, Box 9, Folder 2.
19. Blotner, *Faulkner*, 1368.
20. Blotner, "William Faulkner: Roving Ambassador," 5, 14.
21. These two figures are not unconnected, for the Vanderbilt Agrarians invoked the image of an agrarian Jefferson as part of their creation of a South predicated on agrarian values and opposed to those of industrial societies (see Nicolaisen, "William Faulkner's Dialogue," 66).
22. Nicolaisen, "William Faulkner's Dialogue," 67, 68.
23. Höningshausen, *Faulkner: Masks and Metaphors*, 273, 268.
24. Gordon in Porter, O'Connor, et al., "Recent Southern Fiction," 74–75.
25. U.S. Embassy, Stockholm, to DS, Washington D.C., December 21, 1950; 090.5811/12-2150; Central Decimal Files, 1950–1954; General Records of the DS, RG 59; NARA.
26. Allen, "With Faulkner in Japan," 568, 571.

27. Faulkner, *Lion in the Garden*, 229.

28. Muna Lee, letter to John Vebber, January 25, 1961, Blotner Papers, Box 9, Folder 28.

29. Cecil Sanford quoted in a Muna Lee memo to Mr. Colwell, May 2, 1961, Papers regarding William Faulkner's travels for the U.S. State Department, Accession #7258-a (henceforth, "Faulkner's Travels Papers"), Special Collections Dept., University of Virginia Library, Charlottesville.

30. Charles Harner, letter to Lee, April 4, 1961, Blotner Papers, Box 9, Folder 28.

31. Faulkner, *Lion in the Garden*, 159.

32. See Cohn, "Combating Anti-Americanism."

33. Lee, office memo to Thomas Driver, July 26, 1954, Faulkner's Travels Papers.

34. Translation of article (English title: "Racial Discrimination Is Repugnant to Me, William Faulkner Declared") in *La Nación* (Peruvian newspaper), August 8, 1954, Howland-Faulkner Papers, Dept. of State Papers re: William Faulkner's foreign travel (1954–1955 Sept.).

35. Monteiro, "Faulkner in Brazil," 99.

36. Faulkner, *Selected Letters*, 369.

37. USIS Tokyo, Despatch to DS, Washington, September 27, 1955, Blotner Papers, Box 9, Folder 13.

38. Ibid.

39. See Ono, "Faulkner Studies in Japan," 4–5.

40. Faulkner, *Lion in the Garden*, 144.

41. Blotner, *Faulkner*, 1563.

42. G. Lewis Schmidt, USIS-Tokyo, Despatch to DS/USIA, Washington, September 22, 1955, Blotner Papers, Box 9, Folder 13.

43. Faulkner, "To the Youth of Japan," 187–88.

44. Stecopoulos, *Reconstructing the World*, 132.

45. G. Lewis Schmidt, USIS-Tokyo, Despatch to DS/USIA, Washington, September 22, 1955, Blotner Papers, Box 9, Folder 13.

46. "William Faulkner," *Manila Chronicle*, August 24, 1955, Howland-Faulkner Papers, Newspaper Clippings re: William Faulkner (1955 Aug.–Sept.), Folders 1 and 2.

47. Faulkner, *Lion in the Garden*, 213.

48. Article (title missing) in *Manila Times*, August 25, 1955, Howland-Faulkner Papers, Newspaper Clippings re: William Faulkner (1955 Aug.–Sept.), Folders 1 and 2.

49. Blotner, *Faulkner*, 1569.

50. Quoted in John A. Malley, U.S. Embassy, Manila, Despatch to DS/USIA, September 14, 1955, Blotner Papers, Box 9, Folder 19.

51. John A. Malley, U.S. Embassy, Manila, Despatch to DS/USIA, September 14, 1955, Blotner Papers, Box 9, Folder 19.

52. Faulkner, *Essays, Speeches, and Public Letters*, 222.

53. Ibid., 223.

54. William Gibson, U.S. Legation, Reykjavik, Despatch to Department of State, Washington, October 25, 1955, Howland-Faulkner Papers, Dept. of State Papers re: William Faulkner's foreign travel (1955 Oct.–1957).

55. Polk, *Dark House*, 262.
56. Matthews, "Many Mansions," 11.
57. Woodward, *Burden of Southern History*, 190.
58. Polk, personal communication with the author, April 4, 2009.
59. Blotner, *Faulkner*, 1566.

Works Cited

Allen, Gay Wilson. "With Faulkner in Japan." *American Scholar* 31, no. 4 (autumn 1962): 566–71.

Berghahn, Volker. *America and the Intellectual Cold Wars in Europe: Shepard Stone between Philanthropy, Academy, and Diplomacy*. Princeton: Princeton University Press, 2001.

Blotner, Joseph. *Faulkner: A Biography*, vol. 2. New York: Random House, 1974.

———. "William Faulkner, Roving Ambassador." *International Educational and Cultural Exchange* 2, no. 1 (summer 1966): 1–22.

Cohn, Deborah. "Combating Anti-Americanism during the Cold War: Faulkner, the State Department, and Latin America." *Mississippi Quarterly* 59, nos. 3 and 4 (summer–fall 2006): 396–413.

Emerson, William. "William Faulkner: After Ten Years, 'A Fable.'" *Newsweek* 44, no. 9 (August 30, 1954): 48–52.

Faulkner, William. "Banquet Speech." Nobelprize.org. http://nobelprize.org/nobel_prizes/literature/laureates/1949/faulkner-speech.html. Accessed January 26, 2011.

———. *Essays, Speeches and Public Letters*. Edited by James B. Meriwether. London: Chatto and Windus, 1967.

———. *Lion in the Garden: Interviews with William Faulkner*. Edited by James B. Meriwether and Michael Millgate. Lincoln: University of Nebraska Press, 1968.

———. *Selected Letters of William Faulkner*. Edited by Joseph Blotner. New York: Vintage Books, 1977.

———. "To the Youth of Japan." *Faulkner at Nagano*. Edited by Robert A. Jeliffe. Tokyo: Kenkyusha, 1956. 185–88.

Gray, Richard. *Southern Aberrations: Writers of the American South and the Problems of Regionalism*. Baton Rouge: Louisiana State University Press, 2000.

Hönnighausen, Lothar. *Faulkner: Masks and Metaphors*. Jackson: University Press of Mississippi, 1997.

Kreyling, Michael. *Inventing Southern Literature*. Jackson: University Press of Mississippi, 1998.

Matthews, John T. "Many Mansions: Faulkner's Cold War Conflicts." In *Global Faulkner: Faulkner and Yoknapatawpha, 2006*, edited by Annette Trefzer and Ann J. Abadie, 3–23. Jackson: University Press of Mississippi, 2009.

Monteiro, George. "Faulkner in Brazil." *Southern Literary Journal* 15, no. 3 (1983): 96–104.

"More Trouble in Venezuela." *New York Times*, February 21, 1961. Via NYT ProQuest, http://www.il.proquest.com/proquest/. Accessed June 7, 2007.

Nicolaisen, Peter. "William Faulkner's Dialogue with Thomas Jefferson." In *Faulkner in America: Faulkner and Yoknapatawpha, 1998*, edited by Joseph R. Urgo and Ann J. Abadie, 64–81. Jackson: University Press of Mississippi, 2001.

Nicolaisen, Peter, and Daniel Göske. "William Faulkner in Germany: A Survey." *Faulkner Journal* 24, no. 1 (fall 2008): 63–81.

"Nobel Bedfellows." *New York Times*, November 11, 1950. Via NYT ProQuest, http://www.il.proquest.com/proquest/. Accessed February 12, 2009.

Ono, Kiyoyuki. "Faulkner Studies in Japan: An Overview." In *Faulkner Studies in Japan*, edited and compiled by Thomas L. McHaney, Kenzaburo Ohashi, and Kiyoyuki Ono, 1–12. Athens: University of Georgia Press, 1985.

Pitavy, François. "The Making of a French Faulkner: A Reflection on Translation." *Faulkner Journal* 24, no. 1 (fall 2008): 83–97.

Polk, Noel. *Children of the Dark House: Text and Context in Faulkner*. Jackson: University Press of Mississippi, 1996.

Porter, Katherine Anne, Flannery O'Connor, Caroline Gordon, Madison Jones, and Louis D. Rubin. "Recent Southern Fiction: A Panel Discussion. Wesleyan College, 28 October 1960." In *Conversations with Flannery O'Connor*, edited by Rosemary M. Magee, 61–78. Jackson: University Press of Mississippi, 1987.

Robin, Ron. *The Making of the Cold War Enemy: Culture and Politics in the Military-Intellectual Complex*. Princeton: Princeton University Press, 2001.

Schneider, Ana-Karina. "William Faulkner and the Romanian 'Criticism of Survival.'" *Faulkner Journal* 24, no. 1 (fall 2008): 99–117.

Schwartz, Lawrence H. *Creating Faulkner's Reputation: The Politics of Modern Literary Criticism*. Knoxville: University of Tennessee Press, 1988.

Stecopoulos, Harilaos. *Reconstructing the World: Southern Fictions and U.S. Imperialisms, 1898–1976*. Ithaca: Cornell University Press, 2008.

"Venezuela Quells Rebel Outbreak." *New York Times*, February 21, 1961. Via NYT ProQuest, http://www.il.proquest.com/proquest/. Accessed March 12, 2009.

Wilford, Hugh. *The Mighty Wurlitzer: How the CIA Played America*. Cambridge: Harvard University Press, 2008.

Woodward, C. Vann. *The Burden of Southern History*. 1960. 3rd ed. Baton Rouge: Louisiana State University Press, 1993.

12

The Feeling of a Heartless World

Blues Rhythm, Oppositionality, and British Rock Music

ANDREW WARNES

> While on their way, they would make the dense old woods, for miles around, reverberate with their wild songs, revealing at once the highest joy and the deepest sadness. They would compose and sing as they went along. . . . Into all of their songs they would manage to weave something of the Great House Farm. . . . To those songs I trace my first glimmering conception of the dehumanizing character of slavery. . . . The songs of the slave represent the sorrows of his heart; and he is relieved by them, only as an aching heart is relieved by its tears.
>
> Frederick Douglass, 1845

British rock music incessantly consumes and re-creates the U.S. South.[1] Landmark late 1960s albums, from the Rolling Stones' *Let It Bleed* to *Led Zeppelin II*, flaunt their debt to blues convention, trumpeting their use of a tradition first pioneered by the children of African American slaves. In recent essays I have argued that albums in later subgenres of British rock, such as *The Smiths* (1984) and Tricky's *Maxinquaye* (1995), avoid this flaunting of Delta legend yet continue to draw on southern blues culture at a more epistemological level.[2] Even the appalling racial outbursts of Morrissey, the Smiths' former lead singer, must be considered alongside a songwriting aesthetic that—in its laments, its paralinguistic wails and moans, and its preoccupation with heartbreak and social isolation—reminds us that his first reported recording was of an unidentified Bessie Smith song.[3]

Two possible approaches to British rock's consumption of southern myth have become apparent as a result of this research. One is to focus on those British musicians who parade their blues inheritance and to explore how they inhabit and, in some cases, subvert this tradition. I have no quarrel with the journalists and critics who take this approach, and I have learned much from their examinations. But I also feel that this focus can distract attention from the alternative approach, which is to consider the fuller epistemological debt that *all* British rock owes to U.S. southern culture. The flaunted blues echoes of *Let It Bleed* and *Led Zeppelin II* are invitations; they compel us to acknowledge the debt they owe to the music. And it is no less interesting to consider how, even when British rock musicians have downplayed their blues influences, those influences remain astir, shaping their understanding of what a song is and what it can do.

"The blues," after all, means much more than just a genre. No other tradition in popular music (except, perhaps, rap) spends quite so much time defining its own name. Bessie Smith's complaint of having "blues on my brain" on "Chicago Bound Blues" and Robert Johnson's declaration that the blues is at once a "low down shaking chill" and an "aching old heart disease" on "Preaching Blues (Up Jumped the Devil)" are just two particularly famous examples of this widespread definitional activity.[4] Such definitions remind us that the blues cannot be reduced to a particular combination of lyrical and musical structures, and that these generic structures themselves very often direct attention toward a temper or perspective on life also known as "the blues." Some of the most illuminating gestures toward this perspective occur when blues culture's definitional impulse spills into literature. Langston Hughes' "The Weary Blues" (1926), for example, does more than evoke a genre; it also elevates what stands behind and results in that genre, his poem's apostrophes to "Sweet Blues!" and "O Blues!" imagining it as an emotional mood meriting an ode.[5] A still more suggestive definition appears in Ralph Ellison's famous review of Richard Wright's 1945 autobiography *Black Boy*. Here, Ellison suggests that the blues is "an impulse to keep the painful details and episodes of a brutal experience alive in one's aching consciousness, to finger its jagged grain, and to transcend it, not by the consolation of philosophy but by squeezing from it a near-tragic, near-comic lyricism. As a form, the blues is an autobiographical chronicle of personal catastrophe expressed lyrically."[6] Ellison's musical training at Tuskegee, like his formative exposure to Oklahoma City's blues scene, urges us to associate his commentary with the blues definitions proliferating in the music itself.[7] This proliferation, moreover, indicates that blues epistemology will always remain ineffable, with none of these definitions ever proving final. Ellison nonetheless comes closer than most, establishing that this blues epistemology consists in the persistence of an articulate voice amid obliterating pain. He orients our attention toward an underlying impulse that, if epitomized in blues songs, also becomes manifest in any cultural text that, like *Black Boy*, "provide[s] no solution" but expresses "both the agony of life and the possibility of conquering it through sheer toughness of spirit."[8] For Ellison, then, the blues in essence describes a cultural response to the brutal terms of racist life and, as an epistemological impulse, can arise in cultural texts even when blues conventions remain absent.

This shift reconnects the blues with what preceded it. The songs that Frederick Douglass recollects hearing in "the dense old woods" might or might not have sounded like close ancestors of modern blues. Emotionally, however, they too appear to have fingered life's "jagged grain," improvising amid a "brutal experience" an articulate human voice very like that Ellison found in *Black Boy*. Such are the grounds on which Ellison defines "the blues" philosophically, as a cultural performance that not only mollifies but upends dehumanizing experience. But they are also the grounds on which I would like to base this essay's central assertion. For even those British rock musicians who have been distanced or who have distanced themselves from the blues have continued to consume this southern cultural tradition, and for the simple reason that they too have, time after time, grasped in song a defense against pain. They too have harnessed rhythm to recuperate identity; they too have fingered the "jagged grain" of "brutal experience"; and they too have presented their own articulate voice as a provisional, improvised response to ongoing crisis. Even when avoiding deliberate blues echoes, in other words, British rock musicians of all kinds have consumed and re-created the epistemological imperative of this southern songwriting tradition.

Many problems arise from this less obvious blues inheritance, and this essay will conclude by reflecting a little on them. Before I can consider this transatlantic identification, however, I must first establish its existence. The first section of the essay as such explores blues epistemology. It then turns to British rock music, focusing on a postpunk group, Wire, that made a point of removing obvious blues echoes from their work. But it shows that, despite this avoidance, "Heartbeat" and other Wire songs remain immersed in blues epistemology, and not least because they continue to present their lyrics as recuperating responses to emergency or pain. Even the least "bluesy" British rock continues to approach the song as a chance to combat agony, in the process maintaining a distant but deep connection to the "wild" songs that Douglass overheard in the antebellum U.S. South.

Blues Oppositionality

> It was just what came in the ears and, my, what it did to you. And then I slowly realised that what these cats were doing was closely related to what I'd grown up listening to. You know, it was more stripped down, it was more rural. . . . Then I got into Muddy Waters and then, before I knew it, that leads you immediately to Robert Johnson . . . [And] we just thought it was our job to pay back, to give them what they've given us. They've given us the music and the friendship, and let's stand up, be men, and give them a blues.
>
> Keith Richards, *BBC Blues Britannia* (2009)

British rock musicians name-check the blues so often as to endorse Zora Neale Hurston's 1934 assertion that, when it comes to music history, the juke joint "is the most important place in America."[9] Keith Richards' sense of wonder is just the most obvious example of how performances in "rural" southern juke joints—or at least, their mythic approximation in recorded form—continue to provide an alternative idea of culture, liberating and sexual, out of which British rock artists have shaped new form. Yet because such tributes lead so readily to a southern myth of blues authenticity, they obscure as much as they reveal.[10] *Let's stand up, be men*: the tendency, no less pronounced among musicians today than in the 1960s, to contrast this "authentic" southern blues tradition with "cosmopolitan" jazz tends to mask the fact that the blues, too, arose not in utter isolation but from the antagonistic yet intimate dialogue that the Old South staged between its black and white communities. Recent blues scholarship indeed restates, in the face of Richards' lifelong yearning to melt into blues "genius," the extent to which that "genius" took shape from what Elizabeth Abel has called the "multidirectional racial formation" of Jim Crow society.[11] Landmark studies by Angela Y. Davis, Adam Gussow, Leon F. Litwack, and Elijah Wald place blues performers back into their social world, seeing them not as mythic creatures but as artists who subjected the protocols of southern society to a constant, if often coded, critique. Gussow's *Seems Like Murder Here* (2002), in disclosing the "linkage between lynching and blues lyricism," exemplifies these attempts to bring the critical faculties of the blues back into view. These studies remind us that, even when in flight from the everyday pressures of racial injustice, this music delivered a kind of rebellious, and even dialectical, response to it.[12]

This critical capacity to respond—to answer back, even—can be related to an oppositional aesthetic long apparent in African American culture. For the powerful rebuttals that blues songs made to the dehumanizing spectacles of lynching culture during the 1910s and 1920s were not isolated incidents of political critique, nor did they graft such critique on to a blues paradigm otherwise insulated from social currents in the U.S. South. They were, instead, deliberate instances of a tendency not just to rebel against but to *oppose* dominant white southern racist culture—a tendency that shapes the blues aesthetic at subtler and more musical levels, and that connects this aesthetic to black expressive culture more broadly. Lyrical examples of what Gussow calls bluesmen and women's "public struggle" against "what would annihilate" them merely place onto a rhetorical footing (and thus make more audible) a mode of reversal as old as the plantation, transforming again some of the radically new uses of culture that those in bondage crafted in the name of group survival.[13] Ma Rainey's redemptive inversion of the cultural repertoire of racial terrorism, like Robert Johnson's lyrical response to (in Leon F. Litwack's words) "the elaborate apparatus that circumscribed the actions of black Southerners," exhibits an oppositionality whose origins lie in what Sidney Mintz and Richard Price once called "the birth of African American culture."[14] As Mintz and Price put it in 1976,

> we must draw our distinctions between the slaves and free groups carefully. That they were usually locked into an intimate interdependence is, in our view, inarguable. But we have sought to stress the often quite striking incomprehension of the true nature of this interdependence on the part of the masters. . . . We are not as certain—in fact, we doubt very much—that the slaves were similarly uncomprehending. . . . the institutions created by the slaves to deal with what are at once the most ordinary and most important aspects of life took on their characteristic shape *within* the parameters

of the masters' monopoly of power, but *separate* from the masters' institutions.[15]

Here, then, I am making two interconnected claims: first, that the moments of dialectical opposition that Gussow and others discern in the lyrics of particular blues songs are just the worded manifestations of an aesthetic whose operation cuts into and shapes the music as a whole; and second, that the constant operation of this oppositional aesthetic confirms that the blues belongs to that older and larger black cultural paradigm that grew out of the peculiar mix of isolation and interdependence that first took hold in plantation slavery. A longer sense of the tradition thus comes into view. The blues of oppositional recovery—the blues to which Hughes apostrophized—no longer seems confined to the twentieth century but appear a close descendant of the field hollers and sorrow songs that U.S. literature before 1900 brings to our attention.[16]

Black southern culture, of course, continued to operate under "terrible and usually inescapable constraints" long after abolition.[17] "We can be as separate as the fingers, but one as the hand in all things essential to material progress": far from being a call for reform, Booker T. Washington's famous metaphor sought to reconcile black and white southerners to an existing reality, and in doing so it illustrates the continuing relevance, throughout the Jim Crow era, of Mintz and Price's formulations.[18] For here, too, black southern culture developed amid a kind of forsworn intimacy. It continued to operate in separate spaces that remained ever subject to the observations and intrusions of white power.

Marion Post Wolcott's famous 1939 photograph of a Clarksdale juke joint (see Figure 12.1) illustrates well this historical continuity. This is a photograph in search of a documentary aesthetic. Initially, we can see, Wolcott has focused on a crowd that appears too engrossed in the jitterbugging couple to notice her camera. Vantage point and the lack of apparent posing by her subjects indicate that she is pursuing a documentary fantasy, urging us to forget her involvement and accept the photograph as a window on natural life. To the extent that she succeeds in producing such a shot—a photo that seems neither to touch nor intrude upon the image it captures—Wolcott delivers a mythic vision of the juke joint already familiar from the literature of her period. Her vanishing act, the camera's spiriting away, makes the juke joint look like an island in a Jim Crow

Figure 12.1. Marion Post Wolcott, "Negroes jitterbugging in a juke joint on a Saturday afternoon, Clarksdale, Mississippi" (Original caption, 1939) LC-USF34-052479-D, http://www.loc.gov/pictures/item/fsa2000032907/PP/.

sea, "a haven from white surveillance," where authentic black culture can flourish undisturbed.[19] The policeman in the doorway as such ruins much more than the photograph's aspirations toward documentary truth. His appearance also destroys that mythology of the juke as a sanctuary, a place of fleeting but magnificent isolation, that Wolcott cultivates through her pursuit of this aesthetic. His direct, confronting stare reminds us that such isolation always existed in antagonistic dialogue with, and could never really forget, the disciplinary power surrounding it. Pure isolation—the voyeuristic fantasy that we might be looking in on an undisturbed black southern culture—here remains suspended, forever trying and failing to resist the knowledge awakened as the lens and policeman's eye meet.

So it is interesting that, simply by placing our thumb over the policeman's face, we can restore this photograph to a state of documentary "truth." His arrival, in other words, heralds no crisis for those in the room. The fun goes on uninterrupted. The dancers continue to dance; the onlookers continue to smile; and their enjoyment alone suggests that the policeman's ability to call a halt to proceedings any time he wants is not accompanied by any deeper or more insidious capacity to unsettle the crowd. Their faces betray no sense of being caught unawares. The policeman's appearance in the doorway, far from heralding the sudden incursion of disciplinary power onto the dance floor, merely reveals that this power was already there. The emphasis Wolcott's caption places on the time of the dance (. . . . *On a Saturday afternoon, Clarksdale, Mississippi*) strengthens this impression. For all laborers used to working Saturday mornings, of course, Saturday afternoons and evenings can represent a magic interval, and the places in which they spend such precious leisure time, from English soccer terraces to Jamaican dancehalls, can acquire resonant, if fleeting, connotations of freedom. But the importance that energetic forms of dance so often assumed on black southern Saturdays indicates that these interludes in particular were seized as opportunities, not just for benumbing pleasure, but for the performance of a redeeming, oppositional humanity. The vigorous sexual dancing that famously took place in these juke joints supports Gussow's view that such venues were sites where revelers did not just forget their troubles but could directly "contest economic expropriation" and "reclaim their bodies" through rhythm.[20] The fact that some of the younger men in the crowd look like they have come straight from work, not even changing out of their denim overalls, certainly indicates that this particular juke joint is hosting a rather pointed dance whose participants and onlookers alike are regaining a command over their own bodies that has been lost in the long routines of tedious and tiring labor. It might be true that what we are seeing here is escapism. But surely it is anything but "mere" escapism. On the contrary: Wolcott's caption emphasizes that the blues dance she has photographed occurs in the immediate aftermath of work and is replacing the grueling monotony of manual labor with a very different, and oppositional, physical activity.

Wolcott's photograph helps to bring into view the broader pattern of blues oppositionality in black southern culture. These conditions of isolation in themselves resulted from southern racial protocols, and were from the start enforced in order to curb and alleviate the racial intimacy that in other ways lent shape, through a fraught dialectical process, to the sound of the blues, and to the meaning of that sound in the minds of those who performed it. Privileged whites in both the new and old South were more attached than other social groups in the modern United States and Europe to aristocratic ideas of civilization. Following the example of Thomas

Jefferson, they too tried to weigh southern culture's worth according to a handful of civilized pursuits that could happen only after an unusually large amount of surplus labor had been concentrated into the hands of a leisured class. A tendency to talk about music in the most spiritual terms possible often accompanied this anxious investment in civilization. *Pure, exquisite, divine, serious*—such breathless adjectives, applied in reference to Mozart and Beethoven, and precious few others, often led to a negative comparison with another music, with the Ma Raineys and Big Bill Broonzys of the world, whose work appeared to oppose such qualities.

Even when left unspoken, however, the comparison remained crucial. It was no accident that this exaggerated investment in Eurocentric notions of cultural capital developed in such close proximity with a blues sensibility that celebrated the earthly pleasures of the working poor. It was no accident that the white southern fascination with invented chivalric traditions and the cult of Walter Scott arose cheek by jowl with a blues tradition that eyed such romantic idealism with suspicion, even redefining love in terms of lust, violence, and emotional dependency. It was no accident that, as southern elites privileged classical training, blues musicians took delight in recollecting the makeshift musical tutorials and techniques that they improvised in any time they could snatch between performances and other jobs. It was no accident that a commitment to a model of culture-as-civilization by which privileged whites justified the surplus labor they concentrated into their own hands developed in such close proximity to a culture-as-respite in which plantation workers harnessed the distracting power of song to help themselves through the working day. All of these oppositional phenomena instead indicate the existence of an underlying southern dialectic in which the two parties, one black and one white, found their shape in and took heart from their rebuttal of the other. The conditions of isolated interdependence that continued long into the postbellum era provided the grounds from which African Americans launched their critique of the master culture that condemned them; and blues pioneers knew perfectly well that, in advancing such a critique, they were articulating nothing less than their right to exist.

And yet the blues, of course, has outlived the immediate conditions of its birth and long ago came to seem what Alan Lomax once called "the main musical form of the whole human species."[21] In fact it can seem as though the blues' capacity to conquer what Ellison called "the agony of life . . . through sheer toughness of spirit" deposited into the very conventions of the genre a notion of democratic and universal culture that, wherever it becomes felt, continues to contest the Eurocentric or "civilized" culture it once opposed on southern grounds. For the blues still appears to many not just authentic but affirmative; and in the course of learning their chord progressions and signature vocal styles, musicians far and wide have also imbibed their epistemological imperatives, their radical redefinition of song. It is these epistemological imperatives that require attention today. Even those British rock musicians who have paraded their debt to the blues have proven reluctant to acknowledge its political oppositionality. Keith Richards, Eric Clapton, and several other 1960s stalwarts, while sometimes acknowledging the unimaginable brutality of Jim Crow, have proven less willing to talk about how the blues they cherish negotiated and repudiated that deliberately dehumanizing southern social system. This silence is all the more absolute in the case of those later British rock acts, from the Slits to Wire, who have sought to reject any identification with the blues. Yet these younger British rock musicians, even while trying to strip their songs of blues echoes, continued to "chronicle . . . personal catastrophe," filling their songs with what Ellison called a "near-tragic, near-comic lyricism." Even when in flight from southern U.S. culture, British rock musicians have continued, at a fundamental level, to consume it.

Mesmerizing Heartbeat

One leading assumption about British rock tradition is that the movement from U.K. punk's Year Zero, 1976, toward diffuse postpunk experimentation was fueled by an increasingly total rejection of blues influence. Indeed, according to leading journalists as well as musicians, 1976 marked the moment British rock *stopped* consuming the U.S. South, or at least started to absorb several alternative lineages, from Manhattan disco to Jamaican dub, instead. This is certainly the view Simon Reynolds takes throughout *Rip It Up and Start Again: Postpunk 1978–1984* (2005), an influential history that depicts the transition from punk to postpunk as a kind of purging of the blues and rock 'n' roll debts that had hitherto dominated British rock.

[T]he post-punk bands were firmly committed to the idea of making modern music. They were totally confident that there were still places to go with rock, a whole new future to invent. For the post-punk vanguard, punk had failed because it attempted to overthrow rock's Old Wave using conventional music (fifties rock 'n' roll, garage punk, mod) that *predated* the dinosaur megabands like Pink Floyd and Led Zeppelin.

One curious byproduct of this conviction that rock 'n' roll had outlived its usefulness was the mountainous abuse heaped on Chuck Berry. A key source for punk rock . . . Berry became a negative touchstone, endlessly name-checked as a must-avoid. Perhaps the first example of Berry-phobia occurs as early as the Sex Pistols demos exhumed on *The Great Rock 'n' Roll Swindle*. The band begins jamming on "Johnny B. Goode." Then Johnny Rotten—the group's closet aesthete, who'd go on to form the archetypal post-punk outfit Public Image Ltd—half-heartedly jabbers the tune before groaning: "Oh fuck, it's *awful* . . . Stop it, I fucking hate it . . . AAARRRGH." Lydon's howl of disgusted exhaustion—he sounds like he's choking, suffocated by dead sound—was echoed by scores of post-punk groups: Cabaret Voltaire, for instance, complained, "rock 'n' roll is not about regurgitating Chuck Berry riffs."

Rather than . . . bluesy chords, the post-punk pantheon of guitar innovators favoured angularity, a clean and brittle spikiness.[22]

Certain gestures by musicians of the punk and post-punk period support Reynolds' account. Given the Clash's later hybrid experiments, we can easily hear Joe Strummer's chorus of "I'm so bored with the USA" (from the Clash's 1977 debut LP) not just as a statement of political outrage, but also as a declaration of intent from a vocalist wanting to escape the "back-to-basics rock 'n' roll" echoes that for now encase him.[23] Viv Albertine of the Slits has remembered the immediate aftermath of punk as a moment in which the pursuit of new forms required musicians "to be strict," and to ensure that "there was no sign of a twelve bar in anything you did."[24] Moreover, on their 1977 song "Lowdown," Wire not only avoided "bluesy chords" but lyrically reported the fact, elevating it into a sort of article of faith.

Another cigarette
Another day

From A to B,
Again avoiding C, D, and E,
Because E is where you play the blues
Avoiding a death
Is to win the game
To avoid relegation
The big E
Drowning in the big swim
Rising to the surface
The smell of you
That's the lowdown

This rejection of the blues, however, never quite convinced. One hardly needs to read Julia Kristeva to notice that, far from "Berry-phobia," the postpunk figureheads whom Reynolds quotes are actually expressing *Berry-nausea*: Lydon's "disgust" and "choking" noises, like Cabaret Voltaire's reference to "regurgitation," do not suggest a need to defend the body against external threat, but rather a horror at what already lies within. Similarly, in urging themselves against bluesy chord combinations, we can hear Wire fighting temptation, talking their fingers out of reaching for "the big E." Indeed, as this potent chord looms larger and larger in the lyric, it becomes hard not to notice that Wire has placed their disavowal of blues form under the profoundly bluesy title "Lowdown," a word we have already seen in Robert Johnson's "Preaching Blues (Up Jumped the Devil)." In 1977 and 1978, then, Wire could sound like a band who, far from summarily rejecting the blues, seemed to do so in response to the confusing and contradictory passions this music inspired in them. Their decision, on 2007's "No Warning Given," to retract their original rejection of the blues was thus not altogether surprising.

Dig close to the tree,
If you're looking for roots,
Hey! John Lee Hooker,
I've borrowed your boots.

This belated lyrical tribute suggests that, in their original injunction against bluesy chord progressions, Wire had been protesting too much. But it also maintains a certain distance from Robert Johnson and the crossroads myth often emphasized by Richards and Clapton among other leading British rock artists of the previous generation.[25] If only by focusing on John Lee Hooker, the tribute opens another line of inheritance, one that connects Wire's 1990s experiments in dance music with what Fernando Benadon and Ted Gioia have called the especially "hypnotic qualities" of Hooker's "rhythmic" innovations.[26] Still, this new line of inheritance raises the suspicion that even in the late 1970s Wire had not been reacting against the blues per se, so much as the way in which Britain's existing rock establishment had made the blues play host to a series of guitar solos that seemed, almost heretically, to sacrifice the integrity of blues rhythm in order to create opportunities for egotistical self-expression. This, together with the purgative language of Lydon and Cabaret Voltaire, might in turn suggest that, far from being enemies of the blues, postpunk artists could see themselves as true believers who wished to cleanse the music of narcissistic indulgence and restore it to its original epistemological imperatives. Loyalties, at the very least, seem divided here, and considerably more complicated than a reading of *Rip It Up and Start Again* would suggest. This becomes evident in the course of an interview that Reynolds elsewhere conducts with the Gang of Four guitarist Andy Gill.

> *But if you think of . . . rock in the mid-seventies, people would write about love and sexuality still in this blues-derived, funky, rock 'n' roll way. And [Gang of Four's] approach was much more dispassionate and diagrammatic, observing these couples struggling . . . with a cold, dry, distanced eye. In rock music, this was a shockingly new way of looking at stuff. . . .*
>
> Take the band Free, for example. I loved them in the early seventies—it was very rhythmic and stripped down. I loved the minimalism. But [Free vocalist] Paul Rodgers would be singing about his car and his woman. That's part of the package, you go along with it. You loved Free and yet were completely aware of the utter idiocy of the lyrics. So there was an element of suspended disbelief. . . .
> *Your guitar style is pretty unprecedented. Didn't you have certain standard guitar things that you adamantly refused to do, like solos?*
> We called them anti-solos. When you stopped playing, you just left a hole.
> *Did you avoid other things, like certain bluesy chord progressions? . . .*
> Certainly, to begin with. . . . . The drums and bass and guitar all kind of coexisted. We *built* something out of the interaction of

those things. It wasn't about layers. The instruments are on the same level. . . .
I read somewhere you talking about having a thought-out approach even before you picked up the instruments to write a song. . . . So would it be fair to say that Gang of Four approached songwriting in this structuralist way, as opposed to tunes emerging out of jamming?
Definitely. Jamming was the J-word. . . .
So on some level you were resisting the mystique of the artist's intuition and creativity pouring forth from deep within . . . and proposing a different model where songs are art objects that are constructed.

The idea of sitting around and "Let's just see what happens"— it seemed to relate to some older ethos that was basically alien to us. Having said all that, there are practical reasons for just messing about with instruments: you do that and you quickly just come up with other ideas. I'm not knocking improvisation; that's a whole other thing. I like a lot of jazz. But rock bands who sit about and jam, usually it goes hand in hand with bluesy noodling about.[27]

Emerging here is a more complicated picture than either interviewer or interviewee will allow. On first impression Gill's comments indicate that alternative musicians like him felt a straightforward aversion toward the blues. Read more closely, however, his distaste in fact centers more particularly on the way in which certain U.S. and British rock musicians of the previous generation seemed to see the blues as granting them permission, first, to indulge in ludicrous cock rock posturing and, second, to understand improvisation or jamming not as a collaborative act but a chance for some individual genius to step forward and strut his stuff. Interestingly, however, Gill, having shifted the focus away from the blues per se, then proves unable to completely dismiss the excesses of 1960s and early 1970s rock. That derision instead sits alongside a fascination with British rock's exaggerated version of the southern blues. Even as he shudders at their indulgent solos and other clichés, Gill evidently remains a great admirer of Free in particular, and of their ability to reproduce the integral blues rhythm he calls "minimalist." In the central importance such rhythm assumes here—in Gill's inclination to install rhythm as the measure by which to judge 1960s bands—we begin to hear another response, one that bypasses British punk and postpunk's anti-American stance to salute the blues' ability to equate dance with an oppositional humanity.

For Reynolds, Wire, even more than Gang of Four, epitomizes the post-punk movement. *Rip It Up and Start Again* sets great store in the fact that, instead of Liverpool or some other vibrant port, Wire came from suburban Watford, a provincial town famed for its motorway connections and multistory car parks. These unglamorous credentials are, for Reynolds, reinforced by the fact that the band met at art college, that they know their Theodor Adorno and situationist theory, and that they were likelier to write songs about map references or the shipping forecast than about women, trains, flight, or sex. For Reynolds, tracks like "Heartbeat"—from Wire's second LP, *Chairs Missing* (1978)—move rock music beyond *Never Mind the Bollocks*, beyond bluesy chord progressions and sexual preoccupations, and into a brave new world of automatic rhythms, dub echoes, and more egalitarian collaboration.

I feel icy
I feel cold
I feel old
Is there something behind me?
I'm sublime

I feel empty
I feel dark
I remark
I am mesmerised
By my own beat
Like a heartbeat
In its own beat.

There are some grounds for Reynolds' reading of "Heartbeat." The nihilism from which "Heartbeat" just about manages to pull back differs markedly from the unhappiness to be found in many blues lyrics. Misery in the blues often requires and receives explanation, but Wire here shuns any such storytelling impulse, plunging the singing "I" into an empty universe, and allowing no explanation to interfere with the absolute fact of despair. Against a model of blues rhythm that might resist this invading misery, Wire envisions a coldness building from within. Two of Reynolds' favorite adjectives consequently seem apt. Misery here seems properly Beckettian and properly Ballardian, and to evoke something akin to what

William S. Burroughs called J. G. Ballard's vision of a "whole random universe . . . breaking down into cryptic fragments."[28]

Reynolds' approach works best, however, if you conceive of the blues in the generic terms mentioned at the start of this essay. If we think of the blues only as a set of repeatable lyrical and musical structures that remain static across time, it becomes apparent that Wire has here managed to avoid chord E, stripping "Heartbeat" of all blues echoes. Once we recollect the pronounced definitional impulse of blues lyrics, however, and remember that they themselves regularly refer to a mood or perspective that they also call the blues, the situation grows less settled. If we recognize that the blues is composed not just of dyadic apostrophes and twelve-bar structures—if we accept that it also refers to a full-blown structure of feeling that is grounded in a notion of redemptive oppositionality sourced but reworked from the black southern experience—then "Heartbeat" starts to seem quite different. It starts to seem, indeed, like a return of the repressed: the moment where all those alluring blues echoes that Wire elsewhere avoided return to the surface, joining together to seize control of the song.

A tendency to elevate the status of the heart above that of other internal organs is strikingly universal across diverse human cultures. Biblical psalms, *Paradise Lost,* Native American political rhetoric and Buddhist scripture all endow the heart with the kind of special status on which Marx drew in his famous definition of religion under modern capitalism: "Religion is the sigh of the oppressed creature, the feeling of a heartless world, and the soul of soulless circumstances. It is the opium of the people."[29] But this common sentimentalizing of the heart ultimately requires us to confront again its physiological functions, for, as Fay Bound Alberti suggests, we know that "we cannot understand the heart's emotional status" by removing it and "holding it up to scrutiny"; "it needs to be understood *in situ.*"[30] Compared to the mysteries of the liver or the kidney, this organ actually performs quite a straightforward function: it pumps blood. Persistent across different cultures, then, is an attempt to harness the simple function of the heart to an array of abstract notions of emotion, passion, and love, thereby entangling the obviously physiological and the profoundly philosophical in a way that would seem essential to our sense of human identity. The heart, perhaps the simplest of internal organs, becomes the profoundest as a result of its persistent cultural transformations. Something that we share with other animals here becomes the site of those emotions that, we imagine, set us apart from them.

The long cultural war that African Americans were forced to fight against white supremacist culture surely found no fiercer battleground than over the meaning of the African heart. The epigraph to this essay suggests that Frederick Douglass always understood this. By necessity, he saw, slavery involved a cultural campaign that sought to deny Africans access to the rich and dualistic understanding of the heart that would appear a cultural universal and a fundamental human right. But this epigraph also brings us to the limits, indeed the ultimate failure, of that racist campaign. Recollecting how the "wood" would reverberate with the "wild songs" of his fellow slaves, Douglass is brought to full human consciousness: it is to "those songs I trace my first glimmering conception of the dehumanizing character of slavery." The remarkably modern language testifies to a remarkable observation. For Douglass here is grasping that slavery does not recognize the humanity of his "heart" and its "sorrows," and would describe that heart as little more than a pump or a machine. But he is also showing us that the songs he has heard opposed this reduction. Rhythm, reverberating in the very landscape, restores a dualistic capacity to slaves' hearts, in itself resisting the process of racial dehumanization.

The remarkable effect of "Heartbeat" is to distill this epistemological process of crisis and human recovery into the form of a short pop song. Here, in the world of the lyric, Wire proceeds from a situation of obliterating and annihilating pain. The "I" of the lyric blames himself for his own deterioration, his own shortcomings, as a human. This sense of deficiency propels him toward the brink, forcing him to consider suicide and thus to follow in the footsteps of countless personas of countless blues lyrics. Then the rhythm of his own heartbeat, converted and drummed back to him, offers, as he nears this precipice, sudden and unexpected respite. For to hear the beat, to hear it strengthen, is what makes recovery begin to seem possible to him. Rhythm, yoked to a heartbeat, begins to conquer the threatened obliteration of identity, allowing the singer to assert his own "mesmerizing" individuality. As he does so, his heart too, thanks to this redemptive and oppositional aesthetic, regains its dual structure, becoming once more both a simple physiological machine and the seat of emotion. A kind of recovery of hope, of affect, occurs. The lyric, if beginning in a Ballardian realm of agony, soon begins to enact a recovery of human identity, a recuperation of affect that is wholly and obviously absent from Ballard's classics *The Atrocity Exhibition* (1970) and *Crash* (1973). Existential hopelessness withdraws from the scene. The lyric exhibits not just "the agony of life" but also "the possibility of conquering it through sheer toughness of spirit," and in doing so it, like Wright's *Black Boy*, comes to appear another text that, if devoid of obvious blues echoes, continues to meet the terms of Ellison's classic blues definition.

The ongoing debate about the uses and abuses of Black Atlantic music can still seem somewhat polarized. Paul Gilroy might be right to deride those who mistake "culture as a form of property," but many of us might feel less surefooted about resisting the countervailing position that Public Enemy voiced on "Who Stole the Soul?"[31] To the extent that this essay has tried to crystallize the blues as a form that recovers an articulate human voice amid obliterating pain, these ethical uncertainties have, perhaps, begun to crystallize too. For even British rock artists not often associated with the blues have harnessed a blues epistemology in their approach to songwriting; by doing so, they have drawn a line of identification between the circumstances of Jim Crow and their own experiences of social alienation. The moral status of that connection remains questionable. The engulfing "pain" at the beginning of "Heartbeat," we might feel, is not straightforwardly comparable to what Ellison called the "agony of life." Whatever its ethical status, however, such identification occurs at a deep and epistemological level in much British rock music. Even when it is trying *not* to sound like the blues, that music takes shape from a blues epistemology it associates with a mythologized Jim Crow South.

Notes

1. I would like to thank the participants of the "Creating and Consuming the U.S. South" conference at the University of Copenhagen, August 2010, and particularly its organizers Martyn Bone and Brian Ward, for their close and constructive criticisms of the paper on which this chapter is based.
2. See Warnes, "Black, White and Blue," and "Tricky's *Maxinquaye*."
3. See Kent, "Dreamer in the Real World."
4. Smith, "Chicago Bound Blues"; Johnson, "Preaching Blues (Up Jumped the Devil)."
5. Hughes, "Weary Blues," 1294.
6. Ellison, "Richard Wright's Blues," 1539.
7. Rampersad, *Ralph Ellison*, 28.
8. Ellison, "Richard Wright's Blues," 1548.
9. Hurston, "Characteristics of Negro Expression," 1049.

10. Wald, *Escaping the Delta*, 7.
11. Abel, *Signs of the Times*, 19.
12. Gussow, *Seems Like Murder Here*, 57.
13. Ibid., 23.
14. Litwack, *Trouble in Mind*, 411.
15. Mintz and Price, *Birth of African-American Culture*, 38–39.
16. See Douglass, *Narrative of the Life of Frederick Douglass*, 8–9; Du Bois, *Souls of Black Folk*, 250; *Slave Songs of the United States*, 7.
17. Mintz and Price, *Birth of African-American Culture*, 67
18. Washington, "Booker Washington Promotes Accommodationism," 160.
19. Daniel, *Lost Revolutions*, 125.
20. Gussow, *Seems Like Murder Here*, 181.
21. Lomax quoted in *American Roots Music*.
22. Reynolds, *Rip It Up*, xix.
23. Ibid., xvi.
24. Viv Albertine quoted in Savage, *England's Dreaming*, 248.
25. Wald, *Escaping the Delta*, 247–78.
26. Benadon and Gioia, "How Hooker Found His Groove," 20.
27. Reynolds, *Totally Wired*, 109–12.
28. Burroughs, "Preface," vii.
29. Marx, "Towards a Critique on Hegel's Philosophy of Right," 72.
30. Alberti, *Matters of the Heart*, 161.
31. Gilroy, *Between Camps*, 24.

Works Cited

Abel, Elizabeth. *Signs of the Times: The Visual Politics of Jim Crow*. Berkeley: University of California Press, 2010.

Alberti, Fay Bound. *Matters of the Heart: History, Medicine, Emotion*. Oxford: Oxford University Press, 2010.

American Roots Music. Directed by Jim Brown. PBS, 2001.

Benadon, Fernando, and Ted Gioia. "How Hooker Found His Boogie: A Rhythmic Analysis of a Classic Groove." *Popular Music* 28, no. 1 (2009): 19–32.

Blues Britannia: Can Blue Men Sing the Whites? Directed by Chris Rodley. BBC, 2010.

Burroughs, William S. "Preface." In *The Atrocity Exhibition* by J. G. Ballard. London: Flamingo, 1993.

The Clash. "I'm So Bored with the USA." *The Clash*. CBS, 1977.

Daniel, Pete. *Lost Revolutions: The South in the 1950s*. Chapel Hill: University of North Carolina Press, 2000.

Douglass, Frederick. *Narrative of the Life of Frederick Douglass*. New York: Dover, 1995.

Ellison, Ralph. "Richard Wright's Blues." In *Norton Anthology of African American Literature*, edited by Henry Louis Gates and Nellie Y. McKay, 1538–48. New York: Norton, 2004.

Gilroy, Paul. *Between Camps: Nations, Cultures and the Allure of Race.* London: Penguin, 2001.
Gussow, Adam. *Seems Like Murder Here: Southern Violence and the Blues Tradition.* Chicago: University of Chicago Press, 2002.
Hughes, Langston. "The Weary Blues." In *The Norton Anthology of African American Literature,* edited by Henry Louis Gates and Nellie Y. McKay, 1294. New York: Norton, 2004.
Hurston, Zora Neale. "Characteristics of Negro Expression." In *The Norton Anthology of African American Literature,* edited by Henry Louis Gates and Nellie Y. McKay, 1041–53. New York: Norton, 2004.
Joyner, Charles. *Down by the Riverside: A South Carolina Slave Community.* Urbana: University of Illinois Press, 1985.
Kent, Nick. "Dreamer in the Real World." *The Face,* May 1985. http://www.rocksback pages.com/Library/Article/the-smiths-dreamer-in-the-real-world. Accessed July 29, 2013.
Led Zeppelin. *Led Zeppelin II.* Atlantic, 1969.
Litwack, Leon F. *Trouble in Mind: Black Southerners in the Age of Jim Crow.* London: Vintage, 1999.
Marx, Karl. "Towards a Critique on Hegel's Philosophy of Right." In *Karl Marx: Selected Writings,* edited by David McLellan, 71–82. Oxford and New York: Oxford University Press, 2007.
Mintz, Sidney W., and Richard Price. *The Birth of African-American Culture: An Anthropological Perspective.* Boston: Beacon, 1992.
Oliver, Paul. *The Story of the Blues.* London: Barrie and Jenkins, 1970.
Pollitt, Tessa. Interview. *Punk 77.* http://www.punk77.co.uk/groups/slitstessapolittinter view.htm. Accessed July 26, 2013.
Public Enemy. "Who Stole the Soul?" *Fear of a Black Planet.* Def Jam, 1990.
Rampersad, Arnold. *Ralph Ellison: A Biography.* Alfred A. Knopf: New York, 2007.
Reynolds, Simon. *Rip It Up and Start Again: Post-Punk, 1978–84.* London: Faber and Faber, 2005.
———. *Totally Wired: Post-Punk Interviews and Overviews.* London: Faber and Faber, 2009.
The Rolling Stones. *Let It Bleed.* Decca, 1969.
Savage, Jon. *England's Dreaming: Sex Pistols and Punk Rock.* London: Faber and Faber, 1991.
The Sex Pistols. "Seventeen." *Never Mind the Bollocks.* Virgin, 1977.
Wald, Elijah. *Escaping the Delta: Robert Johnson and the Invention of the Blues.* New York: Amistad, 2004.
Warnes, Andrew. "Black, White and Blue: The Racial Antagonism of The Smiths' Record Sleeves." *Popular Music* 27, no. 1 (2008): 135–49.
———. "Tricky's *Maxinquaye*: Rhythm, Reification and the Resuscitation of the Blues." *Atlantic Studies* 6, no. 2 (2009): 223–37.
Washington, Booker T. "Booker Washington Promotes Accommodationism, 1895." In

Major Problems in African-American History, edited by C. Holt and Elsa Barkley Brown, 159–60. Boston: Houghton Mifflin, 2000.
Wire. "Lowdown." *Pink Flag.* Harvest, 1977.
———. "Heartbeat." *Chairs Missing.* Harvest, 1978.
———. "No Warning Given." *Read & Burn 03.* EP. Pinkflag, 2007.
———. "Used To." *Chairs Missing.* Harvest, 1978.

13

Me and Mrs. Jones

Screening Working-Class Trans-Formations of Southern Family Values

JOHN HOWARD

Filmed in contemporary rural Rankin County, Mississippi—amidst continuing reports of gay bashings, homosexual panic defenses, repressed demagogues, and Lott-legacy politicians filibustering for "Don't Ask, Don't Tell" closets—English director Moby Longinotto's documentary short *The Joneses* (2009) depicts a working-class household of three who are trans-forming southern family values.[1] Acknowledging a cultural context of mutual discretion and quiet accommodation, the film offers partial disclosures as it creates a counterdiscourse to conservative evangelical ethics and circulates on an international avant-garde film-festival circuit of often radical left politics. Premiering in Britain at the Sheffield Doc/Fest, in mainland Europe at Hamburg's International Short Film Festival, and in North America at Toronto's Hot Docs Canadian International Documentary Festival, *The Joneses* is meant to be consumed as much outside as within the U.S. South. In this sense and many others, the Joneses are *screened*—revealed in all their transgressive potential to selected spectators far and wide, and shielded from potentially hostile trailer-park neighbors, area preachers, and employers back home.[2]

The Joneses depicts a sixty-nine-year-old matriarch beloved by her two cohabiting sons. As the elder, forty-year-old, developmentally disabled brother obliquely articulates the advantages of having two mothers—which goes unexplained until near the end of the film—the light-hearted tale becomes a mystery, designed to destabilize the normative nuclear family. As viewers attempt to categorize the feisty heroine (step-mother?

lesbian? transsexual?), the dialogue prompts them to reflect on back stories and speculate about future prospects for all three of the relatives. Outside the tight confines of the manufactured home, a concluding afternoon drive, a simple excursion to the river and back, might be seen to symbolize stasis: this family unit is going nowhere. However, as nondialogic audio-visual elements make clear, the Joneses both know the limits of their time and place and imagine better worlds beyond them.

The Joneses is a work that confounds both hetero- and homo-normative expectations of southern domestic life. This essay utilizes close readings as well as related oral histories; engages *The Joneses*' critical as well as audience reception; and contextualizes the film with reference to the new queer cinema, Hollywood representations, and the Indiana school of rural queer studies. By chronicling conflict and change, estrangement and reconciliation, Longinotto's short film takes the long view, charting an evolution in white working-class values over the lifespan of the protagonist, mother Jones. For at least this one local family, a rural queer cosmopolitanism—as set against the critical mass of an urban gay provincialism—involves regular communication with a wider realm, combined with an overseas travel schedule which, though undertaken infrequently, proves crucially enabling and transformative, a testament to new modes of familial love and Christian redemption.[3]

As scholar Donna Jo Smith has persuasively argued, the mythological/analytical categories of *southern* and *queer* often can conflict as "ideological opposites"—conservative versus radical—to the point of becoming oxymoronic; however, "depending on perspective," they also can conflate as "deviance multiplied." In countless twentieth-century novels and screen adaptations, sectional and sexual deviances intermingle with the macabre and otherworldly to form the genre known as the Southern Gothic, avidly consumed by audiences worldwide. Outside North America, key works in a Southern Gothic tradition have been instrumental in shaping understandings of a backward South filled with back-assward perversions—especially James Dickey's *Deliverance* (1970), available in countless translations and subtitled reels. Even queer writers have crafted exoticizing if not wholly stigmatizing accounts of a queer South, from Carson McCullers' *Reflections in a Golden Eye* (1941) to Truman Capote's *Other Voices, Other Rooms* (1948).[4] Against this context of cultural production, *The Joneses*' southern queer household is portrayed with a matter-of-fact relaxed tone and a true-to-place unhurried pacing, yielding an alternate menu in globalizing formats of consumption and spectatorship. The Joneses' nonconformity is made routine but interesting in its everyday rituals, with external societal prejudices only implied. Produced and consumed mostly outside the U.S. South, *The Joneses* reshapes popular conceptions of the section, representing the *southern* and the *queer* in a state of peaceful coexistence.

Heavenly Father, Earthly Mother

A new day seems to dawn in the opening sequence of *The Joneses*. Before the plain white sans-serif production title is screened on a black ground, we hear and then see a lone dog barking, as if to suggest the first sounds of the morning. A second exterior shot depicts sunlight breaking over leafless trees and mobile homes, with a prominent mailbox both naming this particular household and gesturing to a world beyond it, with which it corresponds. Inside, blinds are curiously closed, curtains drawn. But as the film shifts to an interior shot, we see family members sitting around the table and holding hands while the mother says grace in a distinctly southern accent: "Dear Heavenly Father, We thank you for this day and for this food and for the privilege of sharing all this together: the joy and the sorrow, the good food, the laughter, another day together. And we pray for many more to come. In the name of Jesus, we pray. Amen." This platinum-blonde matriarch's veiny, liver-spotted arms reach out to two younger men, one bearded, the other heavily stubbled, who seem fairly clearly to be her sons. Notably, there is no father in sight, whether heavenly or worldly.

Thus, Longinotto economically establishes at the outset of this fourteen-minute, day-or-two-in-the-life observational documentary the patriarchal Protestant context for a set of seemingly sedentary lives that, we quickly learn, are marked by concerns over mental and physical well-being, even as the kinfolk look expectantly to the future "together." Already here at the start, however, as audience attentiveness is formed and focused, nondialogic aural and visual components complicate the picture, unsettling conventional notions of gender and family, class and consumerism, section and nation. For starters, it transpires that this opening sequence takes place in the early evening, during dinner, not over morning breakfast. Mismatched cups of plastic and faux cut glass demonstrate a decided lack of middle-class pretensions. Music can be heard underneath the prayer, likely from a compact disc player. Hardly the twangy blues guitar of down-and-out southern stereotype, it is an upbeat salsa number from farther south—south of the U.S. border. Bowls are filled not with cereal, we see, but chili. Though wintertime, the three all wear short sleeves: the men in T-shirts, their mother sporting a satiny pink blouse. Her cooking obviously heats up this tight spot. As she concludes the prayer, she leans down to the family dog as he insinuates himself into the lower-left corner of the frame. In a comic element, matriarch and dog kiss. It is the only kiss in the film.[5]

Exhibiting an "ordinary" southern family's strong spiritual values, the eponymous Joneses also have one of the most common surnames in the United States. The name and the film's title imply an ironic all-American authenticity and normalcy, a suggestion accentuated throughout the film by shots of American flags. Indeed, *The Joneses* is the title of another film from 2009, but that full-length Hollywood feature starring Demi Moore and David Duchovny centers on a fully fabricated, upper-middle-class nuclear family of four, who secretly market high-end products to unsuspecting suburbanites. In rural Mississippi, the real-life Joneses upset dominant notions not only of gendered comportment and domestic organization, but also of envy-induced acquisitiveness and conspicuous consumption. Indeed, the aforementioned meal is the only object of consumption in the film. Laden as it is with ready-made, store-bought fat and preservatives, the meal becomes associated with the younger brother's depressive flabbiness, as well as the older brother's life-threatening obesity. Obesity killed his grandmother, the older brother tells us, along with his mother, who now "looks down on" him from heaven. He adds, "I may have grew up without a father, but I've always had two loving mothers." Who, then, the viewer wonders, is this mother we see onscreen? Might she have been the biological father? Is the director making a deliberate choice to withhold this information?[6]

Anticipating and interrupting a key Marxist-feminist critique of many documentary projects—that they obscure the labor that makes lives possible[7]—the film dwells upon the mother's varied employment history, as she dresses for work and describes her colorful past: "Oh, did I tell you, I used to be a hairdresser, cosmetologist? For about six years, oh yes. School teacher, nine years. An accountant. I've done everything but be a stripper. I haven't tried that yet. I'm not real good about swinging around poles." As mother Jones's joke implies, even at age sixty-nine, employment options continue to be weighed: she might "yet" try most anything. She also subtly alludes to a past marked by job discrimination and reskilling, regularly depleting her savings, and requiring her to start over. Retirement, we intuit, is not an option. She "can't be with [her disabled elder son] twenty-four hours a day to watch what he eats," to monitor his consumption of the fruits of her labor, because, "you know, I have to work." Thus, whereas the family may offer thanks to a heavenly father, the three members know full well that it is this earthly mother's hard work that primarily sustains them. And yet no mention is made of her *current* employer. The film does not enter that workplace.

At this juncture I should acknowledge my own subject position vis-à-vis the film's protagonist, which encompasses some three decades of personal history and which means that, rather than being merely an academic critic of *The Joneses*, I played an integral role in the film's production. For as it happens, I first met J. Jones, as I will refer to her, in 1979, in Jackson, Mississippi, at yet another place of work: the bus station owned and operated by my uncle. What for me was a Christmas and summer job between semesters at high school and university was for J. the principal means of survival, after moving up from her parents' chicken farm in Smith County. In class-stratified Mississippi during the stagflationary recession of the late 1970s, J. Jones augmented her income with night-time earnings performing at Mae's Cabaret, also in Jackson, capping a day-and-night double shift much more onerous than my own full-time work/study arrangement.

As one of many people or social forces who now mediate her narratives, and in an effort to extend interpretation, I would like to offer additional—but never definitive—explanations of extraordinary moments and opportunities in twentieth- and twenty-first-century southern lived experience, to supplement the medical-surgical and filmic-ethnographic interventions in J.'s life with my own personal-historical accounts. As a longtime friend of the protagonist; a cocreator of several of her oral histories; a displaced southerner attuned to that setting; and a documentarian committed to articulating my own (necessarily partial) truths, I can assert that—just as that opening sunrise in *The Joneses* is in fact a sunset, the breakfast instead a dinner—the constructed nature of our narratives (beginning-middle-end) can and should be exposed, our attempts at coherence and closure thereby acknowledged as inevitably incomplete. For through their continual re-articulations, queer transnational lives and relationships—exemplified by the case of me and Mrs. Jones—may be uniquely instructive in their testing of social conventions.[8]

Smalltown Boys, Country Girls

Though they only once have been screened together—at the New York LGBT Community Center in February 2012—Longinotto's *The Joneses* makes a logical companion piece for his previous short *Smalltown Boy* (2007), in which a fifteen-year-old English boy in foster care cross-dresses as a Somerset village carnival queen. The two films also fit comfortably with the longer trajectory of Longinotto's oeuvre of quarter-hour, half-hour, and hour-long documentaries, the very titles of which indicate consistent thematic interest in issues of identity, gender, and family. These films include, in the last decade alone, *Make Me Proud* (2001), *Waiting for Khyron* (2002), *Bad Boy* (2003), *A Big Deal for the Charles Family* (2004), and *No Time for Tea at Raj TV* (2005). Indeed, these shorts and longer works all contribute to a family tradition of cinema verité, as Moby's mother Kim Longinotto, perhaps Britain's most celebrated feminist filmmaker, has addressed similar issues in the Tours-award-winning *Pride of Place* (1976), about abuses at the Buckinghamshire boarding school she attended (and which was subsequently shut down); the Houston-award-winning *Shinjuku Boys* (1995), about three trans males working in a Tokyo host bar; the BAFTA-award-winning *Divorce Iranian Style* (1998), about wives personally pleading their cases in Tehran; the Cannes-award-winning *Sisters in Law* (2005), about female court justices pursuing indictments for rape and spousal abuse in Kumba, Cameroon; and the Sundance-award-winning *Rough Aunties* (2008), about child welfare advocates in Durban, South Africa.[9]

However, it was *Smalltown Boy*, in particular, that led playwright/producer Ash Kotak and me to select Moby to direct *The Joneses*, rather than an Oscar-nominated documentary director we had previously interviewed. Otherwise, my involvement in the film was limited to pre-production, such as shooting location stills and brainstorming with Kotak about thematic concerns. Because I had written about J. Jones in my monograph *Men Like That: A Southern Queer History* (1999), and because my friend Ash was interested in seeing J.'s story depicted onscreen, we approached Faction Films in London to produce what was then only a cluster of ideas. Neither of us was involved in filming, editing, post-production, marketing, or distribution. We did not even have input into the choice of title (which, in fact, may have breached confidentiality assurances made to the family). Thus I feel well situated—indeed, privileged and obligated—to undertake close readings of the finished product as a film studies scholar might, but armed with an advantage that we writers and readers of film criticism rarely have: in-depth knowledge of what lies beyond the text, the extradiegetic material that makes authorial/directorial choices all the more significant.[10]

Smalltown Boy and *The Joneses* share a number of traits—as quarter-hour films addressed to gender nonconformists living in non-normative familial arrangements in rural settings and as documentaries that perhaps could be made only in the twenty-first century. They also share problematic elements. For example, just as the long, solitary, smalltown walks of David could be seen to exaggerate his loneliness and despair by giving little sense of the friends and queer community that support him, so too the Joneses' afternoon drive to the Mississippi river and back, with which Longinotto concludes the later short, might suggest that, in truth, J. and her sons have nowhere to go. Yet just as David's very participation in the village carnival—and the permission he grants to Longinotto to film it—demonstrate that he aims to reach larger audiences, both local and international, so too does J.'s very participation in the film project show that she has broader commitments, obligations, and ties, extending well beyond her current circumstances. As we see, though often couched in a language of indirection and dissemblance, J. Jones feels compelled—in a variation of the Faulknerian phrase explored by Fred Hobson—to tell about the (queer) South.[11]

On the banks of the Mississippi, referencing one of the South's mythic white travelers while overlooking his black travel companion, Jim, J. Jones asks her sons, "Wouldn't you like to be like Huckleberry Finn?" Pointing south, she adds, "And that will take you all the way to New Orleans, down that way." Following an ordinary family dispute about a missed exit and calling to mind the most notorious queer port destination in the south, this scene stages, quite self-consciously, a moment of reaffirmed solidarity and love between the family members, who then head back home together. For a variety of reasons, all three can understand the allure of cosmopolitan New Orleans. "Oh, yeah," the elder brother affirms. Still, none has chosen to move away to the big city. Though marked by economic, familial, and sexual ambivalences—all interrogated in the next two sections of this essay—the Joneses have chosen to stay together and to forgo the illusory promises of country-to-city migration.

Twelve minutes into the fourteen-minute film, and just before she gets behind the wheel and drives west toward Vicksburg into an actual sunset, J. Jones, reclining on her bed, speaks directly to camera, finally identifying herself, it would seem, as a former gay man and now a male-to-female transsexual: "We make a big issue about gay people. Or transgender. Whatever. But I'm at peace now. I'm at peace with this conflict. I was estranged from my children for awhile. But now we've been reconciled. And we're together. And we have a close family unit. So life is not too bad." Just before he gets into the backseat for the drive to the river, her younger son speaks directly to camera and seems to intimate that this mother was, in fact, his biological father: "I think J.'s a terrific mother. I really do. I feel very blessed to have, uh, her as my parent." Despite this pronoun equivocation around a non-gender-specific "parent," it is the explicit claiming of J. now as his mother—moreover, his assessment of her as "a terrific mother," with no further reference to the obese, deceased, and apparently biological mother—that constitutes the most important moral, ideological, and political work of the film. Combined with the older brother's earlier testimony of feeling, likewise, "very blessed" to have had "two loving mothers," it asserts a tight-knit, mutually dependent, working-class, and divinely ordained familial love as the best means of overcoming a regionally specific, systemic, institutionalized environment of bigotry and discrimination.[12]

Sounds Queer

With economical utility, the soundtracks for *Smalltown Boy* and *The Joneses* serve to evoke a wider world, with hints of disco, pop, opera, and so-called world music. They gesture toward queer communities scattered across countless urban and nonmetropolitan sites, crucially connected by successive technologies such as radio, television, music video, and the Internet. They demonstrate that these two protagonists, David and J., are neither isolated nor alone, but rather are bound up in networks of transportation and communication, "virtual" and "real," that obliterate boundaries to form (and sometimes delimit) transgender worlds of possibility.[13]

Smalltown Boy features original music composed by Chris White. A solemn minimalist score accompanies David's reminiscences about school bullying and foster family difficulties, as well as the film's present-day observations of homophobia on the village streets. As intertitles count down the number of days until the carnival, tension mounts, violence is anticipated, and viewers wonder if David might withdraw from the festivities, even as he comically primps and preens in preparation. In the end, David appears, true to his word, in purple gown and tiara, as the "alternative" carnival queen, and the music swells to a lively affirming disco beat, as he waves and interacts with the crowd from the back of an open-top convertible.

The title of the film comes from the 1984 synthpop/disco anthem by Britain's Bronski Beat, the video for which is a classic rural-to-urban gay migration narrative. Falsetto lead singer Jimmy Somerville plays the proverbial smalltown boy, who, acknowledging his crush on a school swim team member, is subsequently cornered by teammates in an alley and apparently assaulted. "Mother will never understand why you had to leave," the gay Scot sings, on a train bound for London, "but the answers you seek will never be found at home, the love you need will never be found at home." With this second-person pronoun construction, the video becomes not just an individual autobiographical account, but a larger cultural imperative. What "you" must do—what rural gay youth are advised—is "run away, turn away, run away, turn away, run away." As if following the commandment, the orphaned David, meeting with adult hostility in the opening sequences of *Smalltown Boy*, declares that he does not "belong in the countryside." "It's the wrong place for me."[14]

By contrast, *The Joneses* generationally reverses the scenario, with children made to comprehend their mother's gender "conflict" and sexual predilections on their own home turf. The film makes clear that J. Jones is unlikely to ever leave the trailer park—permanently leave, that is. What cannot be explained in a mere quarter of an hour—what instead are implied by music and funny yarns—are her connections to multiple communities and multiple places. Preparing the Mexican dinner, imagining herself as a seductive "chiquita," mother Jones twists and twirls to the salsa beat and declares, "I don't have a partner, but I can dance," never letting on that (as she has told me) she and the family take affordable vacations in the Yucatán, where she likely procured the CD. Detailing an actual seduction in Mississippi, from days gone by, she describes how she once met an attractive "John Wayne" type "so masculine and so fine" and "somehow . . . ended up at his motel room." Revealing her investment in the standard gender binary and the limits of her sexual practice, J.'s anecdote reaches its comic conclusion with an almost transphobic disruption. Lo and behold, the man "was wearing ladies' undergarments and . . . throwing himself on the bed and hollering, 'Spank me! Oh!' . . . He was into some kind of weird scene. So I got out of there real quick and went home."

Though an important feature of the new queer cinema of the 1990s, erotic spanking gets no further mention in *The Joneses*. Thus, the potential affinity, even homoerotic activity, between two male-born, possibly trans-identified individuals is worrisomely foreshortened. (As of this moment in the 1970s or 1980s, J. Jones had not fully transitioned to female.) Also charting the limits of her cosmopolitanism, the director admirably leaves in, and forces spectators to ruminate upon, mother Jones's complicated, borderline racist-sexist parody of Mexican femininity, as she mock-seduces her younger son and threatens to "kill" the "Yankee pig" if he doesn't return her affections. Associating Mexicans with violence, and Mexican women specifically with murderous jealousy, this yarn demonstrates how mere exposure to cultures of the global South ensures neither sympathy nor understanding of related discourses of degradation around sex, class, race, and gender.[15]

Where did J. Jones and her would-be John Wayne meet? "At the disco"—surely the white, gay-owned disco in Jackson, a short drive away. The disco era is further evoked through J.'s exercise routine, again in her narrow kitchen. Though she has dressed for work to the strains of opera on Mississippi public radio, she later does her aerobics—in black tights, pink shorts and top, and green cosmetic mask—to another recognizable disco anthem, a recent techno remix of the 1974 Hues Corporation track "Rock the Boat," thus recalling the time when J. first would have danced to it. Whereas writer Wayne Koestenbaum has outlined the contours of gay male cultures of opera-going and fandom, scholar Richard Dyer has perceptively noted how, from its earliest days, disco was freighted with troublesome transgressive implications; as such, the "Disco Sucks" backlash harbored racist, antifeminist, antiqueer elements in reaction to the music's appeal among nonwhite, female, and queer dancers, and given the successes of these marginalized groups as performers (the Village People, Sylvester, and so on).[16]

Disco's driving beat is heard in *The Joneses* only from J.'s boom box, during her aerobic workout, not on the soundtrack itself. It is, at that moment, *her* choice of music. By contrast, *Smalltown Boy* briefly overlays a disco track onto the footage of David in the carnival parade, whereas the actual parade music is little more than a rote drumbeat and xylophone. As the Chris White disco instrumental reaches its crescendo, with David smiling and waving to bystanders, a filmic climax is constructed—and constructed as gay (not trans). "The good" of the day, David recounts, "overrode the bad." The film thus has its happy ending, courtesy of disco, even as David disavows transgenderism. Not unlike J.'s snub of her cross-dressing John Wayne from the disco, David concludes, "I just don't want people to think I'm a woman now."

Because *The Joneses* relies on ambient music, with no original score, the audience is spared the clichés of regionally "authentic" country-and-western and rhythm-and-blues or hackneyed approximations thereof. More importantly, by tuning her radio to, and loading her CD player with, classical, dance, and world music, J. Jones—like so many other people in the postmodern age—demonstrates her affinity with and her relationships to a variety of groups and sites at home and abroad. At the film's end, driving home from the Mississippi river, she speaks directly to the camera and implores the audience to think back, to engage with musical history—including her own history as a drag performer, only implied—as she skillfully sings the 1931 tune made famous by Pat Boone in 1957, "Love Letters in the Sand." "You remember that one," she insists. Of course, many younger viewers will not. As they search the Internet for the song, for originals and covers of disco classics, and for these very Longinotto films and more, the comments they leave may sometimes reflect a "global village" in purported harmony. However, queer-identifying young people will have to proceed with caution, given a proliferation of hate speech online that is well in excess of "disco sucks"—not least in the comments section on Journeyman Pictures' official YouTube pages for *Smalltown Boy* and *The Joneses*. Utilizing this latest communication medium, as they did prior ones, to expand both local and extralocal networks, queers young and old will have to test the efficacy of a careful cosmopolitanism that finds allies where it can, by whatever technological means available. They will chart the lengths and distances to which some must go, as J. Jones has gone over time, to find solidarity, community, and family.[17]

Invisible, You Treat Me Like I'm Invisible

In the Joneses' mobile home, photo albums are on the bookshelves, while the walls, tabletops, and chests of drawers are covered with framed photographic portraiture. That some of the pictures are group shots, while most are individual portraits, reflects a tension between family cohesion and personal autonomy in the film. In the bedrooms of J. Jones and her thirty-two-year-old son, the film lingers on three solo portraits, two of the former, one of the latter, insinuating that this quarter-hour film, at its best, will provide suggestive character sketches. Indeed, these one- or two-second close-ups, carefully edited, gesture toward complex back stories and deep psychological states. With prominent palm fronds, the roughly sixteen-by-twenty-inch studio portrait of the son, for example, is spliced into a monologue in which he expresses his sense of constraint and underachievement, his occasionally "feel[ing] worthless" and "inferior," perhaps as compared to his energetic, sometimes overbearing mother. An exterior shot of him at the backdoor, a well-constructed birdhouse framed in, exaggerates this point, as it cuts to a shot of a large treetop with birds taking flight. Later the son confesses, "I hope to get married. And I hope to find that special person. And I hope to have kids. And I hope to have a family"—as if he does not have a family already. He adds, "I haven't found that [interestingly, non-gender-specific] person yet. But like I said, I hope to."

As the film (like the son) cedes the spotlight to J., it perhaps overstates her bossiness during her preparation of the Mexican dinner. The older brother has misplaced her chili seasonings, and the younger is sent to the supermarket for more. "And hurry up," the mother commands, "because I don't intend to be up all night with this now. And don't be gone long. You know how you are. You'll go and stay an hour or two. . . . I mean go and come back in a hurry!" Spoken to a thirty-two-year-old adult, this seems excessive. But there is much that the film cannot reveal, as it rightly refuses to take its attention-generating camera to the mother's and son's workplaces, for fear of transphobic reprisals: the commonplace employment discrimination mentioned earlier. The son (I know, as a family friend) is employed in the self-same supermarket. If he strikes up a leisurely conversation with a coworker or regular customer, the dinner, already on the stovetop, may never be finished. Near the film's end, the camera ameliorates this ostensibly testy mother–son relationship, as it captures his wall plaque addressed to her: "MOM, You have always been more than a mother to me. You have also been my best friend." J. Jones echoes these sentiments as she reflects on these routine squabbles: "We bicker and we fuss and we argue. But we love each other. We're very supportive.... We always come through for each other."[18]

Though *The Joneses* provides tangible evidence of the older son's workday—washing the dishes, walking the dog—it does not linger in his bedroom or speculate about his erotic life, a common problem in many representations of the developmentally disabled. However, with its unwavering emphasis on this particular home and everyday home-life therein, the film resists a steep dramatic arc: there is no recourse to a weighty present-day dilemma that motivates action, or a "journey of discovery" that ends with redemption. The film offers no pat resolution, providing instead a respectful rendering of the household's distinctiveness—"charming," according to London-based daily national newspaper the *Independent,* a summation repeated by many festival-goers.[19] As Robert McRuer asserts in his incisive conjoining of queer theory and disability studies in *Crip Theory* (2006), if a national lesbian and gay political agenda unduly stresses an assimilationist politics of same-sex marriage, it does so to the detriment of the unique domestic configurations suggested by the Joneses. It "obscures the fact that we have already proliferated multiple queer alternatives to straight ways of relating." In this short film, that fact is depicted and richly elaborated.[20]

Why has *The Joneses* yet to be screened at film festivals in the United States? Why have I refused to name the family members depicted onscreen? Because over the duration of this three-year project, J. Jones and her younger son have expressed contradictory impulses of revelation and reserve, disclosure and discretion. They have been concerned foremost about the possibility that neighbors and employers might see the film and seek to harm them as a result. Potential antiqueer violence and discrimination, we see, are constantly negotiated, here in Mississippi as elsewhere. Mary L. Gray, part of a collective of rural queer studies scholars based at Indiana University, brilliantly assesses the fundamental tensions between the "politics of visibility" prized by urban lesbian and gay rights advocates, and the bonds of family and familiarity crucial to rural and small-town diplomacy. Lacking the critical mass and financial wherewithal of big-city campaigning, working-class queers in the countryside must constantly "manage the delicate calculus of . . . visibility's benefits and risks." Indeed, in all settings, it seems all queer citizens must perpetually practice a "selective visibility," carefully modulating outward signs of transgression, weighing personal integrity against bodily safety, as well as economic practicalities. But there seems an even greater investment in ensuring genial relations in sparsely populated areas with meager resources and few neighbors.[21]

Without state employment protections in the South, without gender-identity provisions in the proposed federal lesbian and gay Employment Non-Discrimination Act, many working-class trans Americans such as J. Jones, after transitioning, must build new employment histories in organizations that may react adversely to knowledge of former identities. Therefore, to call J. Jones a "stealth" trans woman—with its connotations of surreptitious furtiveness—would be to diminish these very real, very serious considerations; put simply, it would be to demean her integrity and sincerity. Under such conditions, as large-scale political battles are fought in the media and in metropolitan centers, rural queers and their families carry out the mundane business of getting by and making do, day in and day out. The changes they witness—and help forge—attest to the power of their beliefs and principles, as transformed through what Michel Foucault termed "the little tactics of the habitat."[22]

Conclusion: Long Distance

Mixing humor, pathos, and ambiguity, Moby Longinotto's *The Joneses* imagines familial and regional spaces radically transformed over the course of its sixty-nine-year-old heroine's lifetime. It hints at larger transnational contexts and global cultural networks, as dialectically shaped and reflected by immediate everyday practices. Even though we see only three individuals onscreen and little beyond their trailer park, this pathbreaking trans woman's extensive connections and vast associations—and through her, her family's rural queer cosmopolitanism—are readily inferred. To all appearances rooted, if not stuck, in place, the Joneses in fact have ranged widely, and their stories now circulate broadly. Even though we catch only glimpses of her computer, not in use, Internet access for J. Jones has proven important in crafting her ever-expanding circle of acquaintances and advisors. Certainly, this film's production would have been difficult without it. Moreover, J. Jones's most significant bodily transformation—what she has called "freedom day"—was crucially facilitated by it. However, that day was a quarter-century in the making.[23]

In 1976, J. Jones journeyed outside the region for the first time in her life to consult with doctors at Johns Hopkins University Hospital in Baltimore about hormone therapy. At the dawn of the new millennium, at the age of sixty, J. Jones journeyed to Europe for the first time to finally undergo sex reassignment surgery, or SRS. Given the sad state of U.S. health care and insurance coverage, it was cheaper to seek SRS in Belgium, she discovered online, than in the United States, even calculating the airfare and the recovery period in a hotel. From my home in England, I traveled over to Brussels to be with her, the only friend or family member who could afford to do so.

Right after the procedure, as J. had requested, I rang her eighty-six-year-old mother back in Smith County, Mississippi. Reverting to my old southern accent, the old ways of speaking, I said, "Miz Jones? This is John Howard. I'm calling long-distance from Brussels, Belgium. I just wanted to let you know that the surgery was a success. J.'s still unconscious, but doing fine."

"He is?" she asked.

"Yes, ma'am," I said, "*she*'s doing all right."

"Well," she hesitated, "that's good. Please tell her I love her."

The political efficacy of coming out has long been established for lesbians, gays, bisexuals, and transgender persons, as has the personal significance of medical procedures for *some* trans Americans, with many intersexuals and gender-queer activists calling instead for a dissolution of the gender binary. Mainstream film depictions of trans lives can appear fixated on SRS, especially for the young. As decades pass, however, pressing concerns about queer aging are mounting, and the enduring problems of economic inequality—vast income disparities that are only exacerbated in the Deep South—are shown here to impact in thorny ways upon rural trans and disabled households. These systemic inequities require structural solutions, rather than relying on the individualized make-over suggested by so many representations of the before-and-after "miracle" of SRS as a postmodern gender conversion narrative. Indeed, such SRS procedures, in fact, can happen only within broad contexts of collective struggle. Queer communities small and large, local and global, continue to act as the crucial agents of change, renegotiating and trans-forming intergenerational bonds in ways that dovetail with J. Jones's new reckonings and reconciliations: "her" extraordinary mother-and-child reunions.[24]

Notes

Author's Note: This essay would not have been possible without the outstanding editorial guidance of Martyn Bone.

1. On the murder of white supremacist Richard Barrett and the homosexual panic defense employed by the man charged with his killing, see Mohr, "Suspect," and "Investigator." On Senator Roger Wicker's record of antigay campaigning, see Benen, "GOP Prepared to Filibuster," and Koppelman, "Republican Senator Releases Gay-Baiting Ad." Though not directly referenced in *The Joneses*, these events were reported in international media and would have been seen by some spectators around the same time. On local historical precedents for the homosexual panic defense, see Howard, *Men Like That*, 132–42.

2. For information on the film festivals at which *The Joneses* was premiered, see *Sheffield Doc/Fest* website, https://sheffdocfest.com (accessed October 20, 2010); *International Short Film Festival Hamburg* website, http://festival.shortfilm.com (accessed January 10, 2011); *Hot Docs Canadian International Documentary Festival* website, http://www.hotdocs.ca (accessed January 10, 2011). As of this writing, the film also has been screened at festivals in Brazil, Ireland, Italy, Sweden, and Switzerland, as well as Glasgow and London. On strategies of mutual discretion, see Kennedy and Davis, *Boots of Leather*, 58–60. On quiet accommodation, see Howard, *Men Like That*, xvii, 227.

3. To describe the great complex of normalizing forces accompanying heterosexuality (including, for example, married monogamous cohabiting coupledom), scholars such as Michael Warner have coined the useful term *heteronormativity*. To describe the great complex of normalizing forces accompanying a mainstream, assimilationist homosexuality (including, for example, married monogamous cohabiting coupledom), scholars such as Lisa Duggan have coined the useful term *homonormativity*. Of further relevance to this essay, to describe the great complex of urbanist assumptions accompanying most homonormativity (including the great gay migration narrative mentioned below), scholars such as Judith/Jack Halberstam have coined the useful term *metronormativity*. See Warner, *Fear of a Queer Planet*; Duggan, *Twilight of Equality?*; and Halberstam, *In a Queer Place*. On forms of rural queer cosmopolitanism, as set against an often uncomprehending urban gay provincialism, see my forthcoming essay "Digital Queer History and the Joys and Limits of Gay Sex," in Gray, Johnson, and Gilley, *Queering the Countryside*.

4. Smith, "Queering the South." Though recent documentary films take a deferential and respectful approach to the lived experiences of lesbian and gay Mississippians (*Small Town Gay Bar*, 2006) and trans southerners (*Southern Comfort*, 2001), they also trade on the sensational and scandalous, as when the former slips over the state line to track homophobic preachers and homosexual homicide narratives, and when the latter focuses on phobic doctors' refusals of transgender patients, resulting in undiagnosed and untreated illnesses.

5. Later in the film, J. Jones kisses her younger son, but it is an unreciprocated maternal kiss on the forehead.

6. According to the 1990 census, Jones is the fourth most common surname in the

United States. *US Census Bureau*, May 9, 1995, http://www.census.gov/genealogy/names/dist.all.last, accessed January 13, 2012. The Hollywood film of the same name, *The Joneses*, was directed by Derrick Borte and produced by Roadside Attractions.

7. See, for example, Rabinowitz, *They Must Be Represented*.

8. In my book *Men Like That*, Jones is assigned the pseudonym Rickie Leigh Smith.

9. On Kim Longinotto's documentary practice, see Smaill, *Documentary*, 71–94; Tay, *Women on the Edge*, 61–83; White, "Cinema Solidarity."

10. For *The Joneses*, Kotak and I receive screen credits as executive producers. The film is produced by Caroline Spry and Peter Day. Among extradiegetic material concerning the Jones family, for example, the protagonist has a total of four children, all sons. Living elsewhere, one is married with children, rendering J. Jones a grandmother as well. Yet another is "mentally challenged," as she puts it—institutionalized for schizophrenia, a diagnosis disproportionately visited upon the working-class.

11. Hobson, *Tell about the South*. The phrase "tell about the South" originates in William Faulkner's novel *Absalom! Absalom!* (1936).

12. Referring to this estrangement and reconciliation earlier in the film, J. Jones explains, "We lived apart for several years. . . . I talked them into . . . moving [in] with me, and we would be back together like a family again." She also pointed out the economic advantages to them.

13. This section is informed by, and its title is taken from, the "Sounds Queer" conference, Queer@King's Humanities Research Center, King's College London, June 4, 2010, organized by Ryan Powell.

14. On the rural-to-urban gay migration narrative, see Howard, *Men Like That*, 11–15, and Weston, "Get Thee." The Bronski Beat's "Smalltown Boy" reached number three on the U.K. singles chart. The song was originally released on the album *The Age of Consent* (London Records, 1984).

15. The independently produced, new queer cinema not only portrayed lesbian, gay, bisexual, and transgender figures with a fresh candor, but also dwelled upon radical sex practices such as bondage, domination, and corporal punishment, as with the repeated scenes of spanking in the work of director Todd Haynes. See Aaron, ed., *New Queer Cinema*.

16. See Koestenbaum, *Queen's Throat*, and Dyer, "In Defence of Disco."

17. Of course, I do not propose that there are essential predilections or natural affinities between particular gender and sexual outcasts, on the one hand, and particular genres of music, on the other. To offset limitations to my analysis, see Nadiene Hubbs's forthcoming *Rednecks, Queers, and Country Music*.

18. At the time of filming, J. Jones was employed by the Salvation Army, whose staff, she confided to me, was antagonistic to transsexuality, the key reason there was no filming there. Because she commuted a considerable distance to the workplace, she could legitimately explain that on Sundays her family attended a church closer to home, as was and is the case. Also, an issue elaborated below, her employment history as a woman, though varied, is now of many years' duration.

19. See "Sheffield Doc/Fest opens next week," *Independent*, October 30, 2009.

20. McRuer, *Crip Theory*, 84.

21. Gray, *Out in the Country,* 165. See also Gray, Johnson, and Gilley, eds., *Queering the Countryside.*

22. Foucault, *Power/Knowledge,* 149. I am grateful to Carter Sickels for conversations about "stealth" trans identities in the South. See his insightful study "What Does Masculinity Mean?" On employment discrimination, see Badgett, *Money, Myths, and Change,* and Howard, "Cracker Barrel." As is only obliquely suggested in the film, J. Jones has indeed been subjected to employment discrimination based upon gender identity in the past, stories of which she has shared with me.

23. J. Jones, oral history narrative with the author, Brussels, Belgium, February 3, 2000. As Mary Gray perceptively notes, lesbian, gay, bisexual, and transgender (LGBT) "rural young people use new media not to escape their surroundings but to expand their experience of local belonging [and] enhance their sense of inclusion to broader, imagined queer communities beyond their hometowns" (*Out in the Country,* 15). As we see, that applies to LGBT rural elders as well. In another striking generational reversal, just as queer youth occasionally may be thwarted by parental controls over Internet access, so too queer elders may suffer the intrusions of their adult children. During pre-production of this film, the younger son intercepted one of my emails to J. Jones and replied to me, with all-caps assertiveness, insisting we abandon the project.

24. As evidence of a mainstream fascination with sex reassignment surgery, I would point to the six-part television series *Sex Change Hospital* from 2007, as well as the recent purchase by the Oprah Winfrey Network of a documentary film on the "gender change" of Chaz Bono, born as daughter Chastity to Cher and Sonny Bono. For an enlightening discussion of documentary television and rural trans knowledge, see Gray, *Out in the Country,* 141–64. On issues of queer aging, see the *SAGE: Services and Advocacy for Gay, Lesbian, Bisexual & Transgender Elders* website, http://www.sageusa.org/index.cfm, and the *National Resource Center on LGBT Aging* website, http://www.lgbtagingcenter.org (both accessed January 14 2011).

At the time this essay was completed, plans were under way, with funding in place, to turn *The Joneses* into a feature-length documentary. See http://www.kickstarter.com/projects/1901269862/the-joneses-a-feature-length-documentary for more information, accessed February 18, 2012.

Works Cited

Aaron, Michele, ed. *New Queer Cinema: A Critical Reader.* New Brunswick: Rutgers University Press, 2004.

Badgett, M. V. Lee. *Money, Myths, and Change: The Economic Lives of Lesbians and Gay Men.* Chicago: University of Chicago Press, 2001.

Benen, Steve. "GOP Prepared to Filibuster Troop Funding over DADT." *Washington Monthly,* May 27, 2010.

Duggan, Lisa. *The Twilight of Equality? Neoliberalism, Cultural Politics, and the Attack on Democracy.* Boston: Beacon, 2003.

Dyer, Richard. "In Defence of Disco." *Gay Left* 8 (summer 1979): 20–23.

Foucault, Michel. *Power/Knowledge: Selected Interviews and Other Writings, 1972–1977*. New York: Pantheon, 1980.
Gray, Mary L. *Out in the Country: Youth, Media, and Queer Visibility in Rural America*. New York: New York University Press, 2009.
Gray, Mary L., Colin T. Johnson, and Brian Gilley, eds. *Queering the Countryside: New Directions in Rural Queer Studies*. New York: New York University Press, forthcoming.
Halberstam, Judith. *In a Queer Time and Place: Transgender Bodies, Subcultural Lives*. New York: New York University Press, 2005.
Hobson, Fred. *Tell about the South: The Southern Rage to Explain*. Baton Rouge: Louisiana State University Press, 1983.
Howard, John. "The Cracker Barrel Restaurants." In *Understanding and Managing Diversity: Readings, Cases, and* Exercises, edited by Carol P. Harvey and M. June Allard, 220–28. 4th ed. New York: Prentice Hall, 2009.
———. *Men Like That: A Southern Queer History*. Chicago: University of Chicago Press, 1999.
The Joneses. Directed by Moby Longinotto. London: Faction Films, 2009.
Kennedy, Elizabeth Lapovsky, and Madeline D. Davis. *Boots of Leather, Slippers of Gold: The History of a Lesbian Community*. New York: Routledge, 1993.
Koestenbaum, Wayne. *The Queen's Throat: Opera, Homosexuality, and the Mystery of Desire*. New York: Poseidon Press, 1993.
Koppelman, Alex. "Republican Senator Releases Gay-Baiting Ad." *Salon.com*. October 15, 2008, http://www.salon.com/news/politics/war_room/2008/10/15/wicker_ad. Accessed January 13, 2012.
McRuer, Robert. *Crip Theory: Cultural Signs of Queerness and Disability*. New York: New York University Press, 2006.
Mohr, Holbrook. "Suspect in Death of Miss. Supremacist Speaks Out." *ABC News*, April 26, 2010. http://abcnews.go.com/US/wireStory?id=10479988. Accessed April 26, 2010.
———. "Investigator: Sexual Advances Led to Barrett's Death." *WAPT News*. May 4, 2010. http://www.wapt.com/news/23445744/detail.html. Accessed January 13, 2012.
Rabinowitz, Paula. *They Must Be Represented: The Politics of Documentary*. New York: Verso, 1994.
Sickels, Carter. "What Does Masculinity Mean to You? Trans Males Creating Identities of Possibilities." Master's thesis, University of North Carolina, Chapel Hill, 2010.
Smaill, Belinda. *The Documentary: Politics, Emotion, Culture*. Basingstoke: Palgrave Macmillan, 2010.
Smalltown Boy. Directed by Moby Longinotto. London: Faction Films, 2007.
Smith, Donna Jo. "Queering the South: Constructions of Southern/Queer Identity." In *Carryin' On in the Lesbian and Gay South*, edited by John Howard, 362–84. New York: New York University Press, 1997.
Tay, Sharon Lin. *Women on the Edge: Twelve Political Film Practices*. Basingstoke: Palgrave Macmillan, 2009.

Warner, Michael, ed. *Fear of a Queer Planet: Queer Politics and Social Theory*. Minneapolis: University of Minnesota Press, 1993.

Weston, Kath. "Get Thee to a Big City: Sexual Imaginary and the Great Gay Migration." *GLQ* 2 (1995): 253–77.

White, Patricia. "Cinema Solidarity: The Documentary Practice of Kim Longinotto." *Cinema Journal* 46 (fall 2006): 120–28.

AFTERWORD

After Authenticity

TARA MCPHERSON

My favorite line of this volume comes, perhaps not surprisingly, given his always charming way with words, from Scott Romine's consideration of southern foodways. There he writes, "I believe that the idea of the South has been mostly a bad idea." Such a statement brings to mind Leigh Anne Duck's pronouncement that we need a "Southern studies without 'The South,'" a call referenced in this volume by Jon Smith.[1] Perhaps much of the action (and anxiety) in U.S. southern studies of the past ten years can best be summed up as a struggle around this very notion, the idea that "the South" is, if not an innately bad idea, at least not a particularly useful one for the field. Of course, we are perhaps not really talking about *a* field at all, but a continuum of scholarly practices that encompasses a more traditional southern studies (itself changed across the past twenty years), the New Southern Studies, and even what I apparently once dubbed the "radical fringe caucus" of southern studies, itself an offshoot of the New Southern Studies.[2]

Echoes of all these lineages are to be found in the larger initiative—the "Understanding the South" series of conferences at the universities of Manchester, Florida, Cambridge, and Copenhagen—from which this volume originated. The tensions across them frequently simmer just below the surface of polite conversation, although the essay by Jon Smith included here certainly calls them out quite loudly. They were also quietly on display at the "Creating and Consuming the South" conference in Copenhagen in August 2010. At that event several speakers were at pains to specify that they were not "really" southern studies scholars. I would count John Howard, E. Patrick Johnson, and myself among this number, although there may have been others. The dis-ease we might each feel about locating ourselves as southern studies scholars likely has multiple origins: none of us teaches in a southern university or, for that matter, in a university that much values things "southern"; our primary identities as scholars are within fields that do not much value the South either; and, at least for me, much of my recent work is not (at least on the surface, a point I will return to) about "the South" or even southern studies. Others at the conference more comfortably inhabited some variant of southern studies, and, despite these diverse identifications, the conference did extensively engage things southern.

This volume follows suit. Across its pages, we encounter some usual suspects of more traditional southern studies. Music figures prominently, from jazz to the blues to southern rock to Appalachian folk music. Food makes its appearance too, particularly the MoonPie and the butter bean. New Orleans and Mississippi are noticeably present. There's a dash of Faulkner, a turn to the pastoral, and a dose of the Agrarians (even if partially in claims that we should not be talking about them anymore at all. Nonetheless, they'll figure nicely in the index). We hear tell of community, of place, and of family. There is a curious resilience to many of these themes and objects, even as we may labor or long to displace them. Of course, these usual subjects are not always encountered in the usual ways: John Howard's inversions of the trailer park spring to mind, as does Adam Gussow's remapping of north Mississippi hill country geographies, or Michael Bibler's linking of place to global warming. Unusual suspects are also given their due, including Vietnamese shrimpers, experimental documentary, modern opera, BDSM sex, ecocriticism, and sex change operations. This is as it should be more than a decade into the New Southern Studies. The methodologies are diverse as well, encompassing literary and historical analysis, production studies, oral history, musicology, cultural studies, and even a small dose of psychoanalysis. Most of the essays zero in on a particular moment in time, but a few of the essays, particularly those by Fitzhugh Brundage and Romine, chart changes across a longer temporality.

Across the essays, many Souths take shape, Souths the volume cannot (and should not) easily hold together. Nonetheless, some sense of the South emerges as a perpetual site of (in Andrew Warnes' terms) the "return of the repressed," across the nation, across continents, and in surprising places, including Spain's St. Teresa of Ávila, Cold War Japan, and Britain's post-punk music scene. Reflecting the push against U.S. southern exceptionalism toward transnationalism that aligns the newer southern studies with recent turns in American studies and other fields, several chapters leave at least partially behind the fixed geography below the Mason-Dixon line; in doing so, they build upon Jon Smith's and Deborah Cohn's earlier call to "look away" toward the global South.[3]

Chapters by Warnes and Paige McGinley find the South erupting in contexts seemingly not about the South at all, revealing the degree to which the South travels and does diverse work in terrain far beyond the region or the nation. Each of these two chapters reads its representative texts against the grain to reveal the complexity of the South's power of insistent return. Each also struggles to map the political valences of such maneuvers. Warnes convincingly argues that the blues lurks behind much British rock but stops just short of reading the ethics of such practices (which perhaps cannot be read in the abstract, at any rate). McGinley finds that the modernist opera *Four Saints in Three Acts* cuts two ways, at once "deeply dependent on a black diasporic imaginary" that "formally staged the global flows, migrations, and exiles of both the Middle Passage and the contemporary migration of black Americans to New York from the rural South" and also caught up in "problematic fictions" of a pastoral, frozen region.

Other essays also find the U.S. South traveling abroad, if in less hidden modes, including those by Howard, Deborah Cohn and Helen Taylor. Each of these essays in its own way labors to fix the content and form of this traveling southernness. Warnes likens it to an epistemology, Cohn to a performance, Taylor to a creative prompt, and McGinley to an absent presence. These essays serve to remind us that the U.S. South has always been enmeshed in global circuits of exchange. Moreover, a subset of the essays (especially those by Howard and McGinley) enact this global turn even while interrogating its impulses. They contend that we not simply point out that the U.S. South has "gone global" (like corporate capitalism) but insist instead that we understand what work this global turn is performing. In McGinley's terms, the South often travels in ways that "are not necessarily always detached from the racialist or nationalist thinking" that a turn to transnationalist paradigms "often seeks to debunk."

Clearly, we have here a diverse, productive, and often provocative set of essays. The tensions and overlaps across and between them might be mined in any number of ways. One concept that circulates through a number of the chapters in this volume may produce as much anxiety as the (possibly bad) idea of "the South" itself—the concept of authenticity. Authenticity emerges most explicitly in the chapter by Brundage, evident as it is in his very title. But it is at work in many of the essays and also has a long lineage in the various fields that constitute U.S. southern studies. Across the works collected here we see various figures playing at being authentic, from transsexual Mrs. Jones in *The Joneses*, via various harmonica players and a traveling Faulkner, to the "mock authentic" hero of Scott Elliott's novel *Coiled at the Heart*. Here I consider the role of authenticity in other portions of this volume, suggest some alternate ways we might consider authenticity, and, ultimately, wonder if authenticity is something, like the Agrarians, that we shouldn't be talking about at all.

Circling around Southern Authenticity

If, as Martyn Bone has reminded us in regard to Louis Rubin Jr., an earlier generation of southern scholars tended to "emphasize the 'continuity' of, rather than 'changes' in, 'the South' and 'Southern literature,'" thereby reinforcing an idea of an authentic, enduring quality of southernness, then the authors in our current volume treat the very notion of authenticity with several (if differing) degrees of reserve.[4] Certainly, none of them would overtly champion an eternal and monolithic sense of the South, but they are positioned variously on the issue of whether there is an authentic South at all.

Of the writers collected here, Fitzhugh Brundage most directly takes on the role authenticity has played in points South and in the United States. He argues that "a defining project of twentieth-century [American] culture [is] the pursuit and celebration of the authentic." Brundage qualifies that he is less interested in defining authenticity than in pondering why we care about it and how the term's meaning changed across the twentieth century. He notes a shift in the working of authenticity in the pre- and post–World War II United States, identifying authenticity in the earlier period as about keeping southern culture separate and pure, in isolation from the "solvent of modernity" and commercialism—a separation born of Jim Crow logics. He then maintains that in the later period authenticity might be "held up as evidence of the enrichment of American life that results from pervasive cultural exchange across economic, racial, and social divides." He offers up the Allman Brothers and contemporary cookbooks as evidence of a kind of healing power implicit in such play with authenticity. Brundage concludes that "we can find satisfaction that contemporary Americans find fellowship through southern culture." Even as he hints at the limits of this conclusion, observing that such new-fangled forms of authenticity are "unlikely to resolve the questions of identity and power that have long vexed the South," his mapping is largely a positive and teleological one. Indeed, he uses the word "evolving," signaling a narrative of progress from older forms of authenticity that demanded (an imagined, often racial) purity to newer, more hybrid forms that at least partially free us from these pasts.

In this focus on shifting forms of authenticity, Brundage shares terrain with Romine. In his contribution here, Romine continues the deft engagement with issues of the real and of authenticity that mark *The Real South* (2008), where he pithily suggests that "a mechanically reproduced South is preferable to an authentic one."[5] The affective registers and stylistic tone of Brundage and Romine differ greatly, but there is some degree of coherence in their positions, as each circles frequently (here and elsewhere) around questions of authenticity. In this volume's essays, each prefers syncretic (even fake) culture to the imagined purity of a more "original" culture, but even this turn to the fake works to install some versions of "the South" in very particular ways. While Brundage and Romine rightly resist a nostalgic longing for a "purer" South of old (that they and we know never really existed anyway), they find cause for celebration in our newer syncretic Souths, suggesting that they provide, on the one hand via Brundage, a space for "pervasive cultural mixity" or, on the other à la Romine, at least a path to staying out of each other's way. In each case there tends to be an overemphasis on the upside of syncretism, rather than a sustained engagement with the many ways such relaxed modes of authenticity feed into and spring from larger systems of power, economics, or ideology (i.e., the machinations of late capital). There is also relatively little attention paid to the more repressive wieldings of authentic Souths much in evidence today, including the revival of the White Citizens Councils in the more recent Council of Concerned Citizens, with its prominent ties to southern politicians, as well as the continued presence of neo-Confederate organizations such as the League of the South.

If Brundage points out that questions of authenticity are a "defining project" of the past one hundred years of U.S. culture, he also notes that this turn to authenticity is at least partially instantiated through academic fields such as folklore studies in the early twentieth century (in her essay, Anne Dvinge examines the role that jazz record collectors played in this process). This academic obsession with authenticity certainly impacts other fields as well, up until the present. For instance, the editors of the volume *True West: Authenticity and the American West* (2004) also take up the question of authenticity, following Patricia Nelson Limerick in noting that "the search to distinguish 'the real west' from the 'the fake west' has become a nearly impossible quest, a game with ever-changing rules and no winner."[6] Even a field so vested in authenticity as history remains tied to the word, for, as Theodor Adorno observes, "[h]istory does intrude on every word and withholds each word from the recovery of some alleged original meaning." They propose not judging a text's or an author's authenticity, but rather studying how the idea of authenticity gets deployed and argue that "the relation between history and representation, which includes the relations between history and *its* representations, is the most crucial subject for critics" of this (or any) region to engage.[7] In this, they align in key ways with Romine and Brundage.

From the field of performance studies and in his lively *Appropriating Blackness: Performance and the Politics of Authenticity* (2003), E. Patrick Johnson maintains that authenticity "is yet another trope manipulated for cultural capital" but also recognizes that authenticity is a concept with strategic use value, "for there are ways in which authenticating discourse enables marginalized people to counter oppressive representations of themselves." Like the editors of *True West* or Brundage in his essay here, Johnson is less interested in evaluating authenticity than in understanding what its uses are, and he moves further in troubling the concept. He warns us "to be cognizant of the arbitrariness of authenticity, the ways in which it carries with it the dangers of foreclosing the possibility of cultural exchange and understanding."[8] Johnson highlights the possibility that strategic authenticity might equally work to prevent the very kinds of mixity that Brundage emphasizes.

These expansions and inversions of authenticity and its cultural, political, and disciplinary work coincide with recent scholarship that values the impure, the hybrid, and the contingent. Certainly, we see the ripple effects of such revised notions of authenticity across the U.S. South and across decade-old turns in southern studies. In the realm of fiction, Dorothy Allison calls us to rethink the bastard, and, in literary studies, Patricia

Yaeger turns the canon on its head, asking us to mine the value of "dirt and desire" in southern studies. Such work requires us to consider and produce new Souths, Souths intent on fostering, to echo Johnson, new strategic values.

There is a powerful allure to this lingering in and on authenticity, particularly when engaged in the reading (one might say the consumption, albeit in the academic register) of favorite texts or practices. A substantial thread of my 2003 book *Reconstructing Dixie* (the work that, post-publication, finally connected me with the New Southern Studies, since I had written it largely unaware of this then-emerging field) utilized such tactics, reading hybrid Souths like the Mississippi lesbian enclave Camp Sister Spirit and Octavia Butler's novel *Kindred* (1979) as forms of strategic and disruptive Souths intent on modeling new ways of feeling southern. I insisted that these new modes of feeling are as valid, as authentic (if not more so given their hard-won status) than more familiar stereotypical ones. Later, at the 2005 conference of the Southern Intellectual History Circle (SIHC), in a response to Bill Malone's keynote on Mike Seeger and authenticity, I extended Malone's ideas about Seeger's ability to be at once inauthentic (he's not a southerner) and yet authentic all the same (he added to our sense of the South) to call for new and wackier forms of postauthenticity—ones I suspect Malone himself had little use for.[9]

In my SIHC response, I briefly offered up some impure samples of southern music, sounds I claimed for the South even if they were unlikely to pass old-school tests of authenticity. I was at the time interested in how some musicians deployed authenticity to new ends, retooling southernness in the process. The first example was Loretta Lynn, particularly in the hybrid mode represented by her 2004 album *Van Lear Rose*, produced by rocker Jack White (of White Stripes fame) and featuring some heavy drumming and grungy electric guitar. Lynn's album was nominated for five Grammys and won two (for best album and best vocal collaboration), yet it was largely rejected by country music stations and the Country Music Awards. Nonetheless, Lynn said of the album, "It's kind of like my first one. . . . It's back to real country," claiming authenticity for a work that powerfully models hybridity, forging new connections between the South and elsewhere. Jack White sought out Lynn to work on the album, again hinting at the potentially positive role of what Malone, in describing Seeger, had called the "cultural interventionist." The album also asks us to think complexly about place, about who can speak from where. In commenting on the song "Portland, Oregon," Lynn notes, "I was in Portland, Oregon, when I wrote it. I got to thinking that everybody writes about Texas—what's wrong with Portland, Oregon?"[10] In doing so, she serves to remind us that the South (and southerners) travel and that our engagements with various places need not be tightly bound by birthplace. I termed her wielding of her origins and her travels an "inauthentic authenticity."

My second example at the SIHC conference was Steve Earle, particularly for his album, *The Revolution Starts . . . Now*, also a Grammy winner in 2005. Earle is from Texas, so is only marginally a southerner, but has lived in Tennessee for years, through the ups and downs of his career and drug addiction. The album was a spirited attack on the Bush administration, particularly the track "Rich Man's War." In the album's liner notes, Earle claims strategic southernness, locating "me and my boys" "back here in Tennessee" as he describes working on the album during the breaking news of the prison abuse scandals during the Iraq war: "The most important presidential election of our lifetime was less than seven months away and we desperately wanted to weigh in, both as artists and as citizens of a democracy. . . . The day after the election, regardless of the outcome, the war will go on, outsourcing of our jobs will continue, and over a third of our citizens will have no health care coverage whatsoever." He signs the liner notes, "Steve Earle, Fairview, Tennessee," again insisting on the southern location and origin of his very political message, a message we might not ordinarily locate in southern terrain, particularly given the nation's stereotypical understanding of the South as the "red states." Earle forcefully taps into a long tradition of homegrown, southern-style resistance. I called this mode "authentic inauthenticity."

I intended these two quick examples of sonic Souths to suggest the limit of carefully policing the purity or authenticity of southern culture. They also serve to remind us, as folklorist Charles Joyner has, that innovation and tradition are part and parcel of the same process, inseparable from each other. From a different academic positioning, Paul Gilroy has discussed the power of "nontraditional tradition," a riff on tradition that moves beyond repetition to growth and change, where the "same is retained without needing to be reified." In a figure such as Bob Marley, Gilroy finds not African authenticity but a "transnational image" that "invites further speculation about the status of identity and the conflicting scales on which sameness and solidarity can be imagined."[11] In the music of Lynn and Earle, and, more importantly, in their embrace by a broad cross section of the United States both in and out of the South, we might, I argued, explore new paths toward cultural understanding, a call for cultural exchange that seemed all the more necessary following the 2004 U.S. presidential election and the fixing of the South as the "red states."

As the election results were tallied in 2004, my e-mail inbox was flooded with a series of tirades against the South, including links to websites like fuckthesouth.com and to writers decrying the region's homophobia, bigotry, and racism. The writer of one letter urged the South "to finally just go ahead and secede already." On November 2 and 3, 2004, as I watched the solid sea of southern red glaring out from my computer monitor while trawling CNN and MSNBC.com, it was hard not to think of the South as a monolithic space and to feel smug that I had escaped to Los Angeles. Certainly, progressives on both coasts bemoaned Bush's "southern strategy," making it hard to imagine other Souths, and underwriting a feeling that we should just look away from the South and disavow it. Of course, I knew that would not really be a useful tactic, so I reminded myself of several now well-worn mantras of the New Southern Studies. We need to remember that the South is as much a site of change as it is a site of stasis. To freeze the South as simply red, to leave it there, to wish it would just go away, is to miss the chance to understand how it still functions in very important ways in the national imaginary, propping up so many myths of race, gender, and place, so many dynamics of Othering. Further, we can learn a lot about how we manage the borders of self and nation by exploring how the South and its "authenticities" get deployed by both southerners and nonsoutherners. We must, I reminded myself (and the SIHC audience), also remember and emphasize those demographic patterns of change in the South that make speaking in frozen shades of red and blue so very inaccurate, serving once again to disenfranchise all those southerners who do not fit a very stereotypical mold—the very southerners most likely to have been disenfranchised in the 1950s or in current attempts at election tampering. To look at state voting maps by county is to realize that there is no single South. The solid red disappears at the micro level, a level we cannot neglect if we really want to think about the local and the global and the South's currency at different scales—a point also emphasized by Jon Smith in his essay here.

I still believe much of this but am also aware that these points have been made many times now within the New Southern Studies. As Grace

Elizabeth Hale has noted, these mantras can now have a kind of wearying effect, leading her to ask (if only rhetorically), "We know that this thing called the South—a new generation of academics have named it the southern imaginary—runs deep in American culture. We know that it defines, ensnares, and empowers whites and blacks.... What more, I sometimes wonder, is there to say?"[12] She does, of course go on to find more to say, as do we all, but I have grown increasingly skeptical of my own and others' recourse to narratives and examples of authenticity as a particularly useful mode in which to keep talking and writing. I am increasingly asking myself what this focus on authenticity may be precluding.

Missing the Forest for the Fakes, or Why Southern Studies Should Follow the Money

In her comparative study of the role of authenticity in folklore studies, Regina Bendix queries the value of the term for her field (and others), noting that "disciplinary practice has 'nostaligized the homogeneous' and decried 'bastard traditions,' thus upholding the fallacy that cultural purity rather than hybridity" is the norm. She further argues that in "emphasizing the authentic, the revolutionary can turn reactionary, a process too vividly played out in global political movements of the late 20th century." Eyes firmly fixed on the horrors perpetrated in the name of authenticity, particularly in "devastating campaigns of ethnic cleansing," Bendix calls for scholarship to "lay to rest" its uses of authenticity. She writes that "removing authenticity and its allied vocabulary is one useful step toward conceptualizing the study of culture in the age of transculturation." She urges us elsewhere toward new vocabularies beyond the real and the fake, the authentic and its hybrids.[13]

From a space more aligned with the New Southern Studies, Melanie Benson Taylor enacts such a move in *Reconstructing the Native South: American Indian Literature and the Lost Cause* (2012) by avoiding the term *authenticity* almost entirely. Instead she insists that we may need to "deconstruct Natives' ... compensatory fictions" of "tribe and enemy, friend and foe, insider and outsider." She writes, "My aim is to show that the divisive contours of region, tribe, and nation tend to be corrosive byproducts not just of colonial histories but, in fact, of an increasingly damaging post-colonial present." Throughout her introduction, Taylor returns to sentences such as these: "I aim to add to developing conversations about the paradoxical role of regionalism in the wake of broader globalization patterns" and "What *is* fundamentally lost, however, by both groups [the Native community in the South and white southern adherents to the Lost Cause] is the agency, control, and self-definition undone irretrievably by defeat, reconstruction, and now, the exploitative and competitive logic of market capitalism."[14] In short, work such as Taylor's foregrounds not authenticity (in its real or fake variants), but instead larger systems of late capitalism that are often crippling and restrictive. In doing so, Taylor zeroes in on a loss of choice that runs counter to Romine's claim that we live in a world where one might go "with a clicker wherever one wants" within a mediated landscape of "virtualized and free-floating differences."[15] By resisting a language of authenticity, Taylor instead foregrounds that, for many, differences are not free-floating but often grounded, material, painful, and tense. She also focuses our attention on words and phrases that are none too prevalent in a good deal of southern studies (or this volume, really, save Jon Smith's piece) even as they seem to incessantly characterize the new American studies (and the new activist modes of Occupy): neoliberalism, post-Fordism, labor, economics, and global capitalism.[16] If Romine does not exactly celebrate the South's new commodity form (he writes in this volume, "I do not claim that going to market or assuming commodity form is necessarily a good thing for culture to do"), he does seem to consider it, all in all, a good thing for the South, seeing a kind of freedom born of market choices. Authenticity and questions of the real appear to be vectors through which "the South" creeps back into our work even when we have putatively agreed that it is, for the most part, a "bad idea." One begins to wonder if a focus on the real, the fake, and authenticity makes it that much harder to follow the money.

In a brilliant recent essay on the film *The Fugitive* (1932), Leigh Anne Duck has returned our focus to issues of labor, exploitation, and economics. Even while recognizing the limits of the film, she maintains that its "critique of the southern penal system is nonetheless linked to a critique of the nation's capitalism, a form of analysis that has since practically abated in all discourse except that produced by movements to reform or abolish U.S. prisons." She goes on to argue that *The Fugitive* calls attention to "logics of containment" that may be "axiomatic in U.S. society. Through both plot and metaphor, the film describes the chain gang as an intensification of the many social constraints—including class, business-oriented theology, and the heterosexual family—that isolate white men throughout the country, like southern black men, from the possibility of choice and satisfaction in their labor."[17] If these logics of containment were taking shape in the carceral nation of the 1930s, their parsings and seclusions have only intensified in our post-Fordist era of flexible production, niche marketing, increasing service industries, intensifying globalization, and an ongoing valorization of information as the chief product of capitalism. Inspired in part by an early version of Duck's essay, I have recently argued that our readings of southern culture need to be more materialist and less southern, pushing beyond representation and narrative to conditions of production and the flow of capital. My particular example is the rise of Louisiana as "Hollywood South," where I query the relationship of onscreen images of labor in series like *True Blood* to the processes of deregulation, outsourcing, and economic policy that make such television possible in the first place. I see this work as of a piece with other materialist turns within the academy—in southern studies to a small degree but largely beyond it--that attempt to come to terms with the ways that global economic systems, from plantation economies to Wal-Mart, shape the very stories we are able to tell.

A few chapters in this volume attempt to tread similar waters, if in very subtle ways. For instance, Adam Gussow, Helen Taylor, Frank Cha, and Anne Dvinge are each struggling to bring into view forms of negotiation with global capital that occur at the micro level even as they name various forces of oppression that global capital unleashes. Michael Bibler presents us with a hero so caught within the lures of global capital that he ends up paralyzed by "mock authenticity." Cha's Vietnamese shrimpers push beyond black-white binaries to protect local industry from global markets. Gussow's story of getting paid is particularly interesting here, as it explicitly calls out issues of labor and equity and suggests some modes of working within capital. It points out that there are differences within various modes of production and consumption, and that these differences do matter across many levels and scales. Gussow has largely discarded the language of the authentic in his piece, but Taylor and Dvinge circle uneasily around it.

Of course, the essay in this volume that most avowedly engages many of these issues is Jon Smith's. It is probably by now apparent that I agree with his critique of Romine's faith in pluralistic choice, but I am not sure that his return to a Habermasian public sphere is our best alternative. First, I (among many others) am fairly skeptical that such a sphere ever existed, for most folks at any rate, and, second, I suspect that an array of counterpublics might get us further, as Nancy Fraser, Michael Warner, and Mary Gray have variously argued. I am also not entirely convinced by his polemical claims that "studying 'southernness' may thus be a distraction from whatever political effect our academic work is likely to have," though I tend to agree that we need to be studying southernness in relation to many other things: capital, labor, and neoliberalism most certainly. Likewise, I imagine that southernness should not always be our starting point. In my own academic trajectory, things southern have a way of still returning, in modes that frequently surprise me. For instance, in studying the instantiation of digital computing systems in the middle of the twentieth century (the very systems that undergird our post-Fordist economy), I have come to realize that computation imports into its very technological systems the racial logics I have previously described as "lenticular," that is, the covert racial logics of the post–civil rights era. Thus, a racial logic born at least partially of southern struggles (if also, of course, global ones) is expressed in the very early design of contemporary computational systems. That's an argument for a different book than this one, but it certainly suggests that an understanding of "the South" remains relevant within many systems.[18]

Notes

1. Duck, "Southern Nonidentity," 329.
2. Smith, *Finding Purple America*, xiv.
3. See Smith and Cohn, eds., "Introduction: Uncanny Hybridities."
4. Bone, *Postsouthern Sense of Place*, 34.
5. Romine, *Real South*, 2.
6. Handley and Lewis, *True West*, 1.
7. Adorno quoted in Handley and Lewis, *True West*, 3.
8. Johnson, *Appropriating Blackness*, 3.
9. I should note that, due to illness, I did not actually deliver this response myself. Rather, in an act of kind ventriloquism that apparently left him blushing just a bit, Jon Smith read the response for me.
10. "Loretta Lynn Receives Five Grammy Nods."
11. Gilroy, *Against Race*, 31, 132.
12. Hale, "Shaping a Southern Soundscape."
13. Bendix, *In Search of Authenticity*, 9, 8, 227, 8.
14. Taylor, *Reconstructing the Native South*, 20–21, 18, 13.
15. Romine, *Real South*, 17.

16. This is not to say that no such work takes place at all. In his editorial reading of a draft of this afterword, Martyn Bone pointed out that several British southern and American studies scholars have "long since been focused on labor, immigration, and economics in the South." He is, of course, one of them. Other scholars, including Duck and Smith, continue to undertake this work. At stake, I think, is a willingness to push beyond questions of narrative, representation, and visuality toward more systemic modes of analysis that engage modes of production and the circulation of capital, things one cannot always read off the surface of a text.

17. Duck, "Bodies," 98, 80.

18. My first parsing of this argument appears in an essay, "U.S. Operating Systems at Mid-Century: The Intertwining of Race and Unix," in the recent collection *Race after the Internet*.

Works Cited

Allison, Dorothy. *Bastard out of Carolina*. New York: Plume, 1993.

Bendix, Regina. *In Search of Authenticity: The Formation of Folklore Studies*. Madison: University of Wisconsin Press, 1997.

Bone, Martyn. *The Postsouthern Sense of Place in Contemporary Fiction*. Baton Rouge: Louisiana State University Press, 2005.

Duck, Leigh Anne. "Bodies and Expectations: Chain Gang Discipline." In *American Cinema and the Southern Imaginary*, edited by Deborah Barker and Kathryn McKee, 79–103. Athens: University of Georgia Press, 2011.

———. *The Nation's Region: Southern Modernism, Segregation, and U.S. Nationalism*. Athens: University of Georgia Press, 2006.

———. "Southern Nonidentity." *Safundi: The Journal of South African and American Studies* 9, no. 3 (July 2008): 319–30.

Fraser, Nancy. "Rethinking the Public Sphere: A Contribution to the Critique of Actually Existing Democracy." In *The Phantom Public Sphere*, edited by Bruce Robbins, 1–32. Minneapolis: University of Minnesota Press, 1993.

Gilroy, Paul. *Against Race: Imagining Political Culture Beyond the Color Line*. Cambridge: Harvard University Press, 2000.

Gray, Mary. *Out in the Country: Youth, Media, and Queer Visibility in Rural America*. New York: New York University Press, 2009.

Hale, Grace Elizabeth. "Shaping a Southern Soundscape." *Southern Spaces*, July 29, 2010. http://www.southernspaces.org/2010/shaping-southern-soundscape. Accessed March 18, 2012.

Handley, William R., and Nathaniel Lewis, eds. *True West: Authenticity and the American West*. Lincoln: University of Nebraska Press, 2004.

Joyner, Charles. *Shared Traditions: Southern History and Folk Culture*. Urbana: University of Illinois Press, 1999.

"Loretta Lynn Receives Five Grammy Nods." Associated Press, updated December 7, 2004. http://today.msnbc.msn.com/id/6673480/ns/today-entertainment/t/loretta-lynn-receives-five-grammy-nods/#.T2aD3V0cCzd. Accessed March 18, 2012.

Johnson, E. Patrick. *Appropriating Blackness: Performance and the Politics of Authenticity*. Durham: Duke University Press, 2003.

Malone, Bill C. "Reaffirming Authenticity: Mike Seeger and the Rediscovery of Southern Roots Music." Keynote Lecture. Southern Intellectual History Circle Meeting, Sewanee, Tennessee. February 17–19, 2005.

McPherson, Tara. *Reconstructing Dixie: Race, Gender and Nostalgia in the Imagined South*. Durham: Duke University Press, 2003.

———. "Revamping the South: Thoughts on Labor, Relationality and Southern Representation." In *American Cinema and the Southern Imaginary*, edited by Deborah Barker and Kathryn McKee, 336–52. Athens: University of Georgia Press, 2011.

———. "U.S. Operating Systems at Mid-Century: The Intertwining of Race and Unix." In *Race after the Internet*, edited by Lisa Nakamura and Peter Chow-White, 21–37. New York: Routledge, 2011.

Romine, Scott. *The Real South: Southern Narrative in the Age of Cultural Reproduction*. Baton Rouge: Louisiana State University Press, 2008.

Smith, Jon. *Finding Purple America: The South and the Future of American Studies*. Athens: University of Georgia Press, 2013.

Smith, Jon, and Deborah Cohn. "Introduction: Uncanny Hybridities." *Look Away! The U.S. South in New World Studies*, edited by Jon Smith and Deborah Cohn, 1–19. Durham: Duke University Press, 2004.

Taylor, Melanie Benson. *Reconstructing the Native South: American Indian Literature and the Lost Cause*. Athens: University of Georgia Press, 2011.

Warner, Michael. *Publics and Counterpublics*. New York: Zone Books, 2002.

Yaeger, Patricia. *Dirt and Desire: Reconstructing Southern Women's Writing, 1930–1960*. Chicago: University of Chicago Press, 2000.

CONTRIBUTORS

Michael P. Bibler is associate professor of English at Louisiana State University. He is the author of *Cotton's Queer Relations: Same-Sex Intimacy and the Literature of the Southern Plantation, 1936–1968* and coeditor of the essay collection *Just Below South: Intercultural Performance in the Caribbean and the U.S. South* as well as the first critical edition of Arna Bontemps's 1939 novel *Drums at Dusk*. His articles have appeared in *Journal of American Studies, Mississippi Quarterly, Southern Cultures, Philological Quarterly,* and *MFS: Modern Fiction Studies*.

Martyn Bone is associate professor of American literature at the University of Copenhagen. He is the author of *The Postsouthern Sense of Place in Contemporary Fiction* and the editor of *Perspectives on Barry Hannah*. He served as the University of Copenhagen representative of the "Understanding the South" international research network and is coeditor of the two other volumes in this series: *Citizenship and Identity in the Nineteenth-Century South* and *The American South and the Atlantic World*. His articles have appeared in *American Literature, Journal of American Studies, Comparative American Studies, CR: The New Centennial Review,* and other journals.

W. Fitzhugh Brundage is William B. Umstead Professor of History at the University of North Carolina at Chapel Hill. He is the author of *The Southern Past*; *A Socialist Utopia in the New South*; and *Lynching in the New South*. He has also edited several collections of essays, including *Beyond Blackface: African Americans and the Creation of American Popular Culture, 1890–1930*. His articles have appeared in the *Journal of American History, Journal of Southern History, Historical Journal, Canadian Journal of American Studies,* and other journals.

Frank Cha completed his PhD in American studies at the College of William and Mary in 2013. His dissertation focuses on contemporary literature and film to examine the impact of post-1965 Asian immigration on socio-spatial relationships in the U.S. South. His articles have appeared in *Mississippi Quarterly, Global South,* and *Southern Quarterly*.

Deborah Cohn is professor of Spanish and American studies at Indiana University, Bloomington. She is the author of *The Latin American Literary Boom and U.S. Nationalism during the Cold War* and *History and Memory in the Two Souths: Recent Southern and Spanish American Fiction*, as well as coeditor, with Jon Smith, of *Look Away! The U.S. South in New World Studies*. She has published widely on Spanish American and U.S. fiction in journals such as *Latin American Research Review*, *Mississippi Quarterly*, *CR: The New Centennial Review*, *American Literature*, and others.

Anne Dvinge teaches in the Department of Arts and Cultural Studies at the University of Copenhagen. She was the principal investigator for Denmark in the HERA-funded research program *Rhythm Changes: Jazz Cultures and European Identities* (2010–13). Her current monograph project, *Improvising Citizenship: Jazz Festivals and Trans-Atlantic Practices*, investigates jazz festivals as meeting grounds between local and global understandings of jazz. Her articles have appeared in *Journal for Transnational American Studies*, *Jazzforschung/Jazz Research*, and *Amerikastudien/American Studies*.

Adam Gussow is associate professor of English and southern studies at the University of Mississippi, and the author of three blues-themed books, including *Seems like Murder Here: Southern Violence and the Blues Tradition*, a winner of the C. Hugh Holman Award from the Society for the Study of Southern Literature. He is also a professional blues harmonica player and teacher. (His most recent album, *Southbound*, is available on iTunes.) His current book project is a study of the devil and the blues tradition.

John Howard is professor of American studies at King's College London. He is the editor of three books and the author of two—*Concentration Camps on the Home Front: Japanese Americans in the House of Jim Crow* and *Men Like That: A Southern Queer History*. He has received awards and fellowships from the Arts and Humanities Research Council, British Academy, Delfina Studio Trust, Fulbright Commission, Rockefeller Foundation, and King's College London Students Union.

E. Patrick Johnson is the Carlos Montezuma Professor of Performance Studies and African American Studies at Northwestern University. He has published widely in the area of race, gender, sexuality and performance. He has written two award-winning books, *Appropriating Blackness: Performance and the Politics of Authenticity* and *Sweet Tea: Black Gay Men of the South—An Oral History*. He is also coeditor with Mae G. Henderson of *Black Queer Studies: A Critical*

Anthology. He is currently at work on an oral history of black lesbians of the South.

William A. Link is the Richard J. Milbauer Professor of History at the University of Florida, a position he has held since 2004. His publications include *Roots of Secession: Slavery and Politics in Antebellum Virginia*; *Righteous Warrior: Jesse Helms and the Rise of Modern Conservatism*; *Links: My Family in American History*; and *Cradle of the New South: Race and the Struggle for Meaning in the Civil War's Aftermath*.

Paige A. McGinley is assistant professor of performing arts at Washington University in St. Louis. She is the author of *Staging Delta Blues from Tent Shows to Tourism*. Her articles have appeared in *TDR, Performance Research*, and *Theatre Survey*. Her essay "The Magic of Song! John Lomax, Huddie Ledbetter, and the Staging of Circulation," published in *Performance in the Borderlands* (Harvey Young and Ramon Rivera-Servera, eds.), was awarded the Vera Mowry Roberts Prize in Research and Publication by the American Theatre and Drama Society.

Tara McPherson is associate professor of gender and critical studies in the University of Southern California's School of Cinematic Arts. She is the author of *Reconstructing Dixie: Race, Gender and Nostalgia in the Imagined South*, coeditor of *Hop on Pop: The Politics and Pleasures of Popular Culture*, and editor of *Digital Youth, Innovation and the Unexpected*. She is the founding editor of *Vectors*, a multimedia journal, and is a founding editor of the *International Journal of Learning and Media*. She also leads a software lab for the Alliance for Networking Visual Culture, an initiative supported by the Andrew Mellon Foundation.

Scott Romine is professor of English at the University of North Carolina at Greensboro. He is the author of *The Narrative Forms of Southern Community* and *The Real South: Southern Narrative in the Age of Cultural Reproduction*. He has published articles in *Style, Mississippi Quarterly*, and *Southern Literary Journal*, and in several collections.

Jon Smith is associate professor and chair of English at Simon Fraser University. He is the author of *Finding Purple America: The South and the Future of American Cultural Studies* and coeditor, with Deborah Cohn, of *Look Away! The U.S. South in New World Studies*. His work has appeared in *American Literary History, American Literature, Global South*, and *Modern Fiction Studies*, among other journals, and in essay collections on topics ranging from Faulkner to alt-country.

Helen Taylor is professor of English and Humanities Arts and Culture Fellow, University of Exeter. She is the author of *Gender, Race, and Region in the Writings of Grace King, Ruth McEnery Stuart, and Kate Chopin*; *Scarlett's Women: Gone with the Wind and Its Female Fans*; and *Circling Dixie: Contemporary Southern Culture through a Transatlantic Lens*, and coeditor, with Richard H. King, of *Dixie Debates: Perspectives on Southern Cultures*. She is also the author of many scholarly and popular articles about southern transatlantic writing and culture, especially focused on New Orleans. She was honored for her distinguished contributions to American Studies by the award of the British Association of American Studies Honorary Fellowship 2010–11.

Brian Ward is professor in American studies at Northumbria University. His major publications include *Just My Soul Responding: Rhythm and Blues, Black Consciousness and Race Relations*; *Radio and the Struggle for Civil Rights in the South*; and *The 1960s: A Documentary Reader*. He served as director of the "Understanding the South" international research network sponsored by the Arts and Humanities Research Council and is coeditor of two other volumes in this miniseries: *Citizenship and Identity in the Nineteenth-Century South* and *The American South and the Atlantic World*. He is currently working on a book about the relationships between the American South and the world of British popular music.

Andrew Warnes is a reader in American studies at the School of English, Leeds University. He is the author of *Hunger Overcome? Food and Resistance in Twentieth-Century African-American Literature*; *Richard Wright's Native Son*; and *Savage Barbecue: Race, Culture and the Invention of America's First Food*. His articles have appeared in *Atlantic Studies*, *Journal of American Studies*, *Moving Worlds*, and *Popular Music*.

INDEX

Aaron, Daniel, 5
Abel, Elizabeth, 271
Absalom, Absalom!, 305n11
Accilien, Cécile, 230
Acuff, Roy, 39
Adams, Jessica, 230
Adorno, Theodor W., 64–65, 282, 314
Adventures of Huckleberry Finn, 136n22
Afghanistan war, 73
Africana, 239
Agrarians, Nashville, 2, 55, 73, 79, 90n10, 121, 264n21, 310, 312; critique of capitalism, 6–7, 61; neo-Agrarianism, 2, 77, 91, 130, 132; and proprietary ideal, 128; and southern exceptionalism, 78
Ahmed, Sarah, 103
"Ain't Got No Home," 188
Airriess, Christopher, 207
Alabama, 10, 39, 180; HB-56 law, 10
Albert, Magalie, 216–17, 221
Alberti, Fay Bound, 283
Albertine, Viv, 278
Allen, Gay Wilson, 253–54
Allewaert, Monique, 124
Allison, Dorothy, 314
Allman, Duane, 39, 40
Allman, Greg, 39, 40
Allman Brothers, 11, 39–41, 313; and southern rock, 40
American Dreams in Mississippi, 6
American Idol, 4
Americanization of Dixie, The, 2–3
American Literature, 81
American South and the Atlantic World, The, 10, 17–18

American South in a Global World, The, 20n53, 85
Anderson, Benedict, 77
Anderson, Thomas, 229
Angola state penitentiary, Louisiana, 32
Appadurai, Arjun, 56
Appalachia, 27, 30, 35; and folk music, 11; and mountain folklore, 27, 30–31, 35
Appropriating Blackness: Performance and the Politics of Authenticity, 315
Appropriation of black southern culture, 15, 31–34, 37, 44; and the blues, 146–48; British rock's appropriation of the blues, 268–71, 281, 285. *See also* Blues music; British rock music
Arbor Day Foundation, 132–33
Arizona: SB 1070 law, 10
Armstrong, Howard (aka Louie Bluie), 38, 43
Armstrong, Louis, 188, 250
Arsenault, Raymond, 125
Ashton, Frederick, 226, 227, 237, 241
Associated Artists Studio, 166
Atkinson, Connie, 160
Atlanta, 6, 27, 50, 113n1; and consumer culture, 64; and Gay Pride, 111; and suburban sprawl, 134
Atrocity Exhibition, The, 285
Audacity of Hope, The, 86
Austin, Everett "Chick," 227, 235
Authenticity, 18, 27–46, 292, 312–20; and blues music, 271; commodification of, 6, 10–11, 14, 86, 158, 160, 183; and jazz music, 162, 181; and New Orleans, 183, 190; "post-authenticity," 315, 319; production of,

Authenticity—*continued*
27–31, 32, 35–36, 41, 43, 119; and syncretism, 44, 59, 312–13; and southern food, 51, 62; and southernness, 1, 3–4, 6–7, 9, 11, 15, 17, 28, 49–50, 59, 74–75, 87, 89, 121, 232, 249, 253–55, 311–12, 315–16, 321; strategic authenticity, 314
Autobiography of Alice B. Toklas, The, 228, 235

B. B. King Museum and Delta Interpretive Center, 142, 156n6
Bad Boy, 294
Bad Lieutenant, 186
Baez, Joan, 37
Bailey, Brandon, 150–51
Baker, Houston, 72–74
Ballard, J. G., 283, 285
Baltimore, 238, 242–43, 303
Bankston, Carl Leon, 207
Banksy, 14, 180, 194
Barenboim, Daniel, 190
Barg, Lisa, 229
Barker, Danny, 142
Barrett, Richard, 304n1
Bartram, William, 124
Baton Rouge, 107, 203; and Hurricane Katrina refugees, 8, 186
Baxley, Georgia, 102
Baym, Nina, 76, 78
Bean, Terry "Harmonica," 144, 146, 155
Beatles, The, 66
Beckett, Samuel, 190
Beethoven, Ludwig van, 276
Being and Nothingness, 121
Benadon, Fernando, 280
Bendix, Regina, 318
Benjamin, Walter, 43
Benoit, Tab, 188
Benson Taylor, Melanie, 82, 318–19
Berghahn, Volker, 250
Berry, Chuck, 278
"Berry, D.," 111–13
Berry, Wendell, 121, 126–27, 136nn6,17
Besh, John, 214–15
Betts, Dickie, 39, 40
Bharati, Agehananda, 50
Bibler, Michael, 12, 230, 310, 320

Bierman, Lindsay M., 51
Big Bill Broonzy, 276
Big Deal for the Charles Family, A, 294
Big Walter, 143, 147
Biloxi, 14, 203–6, 208–9, 215, 217–21; casinos in, 219–20, 223n41. *See also* Vietnamese Americans
Birmingham, Alabama, 89
Birmingham School of cultural studies, 88
Biscuits, Spoonbread, and Sweet Potato Pie, 28
Bizet, Georges, 235–36
Black Atlantic, 230, 285
Black Boy, 269–70, 285
Black-white racial binary, 9, 12, 98, 260–61
Blake, William, 18
Blanchard, Terence, 186, 188
Blight, David, 5
Blood Dazzler, 192
Blotner, Joseph, 257, 259, 262–63
"Blue Sky," 39
Blues music, 13, 15, 43, 188, 311; and British rock music, 268–85, 311; connection to lynching, 272; development of, 13, 44, 270–71, 276; epistemology, 269–70; hill country, 147; interracial collaboration, 140; Mississippi blues mystique, 13, 145–46, 149; and Mississippi Delta, 11, 35, 36, 43, 142–44, 147, 149, 156; opposed to jazz, 271; oppositionality, 271–73, 276; origins of, 31, 37, 43, 269, 271; parties, 151; and southern rock, 39–40; tourism, 43–45, 140–49. *See also* Authenticity; British rock music; Hill Country Harmonica; Jim Crow
Boas, Franz, 37
Boat People SOS, 218
Bondage/discipline/sadism/masochism (BDSM) sex, 104–5, 310
Bone, Martyn, 73, 74, 79, 82, 91n32, 117, 128, 263, 285, 303, 312, 322n16
Bono, Chaz, 306n24
Bono, Sonny, 306n24
Boone, Daniel, 120
Boone, Pat, 299
Borenstein, E. Lorenz "Larry," 166–67
Borneman, Ernest, 163
Bourdieu, Pierre, 51
Bow, Leslie, 14

Bowers, Jane Palatani, 237
Branch, Billy, 143
Brazil, 251, 255
Bricks without Straw, 53
British Petroleum (BP), 20, 179
British rock music, 15, 268–70, 311; blues epistemology in, 269, 277, 281; and post-punk, 278-80. See also Blues music
Bronski Beat, 297, 305n14
Brown, Clarence "Gatemouth," 38
Brown, Larry, 127
Brown, Michael, 192
Brown, Rob, 158
Brown, Sterling, 164
Brown v. Board of Education Supreme Court decision, 142, 254, 256, 262
Brundage, W. Fitzhugh, 6, 11, 64, 183, 208, 310, 312–14
Brussels, 16, 303
Bryan, Charles, 15
Buffett, Jimmy, 219
Bui, Huynh, 213
Burnside, R. L., 146, 148
Burroughs, William S., 283
Bush, George W., 44, 179, 192, 316; and "southern strategy," 317
Butler, Octavia, 315

Cabaret Voltaire, 278–80
Cable News Network (CNN), 196, 317
Cage, Nicolas, 186
Cajun culture, 37, 41, 159, 203, 214
Calvinism, 31
Camden, South Carolina, 103
Cameron, Don, 184
Camp, Stephanie, 101, 105
Campbell, Olive Dame, 27–28
Cao, Ahn "Joseph," 221
Capitalism, 5–6, 117, 119, 283, 311, 313, 319, 320, 321. See also Neoliberalism
Capote, Truman, 99, 290
Caribbean, climate compared to U.S. South, 124. See also Jazz music; New Orleans
Carmen, 235–37
Carson, Fiddlin' John, 44
Carter, William, 167
Carter Family, 44

Cash, Johnny, 32
Cash, W. J., 55
Catholic Social Services Migration and Refugee Services, 206
Cavalier and Yankee, 45
Celestial Jukebox, The, 10
Certeau, Michel de, 208
Cha, Frank, 14, 320
Chairs Missing, 282
Chapsal, Madeleine, 253–54
Charleston, 6, 19, 32–35, 36, 60–61, 80; and the Charleston Renaissance, 32–35
Chase, Leah, 42
Chaudhuri, Una, 231
Chef Menteur Construction & Demolition Debris (C&D) Disposal Facility, 210–12, 216
Chenier, Clifton, 38
Cher, 306n24
Chicago, 38, 228; blues, 36, 39
"Chicago Bound Blues," 269
Chicago Columbian Exposition (1893), 27
Chicago Tribune, 110
Child, Frances James, 30
Chua Van Duc Buddhist Temple, New Orleans, 209
Circling Dixie: Contemporary Southern Culture through a Transatlantic Lens, 9, 181
Civil rights movement, 4, 7, 12, 38, 40, 73, 89, 145; commodification of, 8, 75, 208; post–civil rights era, 321
Civil War, 32, 75, 101, 253, 257–58; commodification of, 5, 8, 64
Clapton, Eric, 277, 279
Clarke, John, 88
Clarksdale, Mississippi, 16, 144, 149, 155; in Marion Post Wolcott photograph, 274–75
Clash, The, 278
Classical Theater of Harlem, 190
Climate change, 12, 132, 134, 193
Club Cultures, 88
Cobb, James C., 3–4, 74, 149, 161
Coca-Cola, 63–64, 66
Codrescu, Andrei, 184, 191–92
Cohen, G. A., 61
Cohn, Deborah, 15, 80, 85, 168, 311
Coiled in the Heart, 12, 118–22, 126–32, 134–35, 312

Cold War politics, 15, 86, 249, 262, 311; and cultural diplomacy, 168, 175n41, 251, 255, 261; and William Faulkner, 168, 249–58
Coleman, Ornette, 40
Communism, 249–50, 257–59, 261; and anti-communism, 26, 250, 257–58
Confederacy, 9, 17, 64, 123, 208; cyber-Confederacy, 9, 84, 89; neo-Confederate, 313
Confederates in the Attic, 63
Conkin, Paul, 128
Connelly, Marc, 240
Connick, Harry, Jr., 188
Conquest of Cool, The, 88
Cornbread Nation, 46n25, 49, 59
Costello, Elvis, 188
Cotton, James, 147
Cotton Club, 229, 238
Council of Concerned Citizens, 313
Country music, 31, 36, 39–40, 44, 315–16
Country Music Awards, 315
Course in Miracles, A, 140
Cowley, Malcolm, 249
Cox, Karen, 5–6, 74
Cracker Barrel, 306
Crash, 285
Creating Citizenship in the Nineteenth-Century South, 10, 12, 56
Creating the Big Easy, 162
Creole, 162, 164, 188, 203; creolization, 165
Crews, Harry, 7
Crip Theory, 301
Crockett, Davy, 120
Crossroads, 145
Curtis, King, 39

"D.C.," 107–9, 113
Dailey, Jane, 80
Dainotto, Roberto, 233
Dallas, Texas, 140
Dane, Barbara, 37–38
Davenport, Jeremy, 159
Davidson, Donald, 6, 8, 15, 55, 65
Davis, Angela Y., 271
Day, Peter, 305n10
Dean, Jodi, 86, 89
Debord, Guy, 58–59, 61
Deepwater Horizon disaster, 178–80, 184, 195, 221

DeGeneres, Ellen, 99
Delius, Frederick, 15
Deliverance, 290
Democracy and Other Neoliberal Fantasies, 88
Derrida, Jacques, 82
Dickey, James, 290
"Dioneaux, R.," 111
Dirt and Desire, 72, 78
Disco music, 298–99
Divorce Iranian Style, 294
Dixie Emporium: Tourism, Foodways, and Consumer Culture in the American South, 3
DJ Jubilee, 189
Dollard, John, 55
Domino, Fats, 188
Donaldson, Susan, 77, 79–80
Douglass, Frederick, 16, 60, 268, 270–71, 284
Down Beat Magazine, 161
Down on the Bayou Cookbook, 28
"Do You Know What It Means to Miss New Orleans?," 188
Dr. John, 186, 188
Drive-By Truckers, 15
Drury, Theodore, 228
Du Bois, W.E.B., 106
Duchovny, David, 292
Duck, Leigh Anne, 9, 16, 74, 77–79, 80, 82, 85–86, 87, 90n18, 149, 161, 234, 239, 309, 319–20, 322n16
Duggan, Lisa, 304n3
Durkheim, Emile, 56–57, 64
Dvinge, Anne, 13, 36, 183, 314, 320
Dyer, Richard, 298
Dylan, Bob, 32, 37

Eagerson, George (aka "Countess Vivian"), 99–101, 113
Earle, Steve, 316–17. *See also* Tennessee
Ebony magazine, 37
Ecocriticism/environmental criticism, 12, 117–18, 126, 131, 135, 310; and white southern poverty, 127
Ecology of a Cracker Childhood, 127
Edge, John, 59, 61, 62
Edmonds, Lila, 27–28, 35
Edwards, Honeyboy, 142
Egerton, John, 2, 3, 6, 28–29, 42, 59–61, 63, 67
Eggers, Dave, 191–92

Elementary Forms of the Religious Life, The, 56
Elias, Amy, 8
Elliott, Scott, 12, 118–19, 122, 126–29, 131, 134
Ellison, Ralph, 269–70, 277, 285
Encyclopedia of Southern Culture, 36, 59, 67
English Folk Songs from the Southern Appalachians, 30
ER, 187
Ethnomusicology, 36–37
Europe (in Theory), 233
Evers, Medgar, 73
Exxon Valdez disaster, 189

Fable, A, 262
Faction Films, 294
FAME Studios, 39
Farm Security Administration, 193
Faulkner, William, 15, 154–55, 168, 248–63, 295, 305n11, 310; in Brazil, 255; and the Cold War, 249, 254–63; compares Japan and the U.S. South, 257–58; goodwill ambassador for U.S. Department of State, 249, 251, 253–58; in Iceland, 261; in Italy, 260–61; in Japan, 251, 253, 256–58; on the murder of Emmett Till, 260; in Peru, 251, 255; in the Philippines, 251, 258–60; post–Nobel Prize, 15, 248–50; public performance as American, 248, 252, 262, 263; public performance as farmer, 252, 263; public performance as southerner, 248–49, 250, 252–54, 262, 263; in Venezuela, 251, 254, 255. *See also* Cold War politics; Nobel Prize for Literature
Faust, Drew Gilpin, 5, 8–9
Fear of a Queer Planet, 304
Federal Emergency Management Agency (FEMA), 189, 192, 211
Ferguson, Roderick A., 109
Ferris, William, 49–50, 54, 57, 59–60
Fiehrer, Thomas, 163
Finding Purple America, 4, 18, 90
Fish, Stanley, 62–63, 87
Fisk Jubilee Singers, 31
Florida, 5, 10, 39, 41, 223n32
Florida, Richard, 14, 182, 187
Folk music, 32, 37
Folkways, 27, 50, 57
Foster, Hal, 73
Foster, Stephen, 229

Foucault, Michel, 169–70, 302
Four Saints in Three Acts, 15, 226–43, 311. *See also* Global South; Pastoral
Foxfire books, 36
Foxfire Ranch, Waterford, Mississippi, 151–55
Fox News, 88–89
France, 174n18, 186; William Faulkner in, 254; Gertrude Stein in, 237
Frank, Thomas, 88
Franklin, Aretha, 39
Fraser, Nancy, 321
Free (band), 280–81
French Revolution, 30
From Dixie to Broadway, 239
Frost, Robert, 255
Fuchs, Elinor, 231–32, 237
Fugitive, The, 319

Gang of Four, 16, 280–82
Gardner, Dave, 67
Gaston, Paul, 5
Geertz, Clifford, 51
Geographical History of America, The, 232
Georgia, 7, 27, 41, 43, 102, 109; legal battle with Tennessee over water rights, 134; Sea Islands, 124
Gibbs, Spencer, 107
Gill, Andy, 280–81
Gilroy, Paul, 232, 285, 316
Gioia, Ted, 280
Globalization, 3–4, 12, 17–18; and global capitalism, 319–20; and histories of exploitation, 9–10; and New Southern Studies, 84–85; and southern studies, 17
Global South, 10, 80, 124; and concepts of scale, 17; in *Four Saints in Three Acts*, 15, 228–33, 242–44; and global capitalism, 311; and Vietnamese Americans, 204
Godden, Richard, 262
God without Thunder, 54
Gone With the Wind, 7
Gordon, Caroline, 253
Gotham, Kevin Fox, 189, 195
Grady, Henry, 5
Grammys, 315–16
Grand Opera Company, 228
Grant, Madison, 233
Gray, Mary L., 301, 306n23, 321

Gray, Richard, 73, 248, 262–63
Great Britain, 9, 174n18, 289
Great Migration, 164, 230, 239–40
Great Rock 'n' Roll Swindle, The, 278
Green Pastures, The, 15, 230, 237, 239–42. See also Pastoral
Greeson, Jennifer, 2, 4, 77, 80–81, 83, 85, 90n18, 161, 234
Grosser, Maurice, 238
Grounded Globalism, 84
Gulf of Mexico, 178, 190, 209
Gulf South, 203–6, 208, 210–11, 215–19, 221–22
Gullah, 34–35
Gullah Home Cooking the Daufuskie Way, 28
Gussow, Adam, 13, 16, 271–73, 275, 310, 320
Gustav (hurricane), 180
Guterl, Matthew, 240
Gwin, Minrose, 73

Hach, Phila, 63
Hackler, M. B., 204
Halberstam, Judith/Jack, 304n3
Hale, Grace Elizabeth, 317–18
Hall, Gwendolyn Midlo, 181
Hamburg International Short Film Festival, 289
Hamlet, The, 248
Hammond, James Henry, 4, 67
Hampton University, 107
Hansen, James, 134
Harlem Renaissance, 34, 229
Harris, E. Lynn, 113n1
Harris, Jessica B., 44
Harris, Joel Chandler, 5, 130
Harrison, Richard, 242
Hart-Celler Act, 205
Hartford, Connecticut, 226, 227, 235
Hartman, Saidiya, 238
Haynes, Todd, 305n15
"Heartbeat," 270, 282–85
Hegel, Georg Willhelm Friedrich, 82
Heller, Erich, 57
Hendrix, Jimi, 40
Herder, Johann Gottfried von, 30
Heritage Corn Meal Cookery, 28
Heritage tourism, 6–8, 36, 43, 119. See also Plantation South; Tourism
Hersch, Charles, 162, 164

Herzog, Werner, 186
Heteronormativity, 105, 108–9, 120, 290, 304n3
Heyward, DuBose, 33
Higginbotham, Evelyn Brooks, 106
Hill Country Harmonica, 13, 139–40, 151–53, 155–56; development of, 148–49; as invented southern brand, 148; origins of, 144
Historically black colleges/universities (HBCU), 106–10. See also Homosexuality
HIV/AIDS, 99, 110–13
Hobbes, Thomas, 85
Hoberek, Andrew, 78, 87
Hobsbawm, Eric, 77
Hobson, Fred, 77, 80, 295
Hollowell, Annette, 152–53
Hollowell, Annie, 151, 153, 155
Hollowell, Bill, 151–55
Holmes, Jonathan, 192–93
Homonormativity, 290, 304n3
Homosexuality, 67, 97–113; anti-queer violence and discrimination, 297, 298, 301; and black southern identity formation, 12, 98, 106; and black queer subculture in New Orleans, 99–101; and class, 290, 301–2; as "down low," 99, 110, 113, 113n5, 114n14; and HBCUs, 106–7, 110, 114; and landscape, 98, 101–6, 120; and religion, 97–98; and same-sex marriage, 301; and segregation, 99–100; and southern literature, 290. See also Lesbian, gay, bisexual, and transgender (LGBT)
Hönnighausen, Lothar, 252
Hooker, John Lee, 279, 280
hooks, bell, 109
Hope Community Development Agency, 218
Hoppin' John's Lowcountry Cooking, 28
Horton, Big Walter, 147
Horwitz, Tony, 63–64, 66
Hot Docs Canadian International Documentary Festival, 289
Houseman, John, 226
Houston, 6, 216; and Hurricane Katrina refugees, 8, 186, 189, 209; and Mexican food, 62
Howard, John, 16, 310, 311
Howe, Irving, 249
Howlin' Wolf, 147
Hues Corporation, 298
Hughes, Langston, 269, 273
Hulme, Peter, 263

Human Rights Campaign, 110, 114
Humphries, Jefferson, 83
Hurston, Zora Neale, 34, 271
Hutty, Alfred, 33

Idea of the American South, 73, 82
If God Is Willing and da Creek Don't Rise, 186
I'll Take My Stand, 2, 6, 54, 78, 121, 136n18
Immigration to the South, 10, 14, 29. See also Vietnamese Americans
"I'm So Bored with the USA," 278
In a Queer Place, 304
In Dahomey, 239
Independent, The, 301
Indianola, Mississippi, 142
International Congress of Writers, São Paolo (1954), 251, 255
International Short Film Festival, Hamburg, 289
Interracialism, 140–41, 150–51, 153–54, 156; in musical revues, 228; performed on television, 150–51; Vietnamese and African American relations, 206–7, 212, 218. See also Mississippi
Inventing Southern Literature, 73, 76–77
Iraq war, 73, 316
I Say a Little Prayer, 113n1
Isom, Bob, 102, 113

J. Geils Band, 150
Jackson, Maria-Rosario, 182
Jackson, Mississippi, 293, 298
Jaffe, Allan, 167–68
Jaffe, Ben, 161, 162
Jaffe, Sandra, 167
James, Etta, 188
Jameson, Fredric, 82, 90n10, 91n32
Jamestown colony, 123
Japan, 15, 168, 194, 253–54, 256–58, 311. See also Faulkner, William
Jazz: America's Classical Music, 174
Jazz music, 36, 38, 39–40, 181, 183, 188, 314; Afro-Caribbean and creolized sources of, 163; as America's classical music, 159, 167, 173, 174n6; and "audiotopia," 165, 170, 173; and Cold War culture, 250; commercialization of, 12, 158; development of, 36, 44, 158–59, 162, 164–65, 167, 172; and "musick-ing," 169–70, 171–72; opposed to blues, 271; origins of, 12, 31–32, 159, 161–66, 189; and rock music, 39, 281. See also Authenticity; New Orleans; Preservation Hall
Jazz Review, The, 163
Jefferson, Thomas, 121, 252, 264n21, 275–76
Jessye, Eva, 226, 229, 242
Jewel, Buddy, 146
Jim Crow, 29, 44, 106, 273, 312; and blues tradition, 271, 277, 285; and Plessy v. Ferguson, 194
Jimenez, Flaco, 38
Joe, 127
"Johnny B. Goode," 278
Johnson, E. Patrick, 12, 16, 181, 310, 314–15
Johnson, James Weldon, 240
Johnson, Johnny Lee "Jaimoe," 39
Johnson, Robert, 43–44, 145, 149, 269, 271–72, 279
Jones, Anne Goodwyn, 77, 79–80
Jones, J., 16, 291–97, 300–303, 304n5, 305nn8,10,18, 306nn22,23, 312. See also Joneses, The (documentary short film)
Jones, Robert Edmond, 240
Jones, Sissieretta, 228
Jones, Suzanne, 2, 73
Joneses, The (documentary short film), 16, 289–303, 304nn1,2, 305n10, 306n24
Joneses, The (feature film), 292, 305n6
Journal of American Folklore, 27
Journeyman Pictures, 299
Joyner, Charles, 316
Justus, Jennifer, 63

Kabacoff, Pres, 185
Katrina (hurricane), 8, 14, 20n47, 73, 132, 159, 161, 178–96, 203, 205, 208–10, 213, 215–16; cultural responses to, 158–60, 183, 186–93; impact on African American community in New Orleans, 184–86; impact on Vietnamese American community in Gulf South, 204–6, 209–12; post-Katrina New Orleans, 180, 184, 193–95; post-Katrina musical culture in New Orleans, 188; post-Katrina oral testimonies, 190–91; post-Katrina population decline of New Orleans, 132, 178; post-Katrina trauma, 197n28; Vietnamese American activist responses to, 210–12,

Katrina (hurricane)—*continued*
215–18, 221–22. *See also* Mississippi; New Orleans; Vietnamese Americans
Katrina: A Play of New Orleans, 192–93
Kemp, Mike, 41, 42
Kennedy, Liam, 263
Kentucky, 109
Kentucky Fried Chicken, 148
Kenyon Review, 64
Kerouac, Jack, 136n22
Killers of the Dream, 55
Kimbrough, Junior, 146, 148, 151
Kindred, 315
King, B. B., 145
King, J. L., 110, 113
King, Martin Luther, Jr., 64, 80, 141–43, 150–51, 153
King, Richard, 263
King, Stephen A., 145
Kirby, Jack Temple, 7
Koanga, 15
Koeniger, A. Cash, 124–26
Koestenbaum, Wayne, 298
Kotak, Ash, 294, 305
Krauss, Allison, 38–39
Kreyling, Michael, 73, 90n18, 251–52, 262–63; critique of Kreyling's *Inventing Southern Literature*, 86–90
Krips, Henry, 67
Kristeva, Julia, 279
Kummer, Corby, 62
Kun, Josh, 165, 170
Kunetka, James, 136n22

Labor, 60–61, 292–93, 319–22; and black southerners, 141, 275–76; and exploitation, 127; forced, 102, 105, 142, 283; and immigrants, 9–10, 60; and southern penal system, 319–20. *See also* Slavery
LaCapra, Dominick, 65
Ladd, Barbara, 80
Lake Pontchartrain, 180, 209
Landrieu, Moon, 8
"Larry J.," 103–5, 113
Larry King Live, 196
Larue, Edward, 109
Latining America, 84

Law and Order: SVU, 113
Le, Trinh, 220
League of the South, 313
Ledbetter, Huddie ("Lead Belly"), 32, 38
Led Zeppelin, 16, 40–41, 278
Led Zeppelin II, 268–69
Lee, Muna, 255
Lee, Robert E., 63–64, 66–67
Lee, Spike, 186
Legends of Texas Barbecue, 28
Lemann, Nicholas, 187
Lesbian, gay, bisexual, and transgender (LGBT): and church membership, 97–98; LGBT civil rights movement, 108, 114n22, 114n26; and rural communities, 296–97, 301–2, 306. *See also* Homosexuality; Transsexuality
Let It Bleed, 268–69
Levee.org, 194
Lewis, Edna, 58–59
Life and Labor in the Old South, 123
Light in August, 248
Limerick, Patricia Nelson, 314
Lincoln, Abraham, 66—67; Lincoln memorial, 64
Little Joe, 38
Little Walter, 143
Litwack, Leon F., 271–72
Live at the Fillmore East, 39–40
Liverpool, England, 182, 282
Lomax, Alan, 31, 35, 276
Lomax, John, Sr., 31–32
Lomax, John, Jr., 31
Long, Alecia P., 101
Long, Huey, 44
Longinotto, Kim, 294, 305
Longinotto, Moby, 16, 289–91, 294–95, 299, 302
Look Away! The U.S. South and New World Studies, 80–81, 90n18
Los Angeles, 182
Lost Cause, 4–5, 11, 64–66, 121, 319
Louie Bluie, 38
Louisiana, branding of, 183; and coastline pollution, 195; and French colonial heritage, 162, 208; and French language, 36; as "Hollywood South," 320; and Katrina/Deepwater Horizon disasters, 179–80, 184; Lomaxes' re-

cording trips to, 31, 35; and racial categories, 162, 211; and Vietnamese Americans, 204–6, 208, 209, 217, 221
Louisiana: Where Culture Means Business, 183
Louisiana Economic Development, 218
Louisiana Endowment for the Humanities, 193
Louisiana Rebirth: Restoring the Soul of America, 183
Louisiana State Museum, 166
Louisiana Tastes, 28
"Love Letters in the Sand," 299
"Lowdown," 278–79
Luft, Rachel, 217
Lydon, John (Johnny Rotten), 278–80
Lynn, Loretta, 315, 317
Lyotard, Jean-François, 82
Lytle, Andrew, 55, 61–62

MacKethan, Lucinda H., 130
Madea's Family Reunion, 146
Magsayay, Ramon, 259
Make Me Proud, 294
Malley, John A., 260
Malone, Bill, 315
Malvasi, Mark, 55
Manchester, England, 9
Mansion, The, 262
Mardi Gras, 159, 186, 195
Margaritaville Casino and Restaurant, 219, 223
Mark, Rebecca, 73
Marley, Bob, 316
Marranca, Bonnie, 231
Marsalis, Wynton, 161
Marshall, Bill, 181
Marx, Karl, 61, 283
Mary Queen of Vietnam (MQVN) Catholic church, 207, 210, 213, 214
Mary Queen of Vietnam Community Development Corporation (MQVN CDC), 213, 217, 223nn36,37
Matisse, Henri, 234
Matthews, Edward, 229
Matthews, John, 262–63
Maxinquaye, 268
McCarthyism, 259
McCullers, Carson, 290
McDowell, Fred, 147

McGinley, Paige, 15, 311
McKee, Kathryn, 81, 83–84, 85, 242
McPherson, Tara, 2, 7–10, 18, 62, 82, 113, 141–42, 310
McRobbie, Angela, 88
McRuer, Robert, 301
McTell, Blind Willie, 39, 43
McWhorter, Diane, 83
Memphis, 182; and civil rights industry, 8; and racial tensions, 150
Memphis and the Paradox of Place: Globalization in the American South, 14
Mencken, H. L., 29, 32–33
Men Like That: A Southern Queer History, 16, 294, 305
Miami, 6; and casino industry, 223; and Hurricane Katrina refugees, 189
Mia X, 189
Middle Passage, 33, 230, 242, 311
Milian, Claudia, 84
Mills, David, 187
Mills, Ken, 167
Mintz, Sidney, 272–73
Mississippi, 139–55, 156n6, 297–301, 303, 310, 315; black identity in, 7, 146; blues mystique of, 144–45, 148–49; and blues tourism, 140, 145, 149–50, 152; and class, 292–93; and Delta blues, 11, 13, 35, 36, 43, 143–44, 149; and William Faulkner, 15, 154–55, 253, 255, 260; and Hill Country Harmonica, 139–55; and homophobia, 289, 301, 304n4; and Hurricane Katrina, 180, 204–6, 209; immigrant labor in, 10; and interracialism, 141, 148, 153–54, 156n13; negative images of, 142–43, 154; and penal system, 31; and Emmett Till's murder, 15, 260; and transphobia, 304n4, 305nn18,22; and transsexuality, 16, 304n4, 305n18; and Vietnamese Americans, 204–6, 209, 216–21. *See also* Blues music
Mississippi Blues Commission, 145
Mississippi Blues Trail, 145, 152
Mississippi Burning, 145
Mississippi Development Authority Tourism Division, 145, 152
Mississippi Quarterly, 76, 78
Mississippi River, 131, 180, 190, 209, 295, 299; and 1927 flood, 195

Missouri, 242
Mitchell, Margaret, 7
Modernism, 226–27, 230, 231, 237, 253; literary, 239, 250, 253; operatic, 228, 242, 311; theatrical, 243
Monroe, Bill, 39
Monteith, Sharon, 2, 73, 18n9, 231
Montgomery, Alabama, 8
Montgomery, Little Brother, 142
MoonPie, 49–54, 57–59, 62, 67, 310
Moore, Deacon John, 158
Moore, Demi, 292
Morehouse College, 107; and the "Morehouse Man," 107
Moreton, Bethany, 10
Morris, Benjamin, 188
Morrissey, 268
Morton, Jelly Roll, 163
"Mountain Jam," 40
Mozart, Wolfgang Amadeus, 276
MTV, 64, 83
Multiculturalism, 42, 44, 62–63; boutique, 62–63, 66
Muscle Shoals, Alabama, 39
Music of Spain, The, 235–36
Myth of Southern Exceptionalism, The, 75, 82

Nagin, Ray, 210, 212
Naipaul, V. S., 90n18
Narrative Forms of Southern Community, The, 73, 85
Nashville, 36–37, 39; country music, 36–37
Natchez, 8
National Alliance of Vietnamese American Service Agencies, 218
National Association for the Advancement of Colored People (NAACP), 127
National Jazz Foundation, 166
National Resource Center on LGBT Aging, 306
Nation's Region, The, 80, 239
Native American displacement, 129, 134
Native South, 318–19
Nature's End: The Consequences of the Twentieth Century, 136
Nelson, Dana, 72–74
Nelson, Lynn A., 129
Neoliberalism, 11, 18, 88–89, 319, 321. *See also* Capitalism

Never Mind the Bollocks, 282
Neville, Cyril, 188
New Encyclopedia of Southern Culture, 50–51, 57, 59
New Left, 37
New Orleans, 132, 142, 158–73, 180–96, 203–22, 295, 310; and Africa, 162, 178, 181; and the Caribbean, 163, 178; creative economy of, 182–83; cuisine of, 41–42, 214; desegregation of, 100; "Europeanness" of, 13, 161–62, 178, 181, 183–86; French Quarter, 8, 13–14, 99–100, 160, 167–68, 181, 185, 189; and hip-hop, 189; Iberville projects, 185; impact of Katrina on New Orleans cultural production, 14, 161, 178, 182, 186–89, 192; and jazz, 13, 36, 158–73; and Mardi Gras, 159, 195; New Orleans East, 14, 204–5, 207–19; New Orleans exceptionalism, 14, 20n47, 162, 180, 192; Ninth Ward, 190, 194, 195, 210; and promotion of Old South identity, 6; and segregation, 194; and sexual non-conformity, 12, 99–101, 164, 295; Storyville, 101, 185; and tourism, 14, 159–60, 162, 170, 180–81, 193, 195; Treme, 99; Versailles, 205, 206–8, 210–12, 213, 216, 218; Village de l'Est, 205, 206–8, 210–12, 213, 216, 218. *See also* Jazz music; Katrina (hurricane); Preservation Hall; Vietnamese Americans
New Orleans Jazz & Heritage Festival, 174n2
New Orleans Jazz Club, 166
New Orleans Saints, 181
New Orleans Times-Picayune, 163, 164, 166, 191
New queer cinema, 290, 298, 305n15
New South Creed, 5
New Southern Studies, 72, 77, 78, 79–84, 89–90, 244, 309–11, 315, 317; and American studies, 89, 311; and the circum-Caribbean, 230; criticism of, 12, 56, 75, 77, 79–84; debates over future of, 16–18, 74–75; and dialogue with historians, 10, 56, 75, 84; economic focus of, 9; and globalization, 80–81; and postmodernism, 56, 81–82, 84; and scale, 17–18, 20n52; transformation of, 310. *See also* Southern studies
Newsweek, 185, 252
New York City, 35, 140, 144–45, 231; black migration to, 230, 311; Harlem, 226, 228–29, 231, 232; and jazz, 158, 169; and theater, 227–28, 231, 239

New York LGBT Community Center, 294
New York Times, 99, 184, 226, 239, 248–49, 253
Nguyen, Jack, 220–21
Nguyen, Minh, 215, 216
Nguyen, Vien The, 210–11, 215
Nicolaisen, Peter, 252, 262
Nietzsche, Friedrich, 236
Nieves, Evelyn, 209
Nirvana, 32
Nobel Prize for Literature, 248–50, 252–53, 256–57. *See also* Faulkner, William
NOLA RISING campaign, 190
Nonini, Donald, 85
Nora, Pierre, 66, 169, 173
North Carolina, 27, 30
North Mississippi Allstars, 146
No Time for Tea at Raj TV, 294
"No Warning Given," 279
NYPD Blue, 187

Oakley, Berry, 39
Obama, Barack, 86, 180
O'Brien, Michael, 12, 51–53, 66, 73, 75–76; critique of New Southern Studies, 56, 75–76, 79–85; responses to, 77, 79–85
O Brother, Where Art Thou?, 145
Odetta, 37
Offbeat, 186
Ogden Museum of Southern Art, 189
Old Carolina Tobacco Country Cook Book, 28
Old South, 5–6, 33, 42, 44, 141, 271; re-creation of, 119, 130
Olmsted, Frederick Law, 20
O'Neill, Eugene, 240
O'Neill Verner, Elizabeth, 33
Ono, Kiyoyuki, 256
On the Down Low, 110
On the Road, 136n22
Opera, 226–32, 234, 236, 238–43. *See also* Modernism
Opportunity, 242
Oprah Winfrey Network, 306
Oprah Winfrey Show, 110
Ostendorf, Berndt, 181
Other Voices, Other Rooms, 290
Otte, Marline, 194
Our South: Geographic Fantasy and the Rise of National Literature, 2, 80
Overmyer, Eric, 187

Ownby, Ted, 5, 7
Oxford, Mississippi, 59, 140, 151

Page, Thomas Nelson, 5, 130
Palm Beach, Florida, 5
Panama City, Florida, 217, 223n32
Paradise Lost, 283
Paris, France, 231, 235; compared to New Orleans, 162, 184–86; and William Faulkner, 254; and Gertrude Stein, 228, 243
Passing of the Great Race, The, 233
Pastoral, 36, 134, 310; commercialization of southern imagery, 146; in *Four Saints and Three Acts*, 230, 237–39, 241–43, 311; in *The Green Pastures*, 230, 237, 239, 241–42; and Old South mythology, 130–31; and repression of slavery and Native displacement, 130, 134–36; southern "anti-pastoral," 123; southern urban, 150
Peacock, James, 4, 84
Pearl Harbor, 35, 260
Perrine, Matt, 158
Perry, Bill "Howl-N-Madd," 146
Perry, Jonathan, 110
Perry, Tyler, 146
Peters, Clarke, 158
Petty, Audrey, 49
Philippines Herald, 259
Phillips, U. B., 123
Picasso, Pablo, 227, 234–35
Pickett, Wilson, 39
Pierce, Wendell, 158, 187
Pink Floyd, 278
Pitt, Brad, 195
Placing the South, 52
Plantation Revue, 239
Plantation South, 4, 33, 80, 118–19; Agrarians' vision of, 136n18; and capitalism, 128–29; and environmental factors, 123–24, 126–28, 135; and heritage tourism, 6, 8–9, 33, 118–19; and paternalism, 141, 148; plantation economies, 320; plantation fiction, 5, 7, 131; plantation musicals, 229; and slave songs, 276, 320; and slavery, 123, 127–28, 134, 148, 273
Plessy, Homer, 194
Plessy v. Ferguson Supreme Court decision, 194
Polk, Noel, 262–63
Pollock, Jackson, 250

Pope, Alexander, 82
Porgy, 33
Porgy and Bess, 228
Port Huron Statement, 37
"Portland, Oregon," 316
Post-Fordism, 319–21
Postmodernism, 1, 3, 11–12, 76, 130, 148, 162, 299; and capitalism, 2, 86, 129; and gender conversion narratives, 303; and historical-geographical materialism, 91n32; as "indifferent to God," 56; and New Southern Studies, 17, 81–84; as politically neutral, 12; and southern studies, 88, 90n10; and theater, 231
Postmodernism, or, the Cultural Logic of Late Capitalism, 90n10
Post-punk music, 16, 270, 277–85, 311
Postsouthernism, 79, 124; critique of, 75–76; and environmentalism, 117–19, 126, 129; and historical-geographical materialism, 117; and "the late South," 86; and parody, 118, 135; and place, 3, 79, 117–18; "postsouthern agrarianism," 119–20, 128, 130; and southern studies, 11
Postsouthern Sense of Place in Contemporary Fiction, The, 74, 79
Powell, Shannon, & the Preservation Hall Stars, 170–71
"Preaching Blues (Up Jumped the Devil)," 269, 279
Preface to Peasantry, 55
Preservation Hall, 13, 158, 160, 161, 166–73; and "musicking," 13, 160, 169–72
Presley, Elvis, 63, 66
Preuss, Gene B., 190
Price, Derrick, 193
Price, Richard, 272–73
Pride of Place, 294
"Prospect 1. New Orleans," 183–84
Protestantism, 54, 57, 178, 291
Prudhomme, Paul, 27–28
Public Enemy, 285
Public Image Limited, 278

Qawwali music, 39
Queer Phenomenology, 103

Racial Realities in Europe, 233
Raeburn, Bruce, 160, 164, 166, 187–88
Rainey, Ma, 272, 276

Ransom, John Crowe, 6, 54–55, 57–58, 61, 64–67
Raper, Arthur, 55
Rawls, Alex, 186
Ray, Janisse, 127
RC Cola, 49–50, 59
Reagon, Bernice Johnson, 38
Real South, The, 7, 76, 84–88, 89, 313
Reconstructing Dixie: Race, Gender, and Nostalgia in the Imagined South, 2, 141, 315
Reconstructing the Native South: American Indian Literature and the Lost Cause, 318
Redding, Otis, 39
Redford, Robert, 196
Reed, John Shelton, 67
Reflections in a Golden Eye, 290
Refugee Center of Biloxi, 206
Regis, Helen, 160
Reid, Barbara, 167
Reinhardt, Django, 40
Resistance through Rituals, 88
Revolution Starts . . . Now, The, 316
Reynolds, Simon, 277–83
Richards, Keith, 271, 277, 279
Richardson, Riché, 83, 98
"Rich Man's War," 316
Ridgely, J. V., 123
Rieger, Christopher, 117
Rift, The, 136n22
Rip It Up and Start Again: Postpunk 1978–1984, 277–78, 280, 282
Rise of the Creative Class, The, 182
Rita (hurricane), 178, 180, 183, 185
Roach, Joseph, 230
Roanoke colony, 123
Robeson, Paul, 228
Robinson, Marc, 231
Robinson-Wayne, Beatrice, 229
Rock and roll music, 150, 277–78, 280. *See also* British rock music
"Rock the Boat," 298
Rodgers, Paul, 280
Rolling Stones, 16, 40, 266, 268
Romanticism, 30, 51, 56, 140
Romine, Scott, 1, 3, 8–9, 11–13, 28, 36, 42, 73–74, 76, 79, 89–90, 91, 117, 301, 309, 310, 313–14, 319, 320; critique of Romine's *The Real South*, 84–88
Roosevelt, Franklin D., 253

Rose, Chris, 191, 196
Rough Aunties, 294
Rove, Karl, 88
Rubin, Louis D., Jr., 312
Ruffins, Kermit, 186
Rush, Regina, 263
Rushing, Wanda, 14

SAGE: Services and Advocacy for Gay, Lesbian, Bisexual & Transgender Elders, 306
Said, Edward, 82, 190
Saint Augustine, Florida, 5
Sam Morgan Jazz Band, 188
Sanctuary, 248
Sartre, Jean-Paul, 121
Sass, Herbert, 33, 35
Sassen, Saskia, 84
Satchmo Blows Up the World, 175
Savannah, 6, 19, 36
Scale, 1, 3, 9, 14, 17–18, 75, 169, 179, 302, 316–17, 320
Schmidt, G. Lewis, 257
Schwartz, Lawrence, 249–50
Scott, Walter, 276
Seeger, Mike, 315
Seeger, Pete, 37
Seems Like Murder Here, 272
Selma Freedom Choir, 37
September 11, 2001 terrorist attacks, 11, 73, 180, 190
Sesame Street, 83
Sex Change Hospital, 306n24
Sex Pistols, 278
Sharp, Cecil, 30–31
Shearer, Cynthia, 10
Sheffield Doc/Fest, 289
Shinjuku Boys, 294
Shrimping industry, 206, 310, 320
Sickels, Carter, 306n22
Silverman, Jeff, 148–49, 152–55
Simms, William Gilmore, 5
Simon, David, 187
Simpson, Lewis P., 73–74, 122, 130
Singin' Billy, 15
Sissy Nobby, 189
Sisters in Law, 294
Slavery, 4–6, 40, 89, 134, 242, 258; and black culture, 273, 284; and blues music, 270, 272–73, 284; and foodways discourse, 60–61; and heritage tourism, 8; legacies of, in *Coiled in the Heart*, 119, 123, 127, 129–31; modern slavery, 10; and plantation fiction, 130, 284; sexuality and, 101–2, 105; in theater, 229, 238; and whites' performance of spirituals, 34–35. *See also* Plantation South
Slits, The, 277, 278
Small, Christopher, 160, 169
Smalltown Boy (documentary short film), 294–97, 299
"Smalltown Boy" (song), 305n14
Small Town Gay Bar, 304
Smith, Alice Ravanel Hugar, 33
Smith, Bessie, 31, 37, 268, 269
Smith, Charles Edward, 164, 175
Smith, Donna Jo, 290
Smith, Jon, 3–4, 6, 11–12, 16–18, 18n9, 20n50, 32, 74, 79, 82, 85, 90, 124, 139, 309, 311, 317, 319, 320–21, 321n9, 322n16
Smith, Lillian, 55, 62, 80
Smith, Patricia, 192
Smiths, The, 269
Smokehouse Ham, Spoon Bread, and Scuppernong Wine, 28
Society for the Preservation of Spirituals (SPS), 34
Somerville, Jimmy, 297
Son House, 43
Son of Dave, 150
Sontag, Susan, 190
So Red the Rose, 7
Sound and the Fury, The, 248
South Carolina, 32
Souther, J. Mark, 6, 164
Southern AIDS Coalition, 111
Southern Comfort, 304
Southern culture, 9, 29–31, 44, 51; absence of as lack, 66; commodification of, 9, 57, 60–63, 67; critique of, 44, 52; decline and endurance of, 11, 35–36, 52; and fundamentalism, 54–55, 67; in music, 38–39, 275–77; and nature, 122–23, 132; as queer, 290–91, 295; and religion, 97; and sexuality, 97–98; as syncretic, 11, 42–43, 53, 203. *See also* Authenticity
Southern distinctiveness, 1, 3–4, 8, 12, 16, 161; and climate, 124–25, 134; and essentialism, 90

Southern exceptionalism, 78, 83, 132, 311; southern environmental exceptionalism, 122–23, 132, 134
Southern Food: At Home, On the Road, in History, 28, 63
Southern foodways, 11, 28–29, 36, 41–43, 57, 58–63, 309; critique of, 42–43; as discourse, 43, 50, 58–59, 60–63, 67; as multicultural, 42–44, 62–63; and Native Americans, 42
Southern Foodways Alliance, 3, 11, 49, 59–60
Southern food writing, 49–50, 57
Southern Gothic, 290
Southern identity, creation and consumption of, 2, 4, 11–12, 29, 44–45, 56, 85, 119; and black gay identity, 108–9; and black southern identity, 31–33, 44, 97–98, 141, 273, 284; performance of, 7, 50, 250, 252–53
Southern Intellectual History Circle (SIHC), 80, 315–17
Southern Living, 7–8, 50–51
Southern Past, The, 208
Southern Rock Opera, 15
Southern Shrimp Alliance, 206
Southern studies, as an academic field, 1, 11, 72–75, 78, 90, 146, 309–10, 315; critique of, 72, 74–77, 79, 319, 320; as "old southern studies," 78, 87; and postmodernism, 1, 11–12, 76, 81–83, 88; post-postpolitical southern studies, 12, 17, 89–90; southern studies without "the South," 16, 74, 89; and transnational turn, 9, 311. *See also* New Southern Studies
Southern University, 107
South to a New Place, 2, 73–74
Soviet Union, 168, 250, 262
Spain, 15; representation of in *Four Saints in Three Acts*, 228, 230, 231–37, 242, 244n8
Spelman College, 114n22
Spirituals, 31, 34–35. *See also* Fisk Jubilee Singers; Plantation South
Spry, Caroline, 305n10
Stanonis, Anthony, 3, 4, 162
Star Wars, 83
"Statesboro Blues," 39
Stecopoulos, Harilaos, 20n52, 258
Stein, Alan B., 190
Stein, Gertrude, 15, 226–29, 231–39, 241–43, 244nn6,8

Stephens, Randall, 74
Stettheimer, Florine, 226, 237
Sting, 196
Stoddard, Lothrop, 233
Stone Mountain, Georgia, 64, 66
Stonewall riots, 108
Strieber, Whitley, 136n22
Strummer, Joe, 278
Students Promoting Education Action and Knowledge (SPEAK), 107
Subversive Sounds: Race and the Birth of Jazz in New Orleans, 162
Sumner, William Graham, 50, 57
Sunbelt South, 29, 40
Sundquist, Eric, 77–78
"Sweet Home New Orleans," 188
Sweet Honey in the Rock, 38
"Sweet Southern Comfort," 146
Sweet Tea: Black Gay Men in the South—An Oral History, 12, 98, 107, 111, 113
Swenson, John, 187–88
Sylvester, 298

Tang, Eric, 212
Tanoukhi, Nirvana, 17, 20n51
Taylor, Helen, 9, 13–14, 19–20n47, 159, 162, 213, 311, 318–20
Taylor, William, 44–45
Tea Party, 89
Tearoom Trade, 114
Tennessee, 63; in *Coiled in the Heart*, 118, 120, 126, 131; and Steve Earle, 316; legal battle with Georgia over water rights, 134; and music, 38, 43
Tennessee River, 134
Tennessee Williams Literary Festival and JazzFest, 183
Terry, Sonny, 143
Texas, 134, 316
Thomas, Irma, 188
Thomas, Sharde, 148, 155
Thompson, Fred, 60
Thompson, Tracy, 1
Thomson, Virgil, 226, 228–29, 232, 234–37, 242, 244nn6,8
Thornton, Sarah, 88
Till, Emmett, 15, 73, 260
Tin Pan Alley, 38, 44

Toklas, Alice B., 228, 235
Tommasini, Anthony, 228
Tompkins, Jane, 87
Tourgée, Albion, 5, 53
Tourism, 6, 7–8, 14, 33, 140, 170, 179, 182; "disaster tourism," 195; "voluntourism," 187. *See also* Blues music; Heritage tourism; New Orleans
Toussaint, Allen, 186, 188
Tran, Ginni, 217
Transsexuality, 16, 101, 290, 296, 299, 305, 312; and class, 302; and sex reassignment surgery, 16, 303, 306n24, 310; transphobia, 300
Trefzer, Annette, 81, 82, 84, 85, 242
Treme (television series), 158, 159, 186–87, 189, 195
Trethewey, Natasha, 180, 196n2
Tricky, 268
Trucks, Butch, 39
Trucks, Derek, 39
True Blood, 320
True West: Authenticity and the American West, 314
Tulane University, 166, 187; Amistad Research Center, 189
Turner, Otha, 147, 155
Tuskegee, 269
Twain, Mark, 136n22
Twilight of Equality?, 304

United New Orleans Planning program, 218
United States Catholic Conference, 206
United States Information Service, 254, 258, 261
University of Mississippi, 140, 146, 151, 152

Van Lear Rose, 315
Van Vechten, Carl, 226–27, 232, 235–36
Vappie, Don, 188
Venice, Italy, 184
Venice, Louisiana, 184
Verner, Elizabeth O'Neill, 33
Vesey, Denmark, 6
Vietnamese Americans, 9, 14, 203–22, 310, 320; in Biloxi, 204–6; and Buddhism, 209; and Catholicism, 206, 207, 209; community formation of, 205–9; and community outreach, 216–19; culture of, 213–15; displacement of and post-Katrina community rebuilding by, 209–12, 220–21; globalized Gulf South identity, 204, 207, 215–16; in local politics, 221; and "model minority" myth, 204–5; in New Orleans East, 204–6, 210–12
Vietnamese American Young Leaders Association of New Orleans (VAYLA NO), 216
Vietnamese Martyrs Catholic Church, 209
Viet Village Collective Marketing Campaign, 219
Village Called Versailles, A, 212
Village People, 298
Voice of the Wetlands All-Stars, 188
Voices from the Storm, 191
Voices of Witness, 191
Vu, Thao Jennifer, 210

Wadsworth Atheneum, 226, 227
Waiting for Godot, 190
Waiting for Khyron, 294
Wald, Elijah, 271
"Walkin' to New Orleans," 188
Wal-Mart, 10, 320
Ward, Brian, 15, 18, 74, 263, 285
Warday, 136n22
Warner, Michael, 304n3, 321
Warnes, Andrew, 16, 310, 311
War of Independence, 4, 161
War on Terror, 191
Warren, Kenneth, 75, 86
Warren, Robert Penn, 249
Washburne, Christopher, 163
Washington, Booker T., 273
Waters, Muddy, 36, 145, 271
Watson, Jay, 127
"Weary Blues, The," 269
Webb, Barbara, 229
Weber, Max, 54, 57
Wells, Junior, 143
West-Eastern Divan orchestra, 190
"Whammer Jammer," 150
When the Levees Broke: A Requiem in Four Acts, 186, 188
"Whipping Post," 40
White, Chris, 296, 299
White, Jack, 315
White, Michael G., 188
White Citizens' Council, 142, 313

White Stripes, The, 315
Wicker, Roger, 304n1
Wiggins, Phil, 143
Willard-Lewis, Cynthia, 218
Williams, Tennessee, 58, 99, 181; Tennessee Williams Literary Festival, 183
Williams, Walter J., 136n22
Williamson, Sonny Boy, 143, 145, 147
Wilson, Anthony, 118
Wilson, Olly, 172
Winfrey, Oprah, 99, 113n5
Wire, The (television series), 187
Wire (band), 16, 270, 277–80, 282–85
Wolcott, Marion Post, 273–75
Woods, Johnny, 147
Woodward, C. Vann, 262
World War II, 164, 256

Wright, Richard, 60, 269, 285
Writing the South: Ideas of an American Region, 73

Yaeger, Patricia, 72–73, 78, 83, 314–15
Young, Stark, 7
Young Men's Christian Association (YMCA), 103–5

Zeitoun, 191–92
Zeitoun, Abdulrahman, 191–92, 197n28
Zeitoun, Kathy, 191, 197n28
Zhou, Minh, 207
Žižek, Slavoj, 76, 86
Zwigoff, Terry, 38
Zydeco music, 37–38, 188